PROGRAMMING THE 65816

WILLIAM LABIAK

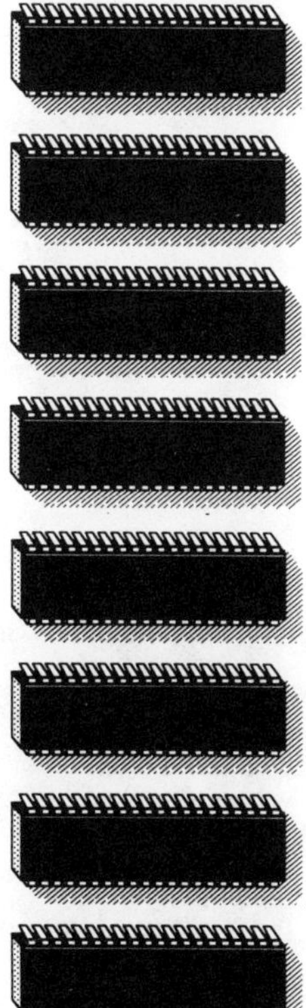

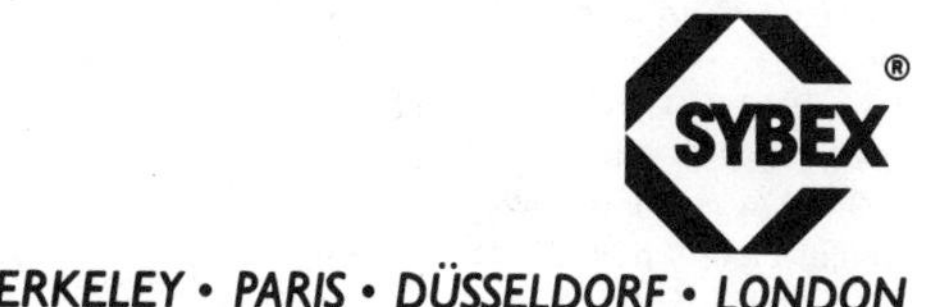

Cover design: Dave Jensen
Book design: Jeffrey James Giese

Library of Congress Card Number: 86-61059
ISBN 0-89588-324-4
Printed by Haddon Craftsmen
Manufactured in the United States of America
10 9 8 7 6 5 4 3 2 1

ACKNOWLEDGMENTS

The author wishes to acknowledge the following people who assisted in the preparation of this book. William Mensch, Jr., of Western Design Center, Inc., provided the author with timely information on the 65816 microprocessor. Dan Tauber reviewed the manuscript and provided helpful suggestions. Tanya Kucak, editor, provided valuable assistance in the preparation of the text.

The staff of SYBEX also provided expert help. In particular, Rudolph Langer (editor-in-chief) suggested the subject and provided valuable support. Thanks also to Jeffrey Giese (design), David Clark and Olivia Shinomoto (word processing), Eileen Walsh and Aidan Wylde (proofreading), Joel Kroman (technical support), and Cheryl Vega and Dawn Amsberry (typesetting).

TABLE OF CONTENTS

INTRODUCTION — X

CHAPTER 1: BASIC CONCEPTS — 1

What Is Programming? 1
Flowcharting 2
Information Representation 4
  Internal Representation of Information 4
  External Representation of Information 22
Exercises 25

CHAPTER 2: 65816 HARDWARE ORGANIZATION — 31

System Architecture 31
Inside a Microprocessor 33
Internal Organization of the 65816 41
Instruction Formats of the 65816 44
Execution of Instructions in the 65816 47
The 65816 and 65802 Chips 48
Summary 51
Exercises 52

CHAPTER 3: BASIC PROGRAMMING TECHNIQUES — 55

Arithmetic Programs 55
BCD Arithmetic 65

Multiplication 71
Binary Division 82
Logical Operations 87
Instruction Summary 88
Subroutines 88
Summary 95
Exercises 96

CHAPTER 4: THE 65816 INSTRUCTION SET 99

Classes of Instructions 99
The 65816 Instruction Set 101
Summary 112
Exercises 112

THE 65816 INSTRUCTIONS: INDIVIDUAL DESCRIPTIONS (ADC–XCE) 114

CHAPTER 5: ADDRESSING TECHNIQUES 207

Possible Addressing Modes 207
65816 Addressing Modes 214
Using the 65816 Addressing Modes 222
Summary 227
Exercises 227

CHAPTER 6: INPUT/OUTPUT TECHNIQUES 229

The 65816 Input/Output Instructions 229
Parallel Byte Transfers 235
Bit Serial Transfer 239
Basic Input/Output Summary 244
Communicating with Input/Output Devices 244

Peripheral Summary 255
Input/Output Scheduling 256
Summary 267
Exercises 267

CHAPTER 7: INPUT/OUTPUT DEVICES 273

The "Standard" PIO 273
Programming a PIO 275
The Western Design Center 65SC21 PIA 276
The 65816 ACIA 278
Other I/O Chips 279
Summary 280

CHAPTER 8: APPLICATION EXAMPLES 283

Clearing a Section of Memory 283
Getting Characters In 284
Testing a Character 284
Bracket Testing 285
Generating Parity 286
Code Conversion: ASCII to BCD 286
Converting Hex to ASCII 287
Finding the Largest Element of a Table 287
Sum of N Elements 288
Checksum Computation 288
Count the Zeros 290
Block Transfer 290
Bubble-Sort 291
Summary 295
Exercises 296

CHAPTER 9: DATA STRUCTURES 301

PART I—THEORY 301

Pointers 301
Lists 302
Searching And Sorting 307
Section Summary 308

PART II—DESIGN EXAMPLES 308

Data Representation for the List 309
Simple List 311
Alphabetic List 313
Linked List 322
Summary 331
Exercises 333

CHAPTER 10: PROGRAM DEVELOPMENT 335

Programming Choices 335
Software Support 338
The Program Development Sequence 339
Hardware Alternatives 342
The Assembler 345
Summary 353
Conclusion 353

APPENDIXES 355

Appendix A: Hexadecimal Conversion Table 355
Appendix B: ASCII Conversion Table 356
Appendix C: Decimal to BCD Conversion Table 357
Appendix D: The 65816 Instruction Set: Operation, Operation Codes, and Status Register 358
Appendix E: Detailed 65816 Instruction Operation 360

Bibliography 364

Index 365

INTRODUCTION

If you want to write assembly language programs for any system based on the 65816, this is the book for you. The 65816 is the 16-bit version of the 6502. In this book, you will find:

- Everything you need to know about the organization and instruction set of this exceptionally interesting microprocessor.
- A complete presentation of the elements of assembly language programming.
- All the essential elementary and intermediate programming techniques that will allow you to begin programming the 65816 on your own.

When you have mastered the material in this book, you will understand how 65816 systems, when properly designed and programmed, can deliver 16-bit performance with 8-bit economy—and you will have gained the knowledge necessary to make the 65816 do this for you.

Programming the 65816 is organized so that the chapters proceed from the simple to the complex. As you read, you will gradually encounter all the concepts and techniques required to build more and more complex programs, to do more and more advanced tasks.

Chapter 1 introduces you to the basics of programming: what it really is, how to keep track of what you are doing, and what you have to do.

Chapter 2 gives the first rundown on the 65816 processor: the registers and the buses, and how instructions are actually executed within the processor.

Chapter 3 gets you into simple programs and teaches you the kinds of arithmetic the 65816 is capable of, as well as logical operations, and the important concept of subroutines.

Chapter 4 is the big one—a complete description of the 65816 instruction set. After a discussion of the classes of 65816 instructions, I present a detailed explanation of each instruction. I discuss the instructions in alphabetical order for easy reference.

Chapter 5 details one of the most important aspects of the 65816: the addressing modes. I begin this essential treatment with a background discussion on the different kinds of addressing possible in microprocessors, and how they work. I then go on to examine the actual addressing modes in this context. Finally, I give concrete examples of the application of each of the modes, to help you completely understand what they can do.

Chapter 6 covers essential input/output techniques, 65816 style, including: the I/O instruction repertory of the 65816, simple serial and parallel I/O programs, some concrete implementations of common I/O tasks, and more advanced techniques.

Chapter 7 considers several I/O chips that are commonly used to interface the 65816 to the external world.

Chapter 8 gets into more extensive application programs. These programs do all sorts of things. But each shows how the 65816 can make simple and fast that which on other microprocessors is cumbersome and slow.

Chapter 9 discusses data structures—another important, though more advanced, area in which the 65816 shines—including pointers, list searching, sorting, and more complex programs and techniques.

Chapter 10 offers a forward look at the world of program development that is now open to you. I compare and evaluate hexadecimal "machine language" coding, assemblers, and high-level languages. I also touch on some available, and more or less desirable, program development environments.

Several useful appendixes and an index bring the book to an end.

Most of the programs in this book were tested on an APLC16 board in an Apple IIe computer using the ORCA/M assembler. Those valuable resources are products of ComLog, of Scottsdale, Arizona, and the Byte Works, of Albuquerque, New Mexico, respectively, which made them available to me for the development of this book. I thank them for thus assuring the accuracy of the programs used throughout this book.

William Labiak

Berkeley, California
Spring 86

BASIC CONCEPTS

1

IN THIS CHAPTER, I introduce the basic concepts and definitions used in computer programming. If you are already familiar with these concepts, you may only want to glance quickly at this chapter, then move on to Chapter 2. I suggest, however, that you read through this chapter, even if you're an experienced programmer, to familiarize yourself with the approach I'll be using throughout this book.

WHAT IS PROGRAMMING?

Given a problem, one normally tries to devise a solution. This solution, expressed as a step-by-step procedure, is called an *algorithm.* An algorithm may be expressed in any language or symbolism, and it must terminate in a finite number of steps. Here is a simple example of an algorithm:

1. Insert key into keyhole
2. Turn key one full turn to the left
3. Seize doorknob
4. Turn doorknob left and push the door

At this point, if the algorithm is correct for the type of lock involved, the door will open.

Once you've expressed a solution to a problem in the form of an algorithm, a computer can then execute the algorithm. Unfortunately, computers cannot understand or execute ordinary spoken English or any other human language. The reason for this lies in the *syntactic ambiguities* of all common human languages. Only a well-defined subset of a natural language, called a *programming language,* can be "understood" by the computer. Converting an algorithm into a sequence of instructions in a programming language is called *programming.* The actual translation phase of the algorithm into the programming language is called *coding.* Programming refers not just to the coding, but also to the overall design of the programs and *data structures* that will implement the algorithm.

Effective programming requires not only an understanding of the possible implementation techniques for standard algorithms, but also the skillful use of computer hardware resources (such as internal registers, memory, and peripheral devices), and creative use of appropriate data structures. I will cover these techniques in the following chapters.

Programming also requires a strict documentation discipline. Well-documented programs are understandable to others, as well as to the author. Documentation must be both internal and external to the program. *Internal program documentation* refers to the comments used in the body of a program to explain its operation. *External documentation* refers to the design documents that are separate from the program, including written explanations, manuals, and flowcharts.

An intermediate step is almost always used between the designing of the *algorithm* and the *program.* It is called *flowcharting.*

FLOWCHARTING

A flowchart is simply a symbolic representation of an algorithm, expressed as a sequence of rectangles and diamonds. On the flowchart, rectangles are used to represent *commands,* or executable statements, and diamonds are used for *tests,* such as: If information X is true, then take action A, else B. Figure 1.1 shows an example of a flowchart. I will not present a formal definition of flowcharts at this point; I will discuss flowcharting in more detail in Chapter 3.

Flowcharting is a highly recommended intermediate step between the specification of the algorithm and the actual coding of the solution. Remarkably, perhaps 10 percent of the programming population can write a program successfully without having to flowchart. Unfortunately, 90 percent of the population believes it belongs to this 10 percent! The result is

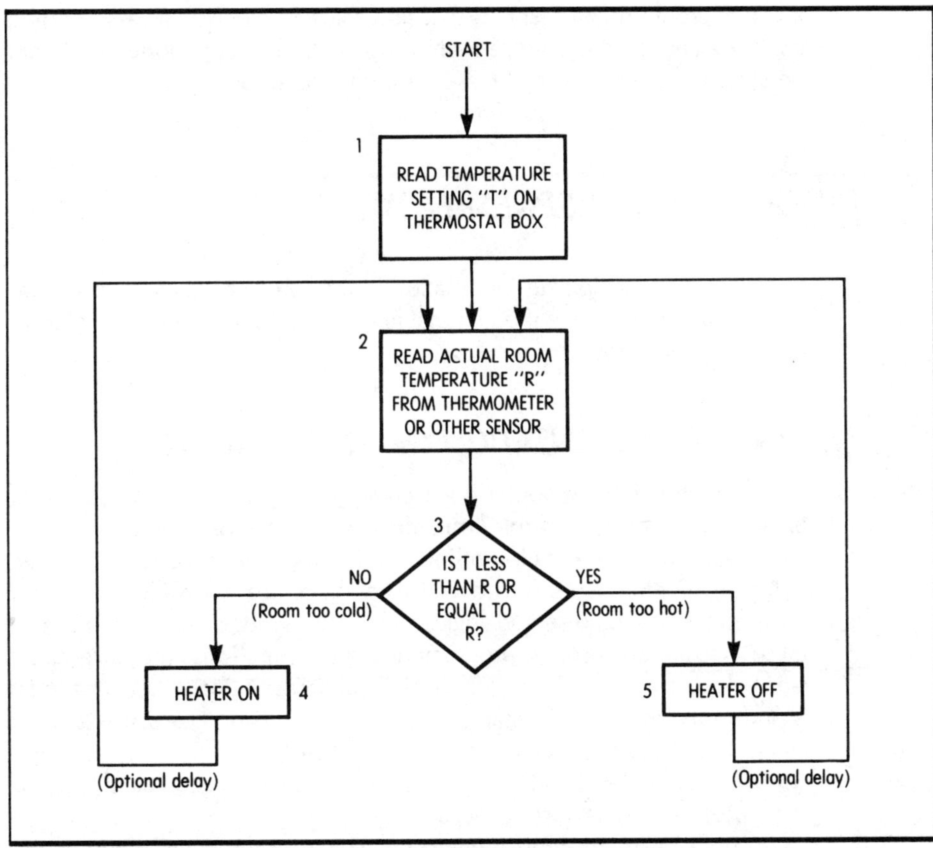

Figure 1.1: A Flowchart for Keeping Room Temperature Constant

that, on the average, 80 percent of these programs will fail the first time they are run on a computer. (These percentages are naturally not meant to be accurate.) In short, most novice programmers seldom see the necessity for drawing a flowchart. This usually results in "unclean" or erroneous programs, and programmers must then spend a long time testing and correcting their programs. (This is called the *debugging* phase.) The discipline of flowcharting is, therefore, highly recommended in all cases. It requires a small amount of additional time prior to the coding, but it usually results in a clear program that executes correctly and quickly. Once flowcharting is well understood, a small percentage of programmers can perform this step mentally, without using paper. Unfortunately, in such cases the programs they write are usually difficult for anyone else to understand, since the documentation provided by the flowchart is not available. As a result, it is universally recommended that flowcharting be used as a strict discipline for any program more than 10 or 15 instructions long. This book provides many examples of flowcharting throughout.

INFORMATION REPRESENTATION

All computers manipulate information in the form of numbers or characters. I will now examine the external and internal representations of information on a computer.

INTERNAL REPRESENTATION OF INFORMATION

All information in a computer is stored as groups of bits. A *bit* stands for a *binary digit.* Because of the limitations of conventional electronics, the most practical representation of information uses two-state logic. The two states of the circuits used in digital electronics are generally *off* and *on*; these states are represented logically by the symbols *0* and *1.* Because these circuits are used to implement logical functions, they are called *binary logic circuits.* As a result, virtually all information processing today is performed in binary format. In the case of microprocessors in general, and of the 65816 in particular, these bits are structured in groups of eight. A group of eight bits is called a *byte.* A group of four bits is called a *nibble.* Two bytes, or 16 bits, form a *word.*

Let's now examine how information is represented internally in this binary format. Two entities must be represented inside the computer. The first is the program, which is a sequence of instructions. The second is the data on which the program operates. The data may include numbers or alphanumeric text. I will now discuss the representation of instructions, numbers, and alphanumerics in binary format.

Program Representation

All instructions are represented internally as single or multiple bytes. A so-called short instruction is represented by a single byte. A longer instruction is represented by two or more bytes. The 65816 is a 16-bit microprocessor, so it fetches bytes successively from its memory. Therefore, a single-byte instruction always has the potential for executing faster than a two- or three-byte instruction. You will see later on that this is an important feature of the instruction set of any microprocessor, and of the 65816 in particular. The limitation to eight bits in length can result in important restrictions; however, the 65816 does not have these restrictions because 16-bit words may be used. This limitation is a classic example of the compromise that often has to be made between speed and flexibility in programming. The binary code used to represent instructions is dictated by the manufacturer: the 65816, like any other microprocessor, comes equipped with a fixed instruction set. The instructions for the 65816 are presented in Chapter 4 and listed with their code in Appendix D. A program is expressed as a sequence of these binary instructions.

Representing Numeric Data

Representing numbers in binary is not a straightforward task: several cases must be distinguished. You must be able to represent whole numbers, then signed numbers (positive and negative numbers or integers), and finally, numbers with a decimal point. Let's now address these requirements and possible solutions.

You can represent integers using a *direct binary* representation. The direct binary representation is simply the representation of the decimal value of a number in the binary system. In the binary system, the rightmost bit represents 2 to the power 0. The next bit to the left represents 2 to the power 1, the next one represents 2 to the power 2, and the leftmost bit represents 2 to the power 7 = 128. For example,

$$b_7b_6b_5b_4b_3b_2b_1b_0$$

represents:

$$b_72^7 + b_62^6 + b_52^5 + b_42^4 + b_32^3 + b_22^2 + b_12^1 + b_02^0$$

The powers of 2 are:

$$2^7 = 128, 2^6 = 64, 2^5 = 32, 2^4 = 16, 2^3 = 8, 2^2 = 4, 2^1 = 2, 2^0 = 1$$

The binary representation is analogous to the decimal representation of numbers, where 123 represents:

$$\begin{array}{rcr} 1 \times 100 & = & 100 \\ + 2 \times 10 & = & 20 \\ + 3 \times 1 & = & 3 \\ \hline & = & 123 \end{array}$$

Note that $100 = 10^2$, $10 = 10^1$, $1 = 10^0$. In this positional notation, each digit represents a power of 10. In the binary system, each binary digit or bit represents a power of 2, instead of a power of 10 as in the decimal system. Let's look at an example of binary. In binary, 00001001 represents:

$$\begin{array}{r} 1 \times \quad 1 = 1\ (2^0) \\ 0 \times \quad 2 = 0\ (2^1) \\ 0 \times \quad 4 = 0\ (2^2) \\ 1 \times \quad 8 = 8\ (2^3) \\ 0 \times \ 16 = 0\ (2^4) \\ 0 \times \ 32 = 0\ (2^5) \\ 0 \times \ 64 = 0\ (2^6) \\ \underline{0 \times 128 = 0\ (2^7)} \\ \text{in decimal: } = 9 \end{array}$$

Let's look at some other examples. 10000001 represents:

$$\begin{array}{r} 1 \times \quad 1 = \quad 1 \\ 0 \times \quad 2 = \quad 0 \\ 0 \times \quad 4 = \quad 0 \\ 0 \times \quad 8 = \quad 0 \\ 0 \times \ 16 = \quad 0 \\ 0 \times \ 32 = \quad 0 \\ 0 \times \ 64 = \quad 0 \\ \underline{1 \times 128 = 128} \\ \text{in decimal: } = 129 \end{array}$$

Therefore, 10000001 represents the decimal number 129. By examining the binary representation of numbers, it is easy to understand why bits are numbered from 0 to 7, going from right to left. Bit 0 is b_0 and corresponds to 2^0. Bit 1 is b_1 and corresponds to 2^1, and so on. The binary equivalents of the numbers from 0 to 255 are shown in Table 1.1.

Decimal to Binary Conversely, I will now compute the binary equivalent of 11 decimal:

$$\begin{array}{l} 11 \div 2 = 5 \text{ remains } 1 \rightarrow 1 \text{ (lowest bit)} \\ \ \ 5 \div 2 = 2 \text{ remains } 1 \rightarrow 1 \\ \ \ 2 \div 2 = 1 \text{ remains } 0 \rightarrow 0 \\ \ \ 1 \div 2 = 0 \text{ remains } 1 \rightarrow 1 \text{ (highest bit)} \end{array}$$

The binary equivalent is 1011 (read the rightmost column from bottom to top). You can obtain the binary equivalent of a decimal number by dividing successively by 2, until you obtain a quotient of 0.

Decimal	Binary	Decimal	Binary
0	00000000	32	00100000
1	00000001	33	00100001
2	00000010	•	
3	00000011	•	
4	00000100	•	
5	00000101	63	00111111
6	00000110	64	01000000
7	00000111	65	01000001
8	00001000	•	
9	00001001	•	
10	00001010	•	
11	00001011	127	01111111
12	00001100	128	10000000
13	00001101	129	10000001
14	00001110		
15	00001111	•	
16	00010000	•	
17	00010001	•	
•			
•			
•		254	11111110
31	00011111	255	11111111

Table 1.1: Decimal-Binary Table

Operating on Binary Data The arithmetic rules for binary numbers are straightforward. The rules for addition are

0 + 0 = 0
0 + 1 = 1
1 + 0 = 1
1 + 1 = (1)0

where (1) denotes a *carry* of 1 (note that 10 is the binary equivalent of 2 decimal). Binary subtraction can be performed by "adding the complement." I will discuss binary subtraction once I show you how to represent negative numbers. Consider the following example involving addition:

```
   10      (2)
 + 01      (1)
 ------------
 = 11      (3)
```

Addition is performed just as in decimal, by adding the columns from right to left. First you add the rightmost column:

```
        10
      + 01
      ----
        11
 (0 + 1 = 1. No carry.)
```

Then the next column:

```
        10
      + 01
      ----
        11
 (1 + 0 = 1. No carry.)
```

Now look at other examples of binary addition:

```
   0010  (2)          0011  (3)
 + 0001  (1)        + 0001  (1)
 -----------        -----------
 = 0011  (3)        = 0100  (4)
```

The last example illustrates the role of the carry. Looking at the rightmost bits: 1 + 1 = (1)0. A carry of 1 is generated, which must be added to the next bits:

```
   001 — column 0 has just been added
 + 000
 +   1   (carry)
 -----
 = (1)0  (where (1) indicates a new carry into column 2)
```

The final result is 0100.

Consider another example:

```
  0111    (7)
+ 0011    (3)
---------------
  1010   (10)
```

In this example, a carry is again generated, up to the leftmost column.

With eight bits, it is therefore possible to directly represent the numbers 00000000 to 11111111—that is, 0 to 255. Two limitations, however, are immediately obvious. First, you can only represent positive numbers. Second, the magnitude of these numbers is limited to 255, if you use only eight bits. Let's now address these limitations in turn.

Signed Binary In a signed binary representation, the leftmost bit is used to indicate the sign of the number. Traditionally, 0 is used to denote a *positive* number and 1 is used to denote a *negative* number. For example, 11111111 represents −127, while 01111111 represents +127. You can now represent positive and negative numbers, but the maximum magnitude of these numbers is only 127. As another example, 00000001 represents +1 (the leading 0 is +, followed by 0000001 = 1) and 10000001 is −1 (the leading 1 is −).

Let's now address the *magnitude* problem. To represent larger numbers, you must use a larger number of bits. For example, if you use 16 bits (two bytes) to represent numbers, you can represent numbers from −32K to +32K in signed binary. (In computer jargon, 1K represents 1,024.) Bit 15 is used for the sign, and the remaining 15 bits (bit 14 through bit 0) are used for the magnitude: 2^{15} = 32K. If this magnitude is too small, you must use three bytes or more.

If you wish to represent large integers, you must use a larger number of bytes internally. This is why most simple BASIC interpreters, and other languages, provide only a limited precision for integers. This way, they can use a shorter internal format for the numbers they manipulate. Better versions of BASIC and some other languages provide a larger number of significant decimal digits at the expense of a large number of bytes for each number.

Let's now solve another problem: the one of speed efficiency. Let's perform an addition in the signed binary representation just introduced. To add +7 and −5:

```
+7 is represented by    00000111
−5 is represented by    10000101
                        --------
The binary sum is:      10001100, or −12
```

This is not the correct result. The correct result is +2. Thus, to use this representation, you must take special actions, depending on the sign. This results in increased complexity and reduced performance. In other words, the binary addition of signed numbers does not work correctly. This is annoying. Clearly, the computer must not only represent information, but it must also perform arithmetic on it.

The solution to this problem is called the *two's complement* representation, which you use instead of the *signed binary* representation for negative numbers. To introduce two's complement, I will first introduce an intermediate step: *one's complement.*

One's Complement In the one's complement representation, all positive integers are represented in their correct binary format. For example, +3 is represented as usual by 00000011. However, its complement, −3, is obtained by complementing every bit in the original representation. Each 0 is transformed into a 1, and each 1 is transformed into a 0. In the example, the one's complement representation of −3 is 11111100.
Let's look at another example:

+2 is 00000010
−2 is 11111101

Note that in this representation, positive numbers start with a 0 on the left, and negative numbers start with a 1 on the left. As a test, add −4 and +6:

```
           −4 is 11111011
           +6 is 00000110
           ---------------
The sum is: (1)00000001
```

where (1) indicates a carry. The correct result should be 2 or 00000010.

Let's try again:

```
           −3 is 11111100
           −2 is 11111101
           ---------------
The sum is: (1)11111001
```

or −6, plus a carry. The correct result is −5. The representation of −5 is 11111010. It did not work.

This representation does represent positive and negative numbers, but the result of an ordinary addition does not always come out correctly. I will now use another representation. It is evolved from the one's complement and is called the two's complement representation.

Two's Complement Representation In the two's complement representation, positive numbers are represented, as usual, in signed binary, just as in one's complement. The difference lies in the representation of *negative numbers.* In two's complement, a negative number is obtained by first computing the one's complement and then *adding one.* Let's examine an example.

Example: +5 is represented in signed binary by 10000101. Its one's complement representation is 11111010. The two's complement is obtained by adding one. It is 11111011.

Let's try a subtraction:

```
  00000011    (3)
+ 11111011   (-5)
--------------------
= 11111110
```

Now, let's identify the result by computing the two's complement:

```
(the one's complement of 11111110 is)     00000001
                              (add 1)   +        1
                                        ----------
    (therefore, the two's complement is)  00000010 or +2
```

The result 11111110 represents −2. It is correct.

Now add +4 and −3 (the subtraction is performed by adding the two's complement):

```
          +4 is 00000100
          -3 is 11111101
          --------------
The result is: (1)00000001
```

If you ignore the carry, the result is 00000001 (1 in decimal). This is the correct result. Without giving the complete mathematical proof, I will simply state that this representation does work. In two's complement, you can add or subtract signed numbers, regardless of the sign. With the usual rules of binary addition, the result is correct, including the sign. The carry is ignored. This is a significant advantage. If this were not the case, you would have to correct the result for sign every time, causing a much slower addition or subtraction time.

For the sake of completeness, let me state that two's complement is simply the most convenient representation to use for simpler processors, such as microprocessors. On more complex processors, you may use other representations. For example, you may use one's complement, but if you do, you need special circuitry to "correct" the result.

From this point on, I will implicitly represent all signed integers internally in two's complement notation. See Table 1.2 for a table of two's complement numbers.

I will now offer examples that demonstrate the rules of two's complement. In particular, C denotes a possible carry (or borrow) condition. (It is bit 8 of the result.) *V* denotes a two's complement overflow; that is, when the sign of the result is changed accidentally, because the numbers are too large. It is essentially an internal carry from bit 6 to bit 7 (the sign bit). I will clarify this below.

The Carry C Here is an example of a carry:

```
  10000000     (128)
+ 10000001     (129)
--------------------
= (1)00000001  (257)
```

where (1) indicates a carry. The result requires a ninth bit (bit 8, since the rightmost bit is 0). It is the carry bit.

If you assume that the carry is the ninth bit of the result, you recognize the result as binary 100000001 = 257. However, the carry must be recognized and handled with care. Inside the microprocessor, the registers used to hold information are generally only eight bits wide. When storing the result, only bits 0 to 7 will be preserved. The 65816 also has 16-bit internal registers, but the carry will still occur if a result is greater than 65535.

A carry, therefore, always requires special action. It must be detected by special instructions, then processed. Processing the carry means storing it somewhere (with a special instruction), ignoring it, or deciding that it is an error (if the largest authorized result is 11111111).

Overflow V Here's an example of overflow:

```
bit 6──────┐
bit 7────┐ │
         ↓ ↓
          01000000    (64)
        + 01000001    (65)
        -------------------
        = 10000001  (−127)
```

An internal carry has been generated from bit 6 into bit 7. This is called an *overflow*. The result is now negative, "by accident." This situation must be detected so that it can be corrected.

+	Two's complement code	–	Two's complement code
+ 127	01111111	– 128	10000000
+ 126	01111110	– 127	10000001
+ 125	01111101	– 126	10000010
. . .		– 125	10000011
		. . .	
+ 65	01000001	– 65	10111111
+ 64	01000000	– 64	11000000
+ 63	00111111	– 63	11000001
. . .		. . .	
+ 33	00100001	– 33	11011111
+ 32	00100000	– 32	11100000
+ 31	00011111	– 31	11100001
. . .		. . .	
+ 17	00010001	– 17	11101111
+ 16	00010000	– 16	11110000
+ 15	00001111	– 15	11110001
+ 14	00001110	– 14	11110010
+ 13	00001101	– 13	11110011
+ 12	00001100	– 12	11110100
+ 11	00001011	– 11	11110101
+ 10	00001010	– 10	11110110
+ 9	00001001	– 9	11110111
+ 8	00001000	– 8	11111000
+ 7	00000111	– 7	11111001
+ 6	00000110	– 6	11111010
+ 5	00000101	– 5	11111011
+ 4	00000100	– 4	11111100
+ 3	00000011	– 3	11111101
+ 2	00000010	– 2	11111110
+ 1	00000001	– 1	11111111
+ 0	00000000		

Table 1.2: Two's Complement Table

Let's examine another situation:

```
  11111111     (−1)
+ 11111111     (−1)
= (1)11111110  (−2)
    ▼
  carry
```

In this case, an internal carry has been generated from bit 6 into bit 7, and also from bit 7 into C. The rules of two's complement arithmetic specify that this carry should be ignored. The result is then correct. This is because the carry from bit 6 to bit 7 did not change the sign bit.

The carry from bit 6 into bit 7 is not an *overflow* condition. When operating on negative numbers, the overflow is not simply a carry from bit 6 into bit 7. Let's examine one more example:

```
  11000000     (−64)
+ 10111111     (−65)
= (1)01111111  (+127)
    ▼
  carry
```

This time, there has been no internal carry from bit 6 into bit 7, but there has been an external carry. The result is incorrect, as bit 7 has been changed. An overflow condition should be indicated.

Overflow can occur in four situations:

1. Addition of large positive numbers
2. Addition of large negative numbers
3. Subtraction of a large positive number from a large negative number
4. Subtraction of a large negative number from a large positive number

Let me now improve the definition of overflow.

Technically, the overflow indicator, a special bit reserved for this purpose and called a *status flag,* is set when there is a carry from bit 6 into bit 7, and there is no external carry. It is also set when there is no carry from bit 6 into bit 7, but there is an external carry. This indicates that bit 7 (the sign of the result) has been accidentally changed. For the technically minded reader, the overflow flag is set by applying exclusive-OR to the carry-in and carry-out of bit 7 (the sign bit). Practically every microprocessor is supplied with a special overflow flag to automatically detect this condition—a condition that requires corrective action.

Overflow indicates that the result of an addition or subtraction requires more bits than are available in the standard 8-bit register used to contain the result.

The Carry and the Overflow The carry and the overflow bits are called status flags. They are provided in every microprocessor. You will learn to use them for effective programming in Chapter 2. These two indicators are located in a special register called the flags or the *status* register. This register also contains additional indicators (as described in Chapter 4).

Examples I'll now give actual examples that illustrate the operation of the carry and the overflow. In each example, V denotes the overflow and C denotes the carry. If there has been no overflow, V = 0; if there has been an overflow, V = 1. (The same is true for the carry C.) Remember that the rules of two's complement specify that the carry be ignored. (The mathematical proof is not supplied here.) Consider the following examples:

Positive-Positive

```
  00000110     (+6)
+ 00001000     (+8)
-----------------------
= 00001110     (+14)  V:0  C:0
(CORRECT)
```

Positive-Positive with Overflow

```
  01111111     (+127)
+ 00000001     (+1)
-----------------------
= 10000000     (-128)  V:1  C:0
```

The above is invalid because an overflow has occurred.
(ERROR)

Positive-Negative(result positive)

```
    00000100      (+4)
+   11111110      (-2)
-----------------------
=(1)00000010      (+2)  V:0  C:1(disregard)
(CORRECT)
```

Positive-Negative (result negative)

```
  00000010     (+2)
+ 11111100     (-4)
-----------------
= 11111110     (-2)  V:0  C:0
(CORRECT)
```

Negative-Negative

```
     11111110     (-2)
+    11111100     (-4)
----------------------
= (1)11111010     (-6)  V:0  C:1(disregard)
(CORRECT)
```

Negative-Negative with Overflow

```
     10000001   (-127)
+    11000010    (-62)
----------------------
= (1)01000011    (+67)  V:1  C:1
(ERROR)
```

In the last example, an *underflow* has occurred, by adding two large negative numbers. The result is −189, which is too large to reside in eight bits.

Fixed Format Representation You now know how to represent signed integers; however, I have not yet resolved the problem of magnitude. If you want to represent larger integers, you need several bytes. To perform arithmetic operations efficiently, you must use a fixed number of bytes, rather than a variable one. Therefore, once you have chosen the number of bytes, the maximum magnitude of the number that can be represented is fixed.

The Magnitude Problem When adding numbers, I've restricted discussion to eight bits, because the processor can operate internally on eight bits at a time and 8-bit examples are easier to understand. However, this restricts you to the numbers in the range −128 to +127. Clearly, this is not sufficient for many applications. The processor can also operate in a 16-bit mode, allowing a range of −32768 to +32767.

You can use multiple precision to increase the number of digits that can be represented. You can then use a two-, three-, or *n*-byte format. For example, let's examine a 16-bit, double-precision format:

00000000	00000000	is 0
00000000	00000001	is 1
01111111	11111111	is 32767
11111111	11111111	is −1
11111111	11111110	is −2

However, this method does have a disadvantage. When adding two numbers, for example, you generally have to fetch them from memory eight bits at a time, as explained in Chapter 2. This results in slower processing. Also, this representation uses 16 bits for any number, even if it could be represented with only eight bits. It is, therefore, common to use the smallest number of bytes possible.

Consider the following important point: the number of bits, *n*, chosen for the two's complement representation is usually fixed for that program. If any result or intermediate computation should generate a number that requires more than *n* bits, some bits will be lost. The program normally retains the *n* leftmost bits (the most significant) and drops the low-order ones. This is called *truncating* the result.

Let's look at an example in the decimal system, using a six-digit representation:

```
    123456
  ×    1.2
  --------
    246912
   123456
  --------
= 148147.2
```

The result requires seven digits. The 2 after the decimal point will be dropped, and the final result will be 148147. It has been truncated. Usually, as long as the position of the decimal point is not lost, this method is used to extend the range of the operations that can be performed, at the expense of precision. (The details of binary multiplication are given in Chapter 3.) The problem is the same in binary. This fixed-format representation may cause a loss of precision, but it may be sufficient for usual computations or mathematical operations.

Unfortunately, in the case of accounting, no loss of precision is tolerable. For example, if a customer rings up a large total on a cash register, it would not be acceptable to have a five-figure total approximated to the dollar. Thus, you must use another representation whenever precision in the result is essential. The solution normally used is BCD, or binary-coded decimal.

BCD Representation The principle used in representing numbers in BCD is to encode each decimal digit separately and use as many bits as necessary to represent the complete number exactly. To encode each of the digits from 0 through 9, four bits are necessary. Three bits supply only eight combinations, and so cannot encode the ten digits. Four bits allow 16 combinations and are, therefore, sufficient to encode the digits 0 through 9. Note also that six of the possible codes are not used in the BCD representation (see Table 1.3). This will become a problem when you perform additions and subtractions. Since only four bits are needed to encode a BCD digit, you may encode two BCD digits in every byte. This is called *packed BCD.* As an example, 00000000 is 00 in BCD, and 10011001 is 99.

CODE	BCD SYMBOL	CODE	BCD SYMBOL
0000	0	1000	8
0001	1	1001	9
0010	2	1010	unused
0011	3	1011	unused
0100	4	1100	unused
0101	5	1101	unused
0110	6	1110	unused
0111	7	1111	unused

Table 1.3: BCD Table

You read a BCD code as follows:

```
                 0010 0001
BCD digit 2 <------┘    |
BCD digit 1 <-----------┘
BCD number 21
```

You use as many bytes as necessary to represent all BCD digits. Typically, one or more nibbles are used at the beginning of the representation to indicate the total number of nibbles—the total number of BCD digits used. Another nibble or byte denotes the position of the decimal point. However, conventions may vary. Here is an example of a representation for multibyte BCD integers:

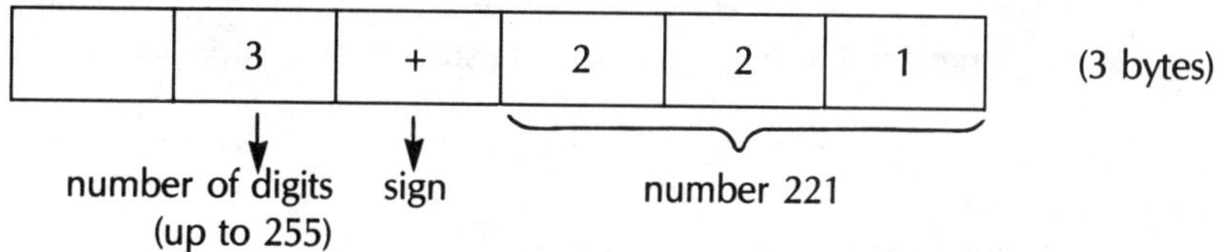

This example represents +221. (The sign may be represented by 0000 for +, and 0001 for −, for example.)

The BCD representation can easily accommodate decimal numbers. For example, +2.21 may be represented by:

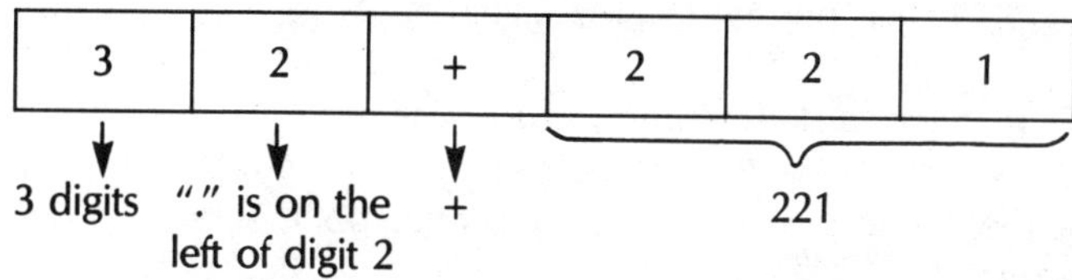

The advantage of BCD is that it yields absolutely correct results. Its disadvantage is that it uses a large amount of memory and results in slow arithmetic operations. This is acceptable only in an accounting environment, but BCD is normally not used in other cases.

The problems associated with the representation of integers, signed integers, and large integers have now been solved. I have even presented one possible method of representing decimal numbers, with BCD representation. Now, I'll examine the problem of representing decimal numbers in fixed-length format.

Floating-Point Representation The basic principle of floating-point representation is that decimal numbers are represented with a fixed-length format. To avoid wasting bits, the representation *normalizes* all the numbers. For example, 0.000123 wastes three zeros on the left before nonzero digits. These zeros have no meaning except to indicate the position of the decimal point. Normalizing this number results in $.123 \times 10^{-3}$, where .123 is the *normalized mantissa* and −3 is the *exponent*. You normalize this number by eliminating all the meaningless zeros to the left of the first nonzero digit and by adjusting the exponent. Consider another example:

Example: 22.1 is normalized as $.221 \times 10^2$. The general form of floating-point representation is $M \times 10^E$, where M is the mantissa and E is the exponent.

You can readily see that a normalized number is characterized by a mantissa less than 1 and greater than or equal to .1 in all cases where the number is not zero. In other words, you can represent it mathematically by:

$$.1 \leqslant M < 1 \text{ or } 10^{-1} \leqslant M < 10^0$$

Similarly, in binary representation:

$$2^{-1} \leqslant M < 2^0 \text{ or } .5 \leqslant M < 1$$

where M is the absolute value of the mantissa (disregarding the sign). For example:

$$111.01 \text{ is normalized as: } .11101 \times 2^3$$

The mantissa is .11101. The exponent is 3.

Now that I have defined the principle of the representation, let's examine the actual format. A typical floating-point representation appears in Figure 1.2.

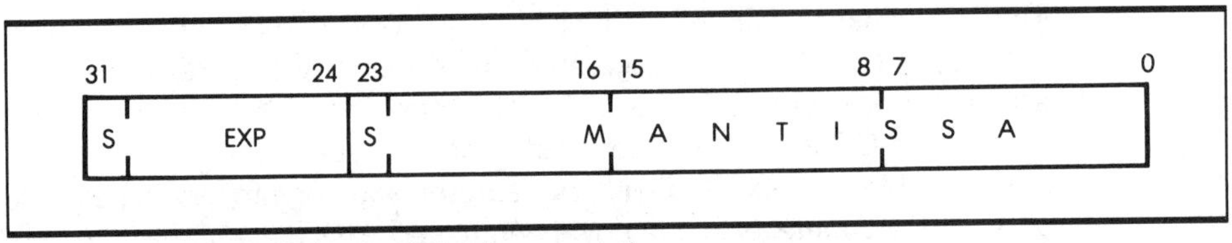

Figure 1.2: Typical Floating-Point Representation

In the representation in Figure 1.2, four bytes are used, for a total of 32 bits. The first byte on the left of the illustration is used to represent the exponent. Both the exponent and the mantissa are represented in two's complement. As a result, the maximum exponent is −128. S in Figure 1.2 denotes the sign bit.

Three bytes are used to represent the mantissa. Since the first bit in the two's complement representation indicates the sign, this leaves 23 bits for the representation of the magnitude of the mantissa.

This is only one example of a floating-point representation. You can use only three bytes, or you can use more. The four-byte representation proposed above is a common one and represents a reasonable compromise in terms of accuracy, magnitude of numbers, storage utilization, and efficiency in arithmetic operation.

I have now explored the problems associated with the representation of numbers and have shown you how to represent them in integer form, with a sign, or in decimal form. Let's now go on to examine how to represent alphanumeric data internally.

Representing Alphanumeric Data

The representation of alphanumeric data—characters—is completely straightforward: all characters are encoded in an 8-bit code. Only two codes are in general use in the computer world; the ASCII code and the EBCDIC code. ASCII stands for American Standard Code for Information Interchange, and it is universally used in the world of microprocessors. EBCDIC is a variation of ASCII used by IBM, and is, therefore, not used in the microcomputer world unless you interface to an IBM terminal.

Let's briefly examine the ASCII encoding. It encodes 26 letters of the alphabet for both uppercase and lowercase, plus 10 numeric symbols, and perhaps 20 additional special symbols. This is easily accomplished with seven bits, which allow 128 possible codes. (See Table 1.4.) All characters are, therefore, encoded in seven bits. The eighth bit, when it is used, is the *parity bit.* Parity is a technique for verifying that the contents of a byte have not been accidentally changed. The number of ones in the byte are counted and the eighth bit is set to one if the count is odd, thus making the total even. This is called *even parity. Odd parity*—writing the eighth bit (the leftmost bit) so that the total number of ones in the byte is odd—can also be used.

As an example, let's compute the parity bit for 0010011 using even parity. The number of ones is 3. The parity bit must, therefore, be a one, so that the total number of bits will be 4—that is, even. The result is 10010011, where the leading 1 is the parity bit and 0010011 identifies the character.

The table of 7-bit ASCII codes is shown in Table 1.4. In practice, it is used "as is"; that is, without parity, by adding a zero in the leftmost position, or else with parity, by adding the appropriate extra bit on the left.

In specialized situations, such as telecommunications, you may use other codings, such as error-correcting codes. However, descriptions of these codings are beyond the scope of this book.

Now that you have seen the usual representations for both program and data inside the computer, let's examine the possible external representations.

HEX LSD	MSD BITS	0 000	1 001	2 010	3 011	4 100	5 101	6 110	7 111
0	0000	NUL	DLE	SPACE	0	@	P	—	p
1	0001	SOH	DC1	!	1	A	Q	a	q
2	0010	STX	DC2	″	2	B	R	b	r
3	0011	ETX	DC3	#	3	C	S	c	s
4	0100	EOT	DC4	$	4	D	T	d	t
5	0101	ENQ	NAK	%	5	E	U	e	u
6	0110	ACK	SYN	&	6	F	V	f	v
7	0111	BEL	ETB	′	7	G	W	g	w
8	1000	BS	CAN	(	8	H	X	h	x
9	1001	HT	EM	)	9	I	Y	i	y
A	1010	LF	SUB	*	:	J	Z	j	z
B	1011	VT	ESC	+	;	K	[	k	{
C	1100	FF	FS	,	<	L	\	l	--
D	1101	CR	GS	—	=	M	]	m	}
E	1110	SO	RS	.	>	N	^	n	~
F	1111	SI	US	/	?	O	←	o	DEL

Table 1.4: ASCII Conversion Table (see Appendix B for abbreviations)

EXTERNAL REPRESENTATION OF INFORMATION

The external representation of information refers to the way information is presented to the *user,* who is generally the programmer. Information can be presented externally in essentially three formats: binary, octal or hexadecimal, and symbolic. Let's examine these formats.

Binary You have seen that information is stored internally in *bytes,* which are sequences of eight *bits* (zeros or ones). It is sometimes desirable to display this internal information directly in its binary format – this is known as *binary representation.* A simple example is provided by light-emitting diodes (LEDs), which are essentially miniature lights on the front panel of the microcomputer. In the case of an 8-bit microprocessor, a front panel is typically equipped with eight LEDs to display the contents of any internal register. A lighted LED indicates a one. An unlighted LED indicates a zero. You may use such a binary representation for the fine debugging of a complex program, especially if it involves input/output, but it is naturally impractical at the human level. This is because, in most cases, it is easier to look at information in symbolic form. For example, 9 is much easier to understand and to remember than 1001. More convenient representations have been devised that improve the interface between people and machines.

Octal and Hexadecimal Octal and hexadecimal encode three and four binary bits, respectively, into a unique symbol. Octal is a format using three bits, where each combination of three bits is represented by a symbol between 0 and 7. (See Table 1.5.)

Binary	Octal
000	0
001	1
010	2
011	3
100	4
101	5
110	6
111	7

Table 1.5: Octal Symbols

For example, 00 100 100 binary is represented by:

```
           00 100 100
           ▼   ▼   ▼
           0   4   4
```

or 044 in octal.

As another example: 11 111 111 is:

```
 11 111 111
 ▼   ▼   ▼
 3   7   7
```

or 377 in octal.

Conversely, the octal 211 represents

010 001 001

or 10001001 binary.

Octal has traditionally been used on older computers that employ various numbers of bits, ranging from 8 to, perhaps, 64. More recently, with the dominance of byte addressed microprocessors, the 8-bit format has become the standard, and another, more practical, representation is used—*hexadecimal* representation.

In the hexadecimal representation, a group of four bits is encoded as one hexadecimal digit. Hexadecimal digits are represented by the symbols from 0 to 9, and by the letters A, B, C, D, E, F. For example, 0000 is represented by 0; 0001 is represented by 1; and 1111 is represented by the letter F (see Table 1.6).

For example, 1010 0001 in binary is represented by

in hexadecimal.

DECIMAL	BINARY	HEX	OCTAL
0	0000	0	0
1	0001	1	1
2	0010	2	2
3	0011	3	3
4	0100	4	4
5	0101	5	5
6	0110	6	6
7	0111	7	7
8	1000	8	10
9	1001	9	11
10	1010	A	12
11	1011	B	13
12	1100	C	14
13	1101	D	15
14	1110	E	16
15	1111	F	17

Table 1.6: Hexadecimal Codes

Hexadecimal offers the advantage of encoding eight bits into only two digits. This is easier to visualize or memorize and faster to type into a computer than its binary equivalent. Therefore, on most new microcomputers, hexadecimal is the preferred method of representation for groups of bits.

Naturally, whenever the information present in the memory has a meaning, such as representing text or numbers, hexadecimal is not convenient for representing the meaning of this information for a human user.

Symbolic Representation *Symbolic representation* refers to the external representation of information in actual symbolic form. For example, decimal numbers are represented as decimal numbers, and not as sequences of hexadecimal symbols or bits. Similarly, text is represented as such. Naturally, symbolic representation is most practical for the user. You use it whenever an appropriate display device is available, such as a CRT display or a printer. (Unfortunately, in smaller systems such as one-board microcomputers it is uneconomical to provide such displays, and you are restricted to hexadecimal communication with the computer if the computer cannot communicate with a terminal.)

Summary of External Representations

Symbolic representation of information is the most desirable, since it is the most natural for a human user. However, it requires an expensive interface in the form of an alphanumeric keyboard, plus a printer or a CRT display. For this reason, it may not be available on the less expensive systems. An alternative type of representation is then used, and in such a case, hexadecimal is the dominant representation. Only in rare cases, relating to fine debugging at the hardware or software level, is the binary representation used. *Binary* directly displays the contents of the registers or memory in binary format.

Now that you have seen how information is represented internally and externally, I will discuss the actual microprocessor that manipulates this information in Chapter 2.

EXERCISES

1-1: *What is the decimal value of 11111100?*

1-2: *What is the binary for 257?*

1-3: *Convert 19 to binary, then back to decimal.*

1-4: *Compute 5 + 10 in binary. Verify that the result is 15.*

1-5: *Compute the result of:*

```
  1111
+ 0001
------
```

Does the result fit into four bits?

1-6: *What is the representation of −5 in signed binary?*

1-7: *The representation of +6 is 00000110. What is the representation of −6 in one's complement?*

1-8: *What is the two's complement representation of +127?*

1-9: *What is the two's complement representation of −128?*

1-10: *What are the smallest and the largest numbers that can be represented in two's complement notation, using only one byte?*

1-11: *Compute the two's complement of 20. Then compute the two's complement of your result. Do you find 20 again?*

1-12: *Complete the following additions. Indicate the result, the carry C, the overflow V, and whether the result is correct or not:*

```
  10111111      (___)              11111010      (___)
+ 11000001      (___)            + 11111001      (___)
= ________      V:___C:___       = ________      V:___C:___
___CORRECT      ___ERROR         ___CORRECT      ___ERROR

  00010000      (___)              01111110      (___)
+ 01000000      (___)            + 00101010      (___)
= ________      V:___C:___       = ________      V:___C:___
___CORRECT      ___ERROR         ___CORRECT      ___ERROR
```

1-13: *Can you show an example of overflow when adding a positive and a negative number? Why or why not?*

1-14: *What are the largest and the smallest numbers that can be represented in two bytes, using two's complement?*

1-15: *What is the largest negative integer that can be represented in a two's complement triple-precision (24-bit) format?*

1-16: *What is the BCD representation for 29? for 91?*

1-17: *Is 10100000 a valid BCD representation? Why or why not?*

1-18: *Using the same convention, represent −23123. Show it in BCD format, as above, then in binary.*

1-19: *Show the BCD for 222 and 111, then for the result of 222 × 111 (Compute the result by hand, then show it in the above representation.)*

1-20: *How many bits are required to encode 9999 in BCD? In two's complement?*

1-21: *How many decimal digits can the mantissa represent with the 23 bits?*

1-22: *Compute the 8-bit representation of the digits 0 through 9, using even parity. (This code will be used in application examples of Chapter 8.)*

1-23: *Complete Exercise 1-22 for the letters A through F.*

1-24: *Using a nonparity ASCII code (where the leftmost bit is 0), indicate the binary contents of the four characters below:*

A
?
3
b

1-25: *What is the hexadecimal representation of 10101010?*

1-26: *Conversely, what is the binary equivalent of FA hexadecimal?*

1-27: *What is the octal representation of 01000001?*

1-28: *What is the advantage of two's complement over other representations used for signed numbers?*

1-29: *How would you represent 1024 in direct binary? Signed binary? Two's complement?*

1-30: *What is the V bit? Should the programmer test it after an addition or subtraction?*

1-31: *Compute the two's complement of +16, +17, +18, −16, −17, and −18.*

1-32: *Show the hexadecimal representation of the following text, which has been stored internally in ASCII format, with no parity:*

MESSAGE

65816 HARDWARE ORGANIZATION

2

TO PROGRAM EFFICIENTLY, you must understand the internal structure of the processor you are using. I will begin this chapter with a discussion of the basic architecture of a microcomputer system. I will then examine the internal organization of the 65816. In particular, I will study the registers of the 65816 and their combined operations. This study is particularly important, because the 65816 has an unusually large number and variety of registers.

SYSTEM ARCHITECTURE

Figure 2.1 shows the architecture of a typical microcomputer system. Appearing on the left of the illustration in Figure 2.1 is the *microprocessor unit* (the *MPU*)—in this case the 65816—which implements the functions of the *central-processing unit* (the *CPU*) on a single chip. The CPU includes an *arithmetic-logical unit* (the *ALU*), plus its internal registers, and a *control unit* (the *CU*), which decodes and internally sequences instructions. (I will discuss the CPU in detail later in this chapter.)

The MPU has three *buses:* an 8-bit bidirectional *data bus* (shown at the top of the illustration in Figure 2.1), a 16-bit unidirectional *address bus,* and a *control bus* (both shown at the bottom of the illustration). I will now discuss the functions of these buses.

The *data bus* carries the data that is exchanged by the various elements of the system. Typically, it carries the data from the memory to the MPU, from the MPU to the memory, and from the MPU to an input/output chip. (An input/output chip communicates with an external device.)

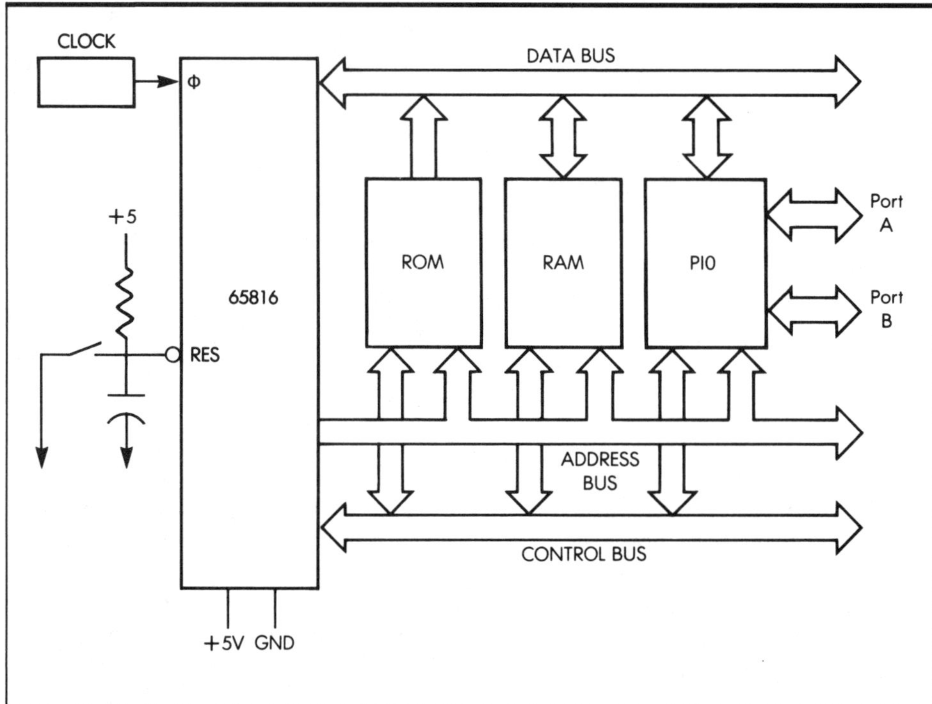

Figure 2.1: A Standard 65816 System

The *address bus* carries an address, generated by the MPU, that specifies the source or destination of the data that transits along the data bus. The *control bus* carries the various synchronization signals required by the system. Now that you know the purpose of the buses, let's connect the additional components required for a complete system.

Every MPU requires a precise timing reference, which is supplied by a *clock.* The clock appears on the left of the MPU box in Figure 2.1.

I will now describe the other elements of the system. Going from left to right on the illustration, you see the ROM, the RAM, and the PIO.

The *ROM* or *read-only memory* stores the *program* for the system. The advantage of ROM memory is that its contents are permanent: they do not disappear when the system is turned off. The ROM, therefore, usually contains a *bootstrap* or *monitor* program to permit initial system operation. In a process-control environment, nearly all programs reside in ROM. This is because they will probably never be changed and must be protected against power failures (they must not be volatile).

The *RAM* or *random-access memory* is the read/write memory for the system. In a hobbyist or program-development environment, most of the programs reside in RAM so that they can be easily changed. Such programs may be kept in RAM, or transferred into ROM, if desired. RAM, however, is volatile. Its contents are lost when power is turned off. In a control system, the amount of RAM is typically small (for data only); however, in a program-development environment, the amount of RAM is large, as it contains programs plus development software. All RAM contents must be loaded, prior to use, from an external device.

Finally, a system also contains one or more interface chips, so that it can communicate with the external world. The most frequently used interface chip is the PIO or *parallel input/output* chip (shown in Figure 2.1). The PIO, like the other chips in the system, connects to all three buses and provides at least two 16-bit ports for communication with the outside world. For simplicity, the connections between the control bus and the various chips do not appear in Figure 2.1.

The functional modules just described need not necessarily reside on a single LSI chip. In fact, you could use *combination chips,* which may include both the PIO and a limited amount of ROM or RAM.

To build an actual system, you need even more components. In particular, you may need to *buffer* the buses. Also, you may need *decoding logic* for the memory RAM chips, and, finally, you may use *drivers* to amplify signals. I won't describe these auxiliary circuits here, as they are not relevant to programming. For more information on specific assembly and interfacing techniques, see reference C207, and for specific information regarding the 65816 system, see Chapter 7.

INSIDE A MICROPROCESSOR

Several microprocessors on the market today implement the same internal architecture. Figure 2.2 shows this architecture. Going from right to left, I will now describe the different modules making up this architecture.

The *control box* on the right of the illustration represents the control unit that synchronizes the entire system. I will describe the role of the control unit later in this chapter.

The *ALU* performs arithmetic and logical operations. Special registers, called *accumulators,* are usually connected to the output of the ALU. The accumulators contain the results of arithmetic operations. Each accumulator has eight bits.

The ALU also provides *shift* and *rotate* facilities. As illustrated in Figure 2.3, a shift moves the contents of a byte by one or more positions to the

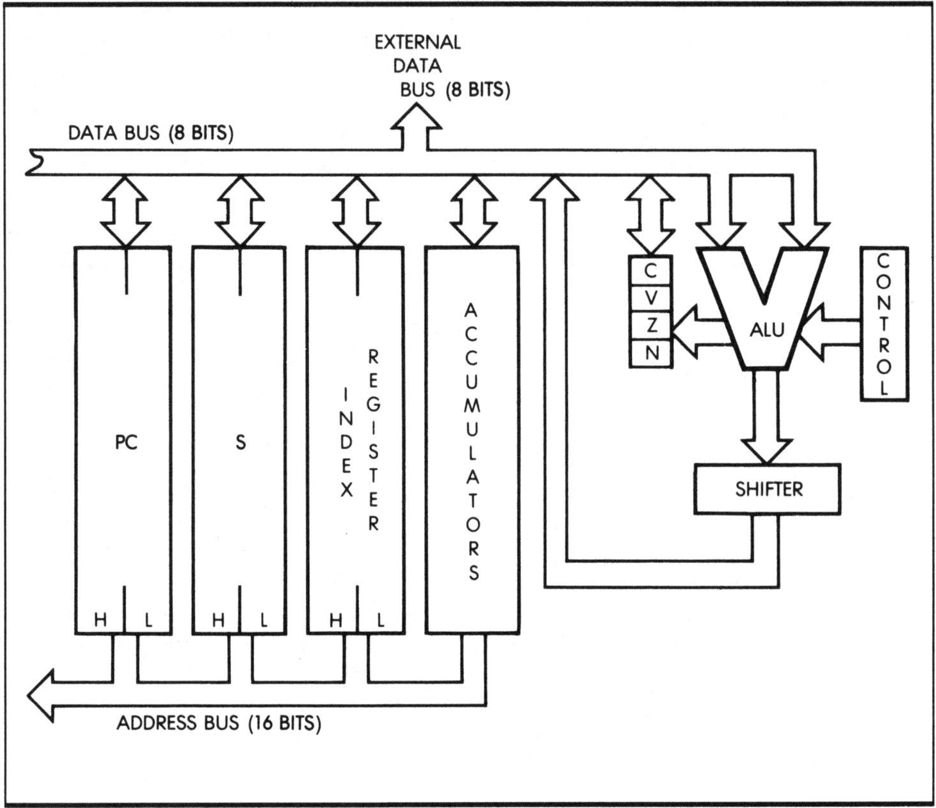

Figure 2.2: Internal Architecture of a "Standard" Microprocessor

left or right. In this illustration, each bit has been moved to the left by one position. The shifter may be on the ALU output, as illustrated in Figure 2.2, or on the accumulator input. I will describe shift and rotate operations in more detail in Chapter 3.

The *status* (or *condition code*) *register* appears to the left of the ALU. Its role is to store exceptional conditions within the microprocessor. The contents of the status register can be tested by specialized instructions, or read onto the internal data bus. A *conditional* instruction causes the execution of a different part of the program, depending on the value of one of the bits in the status register (as shown later).

SETTING STATUS FLAGS

Most of the instructions executed by the microprocessor modify some or all of the status bits. Refer to the chart provided by the manufacturer to learn which bits are modified by what instructions. This information is

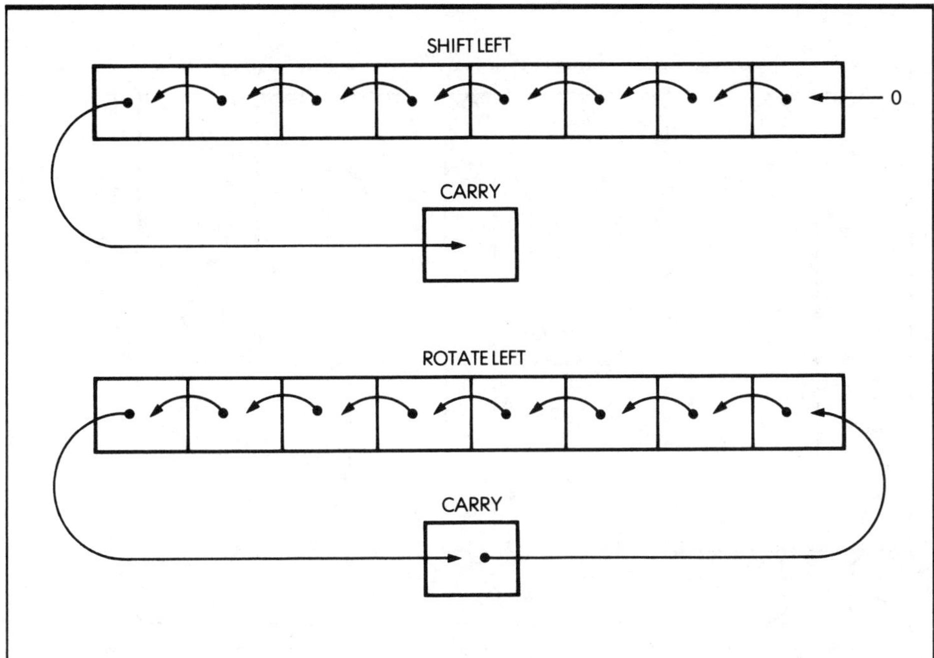

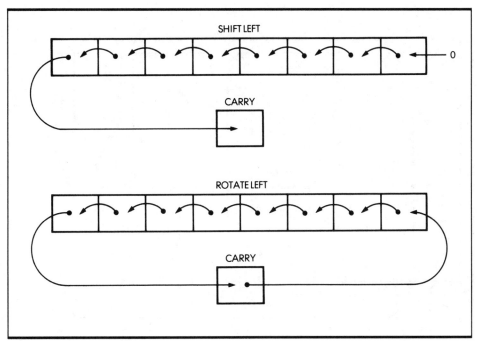

Figure 2.3: Shift and Rotate

essential for understanding the way a program is executed. Appendix D lists this information for the 65816.

THE ADDRESS REGISTERS

Address registers are 16-bit registers used for the storage of addresses. They are also often called *data counters* or *pointers* and are double registers: two 8-bit registers. They are connected to the address bus. The address registers provide the signals for the address bus. Three address registers and an address bus appear in Figure 2.4.

The only way to load the contents of these 16-bit registers is via the data bus (also shown in the illustration). To differentiate between the lower and higher half of each register, each half is usually labeled as L (low) or H (high), denoting bits 0 through 7, or 8 through 15, respectively. Let's examine the three registers shown in the illustration.

The Program Counter (PC)

The *program counter* must be present in all processors, as it is indispensable and fundamental to program execution. It contains the address of the next instruction to be executed.

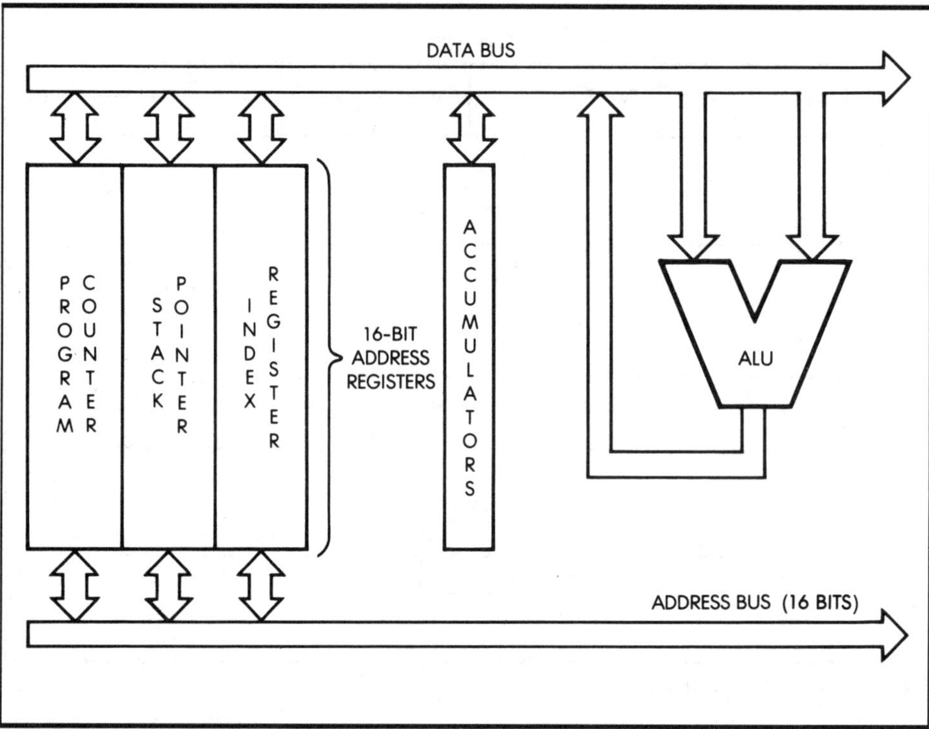

Figure 2.4: The 16-Bit Address Registers Create the Address Bus

Execution of a program is normally sequential. To access the next instruction, the program must bring it from the memory into the microprocessor. The contents of the PC are deposited on the address bus and transmitted toward the memory. The memory then reads the contents specified by this address and sends the corresponding word or instruction back to the MPU. In a few exceptional microprocessors, such as the two-chip F8, there is no PC on the microprocessor. This does not mean, however, that there is not a program counter; for reasons of efficiency, the PC is implemented directly on the memory chip.

The Stack Pointer (S)

The *stack pointer* is used to implement the stack. The stack is described in detail in the next section.

In most powerful, general-purpose microprocessors, the stack is implemented in *software*—within the memory. To keep track of the top of the stack within the memory, a 16-bit register is dedicated to the stack pointer. The S contains the address of the top of the stack within the memory. The stack is indispensable for interrupts and subroutines.

The Index Register (IR)

Indexing is a memory-addressing facility for accessing blocks of data in the memory with a single instruction. It is not always provided in microprocessors. An *index register* typically contains a displacement, which will automatically be added to a base (or it might contain a base, which will be added to a displacement). In short, indexing is used to access any word within a block of data.

THE STACK

A *stack,* formally called an LIFO (last-in, first-out) structure, is a set of registers, or memory locations, allocated to the stack data structure. The essential characteristic of the stack is that it is a *chronological* structure. The first element introduced in the stack is always at the bottom of the stack; the element most recently deposited is on the top. An analogy can be drawn with a stack of plates on a restaurant counter, if you assume there is a hole in the counter with a spring at the bottom, and plates are piled up in the hole. With this organization, the plate that has been put first in the stack is always at the bottom. The one most recently placed on the stack is the one on top. This example also illustrates another characteristic of the stack. In normal use, a stack is only accessible via two instructions: PUSH and PULL (or POP). These two instructions are illustrated in Figure 2.5. The PUSH operation deposits one element on top of the stack; the PULL operation removes elements from the stack. In the case of a microprocessor, it is the *registers* that are deposited on top of the stack. The PULL transfers the top element of the stack into the register specified in the instruction. Other specialized instructions may transfer the top of the stack into other specialized registers, such as the status register. The 65816 is more versatile than most in this respect.

A stack is required for implementing three programming facilities within the computer system: subroutines, interrupts, and temporary data storage. At this point, simply assume that the stack is a required facility in every computer system. The stack may be implemented in two ways:

1. As a hardware stack, where a fixed number of registers may be provided within the microprocessor itself. A hardware stack has the advantage of high speed; however, it has the disadvantage of a limited number of registers.

2. As a software stack. So as not to restrict the stack to a small number of registers, most general-purpose microprocessors, including the 65816, choose the software stack. With the software approach, a dedicated register within the microprocessor, here register S, stores the stack

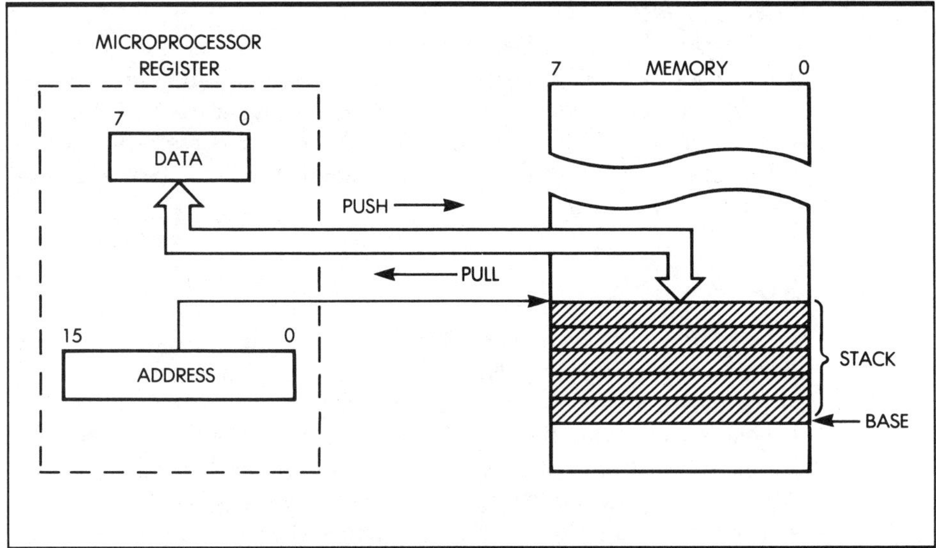

Figure 2.5: The Two-Stack Manipulation Instructions

pointer—the address of the top element of the stack (or, in some cases, the address of the top element of the stack, plus one). The stack is then implemented as an area of memory. The stack pointer, therefore, requires 16 bits to point anywhere in the memory.

THE INSTRUCTION EXECUTION CYCLE

Let's now examine Figure 2.6, where you fetch an instruction from the memory to illustrate the role of the program counter. The MPU appears on the left of the illustration, and the memory appears on the right. The memory stores instructions and data. The memory chip may be a ROM or a RAM, or any other chip that happens to contain memory.

Assume that the program counter has valid contents. It now holds a 16-bit address, which is the address of the next instruction to fetch in the memory.

Every processor proceeds in three cycles:

1. Fetching the next instruction
2. Decoding the instruction
3. Executing the instruction

Let's now follow this sequence.

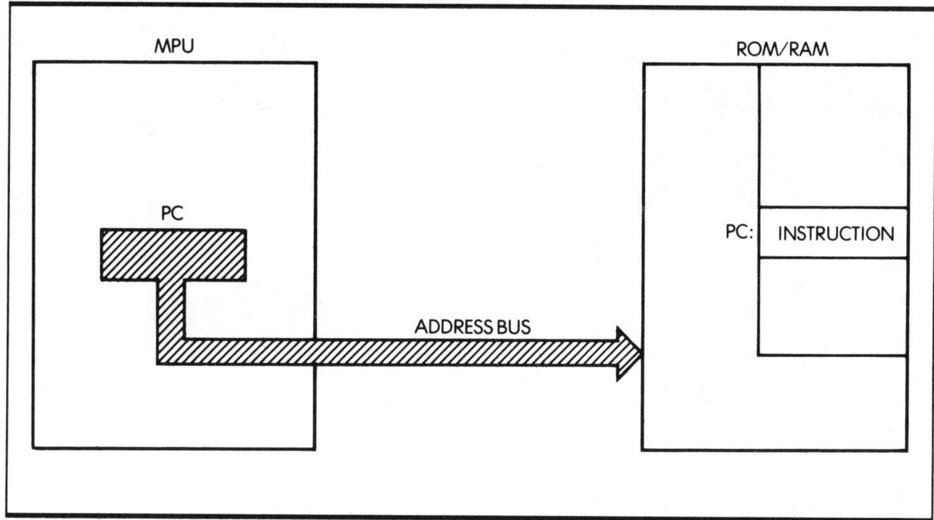

Figure 2.6: Fetching an Instruction from the Memory

Fetching

In the first cycle, the contents of the program counter are deposited on the address bus and gated to the memory (on the address bus). Simultaneously, a read signal may be issued on the control bus of the system, if required. The memory receives the address. The address is used to specify one location within the memory. Upon receiving the read signal, the memory decodes, through internal decoders, the address it has received and selects the location specified by the address. A few hundred nanoseconds later, the memory deposits the 8-bit data corresponding to the specified address on its data bus. This 8-bit word is the instruction you want to fetch. In the illustration in Figure 2.7, this instruction is deposited on the data bus.

Let's briefly summarize the sequence. The contents of the program counter are output on the address bus. A read signal is generated. The *memory* reads, and approximately 300 nanoseconds later, the instruction at the specified address is deposited on the data bus (assuming a single-byte instruction). The microprocessor then reads the data bus and deposits its contents into a specialized internal register, the *IR* or *instruction register.* The IR is eight bits wide and is used to contain the instruction just fetched from the memory.

The fetch cycle is now completed. The eight bits of the instruction are now in the instruction register. The IR appears on the left of Figure 2.7. It is not accessible to the programmer.

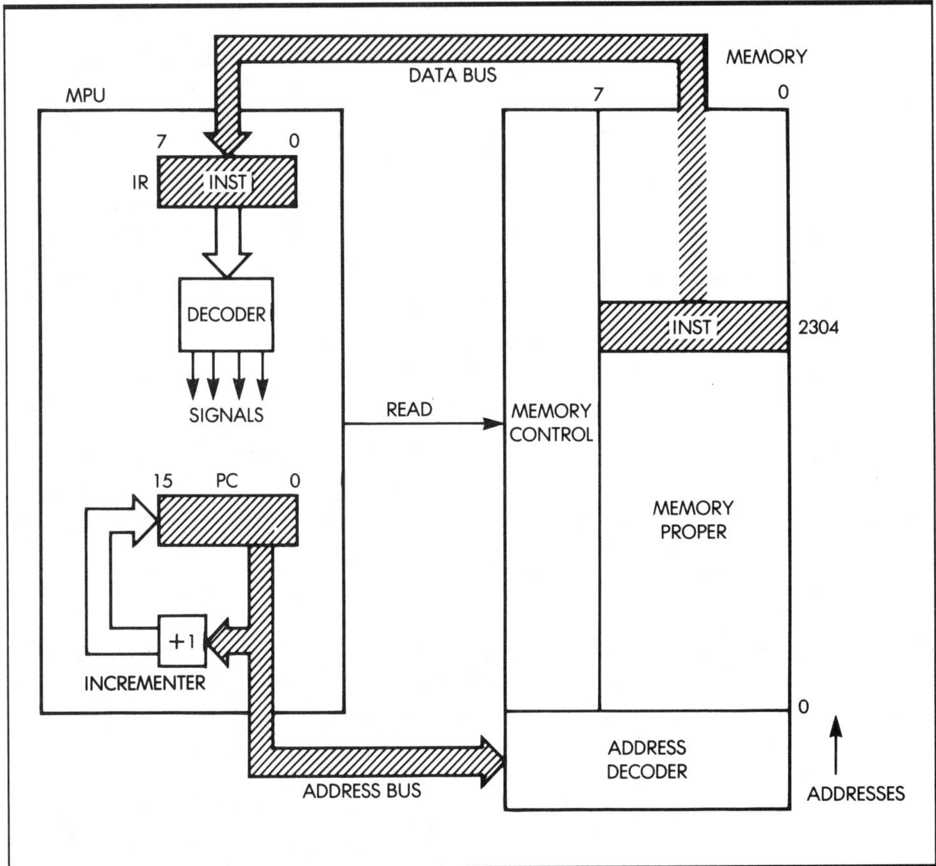

Figure 2.7: Automatic Sequencing

Decoding and Executing

Once the instruction is in the IR, the control unit of the microprocessor decodes the contents and generates the correct sequence of internal and external signals for the execution of the specified instruction. There is, therefore, a short decoding delay, followed by an execution phase, the length of which depends on the nature of the instruction specified. Some instructions execute entirely within the MPU. Others fetch or deposit data from or into the memory. This is why the instructions of the MPU require various lengths of time to execute. This duration is expressed as a number of (clock) cycles. Appendix E lists the number of cycles required by each instruction. Since various clock rates may be used, speed of execution is normally expressed in number of cycles, rather than in number of nanoseconds.

FETCHING THE NEXT INSTRUCTION

I have described how an instruction can be fetched from the memory using the program counter. During the execution of a program, instructions are fetched, in sequence, from the memory. An automatic mechanism must, therefore, be provided to fetch instructions in sequence. This task is performed by a simple incrementer attached to the program counter, as illustrated in Figure 2.7. Every time the contents of the program counter are placed on the address bus, the contents are incremented and written back into the program counter. As an example, if the program counter contains the value 0, the value 0 is output on the address bus. The contents of the program counter are then incremented, and the value 1 is written back into the program counter. In this way, the next time the program counter is used, it is the instruction at address 1 that is fetched. You have just implemented an *automatic mechanism for sequencing instructions.*

I must stress that the above descriptions are simplified. In reality, some instructions may be two or even three bytes long, so that successive bytes will be fetched in this manner from the memory. However, the fetch sequence is identical. The program counter is used to fetch successive bytes of an instruction, as well as successive instructions. The program counter, together with its incrementer, provides an automatic mechanism for pointing to successive memory locations.

INTERNAL ORGANIZATION OF THE 65816

Now that you understand the internal organization of a microprocessor, I will examine the 65816 in particular and describe its capabilities. Figure 2.8 presents a logical description of the internal workings of the 65816. There may be additional interconnections that are not shown. Let's examine the diagram.

In the center of the illustration, you see the *arithmetic-logical unit* (the ALU), recognizable by its characteristic **V** shape. The operation of the ALU will become clear in the next section, when I describe the execution of actual instructions. The *processor status register,* called P in the 65816, appears above and to the right of the ALU. The contents of the processor status register are essentially conditioned by the ALU; however, some of its bits may also be conditioned by other modules or events (see Chapter 4).

The two registers to the left of the ALU are the accumulators, A and B. The accumulators are 8-bit registers, but when the 65816 is in the 16-bit

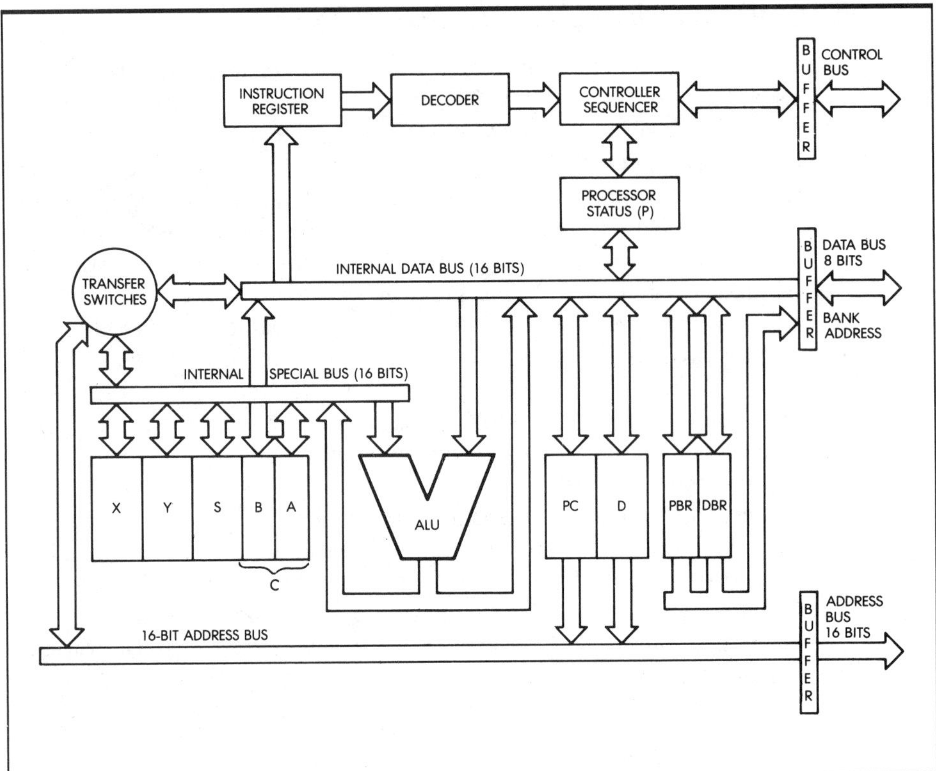

Figure 2.8: Internal Organization of the 65816

mode, they are used together to form the 16-bit C accumulator. Thus, the C accumulator is formed by using the A accumulator as the low byte, bits 0 to 7, and the B accumulator as the high byte, bits 8 to 15. The 16-bit mode for the accumulator is selected by setting the M bit to 0 in the P register. If only 8-bit data is used in a program, the 8-bit accumulator mode is more efficient because only one byte of data needs to be transferred for each operation with the accumulator and memory.

The register immediately to the right of the ALU is the program counter (PC). Recall that the program counter contains the address of the next instruction to be executed. The register shown next to the PC is the *direct page register,* labeled D. The D register is a 16-bit register used to address pages of memory. A *page* is simply a block of 256 words. Thus, memory locations 0 to 255 are page 0 of the memory. Since the 65816 has a 16-bit address bus, there are 256 pages. The D register is added to an 8-bit address in the instruction to form a 16-bit address. The D register allows you to produce faster and more compact programs when using blocks of memory smaller than 256 bytes, especially when the low eight bits of the D register are 0.

To the left of the accumulators are additional address registers. The stack pointer (S) points to the top of the stack in memory. In the case of the 65816, the stack pointer points to the *next available entry* in the stack. (In some microprocessors, the stack pointer points at the last entry.) Also, the stack grows downward—toward the lower addresses. This means that the stack pointer must be *decremented* any time a new word is *pushed onto* the stack. Conversely, whenever a word is removed (pulled) from the stack, the stack pointer must be incremented by one. In the case of the 65816, push and pull instructions involve up to two bytes at the same time, so that the contents of the stack pointer are decremented or incremented by 1 or 2.

Looking at the remaining two registers of the group, you can find another type of register: the *index register.* The two index registers are labeled X and Y. A byte brought along the internal data bus may be added to the contents of X or Y. When using an indexed instruction, this byte is called a *displacement.* Special instructions are provided that will automatically add this displacement to the contents of X or Y and generate an address. This is called *indexing,* as it allows convenient access to any sequential block of data. This feature is also applicable to the S address register.

Now look at the top of the illustration, where the control section of the microprocessor is located. At the top, you find the *instruction register* (IR), which contains the instruction to be executed. The instruction is received from the memory via the data bus and transmitted along the internal data bus to the instruction register. Next to the instruction register appears the *decoder,* which sends signals to the *controller sequencer* and causes the execution of the instruction within, as well as outside, the microprocessor. The control section generates and manages the control bus, which appears at the top of the illustration.

The three buses managed or generated by the system—the data bus, the address bus, and the control bus—all propagate outside the microprocessor through its pins. The external connections are shown on the rightmost part of the illustration. As shown in the figure, the buses are isolated from the outside through buffers.

The 65816 is a 16-bit machine internally, but has an external 8-bit data bus. The two bytes that form 16-bit data are sent out one at a time through the data-bus buffer. The data bus also carries the *bank address* of the 65816. Two registers—the program bank register (PBR) and the data bank register (DBR), shown to the right of the D register in Figure 2.8—are used to make the bank address. The bank-address byte is concatenated with the 16-bit address bus to form a 24-bit address to memory. A bank of memory is 64K, and with an 8-bit bank register, 256 banks or 16M of memory are available. (One *megabyte* [M] is 1,048,576 bytes.) The DBR is used to form the address of data, and the PBR is used to form the address of an instruction. The two registers allow instructions in one bank of memory to use data in another bank of memory. The S and D registers only address data in bank 0.

The special internal bus is used to transfer the contents of the index registers, accumulator, and ALU between each other and the address bus. The internal data bus, address bus, and special bus can be connected by the transfer switches.

I have now described all the logical elements of the 65816. Although you need not understand the detailed operation of the 65816 to start writing programs, you must choose the correct registers and techniques to write efficient codes. To make a correct choice, you need to understand how instructions are executed within the microprocessor. Therefore, I will now examine the execution of typical instructions inside the 65816 and demonstrate the role and use of the internal registers and buses.

INSTRUCTION FORMATS OF THE 65816

Appendix D lists the 65816 instructions. (Note that an instruction specifies the operation to be performed by the microprocessor.) The 65816 instructions may be formatted in one, two, three, or four bytes. From a more simplified standpoint, every instruction may be represented as an opcode, followed by an optional literal or address field, comprising one or two bytes. The opcode field specifies the operation to be carried out. In strict computer terminology, the opcode represents only those bits that specify the operation to be performed, exclusive of the register pointers that might be necessary. In the microprocessor world, it is convenient to call the opcode the operation code itself, as well as any register pointers that it might incorporate. This "generalized opcode" must reside in an 8-bit byte, for reasons of efficiency. This 8-bit opcode is a limiting factor on the number of instructions available in a microprocessor.

Most microprocessors use instructions that are one, two, or three bytes long. (See Figure 2.9.) However, the 65816 can use addresses three bytes long, so some instructions are four bytes long.

Many instructions require that one byte of data, or a part of an address, follow the opcode. In such a case, the instruction will be a two-byte instruction, the second byte being data or part of an address. In other

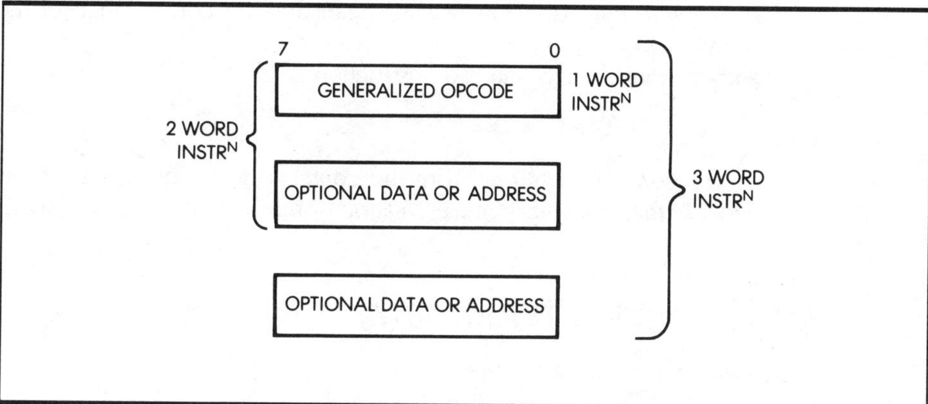

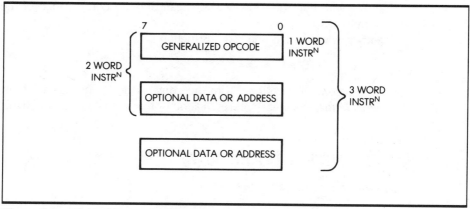

Figure 2.9: Typical Instruction Formats

cases, the instruction might require the specification of an address. An address requires 16 or 24 bits and, therefore, two or three bytes. Thus, the instruction will be a three- or four-byte instruction.

For each byte of the instruction, the control unit must perform a memory fetch, which requires one clock cycle. Thus, the shorter the instruction, the faster the execution.

ONE-BYTE INSTRUCTION (65816)

One-byte instructions require the smallest amount of memory and are, therefore, favored by the programmer. A typical one-byte instruction for the 65816 is an increment, for example:

INC A

which adds 1 to the contents of the A accumulator. This is a typical operation. Every microprocessor is equipped with an instruction like INC A, which allows programmers quickly to add a one to a register, which may then be used as a counter or pointer into memory. Instructions referencing different registers or memory will have different opcodes.

You must represent every instruction internally in a binary format. The above representation, INC A, is *mnemonic,* or symbolic; it is the *assembly-language* representation of an instruction. It is a convenient symbolic representation of the actual binary encoding for that instruction. The binary code that represents this instruction inside memory is 00011010 (bits 0 to 7).

The placement of the bits in the binary representation of an instruction is not meant for the convenience of the programmer, but for the microprocessor, which must decode and execute the instruction. The assembly language representation, however, is meant for the convenience of the programmer.

Another example of a one-byte instruction is:

```
DEC A
```

This instruction subtracts one from the contents of A. You can verify in Appendix D that the binary representation of this instruction is 00111010.

TWO-BYTE INSTRUCTION (65816)

The two-byte instruction

```
LDA #n
```

loads the contents of the second byte of the instruction to the accumulator. The contents of the second byte of the instruction are said to be *literal.* They are data and are treated as eight bits without any particular significance. They could be a character or numerical data—a fact that is irrelevant to the operation.

The code for this instruction is:

10101001 followed by the 8-bit byte *n*

The symbol # is used to indicate an immediate operation. *Immediate,* in most programming languages, means that the next byte or bytes within the instruction contain a piece of data that should not be *interpreted;* that is, the next one or two bytes are to be treated as *literals.*

The control unit is programmed to "know" how many bytes each instruction has. It will, therefore, always fetch and execute the right number of bytes for each instruction. However, the longer the instruction, the more complex it is for the control unit to decode.

THREE-BYTE INSTRUCTION (65816)

The instruction

```
ADC nn
```

requires three bytes. It adds to the accumulator from the address specified in the next two bytes of the instruction. Since addresses are 16 bits long, they require two bytes. In binary, this instruction is represented by:

01101101	8 bits for the opcode
Low Address	8 bits for the lower part of the address
High Address	8 bits for the higher part of the address

EXECUTION OF INSTRUCTIONS IN THE 65816

You have seen that all instructions are executed in three phases: fetch, decode, and execute. The amount of time it takes to execute an instruction depends on the instruction and the type of memory access being done. In the 65816, time is measured in clock cycles. It always takes an integral number of clock cycles to execute an instruction.

Accessing memory requires one clock cycle. Since each instruction must first be fetched from memory, even the fastest instruction requires more than one clock cycle. The fetch phase of an instruction presents the address of the next instruction to the memory. This address is contained in the program counter. When the contents of memory are available, they can be transferred within the microprocessor to the instruction register. The PC is then incremented to point to the next byte in the program.

When the instruction is deposited in the instruction register of the 65816, it is decoded. It takes at least one clock cycle, and possibly more, to decode and execute the instruction. Appendix E gives the execution time for each instruction, describes the address bus cycle-by-cycle activity for each instruction, and shows the external activities of the 65816 while the instruction is being executed. This table offers an in-depth understanding of instruction execution.

EXECUTION OF A ONE-BYTE INSTRUCTION (65816)

Recall that the one-byte instruction

INC A

adds 1 to the A accumulator. This instruction is fetched during the first clock cycle and is decoded and executed during the second cycle. The two-cycle execution time of a one-byte instruction illustrates that all instructions require at least two clock cycles.

EXECUTION OF A TWO-BYTE INSTRUCTION (65816)

Recall that the instruction

LDA #n

described in the previous section, loads to the A accumulator the contents of the byte that immediately follows the instruction. During the first clock cycle, the instruction is loaded into the IR; and the PC increments. During the second clock cycle the instruction is decoded, *while* the next byte, the data, is fetched. The data from this second fetch is loaded into the accumulator before the end of the second cycle. Observe that two activities occurred during the second cycle: the instruction in the IR was decoded, and the next byte was fetched. Since most instructions in the 65816 need this second byte, execution is speeded considerably.

EXECUTION OF A THREE-BYTE INSTRUCTION (65816)

The instruction

ADC nn

is a three-byte instruction. Recall that it adds to the A accumulator the contents of the memory location addressed by nn.

This instruction requires four cycles to execute. The first cycle fetches the opcode. The next decodes the instruction and fetches the low address byte. The third fetches the high address byte. The fourth forms the address of the data on the *internal* address bus (see Figure 2.8) and uses this address to fetch the data from memory and add it to the accumulator. If the processor were in the 16-bit mode, a fifth cycle would be needed to fetch the second byte and add it to the accumulator.

The detailed descriptions I have just presented on the execution of typical instructions should help to clarify the role of the registers and internal buses. A second reading of the preceding section may be helpful in gaining a detailed understanding of the internal operation of the 65816.

THE 65816 AND 65802 CHIPS

The 65816 processor was developed as a 16-bit version of the popular 6502 chip. By setting the E bit in the processor status register to 1, the

65816 will emulate all the instructions of the 6502. When the E bit is 1, the 65816 is in the *emulation mode*. When the E bit is 0, the 65816 is in the native mode and all the additional instructions and addressing modes of the 65816 are available. (See *Programming the 6502* by Rodnay Zaks for more information on the 6502.)

For completeness, I will now examine the signals of the 65816 microprocessor chip. You need not understand the functions of 65816 signals to program the 65816. If you are not interested in the details of hardware, you may want to skip this section.

The 65816 comes in two different forms: the W65C816 and the W65C802. I will first describe the signals of the W65C816. Then I will describe those signals on the W65C802 that are different from those on the W65C816. The instructions for the two processors are identical; only the hardware pinouts are different. Figure 2.10 displays the pinout of the W65C816.

I will now describe the signals, going from the top of the figure to the bottom.

The Φ input is the system clock. The frequency of this clock determines the cycle time of the 65816.

Four W65C816 control signals are related to its internal status or sequencing. IRQ and NMI are the two interrupt signals. IRQ is the usual interrupt signal. You may connect several input/output devices to the IRQ interrupt line. Whenever an interrupt request is present on this line and the internal interrupt bit is enabled, the 65816 will accept the interrupt. NMI is the nonmaskable interrupt. It is always accepted by the 65816.

The ABORT input aborts instructions, usually when there is a problem on the address bus. When the ABORT is active, the instruction will not modify any internal registers and will cause an interrupt when the instruction is complete. The address of the aborted instruction is stored on the stack, and the interrupt will vector to 00FFE8,9 in the emulation mode and 00FFE8,9 in the native mode. The ABORT signal is negative-edge triggered.

Reset (RES) is the signal that initializes the MPU. It moves the contents of address 00FFFC and 00FFFD into the PC. The D, DBR, and PBR, and the high bytes of the X and Y registers, are set to 0, and normal interrupts are disabled. The processor is set to the emulation mode, and the M and X bits in the processor status are set to 1. Reset is usually used after you turn on the computer.

The six bus-control signals are used to control the memory and data buses. The read/write (R/W) is an output that indicates whether data is being read from or written to memory. The memory lock (ML) output indicates a read/modify/write cycle. When a multiprocessor system is used, the other processors should not access memory when the ML signal is active. The vector pull (VP) output indicates that a vector is being

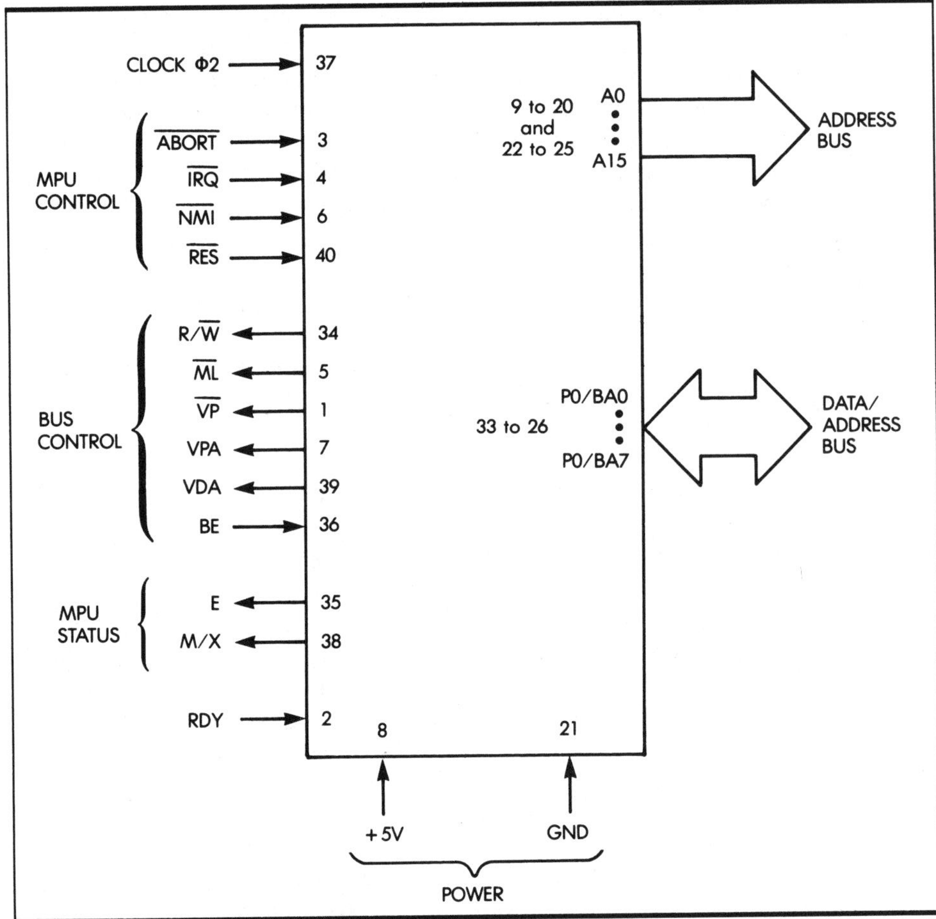

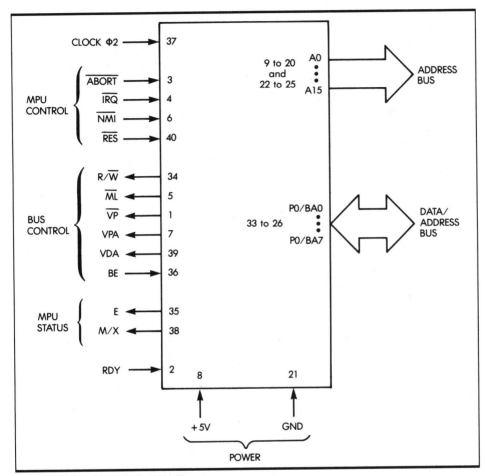

Figure 2.10: W65C816 MPU Pinout

addressed during an interrupt. The valid data address (VDA) and valid program address (VPA) are used to indicate the type of memory being accessed by the address bus. There are four possible combinations of VDA and VPA. They are:

VDA	VPA	
0	0	Internal operation, the address and data buses are available
0	1	Valid program address
1	0	Valid data address
1	1	Opcode fetch

VDA and VPA may be used when you have cache memories in a system. The bus enable (BE) input is used to set the data bus, address bus, and R/W line to the high impedance state to allow external control.

Two signals indicate internal processor status. The first is E, which shows the state of the emulation bit. The second is memory/index (M/X) select status. This multiplexed signal indicates the state of the M and X bits in the processor status register.

The ready (RDY) signal is a bidirectional signal. When the output is active, the ready indicates the processor has executed a wait instruction. If the ready is pulled low externally, the processor will halt execution until the ready signal goes high.

W65C802 CONTROL SIGNALS

The major difference between the W65C816 and W65C802 is that the W65C802 is pin-to-pin compatible with the 6502. The W65C802 does not have the extended bank-addressing registers multiplexed with the data bus, so the W65C802 addresses 64K. The W65C802 is identical internally to the W65C816, and programs are interchangeable as long as the extended-memory feature of the W65C816 is not used. (For compatibility, leave the DBR and PBR registers at 0.) Figure 2.11 displays the W65C802 pinout.

There are three clock signals on the W65C802. The first additional signal is Φ1 out, which provides an inverted clock output for external read and write operations. The second new signal is Φ2 out, which is also used for external read and write operations.

The synchronize (SYNC) output indicates when the processor is fetching an opcode. The set overflow (SO) input sets the overflow bit (V) in the processor status register. All the other pinouts are the same as on the W65C816.

SUMMARY

In this chapter, I have described the internal organization of the 65816. The role of each register is important, and you should fully understand them before you proceed to the next chapter. Chapter 3 introduces the instructions available on the 65816 and many basic programming techniques for the 65816.

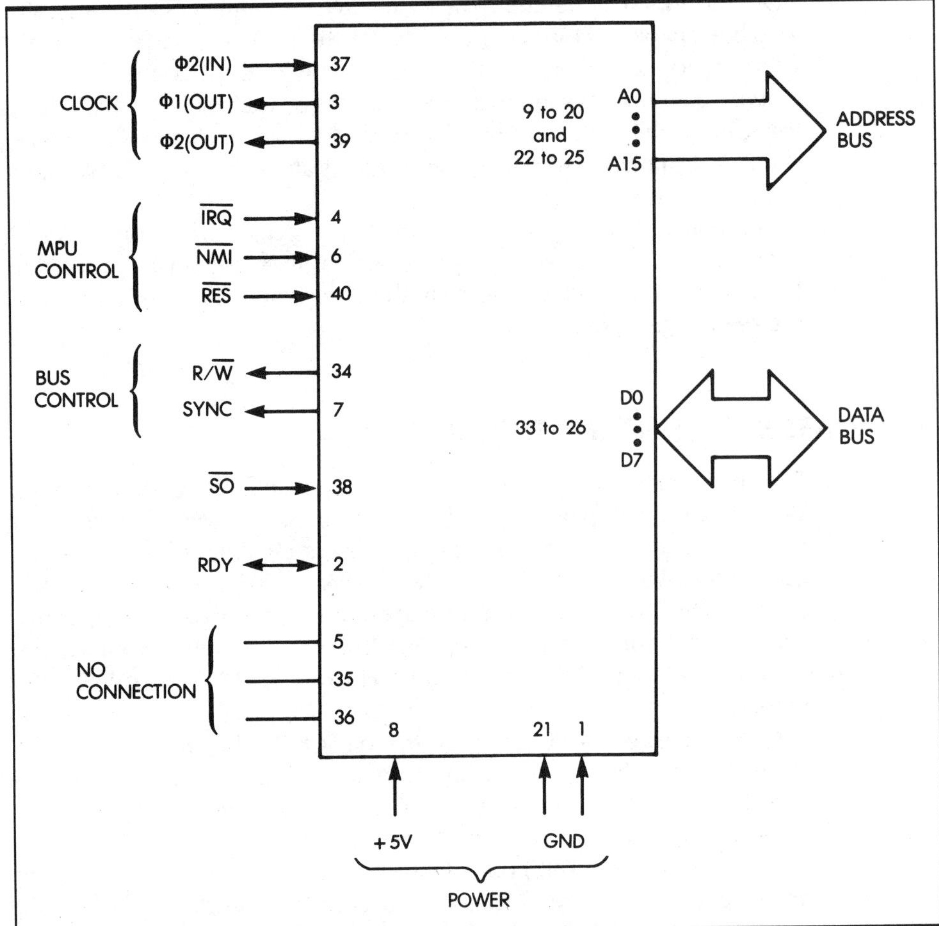

Figure 2.11: W65C802 MPU Pinout

EXERCISES

2-1: *Write the binary code that will increment the index register X, INX. Consult Appendix D for the code. (Note: This table uses hexadecimal notation.)*

2-2: *What is the binary code of the instruction that will clear the contents of the carry bit C in the processor status register?*

BASIC PROGRAMMING TECHNIQUES

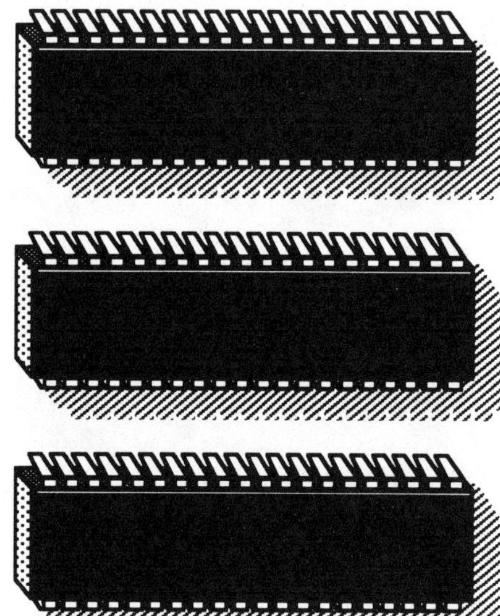

3

IN THIS CHAPTER, I examine the basic techniques necessary for writing a program for the 65816. In particular, I show how to move information between the memory and the MPU, and how to manipulate it within the MPU itself. I develop programs of increasing complexity, so that you can see how various instructions and registers interact.

I will begin by writing simple arithmetic programs. I will then go on to explain the use of the 65816's excellent 16-bit arithmetic capabilities. Finally, I will discuss the important multiply and divide operations.

ARITHMETIC PROGRAMS

The arithmetic programs in this chapter show how to do addition, subtraction, multiplication, and division. Each uses at least one register. Figure 3.1 shows a conceptual diagram of the 65816 registers. These programs perform integer arithmetic on positive binary numbers and on negative numbers represented as two's complement integers. Let's begin with an example of 8-bit addition.

8-BIT ADDITION

Here's a program that performs 8-bit addition:

```
(Instructions)          (Comments)

LDA      ADR1          LOAD OP1 INTO A
ADC      ADR2          ADD OP2 TO OP1
STA      ADR3          SAVE THE RESULT RES AT ADR3
```

In this program, I add two 8-bit operands, OP1 and OP2, stored at memory addresses ADR1 and ADR2, respectively. I call the sum RES and store it at memory address ADR3 (as shown in Figure 3.2).

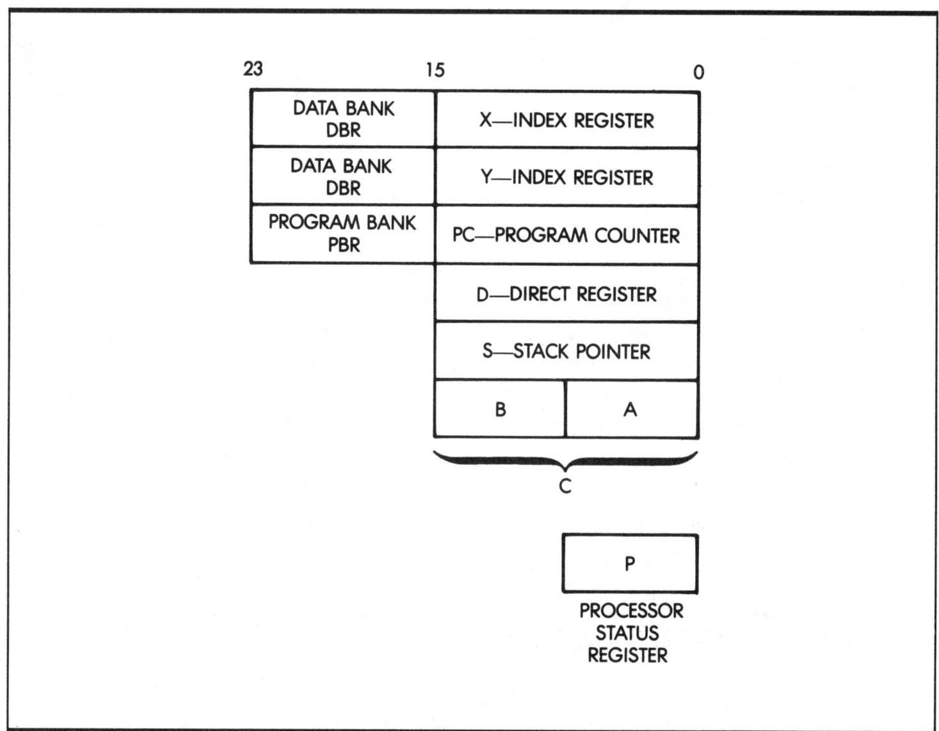

Figure 3.1: The 65816 Registers

Each line of the program, expressed here in symbolic form, is called an *instruction*. Each instruction is translated by the *assembler* program into from one to four binary bytes. For this example, I will *not* discuss this translation; instead I will examine the symbolic representation.

The first line of the program specifies: "load the contents of ADR1 into accumulator A." Figure 3.2 shows that the contents of ADR1 is the first operand, OP1. Thus, the first instruction transfers OP1 from the memory into the accumulator (see Figure 3.3).

ADR1 is a symbolic representation of the actual 16-bit address in the memory. It is defined as being equal to the address 100. The LDA instruction then results in a *read operation* from address 100 combined with the data bank register, DBR (see Figure 3.3); that is, the contents of address 100 are transferred along the data bus and deposited into accumulator A. Recall from Chapter 2 that arithmetic and logical operations operate on the accumulator as one of the source operands. Since you want to add the two values OP1 and OP2, you must first load OP1 into the accumulator; you can then add OP2 to the contents of the accumulator.

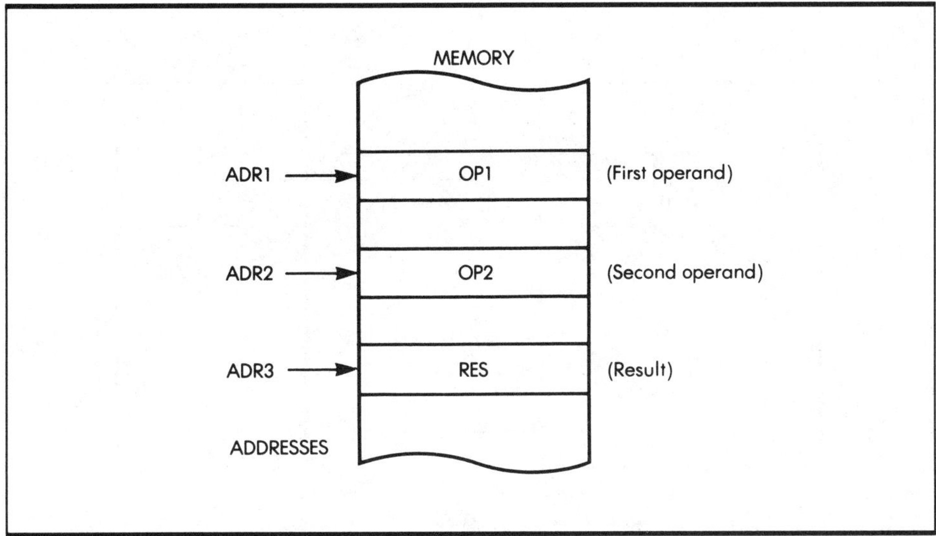

Figure 3.2: 8-Bit Addition: RES = OP1 + OP2

Referring back to the program, let's now examine the rightmost field of each instruction, called the *comment* field. Comments are ignored by the assembler program at translation time; they are useful for program readability. To understand what the program does, it is important to document it with good comments. For the first line of the program, the comment is self-explanatory: the value of OP1, located at address ADR1, is loaded into accumulator A. Figure 3.3 shows the result of this first instruction.

The second instruction

```
ADC    ADR2
```

specifies: "add from ADR2 to accumulator A." Referring to Figure 3.2, you see that the memory location, ADR2, contains the second operand, OP2. When the second instruction is executed, OP2 is fetched from memory and added to OP1 (see Figure 3.4). The sum is then deposited in the accumulator. (*Note:* Remember that in the case of the 65816, the results of the arithmetic operation are deposited back into the accumulator. With other processors, however, it may be possible to deposit these results in other registers, or back into memory.)

The sum of OP1 and OP2 is now contained in accumulator A. To complete this program, you must transfer the contents of A into memory location ADR3, in order to store the results at the specified location. This is done by the third instruction:

```
STA    ADR3
```

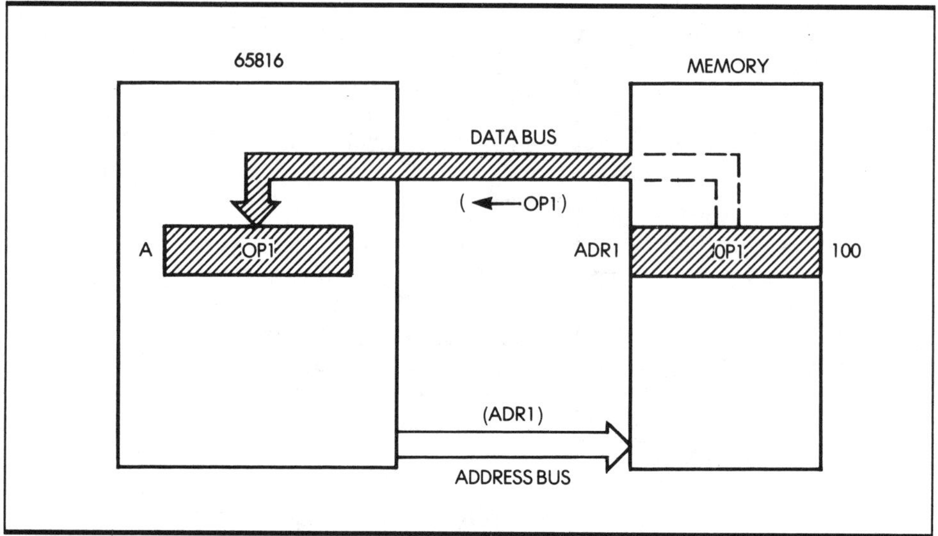

Figure 3.3: LDA ADR1:OP1 Is Loaded from Memory

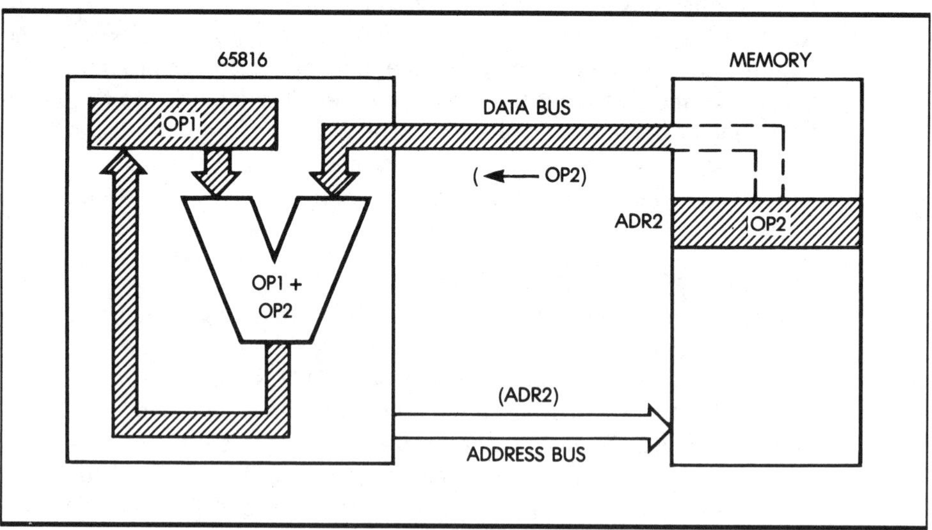

Figure 3.4: ADC ADR2

This instruction loads the contents of A into the specified address, ADR3. Figure 3.5 shows the effect of this final instruction.

Before execution of the ADC operation, the accumulator A contained OP1 (see Figure 3.4). After the addition, a new result was written into

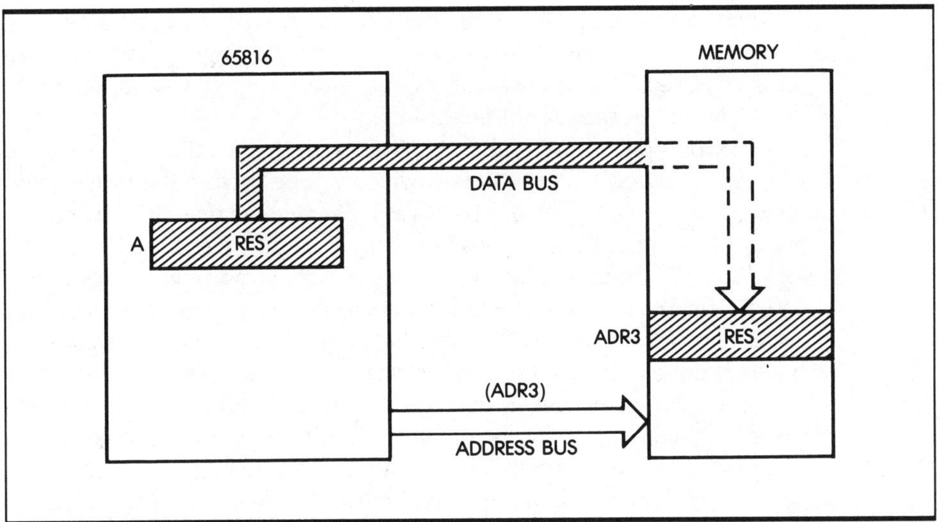

Figure 3.5: STA ADR3

A: OP1 + OP2. Recall that the contents of any register within the microprocessor, as well as any memory location, remain the same after a read operation has been performed on that register. In other words, reading the contents of a register or memory location does not change its contents. Only a *write* operation in the register location changes the contents. In this program, the contents of ADR1 and ADR2 remain unchanged throughout the program. However, after the ADC instruction, the contents of A are modified, because the output of the ALU is written into the accumulator. The previous contents of A are then lost.

65816 PECULIARITIES

The above three-instruction program would indeed be the complete program for most microprocessors. However, two peculiarities of the 65816 exist that will normally require two additional instructions.

First, the ADC instruction really means "add *with* carry" rather than "add." The difference is that a regular add instruction adds two numbers, and add-with-carry adds two numbers plus the value of the carry bit. Since you are adding here 8-bit numbers, no carry should be used, and at the time you start the addition you do not necessarily know the condition of the carry bit (it may have been set by a previous instruction), so you must clear it (set it to zero). This is accomplished by the CLC instruction: "clear carry."

Unfortunately, the 65816 does not have both types of addition operations. It has only an ADC operation. As a result, for single 8-bit additions a necessary precaution is always to clear the carry bit. This is no significant disadvantage but should not be forgotten.

The second peculiarity of the 65816 lies with the fact that it is equipped with powerful decimal instructions, which will be used in the next section on BCD arithmetic. The 65816 always operates in one of two modes: binary or decimal. The state it is in is conditioned by a status bit, the D bit (of register P). Since you are operating in binary mode in this example, you must make sure that the D bit is correctly set. This is done by a CLD instruction, which clears the D bit. Naturally, if all arithmetic within the system is done in binary, the D bit is cleared once and for all at the beginning of the program, and you do not have to set it every time. Therefore, this instruction may, in fact, be omitted in most programs. However, when you practice these exercises on a computer, you may go back and forth between BCD and binary exercises. I have included this extra instruction here because it must appear at least once before you perform any binary addition.

The complete, and safe, 8-bit program is now:

```
CLC                 CLEAR CARRY BIT
CLD                 CLEAR DECIMAL BIT
LDA    ADR1         LOAD OP1 IN A
ADC    ADR2         ADD OP2 TO OP1
STA    ADR2         SAVE RES AT ADR3
```

You may use actual numerical addresses instead of ADR1, ADR2, and ADR3. To keep symbolic addresses, you must use *pseudo-instructions.* Pseudo-instructions specify the value of the symbolic address, so that during translation the assembly program may substitute the actual physical addresses. Examples of pseudo-instructions are:

```
ADR1    EQU   $100
ADR2    EQU   $120
ADR3    EQU   $200
```

In conclusion, an 8-bit addition allows only the addition of 8-bit numbers—numbers between 0 and 255—if absolute binary is used. For most practical applications, however, it is necessary to add numbers having 16 bits or more—to use *multiple precision.* Therefore, let's now look at some examples of arithmetic on 16-bit numbers.

16-BIT ADDITION

For this example, assume the first operand is stored at memory locations ADR1 and ADR1 – 1. Since OP1 is a 16-bit number this time, it requires two 8-bit memory locations. Similarly, OP2 is stored at ADR2 and ADR2 – 1. The result is to be deposited at memory addresses ADR3 and ADR3 – 1. This process is illustrated in Figure 3.6. Note that H indicates the high half (bits 8 to 15), and L indicates the low half (bits 0 to 7).

The logic of this program is exactly the same as in the previous one. First, the lower half of the two operands is added. Any carry generated by this addition is stored automatically in the internal carry bit (C). Then, the high-order half of the two operands is added, along with any carry, and the result is saved in the memory. Here is the program:

```
CLC
CLD
LDA   ADR1       LOAD LOW HALF OF OP1
ADC   ADR2       ADD OP1 AND OP2 LOW
STA   ADR3       STORE RESULT LOW
LDA   ADR1-1     LOAD HIGH HALF OF OP1
ADC   ADR2-1     (OP1+OP2) HIGH + CARRY
STA   ADR3-1     STORE RESULT HIGH
```

The first two instructions are used to ensure that the processor is ready for the type of arithmetic you want to do. The next three instructions are identical to the ones used for the 8-bit addition in the previous section. They add the least significant half (bits 0 to 7) of OP1 and OP2. The sum, called RES, is stored at memory location ADR3 (see Figure 3.6).

Automatically, whenever an addition is performed, any resulting carry (whether 0 or 1) is saved in the carry bit (C) of the processor status register (register P). If the two 8-bit numbers generate a carry, then the C bit will be equal to 1. (It will be set.) If the two 8-bit numbers do not generate a carry, then the value of the carry bit will be 0.

The next three instructions of the program are also identical to those in the previous 8-bit addition program. This time, however, they add the most significant half (the high half, bits 8 to 15) of OP1 and OP2, plus any carry, and store the result at the address ADR3 – 1. After this program has been executed, the 16-bit result is stored at memory locations ADR3 and ADR3 – 1.

At this point, you might ask: "But what if the addition of the high half of the operands also results in a carry?" There are two ways to handle this situation. First, you can assume that this will not happen unless an error has been made, because the program is designed to work for results of

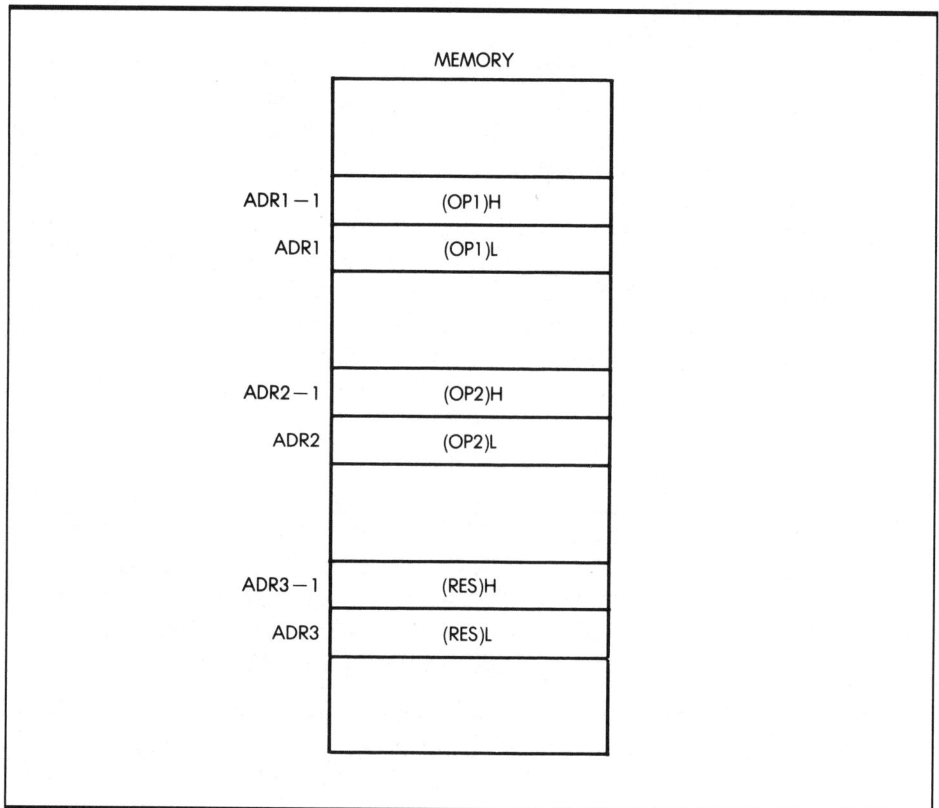

Figure 3.6: Operands for 16-Bit Addition

only up to 16 bits, not 17. Second, you can assume that the program will halt when the carry is set. Or, you can include additional instructions that will handle the extra bit in another word of memory, thus making a 24-bit word. It is up to you to decide on the best route for your purpose—the first of many decisions.

(*Note:* In writing this last program, I have assumed that the high part of the operand is stored "on top of" the lower part—at the lower memory address. This need not always be the case. In fact, the 65816 stores addresses in the reverse manner: the low part is stored in memory first and the high part is stored in the next memory location. To use a standard convention for both addresses and data, I recommend that you also keep data with the low part on top of the high part. This is illustrated in Figure 3.7.)

When operating on multibyte operands, it is important to remember the following information:

1. The order in which data is stored in memory

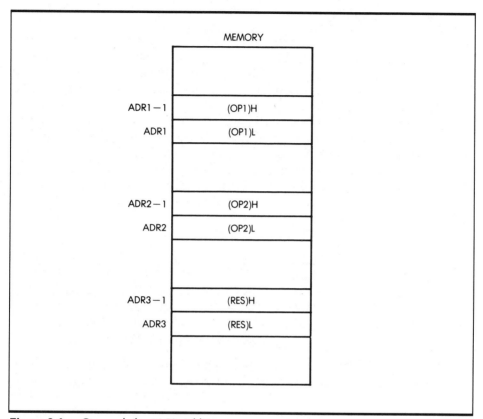

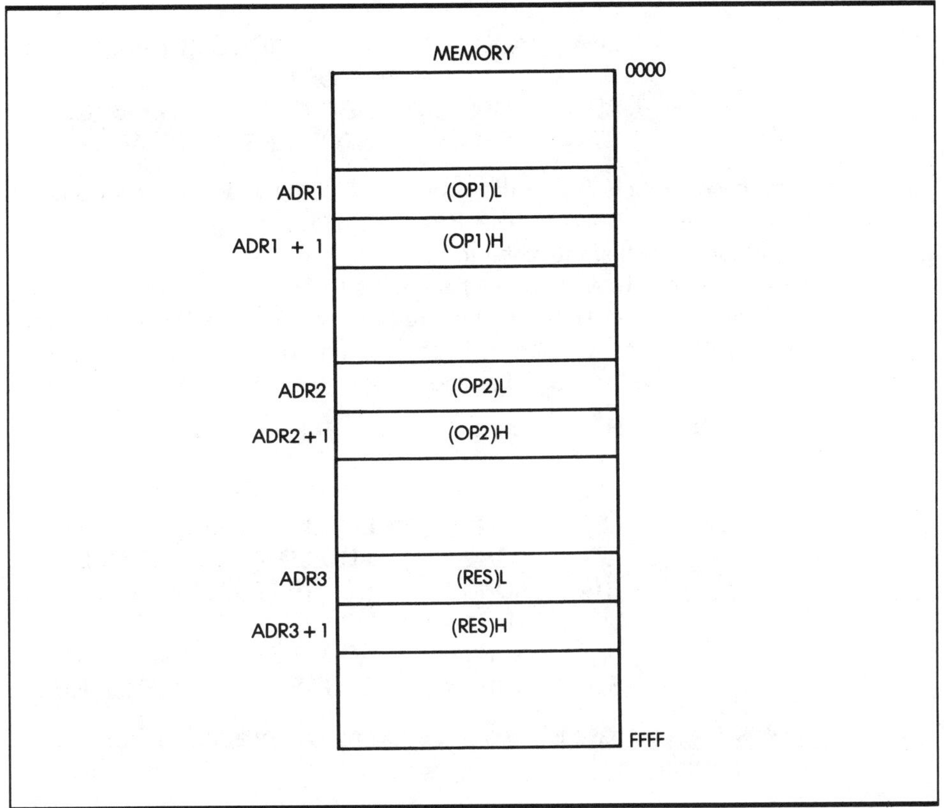

Figure 3.7: Storing 16-Bit Operands in the 65816

2. The location where the data pointers are pointing—to the low or high byte

Similarly, when designing algorithms or data structures, you must decide how to store the 16-bit numbers (low or high part first) and whether address references should point to the low or high half of these numbers.

The programs I have presented so far have been traditional: they use an 8-bit accumulator. I will now present an alternative program for 16-bit addition that does not use the simple 8-bit accumulator. Instead, it uses the 16-bit accumulator mode of the 65816. (Remember from Chapter 2 that C is actually A and B, and that the 65816 allows accumulators A and B to be used as the 16-bit C accumulator.) Operands will be stored as in Figure 3.7. the program is:

```
REP   #$20        CLEAR M BIT IN P
CLC
```

```
CLD
LDA    ADR1       LOAD ACCUMULATOR WITH
                    OP1
ADC    ADR2       ADD OP2 TO OP1 (16 BITS)
STA    ADR3       STORE RES INTO ADR3
```

Notice how much shorter this program is, compared to the previous version. The first instruction, reset P, sets the 65816 into the 16-bit accumulator mode by setting the M bit to 0.

You can readily extend 16-bit numbers to 24, 32, or more bits (always multiples of 8 bits). Let's try an interesting exercise. Use the 16-bit mode I just introduced to write an addition program for 32-bit operands, assuming the operands are stored as shown in Figure 3.8. Here is the program:

```
REP    #$20       CLEAR M BIT IN P
CLC
CLD
LDA    ADR1       LOAD LOW HALF OF OP1
ADC    ADR2       ADD LOW HALF OF OP2
STA    ADR3       STORE LOW HALF RES
LDA    ADR1+2     LOAD HIGH HALF OF OP1
ADC    ADR2+2     ADD HIGH HALF OF OP2
STA    ADR3+2     STORE HIGH HALF OF RES
```

Now that you have learned to perform a binary addition, let's proceed to subtraction.

SUBTRACTING 16-BIT NUMBERS

Performing an 8-bit or 16-bit subtraction is quite simple, so let's try a 16-bit subtraction. As usual, the two numbers, OP1 and OP2, are stored at addresses ADR1 and ADR2. The memory is assumed to be that of Figure 3.7. To perform the subtraction, you use the subtract operation (SBC) instead of the add operation (ADC). The only other change, compared to the addition, is that you use an SEC instruction at the beginning of the program instead of a CLC. SEC means "set carry to 1." This indicates a "no-borrow" condition. The rest of the program is identical to the one for addition. The program is:

```
REP    #$20
CLD
SEC
LDA    ADR1       OP1 INTO A
SBC    ADR2       OP1-OP2
STA    ADR3       RES INTO ADR3
```

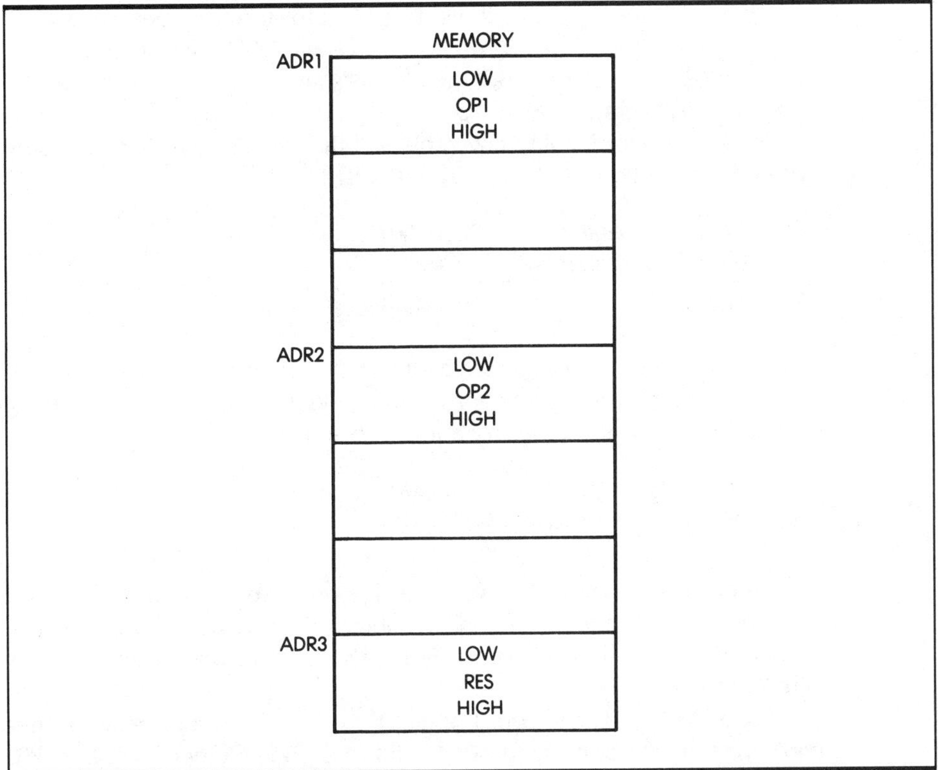

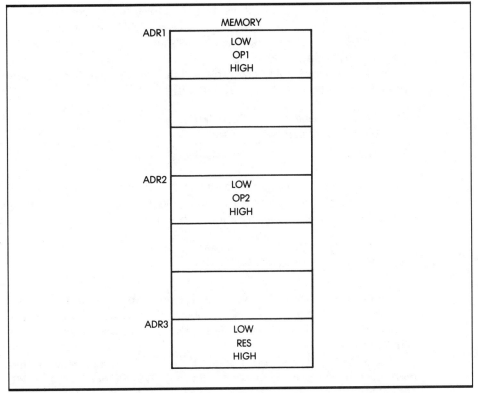

Figure 3.8: A 32-Bit Addition

This program is essentially like the one developed for 16-bit addition.

Recall that in two's complement arithmetic, the final value of the carry indicates a borrow. If a borrow condition has occurred as a result of the subtraction, the carry bit of the processor status register will be zero, and it can be tested.

The examples presented so far in this chapter are simple binary additions and subtractions. However, you may need to use another type of arithmetic, BCD arithmetic.

BCD ARITHMETIC

8-BIT BCD ADDITION

Chapter 1 discussed the concept of BCD arithmetic. Recall that it is essentially used for business applications, where it is imperative to retain every significant digit in a result.

In the BCD notation, a 4-bit nibble is used to store one decimal digit (0 to 9). As a result, every 8-bit byte may store two BCD digits. (This is called *packed BCD*). To see how BCD works, let's add two bytes, each containing two BCD digits (see Figure 3.9).

So that you can identify any problems that might come up, try some numeric examples first. To add 01 and 02:

01 is represented by:	00000001
02 is represented by:	00000010
The result is:	00000011

This result is the BCD representation for 03. (If you are not sure of the BCD equivalent, refer to the conversion table in Appendix C.) Everything worked simply in this case. Try another example:

08 is represented by:	00001000
03 is represented by:	00000011

If you obtained 00001011 as your result, you have computed the *binary* sum of 8 and 3. You have, indeed, obtained 11 in *binary.* But unfortunately, 1011 is an *illegal code* in BCD. The *BCD* representation of 11 is 00010001.

This difference stems from the fact that the BCD representation uses only the first ten combinations of 4 digits to encode the decimal symbols 0 through 9. Thus, the remaining six possible combinations of 4 digits are unused in BCD notation, and the illegal 1011 is one such combination. In other words, whenever the sum of two BCD digits is greater than 9, you must add 6 to the result to skip over the six unused codes.

Let's try another example. To add the binary representation of 6 to 1011:

	1011	(illegal binary result)
	+ 0110	(+6)
The result is:	00010001	

The result is, indeed, 11 in the BCD notation. You now have the correct answer.

This example illustrates one of the basic difficulties of the BCD mode: you must compensate for the six missing codes. You must use a special decimal addition adjust instruction (DAA) to adjust the result of the binary addition on many microprocessors. (Add 6 if the result is greater than 9.) In the case of the 65816, the ADC instruction does it automatically. This is a clear advantage of the 65816 when doing BCD arithmetic.

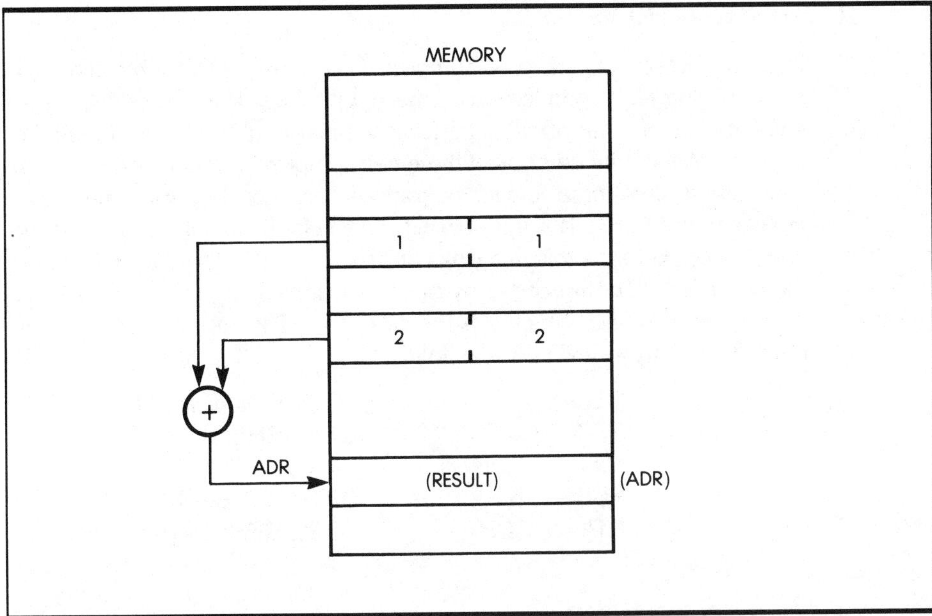

Figure 3.9: Storing BCD Digits

I will use this same example to illustrate another difference. In this example, the carry is generated from the lower BCD digit (the rightmost digit) into the leftmost one. This internal carry must be taken into account and added to the second BCD digit. The addition instruction takes care of this automatically.

Just as in the case of binary addition, you must use CLC and SED to set the processor in the BCD mode. As an example, here is a program to add the BCD numbers 11 and 22:

```
CLC              CLEAR CARRY
SED              SET DECIMAL MODE
LDA   #$11       LOAD LITERAL BCD 11
ADC   #$22       ADD LITERAL BCD 22
STA   ADR        STORE RESULT
```

In this program, I am using two new symbols: # and $. The # symbol means that a *literal* (or constant) follows. The $ sign within the operand field of the instruction specifies that the data that follows is expressed in hexadecimal notation. The hexadecimal and the BCD representations for digits 0 through 9 are identical. The last line of the program stores the result in address ADR.

BCD SUBTRACTION

BCD subtraction appears to be complex. To perform a BCD subtraction, you must add the ten's complement of the number, just like you add the two's complement of a number to perform a binary subtract. You obtain the ten's complement by computing the nine's complement, then adding 1. This typically requires three to four operations on a standard microprocessor. However, the 65816 is equipped with a special BCD subtraction instruction, which performs this in a single instruction. As in the binary example, the program will be preceded by the instructions SED, which sets the decimal mode, and SEC, which sets the carry to 1. Thus, the program to subtract BCD 25 from BCD 26 is as follows:

```
SED              SET DECIMAL MODE
SEC              SET CARRY
LDA    #$26      LOAD BCD 26
SBC    #$25      SUBTRACT BCD 25
STA    ADR       STORE RESULT
```

16-BIT BCD ADDITION

You perform 16-bit addition just as simply as in the binary case. The program for such an addition is:

```
REQ    #$20      SET TO 16-BIT MODE
CLC
SED
LDA    ADR1
ADC    ADR2
STA    ADR3
```

BCD FLAGS

In the BCD mode, the carry flag during an addition indicates that the result is larger than 99. This is unlike the two's complement situation, since BCD digits are represented in true binary. Conversely, the absence of the carry flag during a subtraction indicates a borrow.

PACKED BCD ADDITION

You have now learned how to perform elementary BCD addition and subtraction. However, in actual practice, BCD numbers include any number of bytes. Let's look at a simplified example of a packed BCD addition. Assume that the two numbers, N1 and N2, include the same number of BCD bytes and that that number is called COUNT. Figure 3.10 shows the register and memory allocation. Here is the program:

```
BCDPAK  LDA   #COUNT
        STA   COUNTER
        LDX   #0        CLEAR X REGISTER
        CLC             CLEAR CARRY
        SED             SET DECIMAL MODE
PLUS    LDA   N2,X      LOAD N2 BYTE
        ADC   N1,X      ADD N1 BYTE
        STA   N1,X      STORE RESULT IN N1
        INX             INCREMENT X
        DEC   COUNTER   COUNTER-1
        BNE   PLUS      LOOP UNTIL COUNTER=0
```

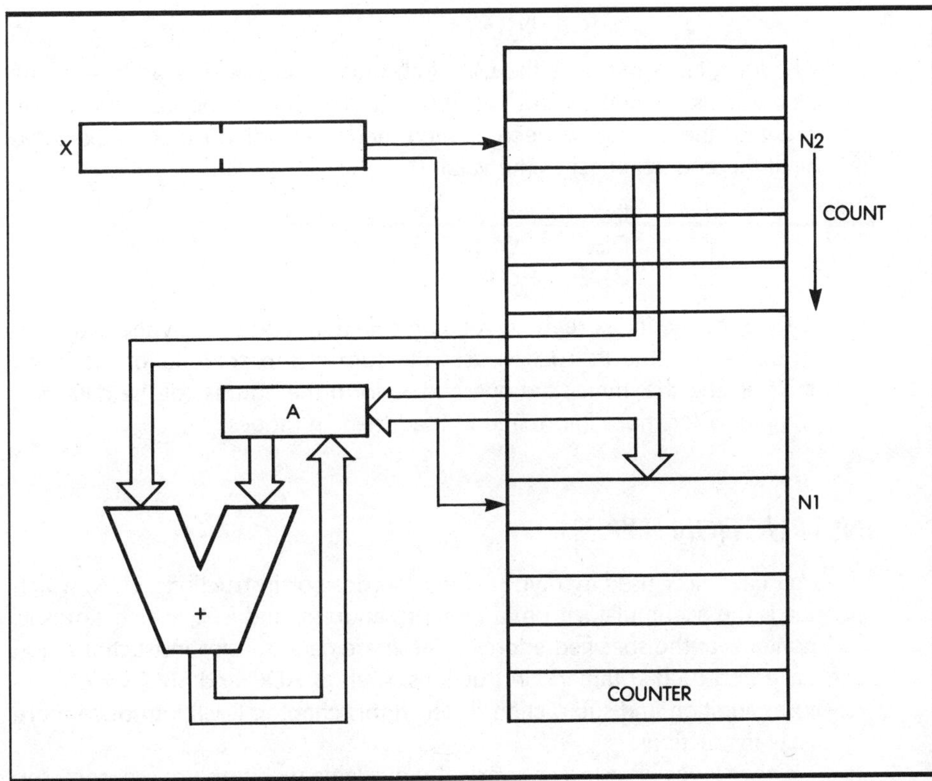

Figure 3.10: Packed BCD Add: N1 ← N2 + N1

N1 and N2 represent the addresses where the BCD numbers are stored. The value COUNT is put into the memory location counter, and the index register X is cleared:

```
BCDPAK  LDA   #COUNT
        STA   COUNTER
        LDX   #0
```

In anticipation of the first addition, the carry bit must be cleared and the processor must be set in the decimal mode:

```
        CLC
        SED
```

The first byte of N2 is loaded into the accumulator, then the first byte of N1 is added to it. The result is then stored in N1:

```
PLUS    LDA   N2,X
        ADC   N1,X
        STA   N1,X
```

The form N2,X indicates the use of absolute indexing. The address of the operand is formed by adding N2 to X. The index registers are incremented, the counter is decremented, and the addition loop is executed until the counter reaches the value 0:

```
        INX
        DEC   COUNTER
        BNE   PLUS
```

By using the index register, you can speed up and simplify the program. In this mode, the instruction uses the sum of the contents of the index register and the immediate operand to form the address of the data. See Chapter 5 for more information on addressing modes.

INSTRUCTION TYPES

You have now used *two* types of microprocessor instructions: LDA, which loads the accumulator from a memory address, and STA, which stores its contents at the specified address. These are *data transfer* instructions. You have also used *arithmetic* instructions, such as ADC and SBC, which perform addition and subtraction. Later in this chapter, I will introduce more ALU instructions.

Other types of instructions are also available within the microprocessor. For example, there is the *jump* instruction. You can use this instruction to modify the order in which a program is executed. In fact, I use it later in an example showing multiplication. Note that jump instructions are often called *branch* instructions for conditional situations—that is, for situations where there is a logical choice in the program. The *branch* derives its name from the analogy to a tree, and it implies a fork in the representation of the program.

MULTIPLICATION

Let's now examine a more complex arithmetic problem: the multiplication of binary numbers. Begin by examining a usual decimal multiplication. To multiply 12 by 23:

```
     12   (multiplicand)
    ×23   (multiplier)
    ---
     36   (partial product)
    +24
    ---
  = 276   (final result)
```

The multiplication is performed by first multiplying the rightmost digit of the multiplier by the multiplicand—3×12 (the partial product is 36); and then by multiplying the next digit of the multiplier, 2, by 12. Then, add 24 to the partial product.

There is, however, *one more operation:* 24 is *offset to the left* (or shifted left) by one position. (The number being added to 36 is really 240.) Equivalently, you could say that the partial product (36) was shifted right by one position before adding. The two numbers, correctly shifted, are then added, and the sum is 276. That was easy. Look at an example of binary multiplication; it is performed in exactly the same way. To multiply 5 × 3:

```
(5)      101   (multiplicand)
(3)     ×011   (multiplier)
        ----
         101   (partial product)
        101
      +000
      -----
(15)   01111   (final result)
```

To perform the multiplication, operate exactly as you have done before. The formal representation of this algorithm appears in Figure 3.11 as a flowchart. Let's examine it.

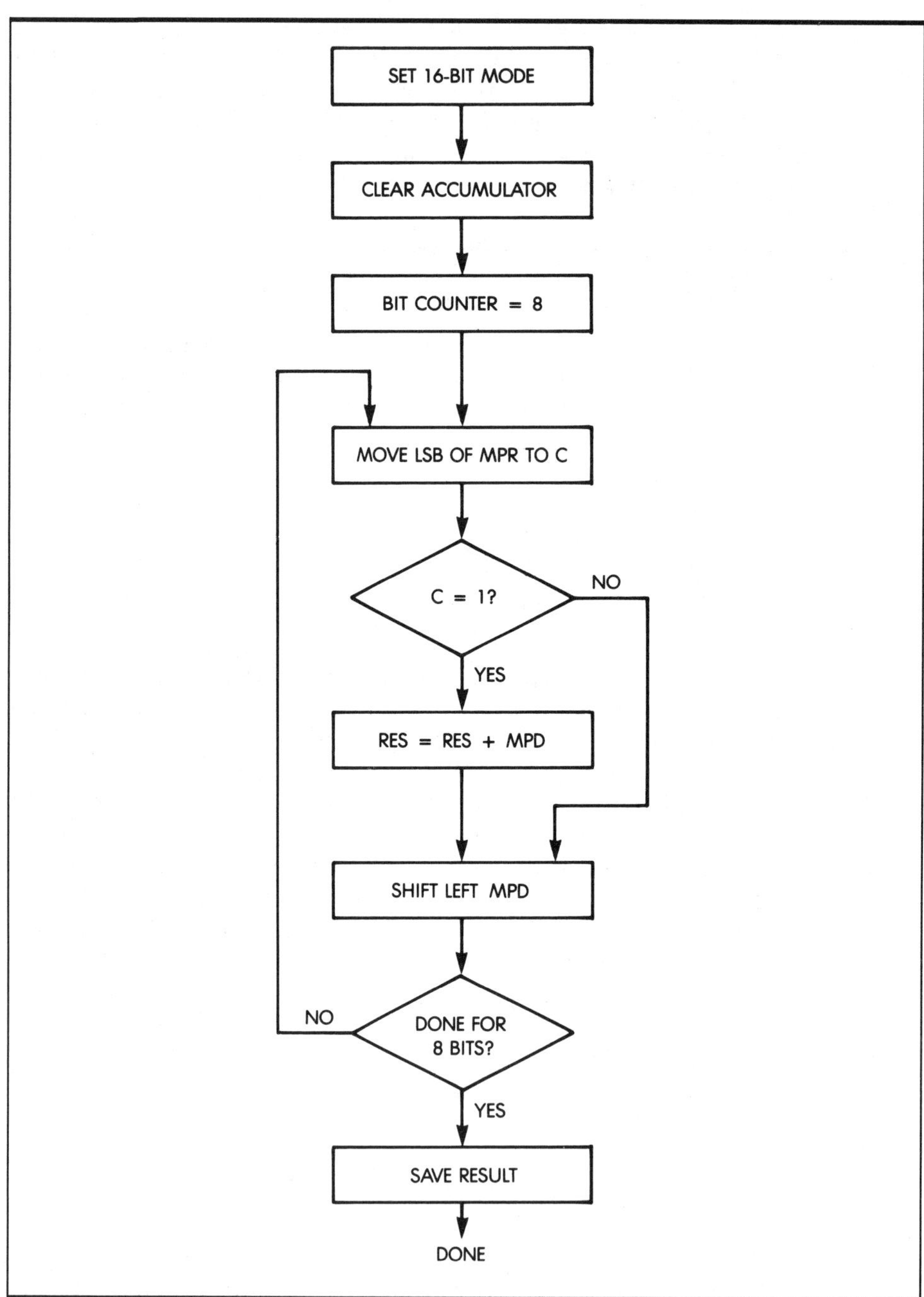

Figure 3.11: The Basic Multiplication Algorithm Flowchart

This flowchart is a symbolic representation of the algorithm I have just presented. Each rectangle represents an order to be carried out and will be translated into one or more program instructions. Each diamond-shaped symbol represents a test being performed—a branching point in the program. If the test succeeds, you branch to a specified location. If it does not, you branch to another location. I will explain the concept of branching later, in the program itself. You should now examine the flowchart and ascertain that it does, indeed, represent the algorithm presented.

Note the arrow coming out of the last diamond at the bottom of the flowchart and going back to the fourth rectangle at the top. It represents the fact that this portion of the flowchart is executed eight times, once for each bit in the multiplier. This type of situation, where execution restarts at the same point, is called a *program loop,* for obvious reasons.

8 × 8 MULTIPLICATION

I will now translate the flowchart in Figure 3.11 into a program for the 65816 and examine it in detail. Note that each box in the flowchart is translated into one or more instructions. (In this program, I assume that MPR and MPD already have a value.)

```
MULT88  REP   #$30     SET REGISTERS TO 16 BITS
        LDA   #0       CLEAR ACCUMULATOR
        LDX   #8       SET COUNTER TO 8
MULT    LSR   MPRAD    SHIFT MPR RIGHT
        BCC   NOADD    TEST CARRY BIT
        CLC            PREPARE TO ADD
        ADC   MPDAD    ADD MPD TO A
NOADD   ASL   MPDAD    SHIFT MPDAD LEFT
        DEX            DECREMENT COUNTER
        BNE   MULT     REPEAT UNTIL COUNTER=0
        STA   RESAD    SAVE THE RESULT
```

Figure 3.12 shows the registers and memory locations used by the program.

The 65816 is set to the 16-bit mode because the result of an 8-bit multiply may be 16 bits. This is because $2^8 \times 2^8 = 2^{16}$. A 16-bit register must therefore be used for the result. The accumulator (A), the index register (X), and three memory locations are used for this multiplication program. The 8-bit multiplier (MPR) is assumed to reside at memory address MPRAD. The multiplicand (MPD) is assumed to reside at memory address MPDAD. The shift count (8) is loaded into X. The accumulator is set to zero.

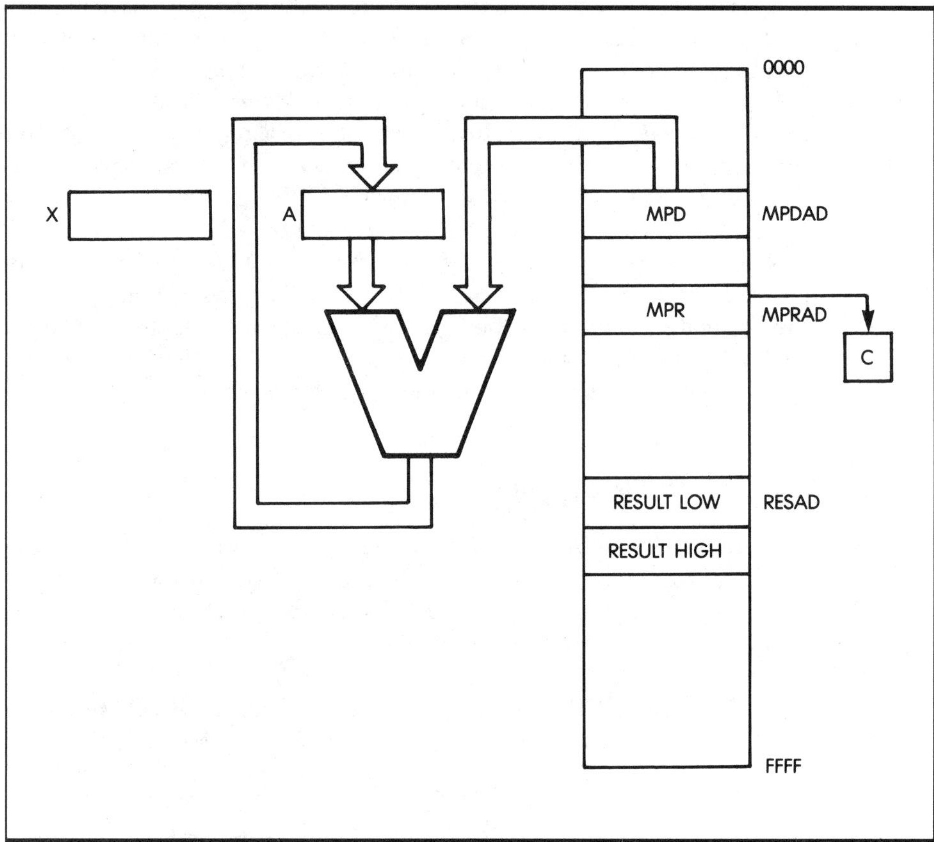

Figure 3.12: Registers and Memory for 8 × 8 Multiplication

The first step is to set the processor registers to the 16-bit mode, clear the accumulator, and load the shift counter, as shown in the flowchart in Figure 3.11. This is accomplished by the following instructions:

```
MULT88  REP   #$30
        LDA   #0
        LDX   #8
```

The first instruction sets the accumulator and index registers to 16 bits. The next instruction clears the accumulator. The accumulator must be set to zero before the multiplicand is added. The third instruction loads the value 8 into the X index register.

Referring back to the flowchart, the next step is to test if the least significant bit (LSB) of the multiplier is one or zero. This is done by shifting the multiplier right, so the LSB goes into the carry bit of the processor status register. The carry bit is then tested to see if an addition should be done. This is done in the next four instructions:

```
MULT    LSR   MPRAD
        BCC   NOADD
        CLC
        ADC   MPDAD
```

A new type of operation, *shift,* is introduced in the instruction LSR. It stands for *logical shift right.* This operation is performed in the arithmetic and logical unit. A shift right always puts 0 in bit 15 (or bit 7 in the 8-bit mode). There are different types of shift operations; I describe them in the next chapter. The effect of the shift is illustrated in Figure 3.13.

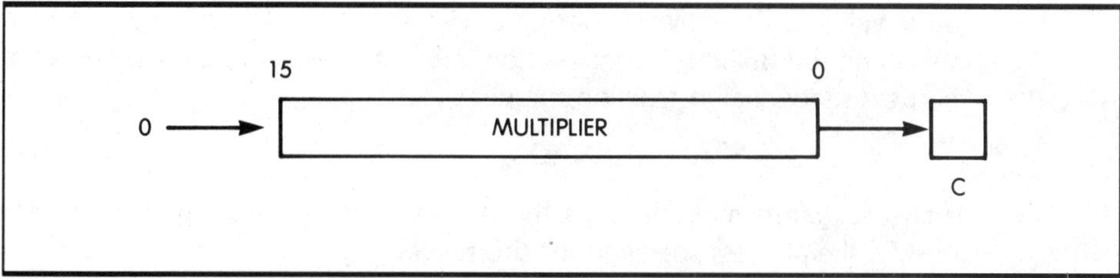

Figure 3.13: Shift-Right Multiplier

The instruction BCC NOADD is a *branch operation.* It means "branch, if the carry bit is clear, to NOADD." If the result of a previous operation sets the carry bit to 0, the program branches to the address NOADD. If the carry bit is 1, no branch occurs, and the next sequential instruction is executed (that is, the instruction CLC is executed).

The instruction CLC clears the carry bit in preparation for the addition done with the instruction ADC MPDAD. This addition uses the 16-bit form of the accumulator, and the word at the address MPDAD is 16 bits long.

The next operation, according to the flowchart in Figure 3.11, is to shift the multiplicand (MPD) left one bit. The instruction

```
NOADD   ASL   MPDAD
```

does the shift, and because the processor is in the 16-bit mode, the whole 16 bits is shifted at once. In an 8-bit microprocessor, extra instructions would be needed to shift.

At this point, you must check to see if all eight bits have been shifted. You can do this by decrementing the bit counter in register X. The register is decremented by the instruction:

```
DEX
```

This decrement instruction has the obvious effect.

You must see if the counter has been decremented to the value 0. You can do this by checking the value of the Z bit. Recall that the Z (zero) status flag indicates whether or not the previous arithmetic operation (such as a decrement operation) has produced a zero result. If the counter is not 0, the operation is not finished, and you must execute the program loop again. This is accomplished by the next instruction:

```
BNE   MULT
```

This branch instruction specifies that whenever the Z bit is not set (NE means "not equal to zero"), a branch occurs to location MULT. This is the program, which is executed repeatedly until the counter is decremented to the value 0. Whenever the counter decrements to the value 0, the Z bit is set, and the BNE MULT instruction fails. This results in the execution of the next sequential instruction, namely:

```
STA   RESAD
```

This instruction merely saves the 16-bit contents of A at the address RESAD, the address specified for the result.

Note that in most cases, the program just developed is a subroutine, and the final instruction in the subroutine is RTS (return from subroutine). I explain the subroutine mechanism later in this chapter.

IMPORTANT SELF-TEST

This program is the first significant program I have presented so far. It includes many different types of instructions, including transfer instructions (LD, ST), arithmetic operations (ADC), logical operations (ASL, LSR), and branch operations (BCC, BNE). It also implements a program loop, in which the seven instructions starting at address MULT are executed repeatedly. It is longer and more complex than the other arithmetic programs, so study it carefully.

To test your understanding of the program, try the following exercise, and complete it correctly before proceeding. It will be your only real proof that you have understood the concepts presented so far. If you obtain a correct result, then you have proven that you understand how instructions manipulate information in the microprocessor, transfer this information between the memory and registers, and process it. If you do not obtain the correct result, or if you do not do this exercise, it is likely that you will experience difficulties later when you begin writing programs yourself. Learning to program requires practice. Please pause now and do the following exercise.

A Sample Exercise

Every time you write a program, you should verify it by hand to ascertain that its results are correct. The goal of this exercise is to do just that by accurately completing Table 3.1.

You may want to write directly on the table, or you may want to make a copy of it. For this exercise, you must determine the contents of every relevant register and memory location in the 65816 after the execution of each instruction in the program. Table 3.1 shows the registers and memory locations used by the previous program. From left to right, they are accumulator A, the index register X, the carry C, and the memory locations for the multiplier, multiplicand, and result. If applicable, you should

Label	Instruction	A	X	C	MPR	MPD	RESULT

Table 3.1: Form for Multiplication Exercise

first complete the label on the left side of this table and then fill in the instructions being executed; then, on the right side of the table, you should fill in the contents of each register after each instruction has been executed. If you do not know the contents of a register, use dashes.

Let's start by filling in the table together. After that, you must fill in the rest of the form by yourself. The first line appears in Table 3.2. Assume that you are multiplying 3 (MPR) by 5 (MPD).

The first instruction to be executed is REP #$30. The M and X bits in the processor status register are cleared to put the accumulator and index registers in the 16-bit mode. Note that the contents of A, X, and the carry bit are still undefined (this is indicated by dashes).

Table 3.3 shows the situation after the first three instructions have been executed (just before the MULT).

The LSR instruction performs the logical shift right, and the rightmost bit of the multiplier falls into the carry bit. Table 3.4 shows that the contents

Label	Instruction	A	X	C	MPR	MPD	RESULT
	REP #$30	—	—	—	3	5	—

Table 3.2: Multiplication after One Instruction

of MPRAD after the shift is 1. The carry bit C is now set to 1. The other registers are unchanged by this operation. Now that you see how the chart works, you should complete it.

Table 3.5 shows a second iteration of the loop.

PROGRAMMING ALTERNATIVES

The preceding program could have been written in several different ways. As a general rule, even the programmer can usually find ways to modify, and often improve, a program. For example, I have used an algorithm that uses shifts and additions; however, I could have used a method that uses only repeated additions. The multiplier is decremented by 1 for each addition done, and the process stops when the multiplier reaches 0. This method is simpler than the first, because it is precisely the definition of multiplication, but it is slower.

Label	Instruction	A	X	C	MPR	MPD	RESULT
	REP #$30	—	—	—	3	5	—
	LDA #0	0	—	—	3	5	—
	LDX #8	0	8	—	3	5	—

Table 3.3: Multiplication after Three Instructions

MULTIPLYING 16-BIT NUMBERS

The 16 × 16 multiplication has a 32-bit product, so the product will require two words of memory. The multiplicand will also require an extra word of memory, because the leftmost bit of the multiplicand must be saved each time it is shifted left. The memory location called TEMP is used to save the bits of the multiplicand and is shown in Figure 3.14. Here is the program for 16 × 16 multiplication:

```
MULT16  REP  #$30      SET TO 16-BIT MODE
        LDA  #0        CLEAR ACCUMULATOR
        STA  TEMP      CLEAR TEMP
        STA  RESAD     CLEAR RESULT LOW
        STA  RESAD+2   CLEAR RESULT HIGH
        LDX  #16       COUNT TO 16 BITS
MULT    LSR  MPRAD     SHIFT MPR LSB TO C
```

Label	Instruction	A	X	C	MPR	MPD	RESULT
	REP #$30	—	—	—	3	5	—
	LDA #0	0	—	—	3	5	—
	LDX #8	0	8	—	3	5	—
MULT	LSR MPDAD	0	8	1	1	5	—
	BCC NOADD	0	8	1	1	5	—
	CLC	0	8	0	1	5	—
	ADC MPDAD	5	8	0	1	5	—
NOADD	ASL MPDAD	5	8	0	1	10	—
	DEX	5	7	0	1	10	—
	BNE MULT	5	7	0	1	10	—

Table 3.4: One Pass through the Loop

```
        BCC   NOADD     TEST CARRY C
        CLC             PREPARE TO ADD
        LDA   RESAD     GET RESULT LOW
        ADC   MPDAD     ADD MPD TO A
        STA   RESAD     SAVE RESULT LOW
        LDA   RESAD+2   LOAD HIGH RESULT
        ADC   TEMP      ADD HIGH BITS OF MPD
        STA   RESAD+2   SAVE RESULT HIGH
NOADD   ASL   MPDAD     SHIFT MPD LEFT
        ROL   TEMP      SHIFT C INTO TEMP
        DEX             DECREMENT BIT COUNTER
        BNE   MULT      REPEAT UNTIL COUNTER=0
```

When the multiplicand is shifted left, the carry bit must be transferred to the word TEMP. This transfer is done by the ROL instruction, which means "rotate left." In a *rotation operation,* as opposed to a shift operation, the

Label	Instruction	A	X	C	MPR	MPD	RESULT
MULT	REP #$30	—	—	—	3	5	—
	LDA #0	0	—	—	3	5	—
	LDX #8	0	8	—	3	5	—
	LSR MPRAD	0	8	1	1	5	—
	BCC NOADD	0	8	1	1	5	—
	CLC	0	8	0	1	5	—
	ADC MPDAD	5	8	0	1	5	—
NOADD	ASC MPDAD	5	8	0	1	10	—
	DEX	5	7	0	1	10	—
	BNE MULT	5	7	0	1	10	—
	LSR MPRAA	5	7	1	0	10	—
	BCC NOADD	5	7	1	0	10	—
	CLC	5	7	0	0	10	—
	ADC MPDAD	15	7	0	0	10	—
NOADD	ASL MPDAD	15	7	0	0	20	—
	DEX	15	6	0	0	20	—
	BNE MULT	15	6	0	0	20	—

Table 3.5: Second Pass through the Loop

bit coming into the word holds the contents of the carry bit C (see Figure 3.15). This is exactly what you want; the contents of C are loaded into the rightmost part of TEMP, and you have thereby transferred the leftmost bit of MPD.

BINARY DIVISION

Division is another complex problem because there is no divide instruction in the 65816. To develop an algorithm for writing a division program for the 65816, let's start by examining a simple decimal division. To divide

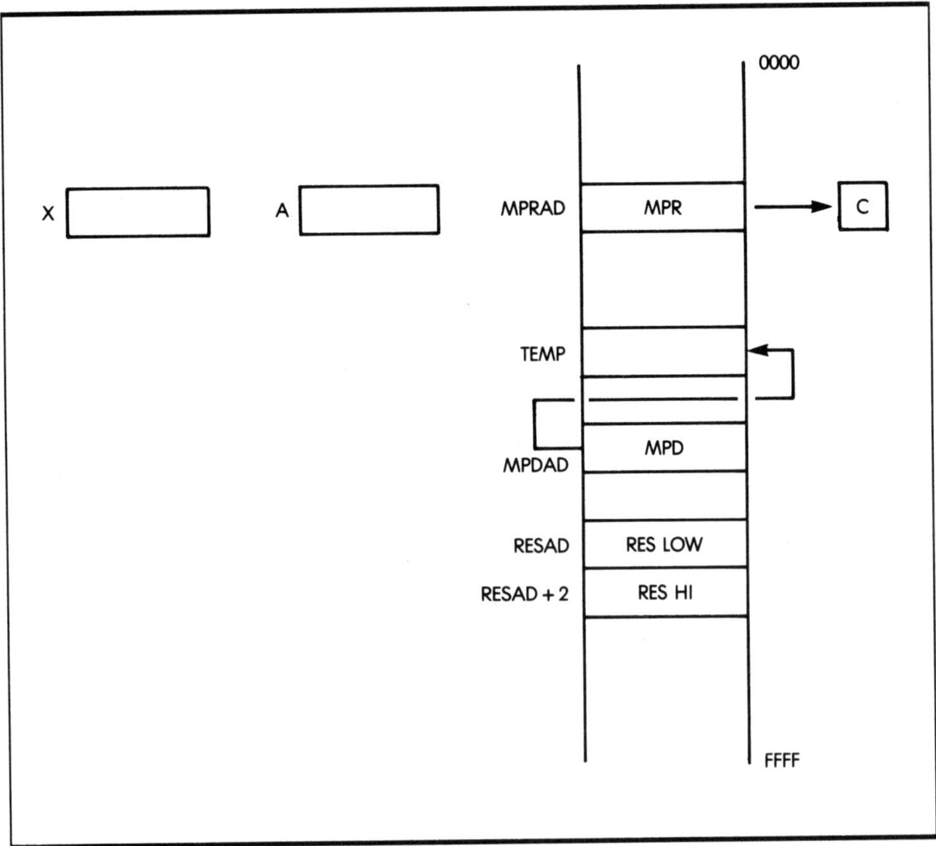

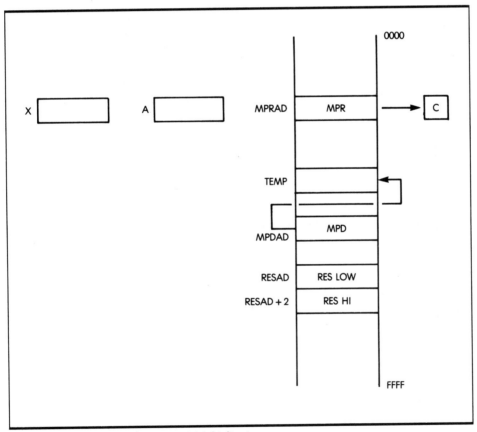

Figure 3.14: Registers for 16 × 16 Multiplication

254 by 12:

```
                  21   (quotient)
(divisor)      12|254  (dividend)
                 24
                  14
                  12
                   2   (remainder)
```

You perform the division by subtracting the largest possible multiple of the divisor from the leftmost digits of the dividend. The new dividend is 14. The multiplier of the divisor becomes the second digit of the quotient. The remainder is the result of the last subtraction.

You make trial subtractions or comparisons to find the largest multiple of the divisor that can be subtracted from the dividend. Note that in determining the first digit of the quotient, the actual number is 20, not 2, and the number subtracted from the dividend is 240, not 24. Leaving the zeros

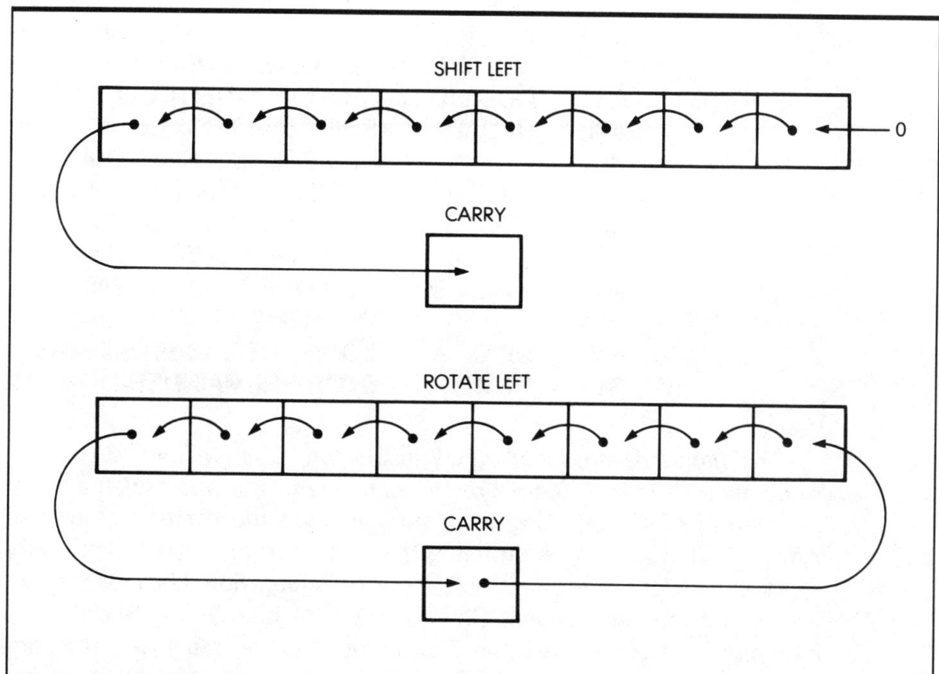

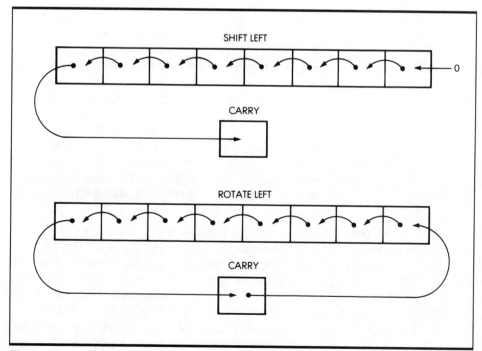

Figure 3.15: Shift and Rotate

out makes the notation convenient, but you must not lose sight of what is actually being done.

Binary division is performed in exactly the same way as decimal division. Let's look at an example. To divide 10 by 3:

```
                   0011   (quotient)
(divisor)       11│1010   (dividend)
                    11
                   ----
                   100
                    11
                   ----
                     1    (remainder)
```

To perform the division, operate exactly as you have done before. The formal representation of this algorithm appears in Figure 3.16. A 16 × 16 division is done, and the register and memory layout is shown, in Figure 3.17. Here is the program:

```
DIV16   REP   #$30     SET TO 16-BIT MODE
        LDX   #16      LOAD BIT COUNTER
        LDA   #0       CLEAR ACCUMULATOR
        STA   QUOTAD   CLEAR QUOTIENT
DIVD    ASL   QUOTAD   SHIFT QUOTIENT LEFT
        ASL   DVDAD    SHIFT DIVIDEND LEFT
        ROL   A        SHIFT DIVIDEND INTO A
        CMP   DVSAD    COMPARE A WITH DIVISOR
        BCC   NOSUB    IF A<DVS SKIP SUBTRACT
        SBC   DVSAD    SUBTRACT DVS FROM A
        INC   QUOTAD   ADD ONE TO QUOTIENT
NOSUB   DEX            DECREMENT COUNTER
        BNE   DIVD     LOOP UNTIL 16 BITS DONE
        STA   REMAD    STORE REMAINDER IN A
```

This program introduces a new instruction, CMP, which is a *compare operation.* It means "compare the contents of the accumulator to the contents of DVSAD." This instruction subtracts the contents of DVSAD from A. It is actually subtracting the divisor from the dividend being shifted into A. It is *not,* however, a normal subtraction, because the contents of A are not changed. Only the status register bits are affected. For example, if A equals DVS, the Z bit in the status register is set. The compare operation does an internal subtraction of two operands, a memory location is subtracted from the accumulator, and the status register is set

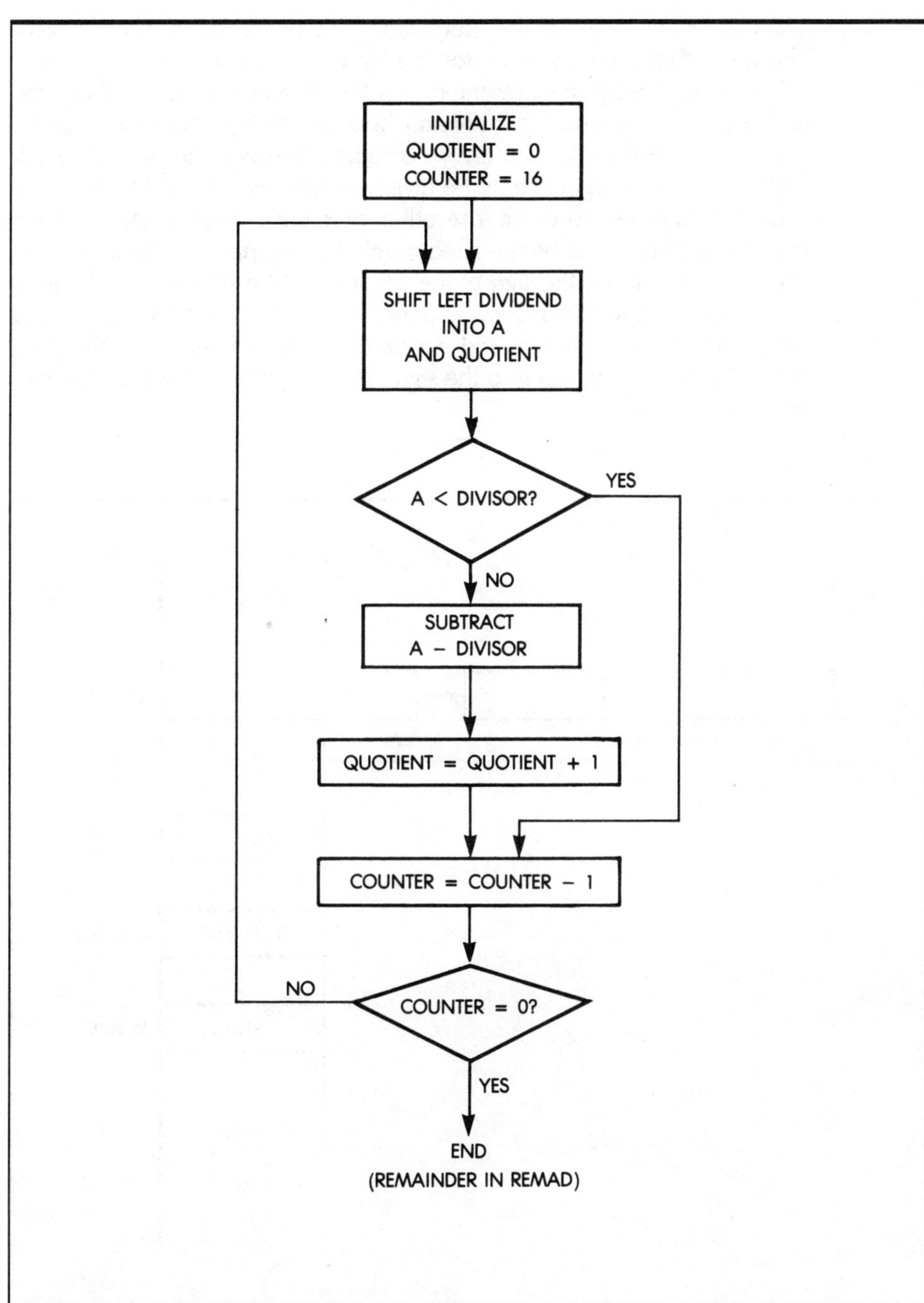

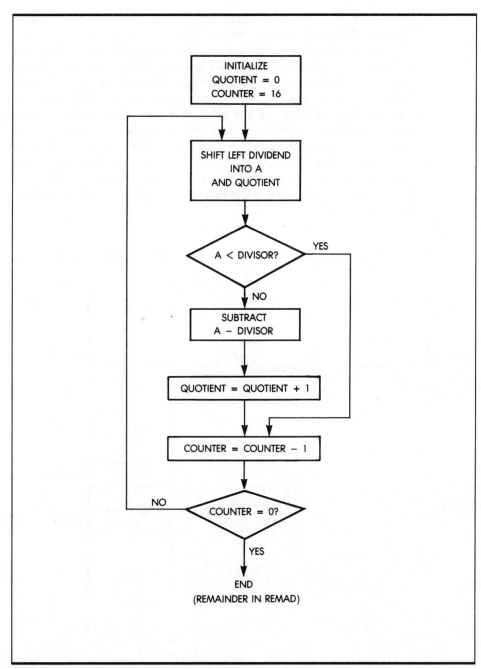

Figure 3.16: 16-Bit Binary Division Flowchart

according to the result of the subtraction. The operands are not changed. The status flags are now ready for use by a *branch instruction.*

The division programs presented thus far have two possible flaws. One is that there is no check for division by zero: division by zero is undefined, and therefore, it is an error condition. The program should check the divisor at the beginning. If the divisor is zero, you should branch to a code that handles the error. The other problem is that all the numbers have been assumed to be unsigned numbers. This problem is usually rectified by determining the sign of the result from the signs of the dividend and divisor before the division is done. Then, convert the dividend and divisor to positive numbers and execute the division program. You then adjust the sign of the result to the sign determined before you performed the division.

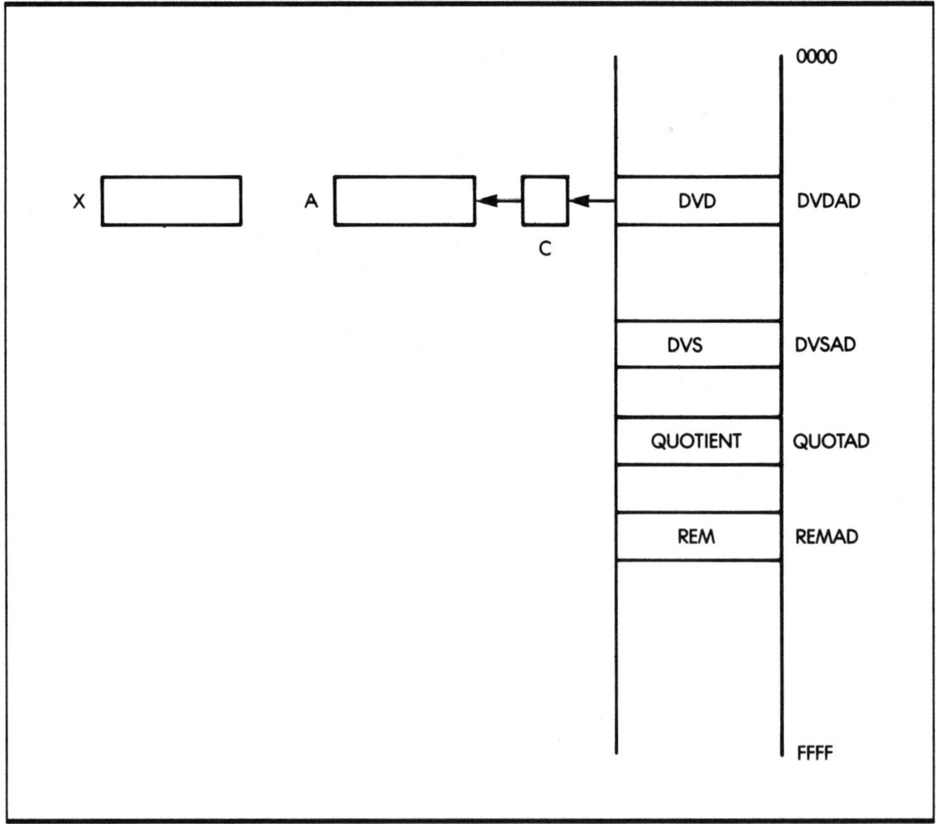

Figure 3.17: Registers for 16 × 16 Division

LOGICAL OPERATIONS

The other class of instructions, which can be executed by the ALU inside the microprocessor, is the set of *logical instructions.* These include AND, OR, and exclusive-OR (EOR). In addition, you can also include the shift and rotate operations, which have already been used, and the comparison instruction (CMP). I describe the AND, OR, and EOR instructions in Chapter 4.

I will now develop a brief program that checks whether a memory location called LOC contains the value 0, the value 1, or something else. This program uses the comparison instruction and performs a series of logical tests. Depending on the result of the comparison, some segment will then be executed.

Let's look at the program:

```
            LDA   LOC     READ CHARACTER IN LOC
            CMP   #$00    COMPARE TO ZERO
            BEQ   ZERO    IS IT A ZERO?
            CMP   #$01    COMPARE TO ONE
            BEQ   ONE     IS IT A ONE?
NONEFOUND   ...
            ...
ZERO        ...
            ...
ONE         ...
            ...
```

The first instruction, LDA LOC, reads the contents of memory location LOC and loads it into accumulator A. The data in LOC is the character you want to test. The instruction

```
CMP   #$00
```

compares the contents of A to the hexadecimal value 00 (the bit pattern 00000000). If this comparison instruction is successful, the Z bit in the status register is set to the value 1. This bit is then tested by the next branch instruction:

```
BEQ   ZERO
```

If this comparison is successful—if the Z bit has been set to one—then the branch succeeds. The program then jumps to the address ZERO. If the test fails, the next sequential instructions are executed:

```
CMP  #$01
BEQ  ONE
```

Similarly, the next branch instruction branches to location ONE, if the comparison succeeds. If none of the comparisons succeed, then the instruction at location NONEFOUND is executed:

```
NONEFOUND ...
```

This program demonstrates the value of the comparison instruction followed by a branch—a combination used in many of the following programs.

INSTRUCTION SUMMARY

I have now introduced you to most of the important instructions of the 65816. You have learned how to transfer values between the memory and registers, perform arithmetic and logical operations on data, and use the loop. I have shown you how to test data, and depending on the results of these tests, execute various portions of the program. In particular, these operations have made full use of the special 65816 features, such as the 16-bit accumulator and the 16-bit memory modes. I will introduce other special instructions throughout the remainder of this book.

I will now discuss another important programming structure, the subroutine.

SUBROUTINES

In concept, a subroutine is simply a block of instructions named by the programmer. From a more practical point of view, a subroutine must start with a label, which identifies it to the assembler. It is terminated by a special instruction called a *return*. I will now illustrate the use of a subroutine to demonstrate its value. Then, I will show how it is actually implemented.

Figure 3.18 illustrates how a subroutine is used. The main program appears on the left of the illustration and the subroutine appears, symbolically, on the right. Let's examine how the subroutine works. In this program, the lines of the main program are executed successively until a new instruction, CALL SUB, is met. This special instruction is the *subroutine call* and results in a transfer to the subroutine. Thus, the next instruction to be executed after the CALL SUB is the first instruction in the subroutine. This is illustrated by arrow 1 in the illustration.

The subprogram within the subroutine executes the same way as any other program, as indicated by arrow 2 in the figure. (I am assuming the subroutine does not contain any other calls.) The last instruction of this subroutine is a RETURN. This is a special instruction, which causes a return to the main program. The next instruction to be executed after the RETURN is the one following the CALL SUB in the main program. This is illustrated by arrow 3 in the illustration. Program execution then continues, as illustrated by arrow 4.

Later, a second CALL SUB appears in the body of the main program. A new transfer occurs, as shown by arrow 5. This means that the body of the subroutine is again executed following the CALL SUB instruction.

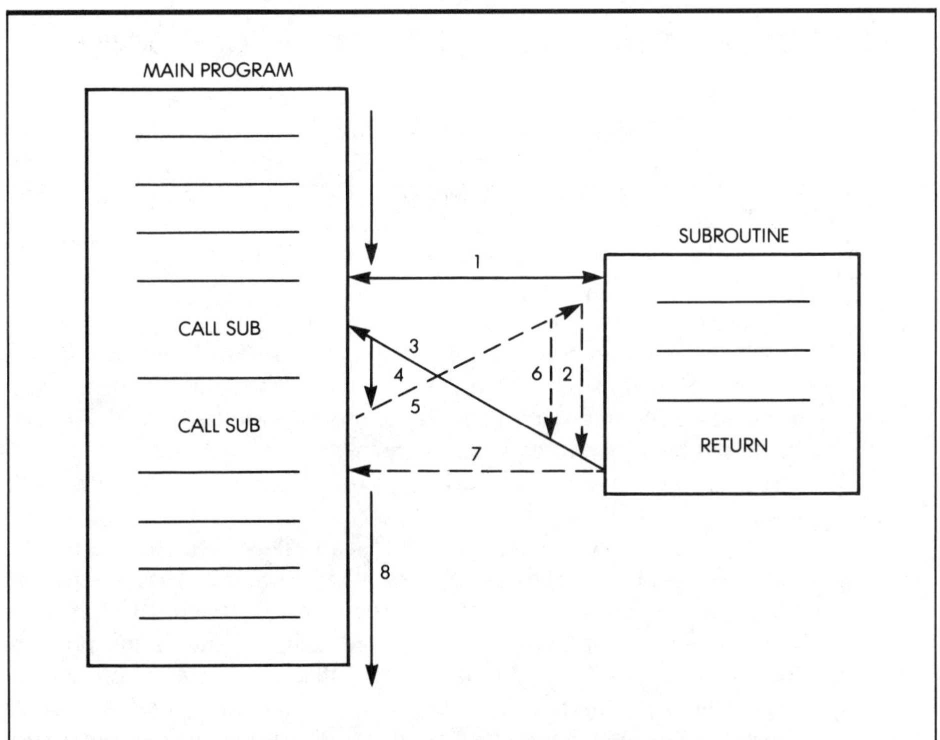

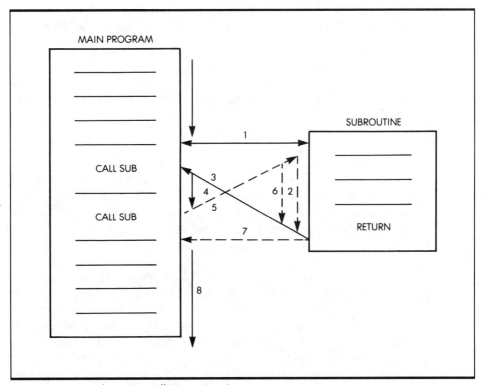

Figure 3.18: Subroutine Calls:Execution Sequence

Whenever a RETURN is encountered within a subroutine, a return occurs to the instruction that follows the CALL SUB being executed. This is illustrated by arrow 7. Following the return to the main program, program execution proceeds normally, as illustrated by arrow 8.

The effect of the two special instructions, CALL SUB and RETURN, should now be clear. The essential value of the subroutine is that you can call it from any number of points in the main program, and use it repeatedly, *without having to rewrite it.* An advantage of this approach is that it saves memory space, since the subroutine doesn't need to be rewritten each time. Another advantage is that the programmer need design a specific subroutine only once, and can then use it repeatedly. This is a significant simplification in program design.

The disadvantage of a subroutine should become clear just by examining the flow of execution between the main program and the subroutine. A subroutine results in *slower execution,* since extra instructions must be executed (the CALL SUB and the RETURN).

IMPLEMENTATION OF THE SUBROUTINE MECHANISM

Let's now examine how the two special instructions, CALL SUB and RETURN, are implemented internally within the processor. The CALL SUB instruction causes the next instruction to be fetched at a new address. Recall that this address is contained in the program counter (PC). This means that CALL SUB substitutes new contents into register PC. In other words, the start address of the subroutine is loaded into the program counter. *Is that really sufficient?*

To answer this question, let's consider the other special instruction: RETURN. This instruction causes a return to the instruction that follows the CALL SUB. This is possible only if the address of this instruction (that is, the value of the program counter at the time the CALL SUB was executed) has been preserved somewhere.

The next problem involves saving this return address: it must always be saved in a location where it will not be erased.

Let's now, however, consider the situation illustrated in Figure 3.19, where subroutine 1 (SUB 1) contains a call to SUB2. That mechanism must work in this case, as well as in other cases, where there may be more than two subroutines—say *n* nested calls. Whenever the program encounters a new CALL, the mechanism that stores the return address must again store the program counter. Therefore, you need at least 2*n* memory locations for this mechanism. Additionally, you need to return from SUB2 first, and SUB1 next. In other words, you need a structure that can preserve the chronological order in which addresses were saved. This structure is the *stack.*

Figure 3.20 shows the actual contents of the stack during successive subroutine calls. The memory layout of the program appears in Figure 3.21. Let's examine the main program first. The first call, CALL SUB1, is encountered at address 100. I assume that, in this microprocessor, the subroutine call uses three bytes. The next sequential address is, therefore, not 101, but 103. The CALL instruction uses addresses 100, 101, 102. Because the control unit of the 65816 "knows" the instruction is three bytes long, the value of the program counter, when the call has been completely decoded, is 103. Therefore, 103 is stored on the stack. The effect of the call is to load the value 280 in the program counter (280 is the starting address of SUB1). In SUB1, the subroutine SUB2 (at location 900) is called at time 2 from the memory address 300. This pushes 303, the return address to SUB1, onto the stack.

I am now ready to demonstrate the effect of the RETURN instruction and the correct operation of the stack mechanism. Execution proceeds within SUB2 until the RETURN instruction is encountered at time 3. The RETURN instruction simply pulls the top of the stack into the program counter. In other words, the program counter is restored to the value it had before entering the subroutine. In the example, the top of the stack is 303. Figure 3.20 shows that, at time 3, value 303 is removed from the

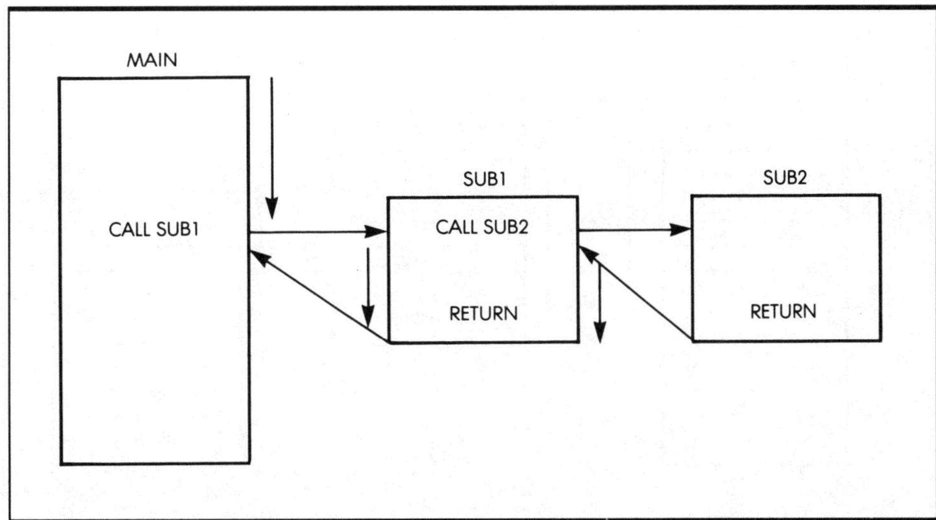

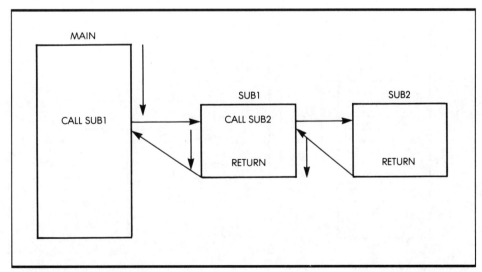

Figure 3.19: Nested Calls

stack and put back into the program counter. As a result, instruction execution proceeds from address 303. At time 4, the RETURN of SUB1 is encountered. The value on top of the stack is 103. It is pulled and installed in the program counter. As a result, program execution proceeds from location 103 in the main program. That is, indeed, the effect you want. Figure 3.20 shows that at time 4 the stack is again empty. Thus, the mechanism to store return addresses works.

The subroutine call mechanism works up to the maximum dimension of the stack. That is why early microprocessors with 4- or 8-register stacks were essentially limited to 4 or 8 levels of subroutine calls.

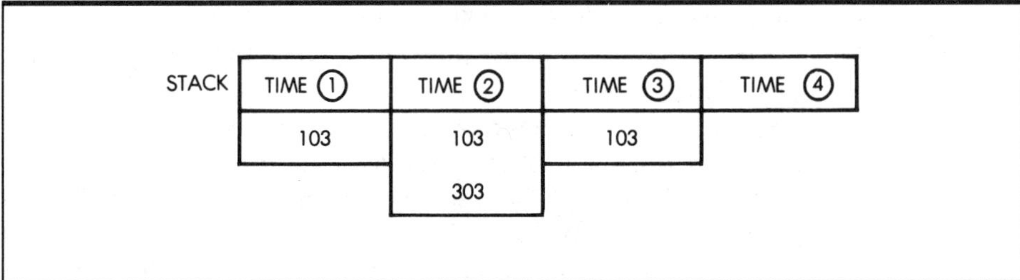

Figure 3.20: Stack versus Time

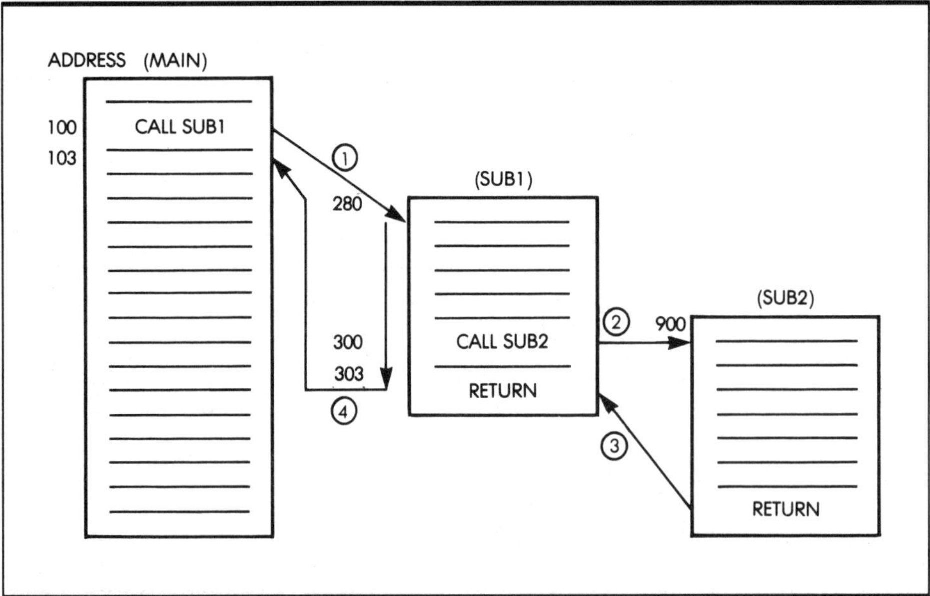

Figure 3.21: The Subroutine Calls, Showing Memory Layout

Note that for clarity, Figures 3.18 and 3.19 show the subroutines to the right of the main program. In reality, the subroutines are typed as regular instructions of the program. When you produce the listing of a complete program, you can list the subroutines at the beginning, middle, or end of the text. For this reason, you must identify them; you do so by preceding each subroutine by a label.

65816 SUBROUTINES

I have now discussed the basic concepts of subroutines. You have seen that a stack is required to implement this mechanism. The 65816 is equipped with a 16-bit stack-pointer register: the hardware stack S. The subroutine call of the 65816 always uses the hardware stack. This stack can reside anywhere within memory and may have up to 64K (1K = 1024) bytes, assuming they are available for that purpose. In practice, the programmer defines the start address for the stack, as well as its maximum dimension, before writing the program, so that some memory area is then reserved for the stack.

In the case of the 65816, there are two subroutine call instructions: JSR and JSL. JSR (jump to subroutine), like the call previously described, contains the address of the subroutine to jump to in the three-byte instruction. However, JSL (jump to subroutine long) differs from JSR in the way the address of the beginning of the subroutine is obtained. In the case of JSL, the three bytes following the opcode form the address of the subroutine. This 24-bit address allows a subroutine to be located anywhere in the 65816 address space.

There are two return instructions that mean "return from subroutine": RTS and RTL. These return instructions operate as previously described. Additionally, there is a special type of return instruction available that is used to terminate interrupt routines. This instruction, RTI, is described in the sections on the 65816 instructions and interrupts in Chapter 6.

SUBROUTINE EXAMPLES

Most of the programs developed in this book would normally be written as subroutines. For example, the division program is likely to be used by many areas of the program. To facilitate and clarify program development, therefore, it is convenient to define a subroutine with a name (for example, DIV16). At the end of this subroutine, then, you would simply add the instruction RTS.

RECURSION

Recursion indicates that a subroutine is calling itself. Recursive programs are not encountered often. Their main application is in artifical-intelligence programming. I will not discuss recursion further in this book.

SUBROUTINE PARAMETERS

When you call a subroutine, you normally expect that the subroutine will work on some data. For example, in the case of multiplication, you have to transmit two numbers, or *parameters,* to the subroutine that performs the multiplication. For example, the multiplication subroutine expects to find the multiplier and the multiplicand in given memory locations. Using fixed memory locations illustrates one of these three methods of passing parameters:

1. Through registers
2. Through memory
3. Through the stack

Let's now examine each method.

Passing Parameters

Registers are often used to pass parameters. This solution is the most advantageous if registers are available, since a fixed memory location is not needed; therefore, the subroutine remains memory-independent.

Using *memory* to pass parameters offers greater flexibility, but results in poorer performance. It also ties the subroutine to a given memory area. The disadvantage of a fixed memory location is that when you use it, other users of the subroutine must be careful to use the same convention. Also, other users must make sure that the memory location is indeed available. That is why, in many cases, a block of memory locations is reserved simply for passing parameters among various subroutines.

Depositing parameters in the *stack* offers the same advantage as using registers: it is memory-independent. The subroutine simply knows that it is supposed to receive, say, two parameters that are stored on top of the stack. Naturally, this method also has disadvantages. It clutters the stack with data and, therefore, reduces the number of possible levels of subroutine calls. It also significantly complicates the use of the stack, and it may require multiple stacks.

The choice is up to the programmer. Generally, it is advantageous to remain independent from actual memory locations as much as possible.

If registers are not available, a possible solution is the stack. However, if a large quantity of information must be passed to a subroutine, this information may have to reside directly in the memory. An elegant way around the problem of passing a block of data is simply to transmit a pointer to the information. Recall that a pointer is the address of the beginning of the block. A pointer can be transmitted in a register, in the stack (two-stack locations can be used to store a 16-bit address), or in one or more given memory locations.

Finally, if neither of the two solutions is applicable, then you can make an agreement with the subroutine to put the data at some fixed memory location (the "mailbox").

SUBROUTINE LIBRARY

There are definite advantages to structuring portions of a program into identifiable subroutines. For example, subroutines can be debugged independently, and they can have a mnemonic name. Also, provided that they can be used in other areas of the program, they become shareable. It becomes advantageous to build a library of useful subroutines. However, there is no general panacea in computer programming. Using subroutines systematically for any group of instructions that can be grouped by function can result in poor efficiency. The alert programmer will have to weigh the advantages against the disadvantages.

SUMMARY

In this chapter, I have described how information is manipulated by instructions inside the 65816. I have introduced increasingly complex algorithms and translated them into programs. I have also discussed the main types of instructions and important structures such as loops, stacks, and subroutines.

By now, you should have acquired a basic understanding of programming and the major techniques used in standard applications. Let's go on to the next chapter and study the instructions available.

EXERCISES

3-1: *Referring only to the list of instructions in Appendix D, write a program that adds two numbers stored at memory locations LOC1 and LOC2, and deposits the results at memory location LOC3.*

3-2: *Rewrite the addition program in Exercise 3-1, using 16-bit numbers and the memory layout indicated in Figure 3.6.*

3-3: *Refer to Figure 3.6. Assume now that ADR1 does not point to the lower half of OP1, but instead points to the higher part of OP1, as illustrated in Figure 3.7. Now write the corresponding program.*

3-4: *Write an 8-bit subtraction program.*

3-5: *Rewrite the subtraction program you wrote in Exercise 3-4, for 16-bit numbers, without using the specialized 16-bit instruction.*

3-6: *Write a subtraction program for a 16-bit BCD number.*

3-7: *Divide 28 by 4 in binary, using a flowchart, and verify that the result is 7. If the result is not 7, try again. Only when you obtain the correct result are you ready to translate this flowchart into a program.*

3-8: *Is it really necessary to clear the quotient at the beginning of a 16-bit division program?*

3-9: *Compute the speed of a division operation using the 16-bit division program. Assume that a branch will occur in 50 percent of the cases. Look up the number of cycles required by each instruction in Appendix E. Assume a clock rate of 2 MHz (one cycle = 0.5 microseconds).*

3-10: *Write a 16 × 16 division program, using the algorithm that subtracts the divisor from the dividend until the divisor is larger than the dividend. The quotient is incremented each time a subtraction is done. Compare it to the 16-bit division program in this chapter, and determine whether this approach is faster or slower than the preceding one. The speeds of the 65816 instructions are given in Appendix D.*

3-11: *Add a check for divide by zero to the 16 × 16 division program.*

3-12: *Make the 16 × 16 division program so that it can handle signed numbers.*

3-13: *Refer to the definition of the LDA LOC instruction in the next chapter. Examine the effect, if any, of this instruction on the status flags. Is it necessary to have the second instruction of the program (CMP $00) illustrate logical operations?*

3-14: *Write a program that reads the contents of memory location 24 and branches to an address called STAR, if there is a* * *in memory location 24. The bit pattern for a* * *in binary notation is assumed to be represented by 00101010.*

3-15: *If DIV16 is used as a subroutine, will it "damage" any internal flags or registers?*

3-16: *Is it legal to let a subroutine call itself? (In other words, will everything work even if a subroutine calls itself?) If you are not sure, draw the stack and fill it with the successive addresses. Then, look at the registers and memory and determine if a problem exists.*

THE 65816 INSTRUCTION SET

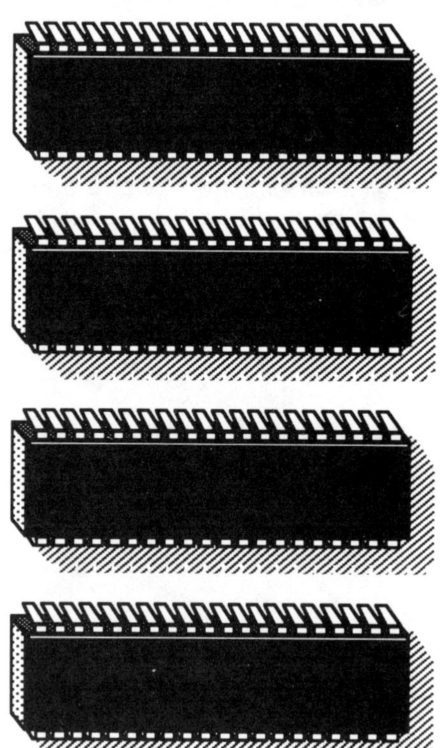

4

IN THIS CHAPTER, I will first analyze the various classes of instructions normally available on a general-purpose computer. I will then examine the variety of instructions that the 65816 offers in each of these categories, and you will see how each of these instructions affects the status register. You will also see these instructions used in various addressing modes.

CLASSES OF INSTRUCTIONS

It is possible to classify instructions in several different ways; there is no standard set of classifications. For the purpose of this discussion, I will distinguish five main categories of instructions:

1. Data transfers
2. Data processing
3. Test and branch
4. Input/output
5. Control

DATA TRANSFERS

Data transfer instructions transfer data between registers, between a register and memory, or between a register and an input/output device. Some registers even offer specialized transfer instructions that can be used to organize data (for example, push and pull operations are provided for efficient stack operation).

DATA PROCESSING

Data processing instructions modify data in the computer. These instructions fall into four general categories:

1. Arithmetic operations (for example: plus, minus)
2. Bit manipulation (for example: set, reset)
3. Logical operations (for example: AND, OR, exclusive-OR)
4. Skew and shift operations (for example: shift, rotate)

TEST AND BRANCH

Test instructions test the bits in the processor status register for values of 0 or 1, and for combinations of these values. It is therefore desirable to have as many flags as possible in this register.

It is useful to have instructions that will test for:

1. Combinations of bits
2. A single bit position in a word
3. The value of a register compared to the value of a memory location (greater than, less than, or equal to)

Generally, microprocessor instructions are limited to testing single bits of the flags register.

Branch instructions generally fall into three categories:

1. The branch, which is restricted to an 8-bit displacement field
2. The jump, which specifies a full 16-bit address
3. The call, which is used with subroutines

It is convenient to have two- or even three-way branches, depending, for example, on whether one operand of a comparison is equal to, greater than, or less than the other operand. It is also convenient to have skip operations, which jump forward or backward by a few instructions. Note that a *skip* is equivalent to a *branch*.

INPUT/OUTPUT

Input/output instructions are specialized instructions for handling input/output devices. In practice, most microprocessors use *memory-mapped I/O,* whereby the input/output devices are connected to the address bus in the same way that the memory chips are connected, and they are addressed as such. (That is, they appear to the programmer as memory locations.)

Memory-type operations (to the address of an I/O device) normally require three bytes and are, therefore, slow. For efficient input/output handling in such an environment, it is usually desirable to have a short addressing mechanism. It is possible to use direct page addressing, which requires only two bytes, if the I/O device addresses are all on the same page of memory.

CONTROL

Control instructions supply synchronization signals. These instructions can suspend or interrupt a program. They can also function as breaks or simulated interrupts. (See Chapter 6 for a detailed description of interrupts.)

THE 65816 INSTRUCTION SET

The 65816 microprocessor was designed as an improved version of the 6502 and, therefore, offers all the capabilities of the 6502, plus several new instructions. In view of the limited number of bits available in an 8-bit opcode, you might wonder how the designers of the 65816 succeeded in implementing additional instructions. They did so by using 255 of the 256 possible opcodes and by not implementing certain address modes with some instructions. By keeping the opcode to one byte, the maximum instruction length is four bytes, and many instructions are only one or two bytes long.

In this section, I will review the various instructions of the 65816, explore capabilities, and group them into logical categories. Let's first examine the capabilities provided by the 65816 in terms of the five classes of instructions just described. Later, I will present an individual, in-depth description of each instruction.

DATA TRANSFER INSTRUCTIONS ON THE 65816

The data transfer instructions on the 65816 fall into three categories: 8-bit transfers, 16-bit transfers, and stack operations. Let's examine each category.

8-Bit Data Transfers

Most 8-bit data transfers use load and store instructions to transfer 8-bit data between memory, the accumulator, and the index registers. For example, the instruction

```
LDA     ADDR1
```

loads accumulator A from memory. Similarly,

```
STX     ADDR1
```

stores index register X in memory. To transfer data between registers, you use the transfer and exchange instructions. The transfer copies the contents of one register to another. For example, the instruction

```
TAX
```

transfers the contents of A to the X register. The exchange instruction works only between the A and B accumulators when the M bit in the processor status register is 1 (8-bit accumulator mode). For example,

```
XBA
```

copies the contents of B to A and A to B.

There are several different addressing modes—*immediate, absolute, direct, indirect indexed, indexed indirect, indexed, direct indirect,* and *stack*—that you can use to access the memory location used in a load or store instruction. I discuss them in detail in Chapter 5.

16-Bit Data Transfers

You can use the same instructions that you used for 8-bit transfers to accomplish 16-bit transfers. The processor must be put in the 16-bit mode for both the accumulators and the index registers. You select the 16-bit mode by setting the M and X bits in the P register to 0. You select the 8-bit mode by setting the M and X bits to 1. For example, you can use the load and store instructions to load three 16-bit registers—C, X, and Y—*from* memory or to store them *in* memory. You can also use the transfer instructions to transfer a 16-bit register to any other 16-bit register, including the direct register D and the stack pointer S. The P register can only be directly modified by the *reset P* and *set P* instructions and by a stack operation.

Stack Operations

Recall from Chapter 3 that the stack operations move data between the top of the stack and the registers or memory. The 65816 has three types of stack instructions: *push, pull,* and *push effective address.* Any of the 65816 registers, except the PC, may be pushed onto or pulled from the stack. For example,

```
PHB
```

pushes the 8-bit program bank register onto the stack. When an 8-bit register is pushed onto the stack, the stack pointer is decremented by 1. Whenever a 16-bit register is pushed onto the stack, the stack pointer is decremented by 2. When a 16-bit register is put onto the stack, the high byte is pushed first. The number of bytes pushed onto the stack for a particular register is dependent on the mode of the 65816. Take care not to push a 16-bit register onto the stack and then switch to the 8-bit mode to pull the register.

The three push-effective-address instructions allow memory locations to be pushed onto the stack. The push effective absolute (PEA) (also called push effective immediate) instruction pushes the two bytes following the opcode onto the stack. The push effective indirect (PEI) instruction pushes the two bytes addressed by the sum of the D register and the byte following the opcode. The push effective relative (PER) instruction adds the two bytes following the opcode to the PC to form the pointer to the two bytes to be pushed onto the stack.

DATA PROCESSING OPERATIONS OF THE 65816

Data processing operations on the 65816 fall into four categories: arithmetic, logical, skew (shift and rotate), and bit manipulation. Let's examine each category.

Arithmetic

There are two main arithmetic operations: addition and subtraction. Both operations use the carry bit, so it is important to remember to clear the carry bit (CLC) before an addition and to set the carry bit (SEC) before a subtraction. You can use both instructions for BCD operations by setting the decimal bit (SED) in the processor status register.

In general, all arithmetic operations modify some of the status register flags (see Appendix D). It is important to note, however, that the INC and DEC instructions, which operate on registers and memory locations, do not modify the C or carry bit. This means that if you increment or decrement past the value 255 (or 65,535 for 16-bit), the C bit will not be changed. If you need to detect a value changing from positive to negative, or vice versa, you must test the N and Z bits.

Logical

The 65816 provides three logical operations—AND, ORA (inclusive), and EOR (exclusive)—plus a comparison instruction, CMP. Let's examine these operations.

AND Each logical operation is characterized by a *truth table,* which expresses the logical value of the result as a function of the inputs. Here is the truth table for AND:

0 AND 0 = 0
0 AND 1 = 0
1 AND 0 = 0
1 AND 1 = 1

or

AND	0	1
0	0	0
1	0	1

The AND operation is characterized by the fact that the output is 1 only if both inputs are 1. In other words, if one of the inputs is 0, the result is guaranteed to be 0. This feature, called *masking,* is used to zero a bit position in a byte.

The AND instruction is useful for clearing or masking one or more bit positions in a byte. Assume, for example, that you want to zero the rightmost four bits in a byte. The program is:

```
LDA     WORD          WORD CONTAINS 10101010
AND     #%11110000    11110000 IS MASK
```

I assume that WORD is equal to 10101010. The result of this program is to leave the value 10100000 in the accumulator. The **%** is used to indicate a binary value.

ORA The ORA instruction is the inclusive-OR operation. It is characterized by the following truth table:

0 OR 0 = 0
0 OR 1 = 1
1 OR 0 = 1
1 OR 1 = 1

or

ORA	0	1
0	0	1
1	1	1

The logical OR, or ORA, is characterized by the fact that if one of the operands is 1, then the result is always 1. The obvious use of ORA, then, is to set any bit in a byte to 1.

Let's set the rightmost four bits of WORD to the value 1. The program is:

```
LDA    WORD
ORA    %00001111
```

Assuming that WORD contains 10101010, the final value of the accumulator is 10101111.

EOR EOR stands for *exclusive-OR*. The exclusive-OR differs from the inclusive-OR in one respect: the result is 1 only if exactly one of the operands is equal to 1. If both operands are equal to 1, then ORA gives a result of 1. The exclusive-OR gives a result of 0. The truth table is:

0 EOR 0 = 0
0 EOR 1 = 1
1 EOR 0 = 1
1 EOR 1 = 0

or

EOR	0	1
0	0	1
1	1	0

You can use the exclusive-OR for comparisons. If any bit is different, then the exclusive-OR of two bytes will be nonzero. In addition, you can use the exclusive-OR to *complement* a byte. You do this by performing the EOR of a byte using all ones. The program appears below:

```
LDA    WORD
EOR    %11111111
```

Assume that WORD contains 10101010. The final value of the accumulator is 01010101. You can verify that this is the complement of the original value.

You can use EOR to advantage as a *bit toggle:* the bits in the accumulator will change, or toggle, each time an EOR is done, if the other byte used does not change.

Skew (Shift and Rotate)

It is necessary here to differentiate between the shift and rotate operations. In a *shift* operation, the contents of the register are shifted to the left or right by one bit position. The bit falling out of the register goes into the carry bit (C), and the bit coming in is 0.

A *rotation* differs from a shift in that the bit coming into the register is the one that falls from the carry bit. The rotation is actually a 9-bit operation. Figure 4.1 illustrates a 9-bit rotation. For example, in the case of a right rotation, the eight bits of the register are shifted right by one bit position. The bit falling off the right part of the register goes, as usual, into the carry bit. Simultaneously, the bit coming in on the left end of the register is the previous value of the carry bit (before it is overwritten with the bit falling out). In mathematics this is called a 9-bit rotation, since the eight bits of the register, plus the ninth bit (the carry bit), are rotated right by one bit position. Conversely, the left rotation accomplishes the same result in the opposite direction. The rotation is 17 bits in the 16-bit processor mode.

Bit Manipulation

I have shown previously how you can use the logical operations to set or reset bits, or groups of bits, in accumulators or memory. You can also use two special instructions for operating on the processor status register: REP and SEP. The REP instruction, meaning "reset status bits," performs an AND function with P and the complement of a byte immediately following the opcode and stores the result in P. Any bit that is set in A will be cleared in P. For example,

```
REP     #$30
```

clears the M and X bits in P to set the processor into the 16-bit mode.

The SEP instruction, meaning "set status bits," performs an OR function with A and P and stores the result in P. Any bit set in A will be set in P. For example,

```
SEP     #$30
```

sets the M and X bits in P to put the processor into the 8-bit mode.

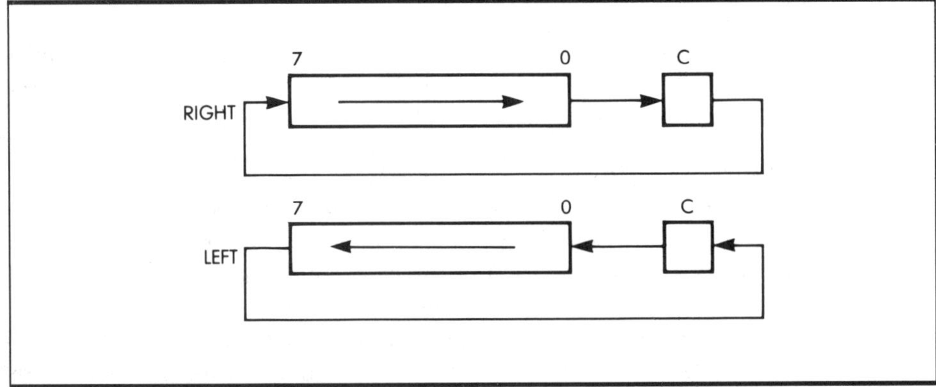

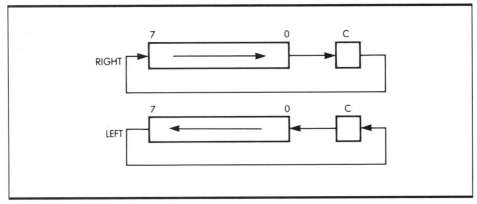

Figure 4.1: 9-Bit Rotation

There are two instructions, similar to REP and SEP, that operate on the accumulator and memory. The TRB instruction means "test and reset bits." This instruction performs an AND function between the complement of A and a memory location, and stores the result in memory. Any bit that is set in A will be cleared in the memory. The other instruction is TSB, meaning "test and set bits," which performs a logical OR between A and memory and stores the result in memory. Any bit set in A will be set in memory after a TSB instruction.

Finally, the bit test instruction, BIT, sets the status register with the result of performing AND on the accumulator and an 8-bit memory location. In the bit test instruction, neither the accumulator nor the memory location is changed. The AND operation changes only the bits in the P register. The N and V bits are set by bits 7 and 6 of the result, respectively. In the 16-bit mode, bit 15 is copied to N and bit 14 is copied to V.

TEST AND BRANCH OPERATIONS OF THE 65816

Since testing operations rely heavily on the use of the status register, I will now describe the role of each of the status flag bits. Figure 4.2 shows the contents of the status register.

C is the carry bit, V is overflow, Z is zero, and N is negative. Bit 2 is used with interrupts. The M and X bits determine whether the 65816 is in the 8-bit or 16-bit mode. When the 65816 is in the emulation (6502) mode, bits 4 and 5 are set for special 6502 operations. The D bit puts the 65816 into the BCD arithmetic mode when it is 1. The E bit determines whether the processor is in the emulation mode or in the native (65816) mode. You can change the E bit by exchanging it with the C bit, using the exchange carry and emulation bits (XCE) instruction. When E is 0, the 65816 is in the native mode. When E is 1, the 65816 is in the emulation mode. You can test the other four codes (C,V, Z, N) in conjunction with

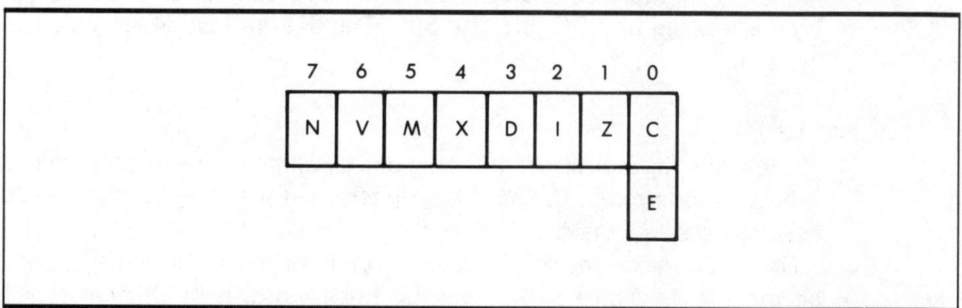

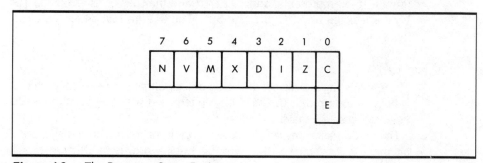

Figure 4.2: The Processor Status Register

conditional branch instructions. I will now describe the role of each status flag bit.

Carry (C)

In the case of nearly all microprocessors, and of the 65816 in particular, the carry bit assumes a dual role. First, it is used to indicate if an addition or subtraction operation has resulted in a carry (or borrow). Second, it is used as a ninth bit in the case of shift and rotate operations. Using a single bit to perform both roles facilitates some operations, such as a division operation. This should be clear from the description of division operations given in Chapter 3.

When you are learning to use the carry bit, it is important to remember that all arithmetic operations either set or reset it, depending on the result of the instructions. Similarly, all shift and rotate operations use the carry bit and either set or reset it, depending on the value of the bit coming out of the word.

In the case of logical instructions, you can use REP, SEP, CLC, and SEC to directly reset or set the carry bit. Instructions that affect the carry bit are ADC, ASL, CMP, CPX, CPY, LSR, ROL, ROR, SBC, and XCE. Also, some data transfer instructions and control instructions, including PLP and RTI, affect the C bit, and all the other status bits, because they load the status register.

Overflow (V)

I described the overflow flag in Chapter 1, when I introduced the two's complement notation. The overflow flag detects if, during an addition or subtraction, the sign of the result was "accidentally" changed, due to the overflow of the result into the sign bit. (Recall that, using an 8-bit representation, the largest positive number and the smallest negative number in two's complement are +127 and −128, respectively. The largest number using a 16-bit representation is +32767 and the smallest is −32768.) The V bit is affected by ADC, BIT, and SBC. The CLV instruction always clears the V bit.

Zero (Z)

The Z status flag indicates if the value of a byte that has been computed or is being transferred, is 0. The Z bit is often used with comparison instructions to indicate a match.

For an operation resulting in a zero result, or for a data transfer, the Z bit is set to 1 whenever the byte, or 16-bit word, is 0. Otherwise, Z is reset to 0.

The following instructions condition the value of the Z bit: ADC, AND, ASL, BIT, CMP, CPX, CPY, DEC, DEX, DEY, EOR, INC, INX, INY, LDA, LDX, LDY, LSR, ORA, PLA, PLB, PLD, PLX, PLY, ROL, ROR, SBC, TAX, TAY, TCD, TCS, TDC, TRB, TSB, TSC, TSX, TXA, TXY, TYA, TYX, and XBA.

Negative (N)

This status bit reflects the value of the most significant bit of a result, or of a byte (or 16-bit data) being transferred. In two's complement notation, the most significant bit represents the sign: 0 indicates a positive number, and 1 indicates a negative number. As a result, bit 7 (or bit 15, for 16-bit numbers) is called the negative bit.

In most microprocessors, the sign bit plays an important role when communicating with input/output devices, because it is usually the most convenient bit to test. When examining the status of an input/output device, reading the status register automatically conditions the negative bit, which is then set to the value of bit 7 of the status register and can be conveniently tested by the program. This is why the status register of most input/output chips connected to microprocessor systems has its most important indicator (usually ready/not ready) in bit position 7.

The following instructions affect the negative bit: ADC, AND, ASL, BIT, CMP, CPX, CPY, DEC, DEX, DEY, EOR, INC, INX, INY, LDA, LDX, LDY, ORA, PLA, PLB, PLD, PLX, PLY, ROL, ROR, SBC, TAX, TAY, TCD, TDC, TSC, TSX, TXA, TXY, TYA, TYX, and XBA. The LSR instruction always clears the N bit.

Summary of the Status Register Bits

The status bits automatically detect special conditions within the ALU of the microprocessor. You can conveniently test them by using specialized instructions, so that specific actions can be taken in response to the condition detected. It is important to understand the role of the various indicators available, since most decisions made within the program are determined by the value of these status bits. All branches executed within a program jump to specified locations, depending on the status of these bits. The only exception involves the interrupt mechanism (described in Chapter 6), which may cause jumping to specific locations whenever a hardware signal is received on specialized pins of the 65816.

At this point, you need only remember the main function of each bit. When programming, you may want to refer to the description of each instruction in this chapter to verify its effect on the various status bits. Most bits can be ignored most of the time, and if you are not yet familiar with them, you should not feel intimidated by their apparent complexity. Their use will become clearer as you examine other application programs.

The Branch Instructions

A *branch instruction* causes a forced branching to a specified program address. It changes the normal flow of program execution from a sequential mode into one where a different segment of the program is suddenly executed. Branches may be conditional or unconditional. An *unconditional* jump is one where the branching occurs to a specific address, regardless of any other condition. A *conditional* branch is one where the branching occurs to a specific address only if one or more conditions are met. This is the type of jump instruction used to make decisions based upon data or computed results.

To describe conditional branch instructions, you must understand the role of the processor status register (explained in the preceding section), since all branching decisions are based upon these status bits. I will now examine the branch instructions in more detail.

The two main types of branch instructions provided by the 65816 are branch instructions within the main program (called branches), and the special branch instructions used to jump to and from a subroutine (JSR and RTS). As a result of any branch instruction, the program counter (PC) is reloaded with a new address, and the usual program execution resumes from that point on. The full power of branch instructions can be understood only in the context of the various addressing modes provided by the microprocessor. (I will cover this topic in Chapter 5 when I discuss addressing modes.) I will consider here only the other aspects of these instructions.

Branches may be either unconditional (always branching to a specified memory address) or conditional. In the case of a conditional branch, one or more of the four status code bits—Z, C, V, N—may be tested for the value 0 or 1.

The corresponding abbreviations for the individual bits are:

BCC	=	carry clear	(C = 0)
BCS	=	carry set	(C = 1)
BEQ	=	equal to zero	(Z = 1)
BNE	=	not equal to zero	(Z = 0)
BMI	=	minus	(N = 1)
BPL	=	plus	(N = 0)
BVC	=	overflow clear	(V = 0)
BVS	=	overflow set	(V = 1)

The availability of conditional branches is a powerful resource in a computer, although this resource is not provided on all microprocessors. This resource does, however, improve the efficiency of programs by implementing in a single instruction what would normally require two instructions. There is, however, one drawback to branch instructions on most computers: the address specified with the branch instruction is only one byte in length. This byte is added to the PC to obtain the new address. This means that a branch may move the PC only 127 bytes forward or 128 bytes backward from the location of the branch instruction. Branching farther is not possible. However, the 65816 does have a special long-branch instruction.

The *long branch* (BRL) specifies a 16-bit address with the instruction. When added to the PC, branching is allowed to any of the 65,536 memory locations in a 64K bank of memory. This type of branch instruction removes the need to branch to a jump instruction (JMP).

Finally, a special return instruction, RTI, is provided with interrupt routines. Chapter 6 will discuss this instruction in detail.

One more type of specialized branch is available: the break (BRK) instruction. The break pushes the contents of the program counter and status register onto the stack. The contents of memory locations 00FFE6 and 00FFE7 are then deposited in PCL and PCH, respectively.

Important: PC + 2 is the value saved on the stack. This may not be the next instruction, and a correction may be necessary. BRK is usually used to patch an existing program where BRK replaces a two-byte instruction. When debugging a program, you generally use BRK to cause an exit to the monitor.

INPUT/OUTPUT INSTRUCTIONS ON THE 65816

You can address input/output devices in one of two ways: as memory locations (using any one of the instructions described previously) or by using specific input/output instructions. Chapter 6 examines input/output techniques in detail. The 65816 has no special instructions devoted to input/output. Usual memory addressing instructions use three bytes: one for the opcode and two for the address. As a result, these instructions execute slowly, since they require three memory accesses. However, if you use the special *direct page* addressing mode, where the address is formed by the direct page register and a byte in the instruction, then the instructions to access an input/output device need only be two bytes in length. This allows faster execution.

CONTROL INSTRUCTIONS ON THE 65816

Control instructions modify the operating mode of the CPU and manipulate its internal status information. The 65816 provides three control instructions: NOP, WAI, and STP.

The NOP instruction is a no-operation instruction that does nothing for two cycles. It is typically used either to introduce a deliberate delay (2 cycles, or 1 microsecond with a 2 MHz clock) or to fill gaps created in a program during the debugging phase.

The WAI instruction is used in conjunction with interrupts. It actually suspends the operation of the CPU. The CPU then resumes operation whenever an interrupt signal is received. A WAI is used to ensure that minimum time elapses between an interrupt and the program servicing that interrupt.

Finally, the last control instruction is stop the clock (STP). The processor and the clock will stop when this instruction is executed. The processor will not be started again until an external reset is done.

SUMMARY

I have now described the five categories of instructions available on the 65816. Specific details on the individual instructions are presented in the following section of this chapter. You need not understand the role of each instruction to start programming. At the beginning, it is sufficient to know a few essential instructions of each type; however, as you begin writing your own programs, you will want to learn all the instructions on the 65816 so that you can make your programs as efficient as possible.

I have not yet described one important aspect of programming: the addressing techniques implemented on the 65816 that facilitate data retrieval within the memory space. I will cover these addressing techniques in the next chapter.

EXERCISES

4-l: *Write a three-line program that zeros bits 1 and 6 of WORD.*

4-2: *What will happen if you use a MASK equaling 11111111 with an AND instruction?*

4-3: *What will happen if you use the instruction ORA #%10101111 and A contains 10101111?*

4-4: *What is the effect of using OR with FF hexadecimal?*

4-5: *What is the effect of EOR, if you use a register with 00 hexadecimal, instead of 11111111, to complement a byte?*

THE 65816 INSTRUCTIONS: INDIVIDUAL DESCRIPTIONS

ABBREVIATIONS AND SYMBOLS FOR INSTRUCTION DESCRIPTIONS

Flags

X — flag changed according to operation or result of instruction
 — flag unchanged (space)
0 — flag cleared by instruction
1 — flag set by instruction

Notation

A, B, C, D, X, Y, S, P, PC — registers

←	— data transfer
⟷	— exchange data
M	— byte or 16-bit word memory operand of valid type for given instruction
ADDR	— address of instruction or data
N	— 8-bit immediate mode operand
NN	— 16-bit immediate mode operand
PCH	— most significant byte of 16-bit register
PCL	— least significant byte of 16-bit register
V	— AND function
Λ	— OR function
( )	— use the operand as a pointer into memory

Add Memory to Accumulator with Carry

Mnemonic: ADC M

Function: A ← A + M + C

Description: The carry bit and memory operand are added into the accumulator.

Status Register:

N	V	M	X	D	I	Z	C
X	X					X	X

Addressing Modes:

Immediate
Absolute
Absolute Long
Direct
Direct Indirect Indexed
Direct Indirect Long Indexed
Direct Indexed Indirect
Direct Indexed with X
Absolute Indexed with X
Absolute Long Indexed with X
Absolute Indexed with Y
Direct Indirect
Direct Indirect Long
Stack Relative
Stack Relative Indirect Indexed

AND

AND Memory with Accumulator

Mnemonic: AND M

Function: A ← A∧M

Description: The AND function operates on accumulator A and the memory location, and the result is stored in A.

Status Register:

N	V	M	X	D	I	Z	C
X						X	

Addressing Modes:

Immediate
Absolute
Absolute Long
Direct
Direct Indirect Indexed
Direct Indirect Long Indexed
Direct Indexed Indirect
Direct Indexed with X
Absolute Indexed with X
Absolute Long Indexed with X
Absolute Indexed with Y
Direct Indirect
Direct Indirect Long
Stack Relative
Stack Relative Indirect Indexed

ASL

Arithmetic Shift Left

Mnemonics: ASL M; ASL A

Function:

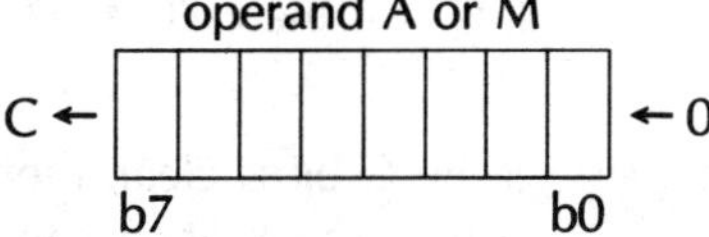

Description: All the bits in the operand are shifted left by one position. Bit 7 is transferred to the carry bit; bit 0 becomes a zero. In the 16-bit mode, bit 15 is transferred to the carry bit.

Status Register:

N	V	M	X	D	I	Z	C
X						X	X

Addressing Modes:

Absolute
Direct
Accumulator
Direct Indexed with X
Absolute Indexed with X

BCC

Branch on Carry Clear

Mnemonic: BCC N

Function: If C = 0 then: PC ← PC + N

Description: If the C bit is clear, then a PC relative branch is executed. The branch can access any instruction in the range +129 to −126 bytes relative to the first byte of the branch instruction.

Status Register:

N	V	M	X	D	I	Z	C

(no change)

Addressing Mode: Relative

BCS

Branch on Carry Set

Mnemonic: BCS N

Function: If C = 1 then: PC ← PC + N

Description: If the C bit is set, then a PC relative branch is executed. The branch can access any instruction in the range +129 to −126 bytes relative to the first byte of the branch instruction.

Status Register:

N	V	M	X	D	I	Z	C

(no change)

Addressing Mode: Relative

BEQ

Branch on Equal

Mnemonic: BEQ N

Function: If Z = 1 then: PC ← PC + N

Description: If the zero bit is set, then a PC relative branch is executed. This is true after a subtract or compare on any binary values, if the register was the same as the memory operand. The branch can access any instruction in the range +129 to −126 bytes relative to the first byte of the branch instruction.

Status Register:

N	V	M	X	D	I	Z	C

(no change)

Addressing Mode: Relative

BIT

Bit Test

Mnemonic: BIT M

Function: A∧M

Description: The AND function operates on the accumulator A and a memory operand, and the result is discarded. Only the status bits are affected; neither operand is affected. In the 8-bit mode, the N bit is set to bit 7 and the V bit is set to bit 6. In the 16-bit mode, the N bit is set to bit 15 and the V bit is set to bit 14.

Status Register:

N	V	M	X	D	I	Z	C
X	X					X	
b7	b6						
b15	b14						

Addressing Modes:

Immediate
Absolute
Direct
Direct Indexed with X
Absolute Indexed with X

BMI

Branch on Minus

Mnemonic: BMI N

Function: If N = 1 then: PC ← PC + N

Description: If the negative bit is set, then a PC relative branch is executed. This condition is true after an operation if the sign bit was set. The branch can access any instruction in the range +129 to −126 bytes relative to the first byte of the branch instruction.

Status Register:

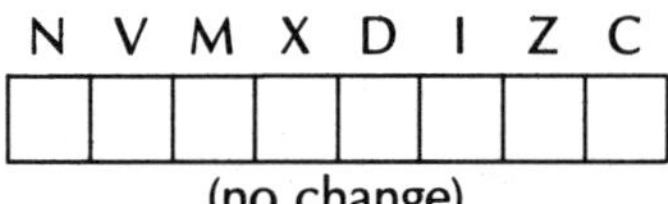

(no change)

Addressing Mode: Relative

BNE

Branch on Not Equal

Mnemonic: BNE N

Function: If Z = 0 then: PC ← PC + N

Description: If the zero bit is clear, then a PC relative branch is executed. This is true after a subtract or compare on any binary values, if the register was not the same as the memory operand. The branch can access any instruction in the range +129 to −126 bytes relative to the first byte of the branch instruction.

Status Register:

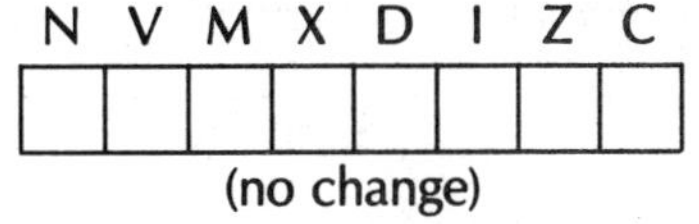

N	V	M	X	D	I	Z	C

(no change)

Addressing Mode: Relative

BPL

Branch on Plus

Mnemonic: BPL N

Function: If N = 0 then: PC ← PC + N

Description: If the negative bit is clear, then a PC relative branch is executed. This condition is true after an operation if the sign bit was clear. The branch can access any instruction in the range +129 to −126 bytes relative to the first byte of the branch instruction.

Status Register:

N	V	M	X	D	I	Z	C

(no change)

Addressing Mode: Relative

BRA — *Branch Always*

Mnemonic: BRA N

Function: PC ← PC + N

Description: A PC relative branch is always executed.

Status Register:

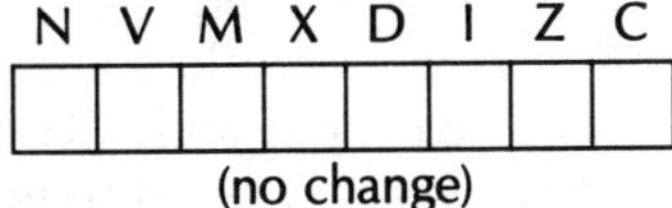

(no change)

Addressing Mode: Relative

BRK

Break

Mnemonic: BRK

Function: (S) ← PBR, (S) ← PC, (S) ← P, PC ← (FFE6,FFE7)

Description: Break operates like an interrupt: the program bank register is pushed on the stack, then the program counter, and finally the status register (P). The contents of memory locations FFE6 and FFE7 are then deposited in PCL and PCH, respectively. The program bank register is set to 0. Important: Unlike an interrupt, break saves PC + 2. PC + 2 may not be the next instruction, and a correction may be necessary.

Status Register:

N	V	M	X	D	I	Z	C
				0	1		

Addressing Mode: Stack

BRL

Branch Long Always

Mnemonic: BRL NN

Function: PC ← PC + NN

Description: A PC relative branch is always executed. The branch long can access any address in a 64K memory bank.

Status Register:

N	V	M	X	D	I	Z	C

(no change)

Addressing Mode: Relative Long

Branch on Overflow Clear

Mnemonic: BVC N

Function: If V = 0 then: PC ← PC + N

Description: If the overflow bit is clear, then a PC relative branch is executed. This condition is true after an operation of two's complement values, if the result was valid (there was no overflow). The branch can access any instruction in the range +129 to −126 bytes relative to the first byte of the branch instruction.

Status Register:

N	V	M	X	D	I	Z	C

(no change)

Addressing Mode: Relative

BVS

Branch on Overflow Set

Mnemonic: BVS N

Function: If V = 1 then: PC ← PC + N

Description: If the overflow bit is set, then a PC relative branch is executed. This condition is true after an operation of two's complement values, if the result was invalid (there was an overflow). The branch can access any instruction in the range +129 to −126 bytes relative to the first byte of the branch instruction.

Status Register:

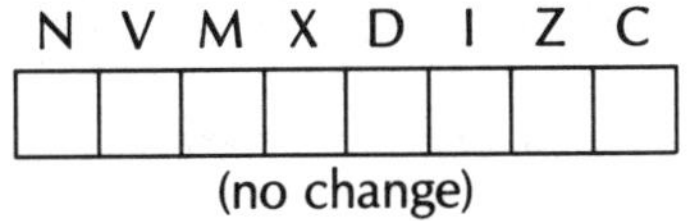

(no change)

Addressing Mode: Relative

CLC

Clear the Carry Bit

Mnemonic: CLC

Function: C ← 0

Description: The carry bit is set to 0. This is often done before an ADC.

Status Register:

N	V	M	X	D	I	Z	C
							0

Addressing Mode: Implied

CLD
Clear the Decimal Bit

Mnemonic: CLD

Function: D ← 0

Description: The decimal bit is cleared, setting the binary mode for ADC and SBC.

Status Register:

N	V	M	X	D	I	Z	C
				0			

Addressing Mode: Implied

Clear the Interrupt Disable Bit

Mnemonic:	CLI
Function:	I ← 0
Description:	The interrupt disable bit is cleared. This enables interrupts. An interrupt handling routine must always clear the I bit, or else other interrupts may be lost.

Status Register:

N	V	M	X	D	I	Z	C
					0		

Addressing Mode:	Implied

CLV

Clear the Overflow Bit

Mnemonic: CLV

Function: V ← 0

Description: The overflow bit is cleared.

Status Register:

N	V	M	X	D	I	Z	C
	0						

Addressing Mode: Implied

CMP

Compare Memory and Accumulator

Mnemonic: CMP M

Function: A − M

Description: The memory operand is subtracted from the accumulator, and the result is discarded. Only the status register bits are affected; neither operand is affected. If A is greater than or equal to M, the C bit is set.

Status Register:

N	V	M	X	D	I	Z	C
X						X	X

Addressing Modes:

Immediate
Absolute
Absolute Long
Direct
Direct Indirect Indexed
Direct Indirect Long Indexed
Direct Indexed Indirect
Direct Indexed with X
Absolute Indexed with X
Absolute Long Indexed with X
Absolute Indexed with Y
Direct Indirect
Direct Indirect Long
Stack Relative
Stack Relative Indirect Indexed

COP — *Coprocessor*

Mnemonic: COP

Function: (S) ← PBR, (S) ← PC, (S) ← P, PC ← (FFE4,FFE5)

Description: Coprocessor operates like an interrupt: the program bank register is pushed on the stack, then the program counter, and finally the status register (P). The contents of memory locations FFE4 and FFE5 are then deposited in PCL and PCH, respectively. The program bank register is set to 0.

Status Register:

N	V	M	X	D	I	Z	C
				0	1		

Addressing Mode: Stack

Compare Memory and Index X

Mnemonic: CPX M

Function: X − M

Description: The memory operand is subtracted from the X index register, and the result is discarded. Only the status register bits are affected; neither operand is affected. If X is greater than or equal to M, the C bit is set.

Status Register:

N	V	M	X	D	I	Z	C
X						X	X

Addressing Modes:

Immediate
Absolute
Direct

CPY

Compare Memory and Index Y

Mnemonic: CPY M

Function: Y – M

Description: The memory operand is subtracted from the Y index register, and the result is discarded. Only the status register bits are affected; neither operand is affected. If Y is greater than or equal to M, the C bit is set.

Status Register:

N	V	M	X	D	I	Z	C
X						X	X

Addressing Modes:

Immediate
Absolute
Direct

DEC

Decrement

Mnemonics: DEC M; DEC A

Function: A ← A − 1 or M ← M − 1

Description: One is subtracted from the specified operand. Note that the carry bit is not affected.

Status Register:

N	V	M	X	D	I	Z	C
X						X	

Addressing Modes:

Absolute
Direct
Accumulator
Direct Indexed with X
Absolute Indexed with X

DEX

Decrement Index X

Mnemonic: DEX

Function: X ← X − 1

Description: One is subtracted from the X index register. Note that the carry bit is not affected.

Status Register:

N	V	M	X	D	I	Z	C
X						X	

Addressing Mode: Implied

DEY

Decrement Index Y

Mnemonic: DEY

Function: Y ← Y − 1

Description: One is subtracted from the Y index register. Note that the carry bit is not affected.

Status Register:

N	V	M	X	D	I	Z	C
X						X	

Addressing Mode: Implied

EOR

Exclusive-OR Memory with Accumulator

Mnemonic: EOR M

Function: A ← A EOR M

Description: The logical exclusive-OR operates on accumulator A and a memory location, and the result is stored in A.

Status Register:

N	V	M	X	D	I	Z	C
X						X	

Addressing Modes:

Immediate
Absolute
Absolute Long
Direct
Direct Indirect Indexed
Direct Indirect Long Indexed
Direct Indexed Indirect
Direct Indexed with X
Absolute Indexed with X
Absolute Long Indexed with X
Absolute Indexed with Y
Direct Indirect
Direct Indirect Long
Stack Relative
Stack Relative Indirect Indexed

INC

Increment

Mnemonics: INC M; INC A

Function: A ← A + 1 or M ← M + 1

Description: One is added to the specified operand. Note that the carry bit is not affected.

Status Register:

N	V	M	X	D	I	Z	C
X						X	

Addressing Modes:

Absolute
Direct
Accumulator
Direct Indexed with X
Absolute Indexed with X

INX

Increment Index X

Mnemonic: INX

Function: X ← X + 1

Description: One is added to the X index register. Note that the carry bit is not affected.

Status Register:

N	V	M	X	D	I	Z	C
X						X	

Addressing Mode: Implied

INY

Increment Index Y

Mnemonic: INY

Function: Y ← Y + 1

Description: One is added to the Y index register. Note that the carry bit is not affected.

Status Register:

N	V	M	X	D	I	Z	C
X						X	

Addressing Mode: Implied

JML

Jump Long

Mnemonic: JML ADDR

Function: PC ← (ADDR) PBR ← (ADDR + 2)

Description: A new address is loaded into the program counter and the program bank register. The immediate two bytes after the opcode point to the three bytes of the new address.

Status Register:

N	V	M	X	D	I	Z	C

(no change)

Addressing Mode: Absolute Indirect

JMP

Jump

Mnemonic: JMP ADDR

Function: PC ← ADDR

Description: A new address is loaded into the program counter. This address can be 16 bits to jump within a bank or 24 bits to jump anywhere in the 16-megabyte address space.

Status Register:

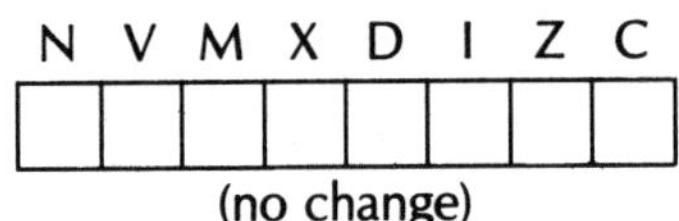

(no change)

Addressing Modes:

Absolute
Absolute Long
Absolute Indirect
Absolute Indexed Indirect

JSL

Jump Subroutine Long

Mnemonic: JSL ADDR

Function:

(S) ← PBR; S ← S − 1
(S) ← PCH; S ← S − 1
(S) ← PCL; S ← S − 1
PC ← ADDR; PBR ← ADDR + 2

Description: The PC and program bank register are pushed onto the stack and a new PC and PBR are loaded from memory. This instruction allows a jump to a subroutine at any address in the 16-megabyte memory space.

Status Register:

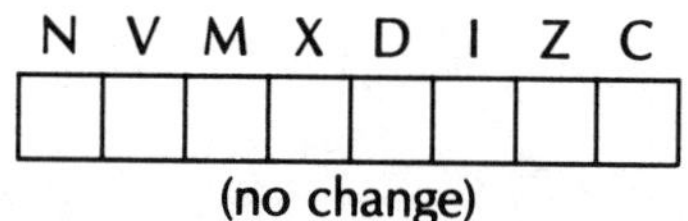

(no change)

Addressing Mode: Absolute Long

JSR

Jump to Subroutine

Mnemonic: JSR ADDR

Function:

(S) ← PCH; S ← S − 1
(S) ← PCL; S ← S − 1
PC ← ADDR;

Description: The PC is pushed onto the stack and a new PC is loaded from memory.

Status Register:

N	V	M	X	D	I	Z	C

(no change)

Addressing Modes:

Absolute
Absolute Indexed Indirect

LDA Load Accumulator from Memory

Mnemonic: LDA M

Function: A ← M

Description: The memory operand is loaded into the accumulator.

Status Register:

N	V	M	X	D	I	Z	C
X						X	

Addressing Modes:

Immediate
Absolute
Absolute Long
Direct
Direct Indirect Indexed
Direct Indirect Long Indexed
Direct Indexed Indirect
Direct Indexed with X
Absolute Indexed with X
Absolute Long Indexed with X
Absolute Indexed with Y
Direct Indirect
Direct Indirect Long
Stack Relative
Stack Relative Indirect Indexed

Load Index Register X

Mnemonic: LDX M

Function: X ← M

Description: The memory operand is loaded into the X index register.

Status Register:

N	V	M	X	D	I	Z	C
X						X	

Addressing Modes:

Immediate
Absolute
Direct
Direct Indexed with Y
Absolute Indexed with Y

LDY — *Load Index Register Y*

Mnemonic: LDY M

Function: Y ← M

Description: The memory operand is loaded into the Y index register.

Status Register:

N	V	M	X	D	I	Z	C
X						X	

Addressing Modes:

Immediate
Absolute
Direct
Direct Indexed with X
Absolute Indexed with X

LSR

Logical Shift Right

Mnemonics: LSR M; LSR A

Function:

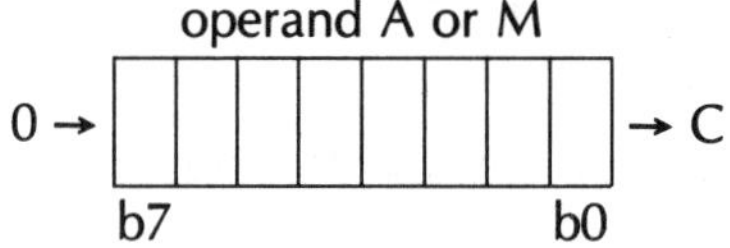

Description: All the bits in the operand are shifted right by one position. Bit 0 is transferred to the carry bit; bit 7 becomes a zero. In the 16-bit mode, bit 15 is set to 0.

Status Register:

N	V	M	X	D	I	Z	C
0						X	X

Addressing Modes:

Absolute
Direct
Accumulator
Direct Indexed with X
Absolute Indexed with X

MVN Block Move Negative

Mnemonic: MVN #NN

Function: M ← M; X ← X + 1; Y ← Y + 1; A ← A − 1; DBR ← N

Description: Move a block of memory starting at a low address and ending at a higher address. The Y index register contains the destination address of the block, and the X register contains the source address. Accumulator A contains the number of bytes to move minus one. The X and Y registers are incremented after each iteration. The A register is decremented after each iteration. The first byte after the opcode is put in the data bank register and used with Y to form the 24-bit address of the destination. The second byte is used as the data bank address for the source.

Status Register:

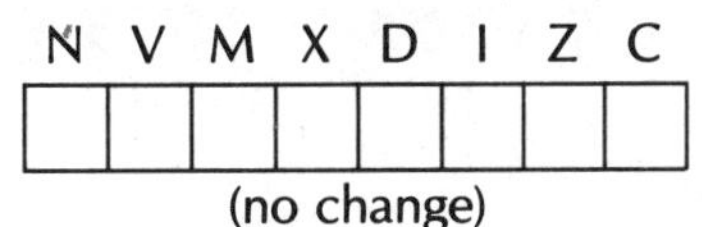

(no change)

Addressing Mode: Block Source Bank, Destination Bank

Block Move Positive

Mnemonic: MVP #NN

Function: M ← M; X ← X − 1; Y ← Y − 1; A ← A − 1; DBR ← N

Description: Move a block of memory starting at a high address and ending at a lower address. The Y index register contains the destination address of the block, and the X register contains the source address. Accumulator A contains the number of bytes to move minus one. The X and Y registers are decremented after each iteration. The A register is also decremented after each iteration. The first byte after the opcode is put in the data bank register and used with Y to form the 24-bit address of the destination. The second byte is used as the data bank address for the source.

Status Register:

N	V	M	X	D	I	Z	C

(no change)

Addressing Mode: Block Source Bank, Destination Bank

NOP

No Operation

Mnemonic: NOP

Function: None

Description: The processor does nothing for two cycles. This instruction is used to introduce delays or to fill patches in a program.

Status Register:

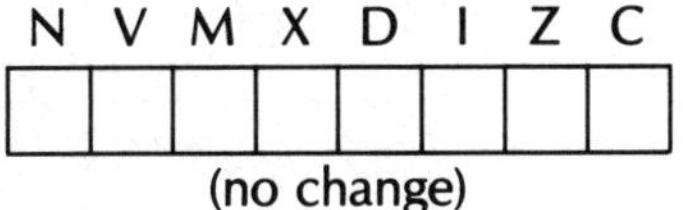

(no change)

Addressing Mode: Implied

OR Memory with Accumulator

Mnemonic: ORA M

Function: A ← AVM

Description: The OR function operates on accumulator A and a memory location, and the result is stored in A.

Status Register:

N	V	M	X	D	I	Z	C
X						X	

Addressing Modes:

Immediate
Absolute
Absolute Long
Direct
Direct Indirect Indexed
Direct Indirect Long Indexed
Direct Indexed Indirect
Direct Indexed with X
Absolute Indexed with X
Absolute Long Indexed with X
Absolute Indexed with Y
Direct Indirect
Direct Indirect Long
Stack Relative
Stack Relative Indirect Indexed

PEA

Push Effective Absolute Address on the Stack
Push Immediate Data Word on the Stack

Mnemonic: PEA #NN

Function: (S) ← PC + 1; S ← S − 1
(S) ← PC + 2; S ← S − 1

Description: The two bytes of data immediately following the opcode are pushed onto the stack.

Status Register:

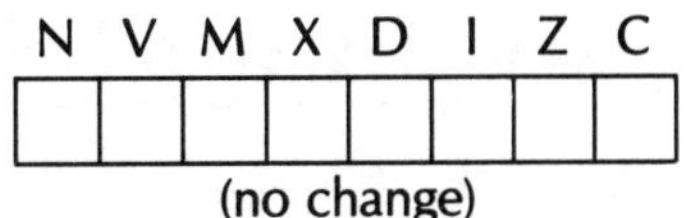

(no change)

Addressing Mode: Stack

PEI

Push Effective Indirect Address on the Stack

Mnemonic: PEI #N

Function:

(S) ← (D + (PC + 1)); S ← S − 1
(S) ← (D + (PC + 1) + 1); S ← S − 1

Description: The byte of data immediately following the opcode is added to the direct register (D), and the D register is used as a pointer to two bytes to be put on the stack. The D register is not changed, and the two bytes must be in bank zero.

Status Register:

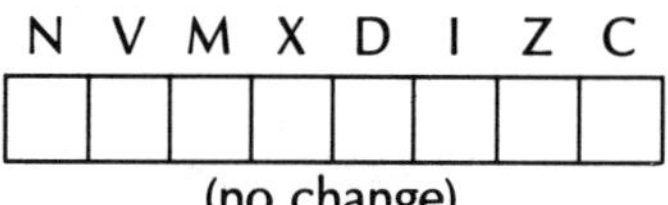

N	V	M	X	D	I	Z	C

(no change)

Addressing Mode: Stack

PER

Push Effective PC Relative Address on the Stack

Mnemonic: PER #NN

Function: (S) ← PC + NN + 2; S ← S − 2

Description: The two bytes of data immediately following the opcode are added to the program counter, after the PC has been updated to point to the next instruction, and this value is then stored on the stack. The PC and program bank register are not changed. The two bytes are actually added to the PC + 2.

Status Register:

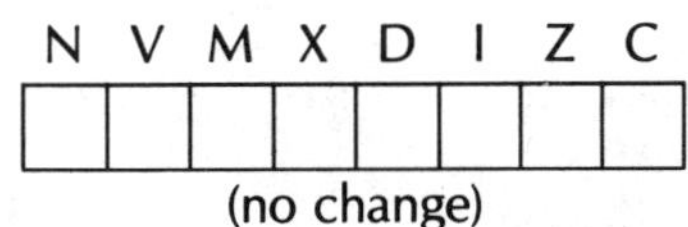

(no change)

Addressing Mode: Stack

PHA

Push the Accumulator on the Stack

Mnemonic: PHA

Function: (S) ← A; S ← S − 1 or S ← S − 2

Description: The contents of the accumulator are pushed onto the stack. If the processor is in the 16-bit memory mode, both bytes are put onto the stack and the stack pointer S is decremented by 2.

Status Register:

N	V	M	X	D	I	Z	C

(no change)

Addressing Mode: Stack

PHB

Push the Data Bank Register on the Stack

Mnemonic: PHB

Function: (S) ← DBR; S ← S − 1

Description: The contents of the data bank register are pushed onto the stack.

Status Register:

N	V	M	X	D	I	Z	C

(no change)

Addressing Mode: Stack

PHD

Push the Direct Register on the Stack

Mnemonic: PHD

Function: (S) ← D; S ← S − 2

Description: The contents of the direct register are pushed onto the stack.

Status Register:

N	V	M	X	D	I	Z	C

(no change)

Addressing Mode: Stack

Push the Program Bank Register on the Stack

Mnemonic: PHK

Function: (S) ← PBR; S ← S − 1

Description: The contents of the program bank register are pushed onto the stack.

Status Register:

N	V	M	X	D	I	Z	C

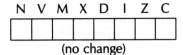

(no change)

Addressing Mode: Stack

PHP

Push the Status Register on the Stack

Mnemonic: PHP

Function: (S) ← P; S ← S − 1

Description: The contents of the processor status register are pushed onto the stack.

Status Register:

N	V	M	X	D	I	Z	C

(no change)

Addressing Mode: Stack

PHX — *Push the Index Register X on the Stack*

Mnemonic: PHX

Function: (S) ← X; S ← S − 1 or S ← S − 2

Description: The contents of the X index register are pushed onto the stack. If the processor is in the 16-bit memory mode, both bytes are put on the stack and the stack pointer (S) is decremented by 2.

Status Register:

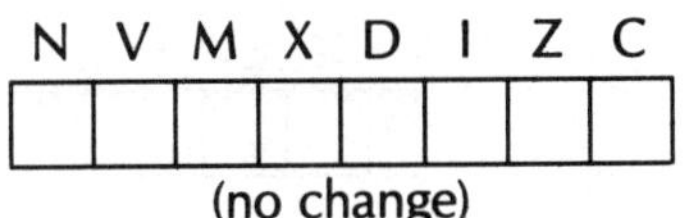

Addressing Mode: Stack

PHY

Push the Index Register Y on the Stack

Mnemonic: PHY

Function: (S) ← Y; S ← S − 1 or S ← S − 2

Description: The contents of the Y index register are pushed onto the stack. If the processor is in the 16-bit memory mode, both bytes are put on the stack and the stack pointer (S) is decremented by 2.

Status Register:

N	V	M	X	D	I	Z	C

(no change)

Addressing Mode: Stack

PLA — *Pull the Accumulator off the Stack*

Mnemonic: PLA

Function: S ← S + 1 or S ← S + 2; A ← (S)

Description: The contents of the accumulator are pulled from the stack. If the processor is in the 16-bit memory mode, both bytes are pulled off the stack and the stack pointer (S) is incremented by 2.

Status Register:

N	V	M	X	D	I	Z	C
X						X	

Addressing Mode: Stack

PLB

Pull the Data Bank Register off the Stack

Mnemonic: PLB

Function: S ← S + 1; DBR ← (S)

Description: The contents of the data bank register are pulled off the stack.

Status Register:

N	V	M	X	D	I	Z	C
X						X	

Addressing Mode: Stack

PLD

Pull the Direct Register off the Stack

Mnemonic: PLD

Function: S ← S + 2; D ← (S)

Description: The contents of the direct register are pulled off the stack.

Status Register:

N	V	M	X	D	I	Z	C
X						X	

Addressing Mode: Stack

PLP

Pull the Status Register off the Stack

Mnemonic: PLP

Function: S ← S + 1; P ← (S)

Description: The contents of the processor status register are pulled off the stack.

Status Register:

N	V	M	X	D	I	Z	C
X	X	X	X	X	X	X	X

Addressing Mode: Stack

PLX

Pull the Index Register X off the Stack

Mnemonic: PLX

Function: S ← S + 1 or S ← S + 2; X ← (S)

Description: The contents of the X index register are pulled off the stack. If the processor is in the 16-bit memory mode, both bytes are pulled off the stack and the stack pointer (S) is incremented by 2.

Status Register:

N	V	M	X	D	I	Z	C
X							

Addressing Mode: Stack

PLY

Pull the Index Register Y off the Stack

Mnemonic: PLY

Function: S ← S + 1 or S ← S + 2; Y ← (S)

Description: The contents of the Y index register are pulled off the stack. If the processor is in the 16-bit memory mode, both bytes are pulled off the stack and the stack pointer (S) is incremented by 2.

Status Register:

N	V	M	X	D	I	Z	C
X						X	

Addressing Mode: Stack

REP

Reset Status Bits

Mnemonic: REP #N

Function: $P \leftarrow P \wedge \overline{N}$

Description: The AND function operates on the status register (P) and the complement of the byte immediately following the opcode, and the result is stored in P.

Status Register:

N	V	M	X	D	I	Z	C
X	X	X	X	X	X	X	X

Addressing Mode: Immediate

ROL

Rotate Left

Mnemonics: ROL M; ROL A

Function:

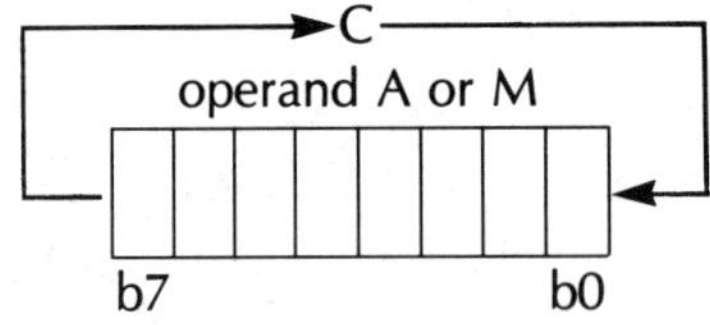

Description: All the bits in the operand are shifted left by one position. Bit 0 comes from the carry bit, and bit 7 is put into the carry bit. In the 16-bit mode, bit 15 is transferred to the carry bit.

Status Register:

N	V	M	X	D	I	Z	C
X						X	X

Addressing Modes:

Absolute
Direct
Accumulator
Direct Indexed with X
Absolute Indexed with X

ROR

Rotate Right

Mnemonics: ROR M; ROR A

Function:

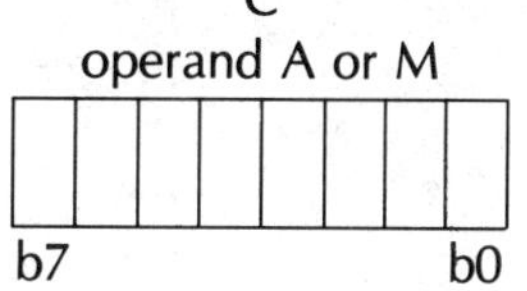

Description: All the bits in the operand are shifted right by one position. Bit 7 comes from the carry bit, and bit 0 is put into the carry bit. In the 16-bit mode, bit 15 is transferred from the carry bit.

Status Register:

N	V	M	X	D	I	Z	C
X						X	X

Addressing Modes:

Absolute
Direct
Accumulator
Direct Indexed with X
Absolute Indexed with X

RTI

Return from Interrupt

Mnemonic: RTI

Function:

S ← S + 1; P ← (S)
S ← S + 1; PCL ← (S)
S ← S + 1; PCH ← (S)
S ← S + 1; PBR ← (S)

Description: The status register, the PC, and the program bank register are pulled from the stack memory. This instruction reverses the action of an interrupt and should be placed at the end of an interrupt routine.

Status Register:

N	V	M	X	D	I	Z	C
X	X	X	X	X	X	X	X

Addressing Mode: Stack

RTL

Return from Subroutine Long

Mnemonic: RTL

Function:

S ← S + 1; PCL ← (S)
S ← S + 1; PCH ← (S)
S ← S + 1; PBR ← (S)

Description: The PC and program bank register are pulled from the stack memory. This instruction reverses the action of a JSL.

Status Register:

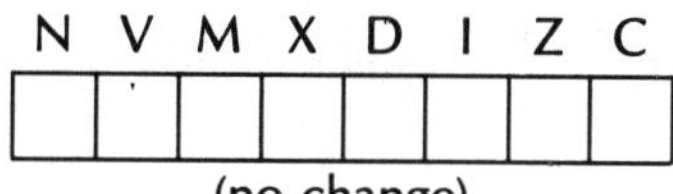

(no change)

Addressing Mode: Stack

RTS

Return from Subroutine

Mnemonic: RTS

Function: S ← S + 1; PCL ← (S)
S ← S + 1 ; PCH ← (S)

Description: The PC is pulled from the stack memory. This instruction reverses the action of a JSR.

Status Register:

N	V	M	X	D	I	Z	C

(no change)

Addressing Mode: Stack

SBC

Subtract Memory from Accumulator with Carry

Mnemonic: SBC M

Function: $A \leftarrow A - M - \overline{C}$

Description: The memory operand and complement of the carry bit are subtracted from the accumulator.

Status Register:

N	V	M	X	D	I	Z	C
X	X					X	X

Addressing Modes:

Immediate
Absolute
Absolute Long
Direct
Direct Indirect Indexed
Direct Indirect Long Indexed
Direct Indexed Indirect
Direct Indexed with X
Absolute Indexed with X
Absolute Long Indexed with X
Absolute Indexed with Y
Direct Indirect
Direct Indirect Long
Stack Relative
Stack Relative Indirect Indexed

SEC

Set the Carry Bit

Mnemonic: SEC

Function: C ← 1

Description: The carry bit is set to 1. This is often done before an SBC.

Status Register:

N	V	M	X	D	I	Z	C
							1

Addressing Mode: Implied

SED

Set the Decimal Bit

Mnemonic: SED

Function: D ← 1

Description: The decimal bit is set to 1, specifying the decimal mode for ADC and SBC.

Status Register:

N	V	M	X	D	I	Z	C
				1			

Addressing Mode: Implied

SEI

Set the Interrupt Disable Bit

Mnemonic: SEI

Function: I ← 1

Description: The interrupt disable bit is set, disabling interrupts. This instruction is used during interrupt handling routines.

Status Register:

N	V	M	X	D	I	Z	C
					1		

Addressing Mode: Implied

SEP

Set Status Bits

Mnemonic: SEP #N

Function: P ← PVN

Description: The OR function operates on the status register (P) and the byte immediately following the opcode, and the result is stored in P.

Status Register:

N	V	M	X	D	I	Z	C
X	X	X	X	X	X	X	X

Addressing Mode: Immediate

STA

Store Accumulator into Memory

Mnemonic: STA M

Function: M ← A

Description: The contents of the accumulator are stored at the memory operand.

Status Register:

N	V	M	X	D	I	Z	C

(no change)

Addressing Modes:

Absolute
Absolute Long
Direct
Direct Indirect Indexed
Direct Indirect Long Indexed
Direct Indexed Indirect
Direct Indexed with X
Absolute Indexed with X
Absolute Long Indexed with X
Absolute Indexed with Y
Direct Indirect
Direct Indirect Long
Stack Relative
Stack Relative Indirect Indexed

STP

Stop the Clock

Mnemonic: STP

Function: Stop processor

Description: The processor and clock stop until a reset is done.

Status Register:

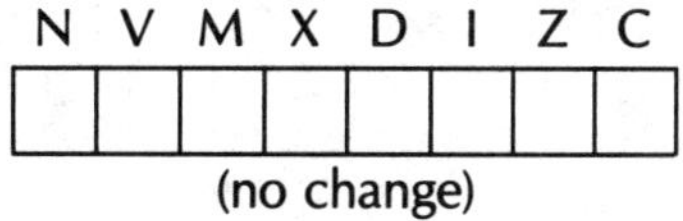

Addressing Mode: Implied

STX

Store Index Register X

Mnemonic: STX M

Function: M ← X

Description: The X index register is stored at the memory operand.

Status Register:

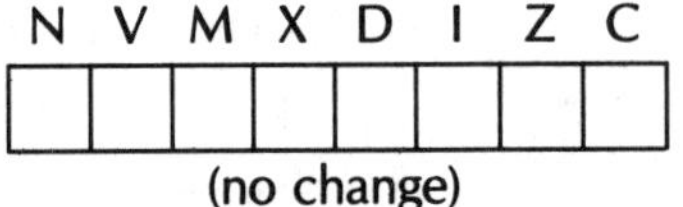

Addressing Modes:

Absolute
Direct
Direct Indexed with Y

STY

Store Index Register Y

Mnemonic: STY M

Function: M ← Y

Description: The Y index register is stored at the memory operand.

Status Register:

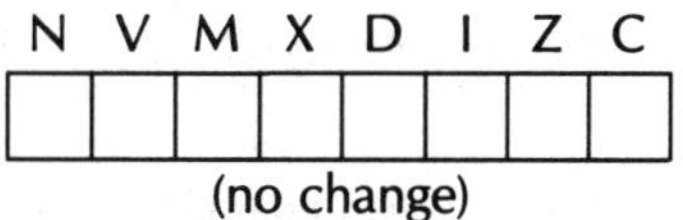

N	V	M	X	D	I	Z	C

(no change)

Addressing Modes:

Absolute
Direct
Direct Indexed with X

STZ

Store Zero in Memory

Mnemonic: STZ M

Function: M ← 0

Description: Zero is stored at the memory operand.

Status Register:

N	V	M	X	D	I	Z	C

(no change)

Addressing Modes:

Absolute
Direct
Direct Indexed with X
Absolute Indexed with X

Transfer Accumulator into X

Mnemonic: TAX

Function: X ← A

Description: The accumulator is transferred into the X index register. The contents of A are not changed.

Status Register:

N	V	M	X	D	I	Z	C
X						X	

Addressing Mode: Implied

TAY

Transfer Accumulator into Y

Mnemonic: TAY

Function: Y ← A

Description: The accumulator is transferred into the Y index register. The contents of A are not changed.

Status Register:

N	V	M	X	D	I	Z	C
X						X	

Addressing Mode: Implied

Transfer Accumulator into Direct Register

Mnemonic: TCD

Function: D ← C

Description: The 16-bit accumulator (C) is transferred into the direct register. The contents of C are not changed.

Status Register:

N	V	M	X	D	I	Z	C
X						X	

Addressing Mode: Implied

TCS

Transfer Accumulator into Stack Pointer

Mnemonic: TCS

Function: S ← C

Description: The 16-bit accumulator (C) is transferred into the stack pointer. The contents of C are not changed. This instruction changes the location of the stack in memory.

Status Register:

N	V	M	X	D	I	Z	C

(no change)

Addressing Mode: Implied

Transfer Direct Register into Accumulator

Mnemonic: TDC

Function: C ← D

Description: The direct register is transferred into the 16-bit accumulator (C). The contents of D are not changed.

Status Register:

N	V	M	X	D	I	Z	C
X						X	

Addressing Mode: Implied

TRB

Test and Reset Bits

Mnemonic: TRB M

Function: $M \leftarrow M \wedge \overline{A}$

Description: The AND function operates on the complement of accumulator A and the memory operand, and the result is stored in the memory operand. Any bit set in A will be cleared in the memory operand.

Status Register:

N	V	M	X	D	I	Z	C
						X	

Addressing Modes:

Absolute
Direct

TSB

Test and Set Bits

Mnemonic: TSB M

Function: M ← M∨A

Description: The OR function operates on the memory operand and accumulator A, and the result is stored in the memory operand. Any bit set in A will be set in the memory operand.

Status Register:

N	V	M	X	D	I	Z	C
					X		

Addressing Modes:

Absolute
Direct

TSC

Transfer Stack Pointer into Accumulator

Mnemonic: TSC

Function: C ← S

Description: The stack pointer is transferred into the 16-bit accumulator (C). The contents of S are not changed.

Status Register:

N	V	M	X	D	I	Z	C
X						X	

Addressing Mode: Implied

Transfer Stack Pointer into Index Register X

Mnemonic: TSX

Function: X ← S

Description: The stack pointer is transferred into index register X. The contents of S are not changed.

Status Register:

N	V	M	X	D	I	Z	C
X						X	

Addressing Mode: Implied

Transfer Index Register X into Accumulator

Mnemonic: TXA

Function: A ← X

Description: The X index register is transferred into accumulator A. The contents of X are not changed.

Status Register:

N	V	M	X	D	I	Z	C
X						X	

Addressing Mode: Implied

TXS

Transfer Index Register X into the Stack Pointer

Mnemonic: TXS

Function: S ← X

Description: The X index register is transferred into the stack pointer. The contents of X are not changed. This instruction will change the location of the stack in memory.

Status Register:

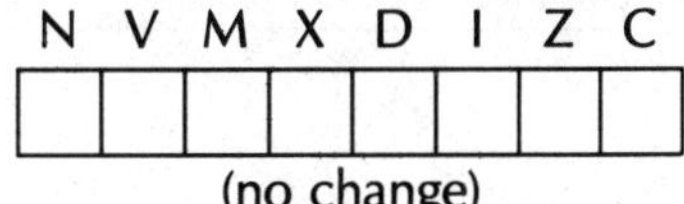

(no change)

Addressing Mode: Implied

TXY

Transfer Index Register X into Index Register Y

Mnemonic: TXY

Function: Y ← X

Description: The X index register is transferred into the Y index register. The contents of X are not changed.

Status Register:

N	V	M	X	D	I	Z	C
X						X	

Addressing Mode: Implied

TYA

Transfer Index Register Y into Accumulator

Mnemonic: TYA

Function: A ← Y

Description: The Y index register is transferred into accumulator A. The contents of Y are not changed.

Status Register:

N	V	M	X	D	I	Z	C
X						X	

Addressing Mode: Implied

TYX — *Transfer Index Register Y into Index Register X*

Mnemonic: TYX

Function: X ← Y

Description: The Y index register is transferred into the X index register. The contents of Y are not changed.

Status Register:

N	V	M	X	D	I	Z	C
X						X	

Addressing Mode: Implied

Wait for Interrupt

Mnemonic: WAI

Function: READY ← 0

Description: The processor stops until an external interrupt occurs. You can use this feature to reduce interrupt latency by putting the WAI instruction at the beginning of the interrupt service routine and setting the interrupt disable bit I. When an interrupt occurs, the instruction after the WAI will be executed.

Status Register:

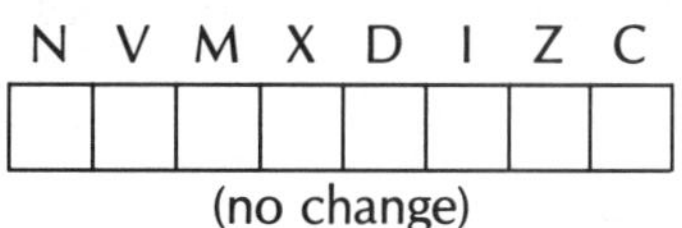

Addressing Mode: Implied

XBA

Exchange the B and A Accumulators

Mnemonic: XBA

Function: A ⟷ B

Description: The A and B accumulators are exchanged. The M bit in the status register should be 1. The XBA instruction is used when 8-bit data is used and an extra register, B, is needed.

Status Register:

N	V	M	X	D	I	Z	C
X						X	

Addressing Mode: Implied

XCE — *Exchange the Carry and Emulation Bits*

Mnemonic: XCE

Function: C ⟷ E

Description: The C and E bits in the status register P are exchanged. This instruction is used to change the 65816 operation between the native mode and the 6502 emulation mode. To set the 65816 into the native mode, execute the following instructions:

```
CLC
XCE
```

To set the 65816 back into the emulation mode, execute the following instructions:

```
SEC
XCE
```

Status Register:

N	V	M	X	D	I	Z	C
							E

Addressing Mode: Implied

ADDRESSING TECHNIQUES

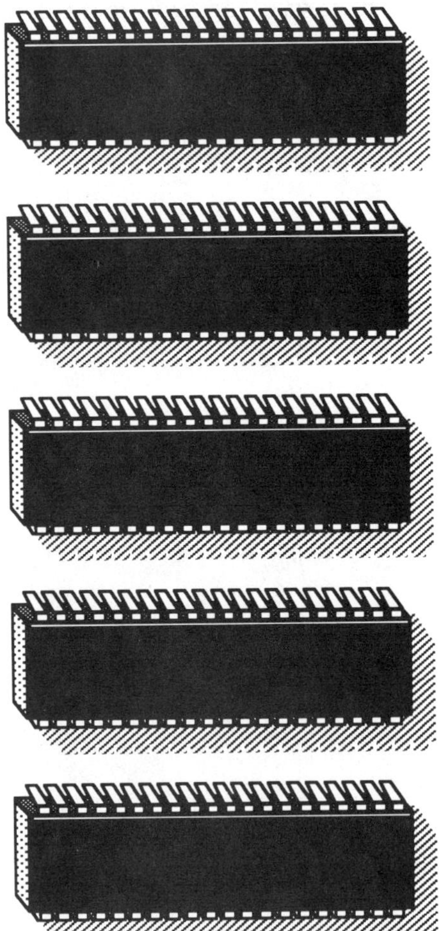

5

IN THIS CHAPTER, I will first discuss the general theory of addressing and examine the various techniques used for accessing data. I will then go on to examine the most important aspect of the 65816's architecture—the area where its special power is most apparent—the extensive 65816 addressing capabilities. The most important of these are indexed, direct, and indirect addressing.

The special registers and modes provided for indexed addressing make the 65816 an excellent machine for writing efficient routines to handle complex data structures. The 65816's relative addressing modes make it possible to write position-independent code (especially important in ROM-based applications)—a task that would be impossible on many other microprocessors.

Although complex data-accessing methods are not necessary in the beginning stages of programming, it is crucial to understand the addressing modes to realize the full power of the 65816. Once you have mastered these addressing techniques, it will then be a straightforward matter to write efficient data-handling routines.

POSSIBLE ADDRESSING MODES

Addressing refers to the specification, within an instruction, of the location of the operand on which the instruction will operate. I begin by examining the six main addressing modes (shown in Figure 5.1).

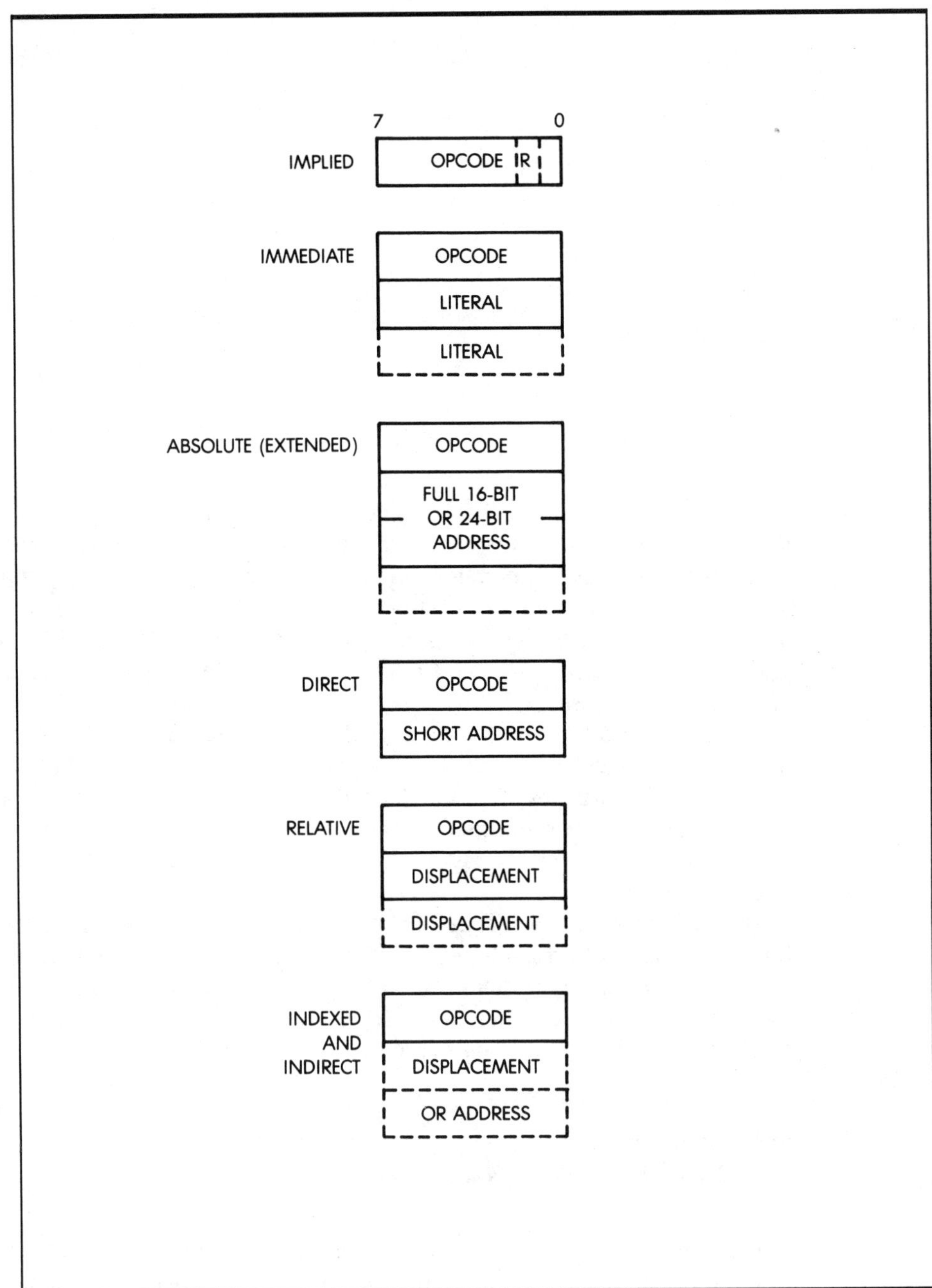

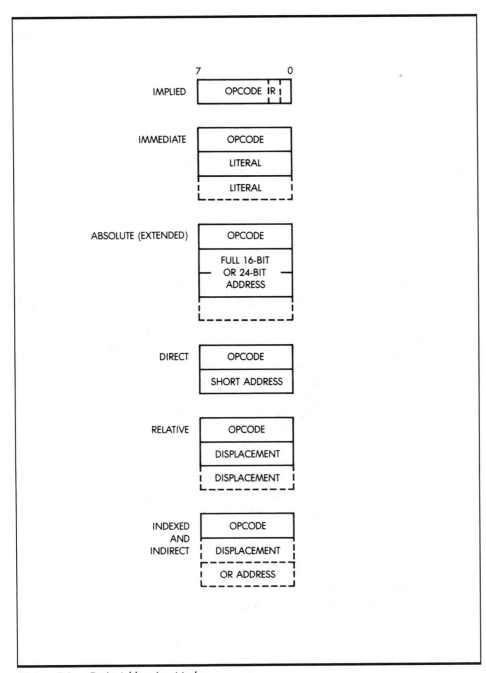

Figure 5.1: Basic Addressing Modes

IMPLIED (INHERENT OR REGISTER) ADDRESSING

Instructions that operate exclusively on registers normally use *implied addressing* (as illustrated in Figure 5.1). An implied instruction derives its name from the fact that it does not specifically contain the address of the operand on which it operates; instead, its opcode specifies one or more registers. Since internal registers are usually few in number (commonly eight), only a small number of bits are needed to specify a particular register in the opcode.

An example of an implied addressing instruction is:

```
DEC   A
```

This instruction specifies "decrement the contents of A by 1."

IMMEDIATE ADDRESSING

In the *immediate addressing* mode, an 8- or 16-bit literal (a constant) follows the 8-bit opcode (see Figure 5.1). Since the microprocessor is equipped with 16-bit registers, it may be necessary to load 8- or 16-bit literals. An example of an immediate instruction is:

```
ADC    #$5
```

The second word of this instruction contains the literal 5, which is added to accumulator A.

ABSOLUTE (OR EXTENDED) ADDRESSING

In *absolute addressing,* the 16-bit address of the operand follows the opcode. Absolute addressing, therefore, requires three-byte instructions. Here is an example using the absolute addressing mode:

```
STA    $1234
```

This instruction specifies that the contents of the accumulator are to be stored at memory location 1234 hexadecimal. Absolute addressing is also called *extended addressing,* because a full 16-bit memory address is specified.

A disadvantage of absolute addressing is that it requires a three-byte instruction. To improve the efficiency of the microprocessor, there may be another addressing mode available, direct addressing, which requires that only one byte be used for the address.

DIRECT ADDRESSING

In *direct addressing*, the opcode is followed by an 8-bit address (see Figure 5.1). The advantage of this approach is that it requires only two bytes, instead of three, for absolute addressing. A disadvantage is that on *most* microprocessors it limits all addressing within this mode to addresses 0 to 255. (*Note:* The 65816 does not have this limitation.) When addresses 0 to 255 are used, this type of addressing is also known as *short* or *zero-page addressing*.

RELATIVE ADDRESSING

You use *relative addressing* with branch instructions. If the state of the status flags satisfies the test made by the branch instruction, then the branch instruction loads the PC with a new address. The byte following the opcode, called the *displacement*, is added to the PC to form the new PC, to which the instruction branches. Figure 5.1 shows the structure of the relative addressing mode.

Since the displacement is a positive or negative number, a relative branch instruction allows a branch forward of 127 bytes or backward of 128 bytes (usually +129 or −126, since the PC will have been incremented by 2). The branch instructions are used in program loops. Because most loops are short, relative branching with a one-byte displacement is the most common. Relative branching usually results in significantly improved performance for short routines.

If you need a larger branch displacement, you can use the long branch instruction with a 16-bit displacement. This instruction is three bytes long (see Figure 5.1). The long branch can branch to any address in the memory because the displacement ranges from −32768 to +32767. Since long branch instructions take longer to execute than the simple branch instructions, you normally use them only when the shorter branch will not work. Relative addressing provides improved speed performance with branch instructions. If a program uses relative addressing, it can be easily moved to different areas of memory. In addition, if you do not use absolute addresses, then you can relocate the program to other areas of memory. The jump instruction (JMP) allows the use of absolute addressing. Generally, you should avoid the absolute addressing mode in favor of relative addressing.

INDEXED ADDRESSING

You use *indexed addressing* to access, in succession, the elements of a block or table. This mode appears in examples given later in this chapter.

With indexed addressing, the instruction specifies both an index register and a base address. The contents of the register and base address are added to provide the final address. In this way, the address could be the beginning of a table in memory. The index register would then be used to efficiently access all the elements of a table successively. However, there must be a way to increment or decrement the index register.

Pre-Indexing and Post-Indexing

There are two modes of indexing: *pre-indexing* and *post-indexing*. Pre-indexing is the usual indexing mode, in which the final address is the sum of a displacement or address, plus the contents of the index register. Figure 5.2 illustrates this approach (assuming an 8-bit displacement field and a 16-bit index register).

On the other hand, post-indexing treats the contents of the displacement field as the *address* of the actual displacement, rather than as the displacement itself. In post-indexing, the final address is the sum of the contents of the index register, plus the contents of the memory word *designated by the displacement field* (see Figure 5.3). This feature, in fact, uses a combination of indirect addressing and pre-indexing. Let's now define indirect addressing.

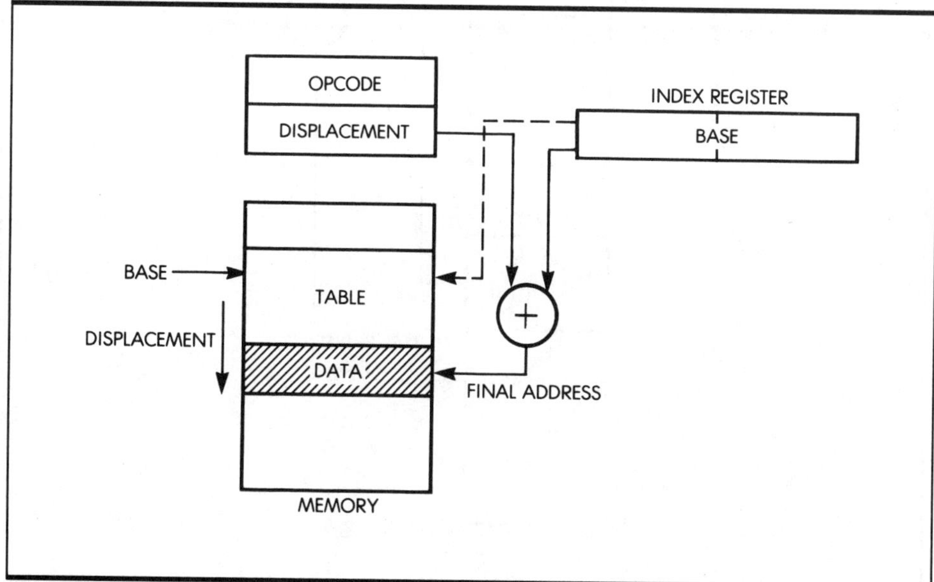

Figure 5.2: Addressing (Pre-Indexing)

Indirect Addressing

At times, two subroutines must exchange a large quantity of data stored in the memory. More generally, several programs or subroutines may need to access a common block of information. To preserve the generality of the program, you should not keep such a block at a fixed memory location. In particular, the size of the block may grow or shrink dynamically; thus, it may have to reside in various areas of the memory, depending on its size. It would, therefore, be impractical to try to access this block using absolute addresses—that is, without rewriting the program every time.

The solution to this problem, then, is to deposit the starting address of the block at a fixed memory location. *Indirect addressing,* therefore, normally uses an opcode (8 bits in the case of the 65816), followed by a 16-bit address. This address is used to retrieve a 16-bit word from the memory. This is used as the address of the operand. Figure 5.4 illustrates

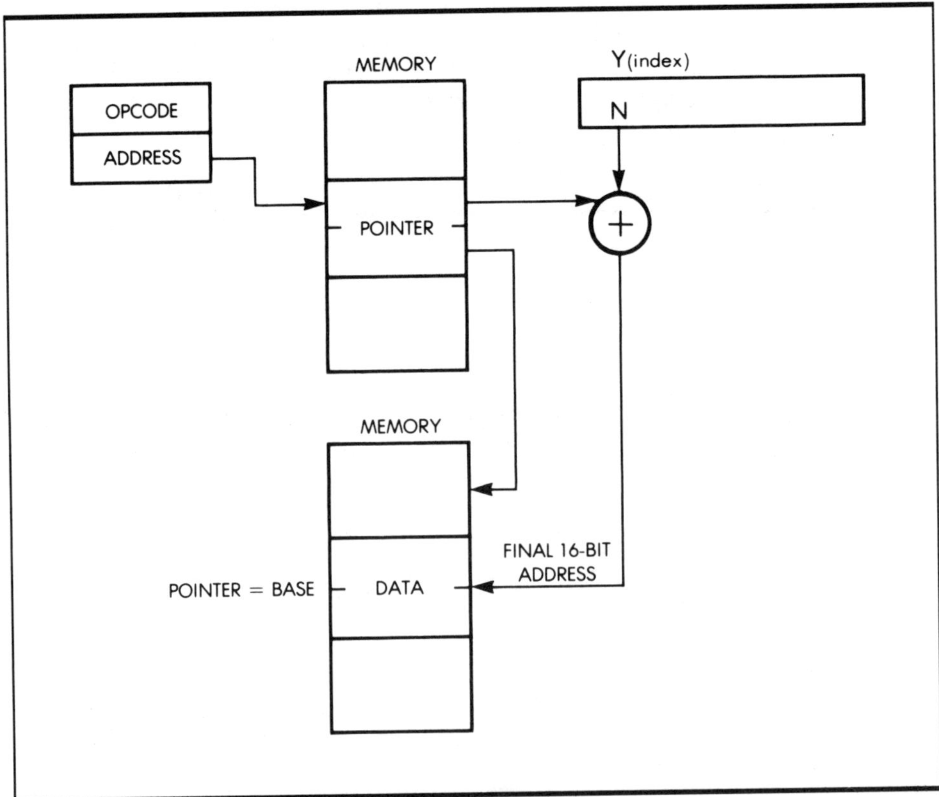

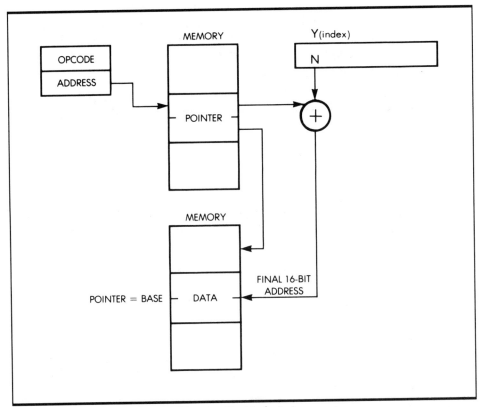

Figure 5.3: Indirect Indexed Addressing (Post-Indexing)

the structure of an instruction using indirect addressing, where the two bytes at the specified address A1 contain A2. A2 is then interpreted as the actual address of the data to be accessed.

Indirect addressing is particularly useful any time pointers are used. Various areas of the program can then refer to these pointers to conveniently and elegantly access a word or block of data. Another form of indirect addressing, *indexed indirect addressing,* uses an index register, rather than a memory location, to contain the address of the desired data.

Long Addressing

Most 16-bit microprocessors can address more than 64K of memory, even though the PC and index registers are 16 bits long, by using *long addressing.* Additional address registers are provided for long addressing. These registers are concatenated with the index registers or PC to form a 24-bit or even a 32-bit address, as shown in Figure 5.5. An absolute long address would require extra bytes in an instruction.

COMBINATIONS OF MODES

You can combine addressing modes. In particular, in a completely general addressing scheme you can use many levels of indirection. For example, in Figure 5.4 the address A2 could again be interpreted as an indirect address, and so on.

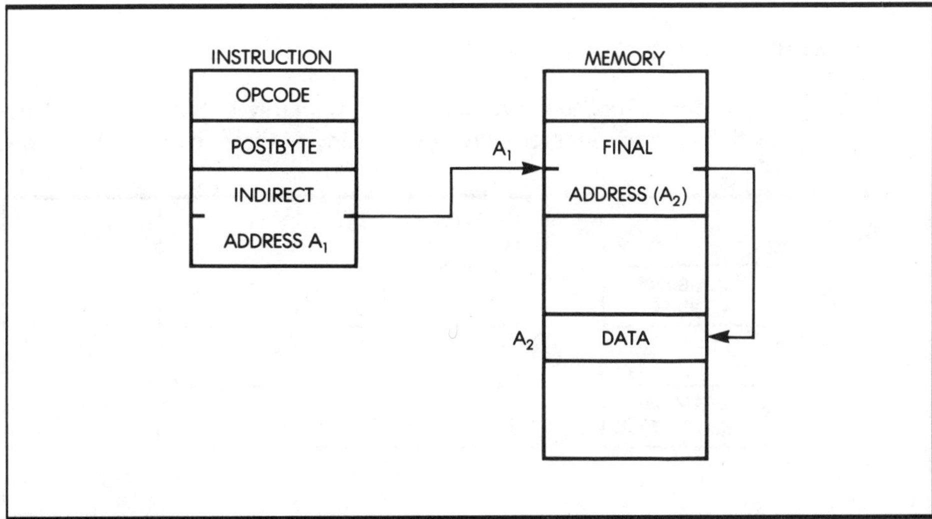

Figure 5.4: Indirect Addressing

You can also combine indexed addressing with indirect access. This allows efficient access to word *n* of a block of data, provided you know the location of the pointer to the starting address (see Figure 5.2).

MODE SUMMARY

You are now familiar with all the usual addressing modes that can be provided in a system. Most microprocessor systems, because of the limitation of the MPU (that it must be realized within a single chip), do not provide all possible modes, but only a small subset of them. The 65816 provides a good subset of possibilities. Let's examine them.

65816 ADDRESSING MODES

The 65816 addressing modes are an important feature of the 65816 processor. You can use them with most instructions to achieve great power and flexibility. The new addressing modes and additional instructions make the 65816 a more versatile machine than its predecessor, the 6502. To make good use of the 65816 processor and to write better programs, it is important to learn to use all the addressing modes.

IMPLIED ADDRESSING (65816)

On the 65816, *implied addressing* is used primarily by single-byte instructions that operate on internal registers. Many of these instructions require

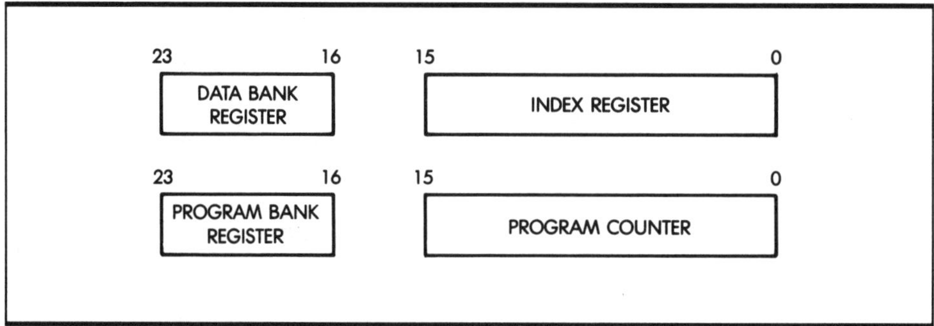

Figure 5.5: Registers for Long Addresses

only two cycles to execute. Table 5.1 shows the instructions that use implied addressing.

Some instructions, such as XBA, require more than two cycles to execute. Implied addressing is also called *register addressing.*

IMMEDIATE ADDRESSING (65816)

Since the 65816 has both single-length (8-bit) and double-length (16-bit) registers, it provides two types of immediate addressing, with both 8- and 16-bit literals. Instructions are then either two or three bytes long.

Here are examples of instructions using the *immediate addressing* mode:

```
LDA   #N     (one byte)
LDX   #NN    (two bytes)
ADC   #NN    (two bytes)
```

The number of bytes needed in the immediate addressing mode depends on the mode of the processor; 8 bits or 16 bits for the accumulator or index registers. The following instructions may use immediate addressing:

- With 8- or 16-bit operands: ADC, AND, BIT, CMP, CPX, CPY, DEC, EOR, LDA, LDX, LDY, ORA, SBC
- With 8-bit operands only: REP, SEP

ASL	INX	STP	TXY
CLC	INY	TAX	TYA
CLD	LSR	TCD	TYX
CLI	NOP	TCS	WAI
CLV	ROL	TDC	XBA
DEC	ROR	TSC	XCE
DEX	SEC	TSX	
DEY	SED	TXA	
INC	SEI	TXS	

Table 5.1: Instructions Using Implied Addressing

ABSOLUTE (OR EXTENDED) ADDRESSING (65816)

By definition, *absolute addressing* requires three or four bytes. The first byte is the opcode, and the next two are the 16-bit address specifying the memory location (the absolute address). If you use the *absolute long* mode, the instruction requires four bytes. The first byte is the opcode, and the next three are the 24-bit address.

Absolute addressing always specifies a particular address, which does not change while the program executes. Input and output programs often use absolute addressing. Examples of instructions using absolute addressing are:

```
LDA   $10
JMP   $1234
```

where the two hexadecimal numbers represent the 16-bit addresses of data or instructions. Instructions that can use the absolute addressing mode are: ADC, AND, ASL, BIT, CMP, CPX, CPY, DEC, EOR, INC, LDA, LDX, LDY, LSR, ORA, ROL, ROR, SBC, STA, STX, STY, STZ, TRB, and TSB.

DIRECT ADDRESSING (65816)

On most microprocessors where it is available, *direct addressing* addresses only the first 256 bytes of memory (page 0, which is addresses 0 to 255). This is because only an 8-bit address is specified, allowing the instruction to use two bytes instead of three. On the 65816, you can address any byte in bank 0 of memory by using direct addressing and manipulating the direct register (D). An example of direct addressing is:

```
ADC   <$10
```

The symbol < denotes direct addressing.

When direct addressing is used, the byte immediately following the opcode is added to the D register to form the address of the operand. By changing the D register appropriately, any page in bank 0 of memory may be addressed. When the D register contains 0, the 65816 direct addressing mode operates in the same manner as the 6502 processor. If the low byte of the D register is not 0, an extra instruction cycle is needed. The following instructions use direct addressing: ADC, AND, ASL, BIT, CMP, CPX, CPY, DEC, EOR, INC, LDA, LDX, LDY, LSR, ORA, ROL, ROR, SBC, STA, STX, STY, STZ, TRB, and TSB.

RELATIVE ADDRESSING (65816)

By definition, relative addressing requires two bytes. The first byte is the *branch relative* opcode; the second specifies the displacement and its sign. A long branch requires an extra byte for the displacement, making a total of three bytes. The instructions that use relative addressing are: BCC, BCS, BEQ, BMI, BNE, BPL, BRA, BRL, BVC, and BVS.

Examine these instructions with caution when you are concerned about timing. Whether a test succeeds or fails (whether there is not or there is a branch), all short branch instructions require two or three cycles, respectively. If you take a branch and cross a page boundary, the instruction will execute in four cycles.

Exercise caution when you are computing the duration of execution of a program segment. If you are not sure the branch will succeed, you must remember that sometimes the instruction will require *two cycles (if the condition is not met)* and sometimes *three or four cycles (if the condition is met).* An average value is often used for the duration of a branch.

This timing problem does not apply to the branch always (BRA) and branch long (BRL) instructions, which do not test any condition.

(*Note:* To differentiate the absolute jump instruction from the relative branch, the jump instruction is labeled JMP.)

There is another type of relative addressing in the 65816 that uses the stack pointer (S). The *stack relative* addressing mode adds the byte immediately following the opcode to the stack pointer to form the address of the operand. The unsigned value of the offset byte is used, so only values from 0 to 255 above the value of S can be addressed. The address must be in bank 0. An example of stack relative addressing is:

```
ADC   $50,S
```

The instructions that can use stack relative addressing are: ADC, AND, CMP, EOR, LDA, ORA, SBC, and STA.

INDEXED ADDRESSING (65816)

The *indexed addressing* mode is very powerful on the 65816 microprocessor. In all indexed addressing, one of the index registers (X or Y) is used to calculate the effective address of the data used by the instruction. There are two different types of indexed addressing: direct indexed and absolute indexed.

Direct Indexed

In the *direct indexed* mode, the byte following the opcode is used as an offset and is added to the direct register, and then the specified index register is added to this sum to form the address of the operand. The operand must be in bank 0. Examples of direct indexed addressing are:

```
ADC   $0,X
LDX   $50,Y
```

Instructions that use the direct indexed addressing are:

- With X: ADC, AND, ASL, BIT, CMP, DEC, EOR, INC, LDA, LDY, LSR, ORA, ROL, ROR, SBC, STA, STY, STZ
- With Y: LDX, STX

Absolute Indexed

The *absolute indexed* mode adds the two bytes following the opcode to a specified index register to form the low 16 bits of the address. The data bank register contains the high 8 bits of the address. The low-order address byte immediately follows the opcode. Examples of absolute indexed addressing are:

```
ADC   $100,X
AND   $1234,Y
```

Instructions that use the absolute indexed mode are:

- With X: ADC, AND, ASL, BIT, CMP, DEC, EOR, INC, LDA, LDY, LSR, ORA, ROL, ROR, SBC, STA, STZ
- With Y: ADC, AND, CMP, EOR, LDA, LDX, ORA, SBC, STA

The *absolute long indexed* mode may be used only with index register X. With this mode, the 24-bit address is stored after the opcode and is added to the X index register to form the effective address of the operand. An example of absolute long indexed addressing is:

```
CMP   $FF1234,X
```

Instructions that use the absolute long indexed mode are: ADC, AND, CMP, EOR, LDA, ORA, SBC, and STA.

INDIRECT ADDRESSING (65816)

The indirect addressing modes in the 65816 use the bytes following the opcode as a pointer to the address of the opcode. There are two types of indirect addressing—absolute and direct.

Absolute Indirect

The *absolute indirect* address mode uses the two bytes following the opcode to form the address that points to the operand used by the instruction. Only the JMP and JML instructions use this mode, so the operand fetched is always the address to jump to. An example of this instruction is:

```
JMP    ($1234)
```

The pointer always points to bank 0 because the address is two bytes long. When you use the jump long (JML) instruction, the program bank register is loaded from the location addressed by the pointer plus two.

Direct Indirect

The *direct indirect* mode adds the byte immediately following the opcode to the direct register to form a pointer to the low-order 16 bits of the address of the operand. The data bank register contains the high-order 8 bits. The 16-bit low-order address pointed to by the direct register must be in bank 0. The direct indirect mode is indicated by parentheses around the offset byte, as indicated in this example:

```
$123456   ADC     ($20)
$000120   $FEEE
$AAFEEE   $02
```

Assume that in the above example, D=$0100 and DBR=$AA. The value $20 will be added to D to fetch the address $FEEE, which is concatenated with $AA to form the address of the operand, $02.

The *direct indirect long* addressing mode uses the pointer formed by the sum of the offset byte and direct register to fetch all three bytes of the address of the operand. Here is an example of the direct indirect long mode:

```
$123456   ADC     [$20]
$000120   $AAFEEE
$AAFEEE   $02
```

The square brackets [ ] are used to indicate long addressing.

The following instructions may be used with both addressing modes: ADC, AND, CMP, EOR, LDA, ORA, SBC, and STA.

COMBINATIONS OF ADDRESSING MODES

The 65816 has five combinations of the direct, indexed, and indirect modes. These modes provide flexibility for passing parameters and arrays of data from one part of the program to another.

Direct Indirect Indexed

The *direct indirect indexed* mode is also referred to as *indirect, Y.* The second byte of the instruction is added to the direct register. The 16-bit contents of the location pointed to by the direct register are combined with the data bank register to form the base address. (The location pointed to by the direct register must be in bank 0.) The Y index register is added to the base to form the effective address of the operand. In the following example

```
$123456    ADC     ($20),Y
$000120    $FF00
$AAFFEE    $02
```

assume that D=$0100, DBR=$AA, and Y=$00EE. The value 2 is added to the accumulator.

The *direct indirect long indexed* mode is similar to the direct indirect indexed mode, except that the sum of the direct register and offset byte point to a 24-bit address, which is added to Y to form the effective address of the operand. The direct register only points to a location in bank 0. The data bank register is not used, as shown in the following example:

```
$123456    ADC     [$20],Y
$000120    $BBFF00
$BBFFEE    $02
```

Assume that D=$0100, DBR=$AA, and Y=$00EE. The value 2 is added to the accumulator. The square brackets [ ] are used to indicate long addressing.

You may use the following instructions with both modes in direct indirect indexed addressing: ADC, AND, CMP, EOR, LDA, ORA, SBC, and STA.

Direct Indexed Indirect

The *direct indexed indirect* mode is often referred to as *indirect, X.* The second byte of the instruction is added to the sum of the direct register and the X index register. This sum points to a 16-bit address in bank 0. The 16-bit address is combined with the data bank register to form the effective address of the operand. The following example adds the value $02 to the accumulator:

```
$123456   ADC    ($20,X)
$005120   $FF00
$AAFF00   $02
```

Assume that D=$0100, DBR=$AA, and X=$5000. You may use the following instructions with the direct indexed indirect mode: ADC, AND, CMP, EOR, LDA, ORA, SBC, and STA.

Absolute Indexed Indirect

The *absolute indexed indirect* mode adds the second and third bytes of the instruction to the X index register to form a 16-bit pointer into bank 0. The pointer is loaded into the PC. The program bank register is not affected. This addressing mode is used with the JMP and JSR instructions, and it allows a single jump or jump-to-subroutine instruction to jump to different locations, depending on the value of the X.

Stack Relative Indirect Indexed

The *stack relative indirect indexed* mode uses the second byte of the instruction to add to the stack pointer, forming a pointer to the low-order 16-bit base address in bank 0. The data bank register contains the high-order 8 bits of the base address. The effective address of the operand is the sum of the 24-bit base address and the Y index register. Here is an example:

```
$123456   ADC    ($20,S),Y
$000120   $FF00
$AAFF22   $02
```

Assume that S=$0100, DBR=$AA, and Y=$22. The value 2 is added to the accumulator. This addressing mode is used with the following instructions: ADC, AND, CMP, EOR, LDA, ORA, SBC, and STA.

ADDRESSING MODE NOTATION

When you are developing a program using assembly language, you must have a notation to indicate which addressing mode is to be used with an instruction. Table 5.2 shows the notation recommended by the manufacturer of the 65816.

USING THE 65816 ADDRESSING MODES

This section contains short program examples illustrating the use of several addressing modes. These programs are often used as parts of larger programs.

USE OF INDEXING FOR SEQUENTIAL BLOCK ACCESS

Indexing is used primarily for addressing successive locations within a table. It is sometimes desirable to limit the table size to 256 so that you can use the

ADDRESSING MODE	OPERAND FORMAT
IMPLIED	none needed
IMMEDIATE	#N or #NN
ABSOLUTE	NN
ABSOLUTE LONG	NNN
DIRECT	N
DIRECT INDIRECT INDEXED	(N),Y
DIRECT INDIRECT LONG INDEXED	[N],Y
DIRECT INDEXED INDIRECT	(N,X)
DIRECT INDEXED WITH X	N,X
DIRECT INDEXED WITH Y	N,Y
ABSOLUTE INDEXED WITH X	NN,X
ABSOLUTE INDEXED WITH Y	NN,Y
ABSOLUTE LONG INDEXED WITH X	NNN,X
ABSOLUTE INDIRECT	(NN)
DIRECT INDIRECT	(N)
DIRECT INDIRECT LONG	[N]
ABSOLUTE INDEXED INDIRECT	(NN,X)
STACK RELATIVE	N,S
STACK RELATIVE INDIRECT INDEXED	(N,S),Y

N *8-bit value*
NN *16-bit value*
NNN *24-bit value*

Table 5.2: Addressing Mode Notation

8-bit index register mode, which is faster than the 16-bit mode.

Let's now search a table of 100 elements for the * character. The starting address for this table is called BASE. The table has only 100 elements. Figure 5.6 shows the algorithm. Here is the program:

```
SEARCH    LDX    #0
TEST      LDA    BASE,X
          CMP    #'*
          BEQ    FOUND
          INX
          CPX    #100
          BNE    TEST
NOTFOUND ...
FOUND     ...
```

This program uses the absolute indexed mode. The same program using the direct indexed mode is shown below. Note that the direct register is loaded through the accumulator.

```
SEARCH    LDA    #BASE
          TCD
          LDX    #0
TEST      LDA    0,X
          CMP    #'*
          BEQ    FOUND
          INX
          CPX    #100
          BNE    TEST
NOTFOUND ...
FOUND     ...
```

When the direct indexed mode is used, the table must be in bank 0.

A BLOCK TRANSFER ROUTINE

In the following program, COUNT is the number of elements in the block to be moved. The number is assumed to be less than 65,536. FROM is the base address of the block, and TO is the base of the memory area where it should be moved. The algorithm is quite simple: you move a byte at a time, and keep track of the byte you are moving by decrementing X. Here is the program:

```
BLKMOV LDX   #COUNT
NEXT   LDA   FROM,X
```

```
STA    TO,X
DEX
BNE    NEXT
```

This program will move words until X equals zero; therefore, the program will not transfer the byte at FROM. The tables TO and FROM must be just *above* where the addresses point to. This block transfer program is designed to work with bytes. To use 16-bit words, the X register must be decremented twice and the processor M and X bits in the status register must be set to 0.

BLOCK TRANSFER INSTRUCTIONS

The block move program was written to illustrate the use of the X index register, but you would generally not use the program on the 65816 because the *block move* instructions are much more efficient. The block move can move up to 65,536 bytes from one part of the 16-megabyte

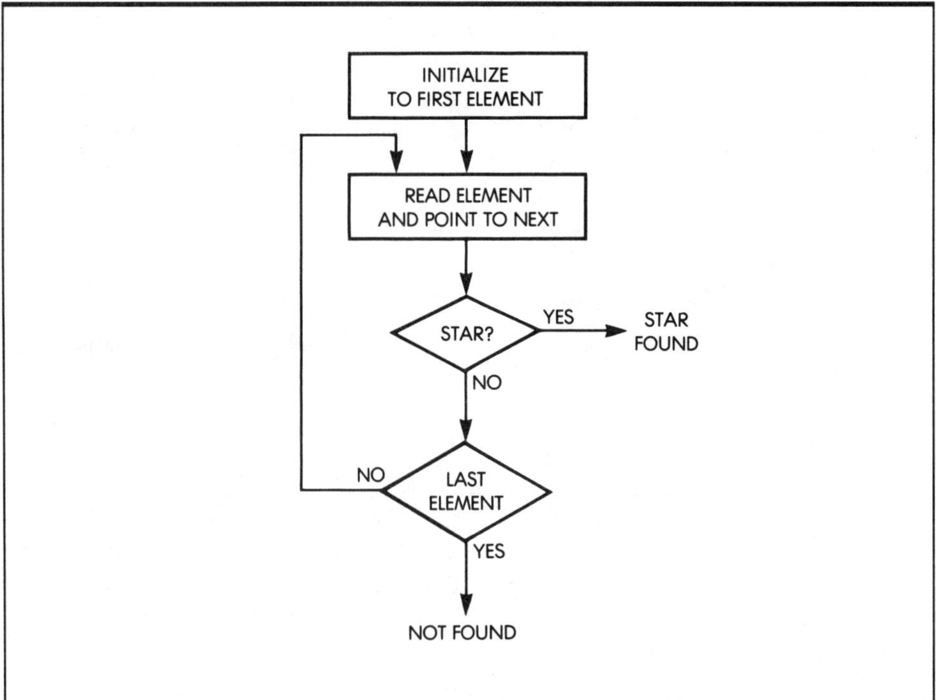

Figure 5.6: Character Search Flowchart

memory space to any other part. The block move uses the X index register to store the low 16 bits of the source address, and it uses the Y index register to store the low 16 bits of the destination address. The second byte of the instruction contains the bank address for the destination address, and the third byte of the instruction contains the bank address for the source bank. The accumulator contains the number of bytes to transfer minus 1. Figure 5.6 shows the memory and register usage for the block move positive (MVP) instruction. Here is an example of block move positive:

```
REP   #$30
LDA   #511
LDX   #SOURCE
LDY   #DEST
MVP   #$0201
```

The first instruction, REP #$30, puts all registers into the 16-bit mode. The byte count in the accumulator shows that 512 bytes will be moved. The source data bank is 1, and the destination data bank is 2. The accumulator will be decremented each time a byte is moved. The X and Y registers will also be decremented each time data is moved. This means data will move first from the highest locations in the source to the highest locations in the destination, as illustrated in Figure 5.7.

The block move negative (MVN) instruction is the same as the block move positive, except the index registers are *incremented* after each byte is transferred. The data bank register will always contain the destination bank address when either instruction is finished.

ADDING TWO BLOCKS

I will now develop a program that adds, element-by-element, two blocks that start at addresses BLK1 and BLK2, respectively, and that have an equal number of 16-bit elements (COUNT). Here is the program:

```
BLKADD LDX   #0
       LOOP  CLC
       LDA   BLK1,X
       ADC   BLK2,X
       STA   BLK2,X
       INX
       INX
       CPX   #COUNT*2
       BNE   LOOP
```

I will now implement the same program using the direct indirect indexed mode. This mode allows the addresses of the blocks to be stored in bank 0 and to be referenced with the direct register. The addresses are stored in bank 0 at PTR1 and PTR2. Here is the program:

```
BLKADD  LDY   #0
NEXT    CLC
        LDA   (PTR1),Y
        ADC   (PTR2),Y
        STA   (PTR2),Y
        INY
```

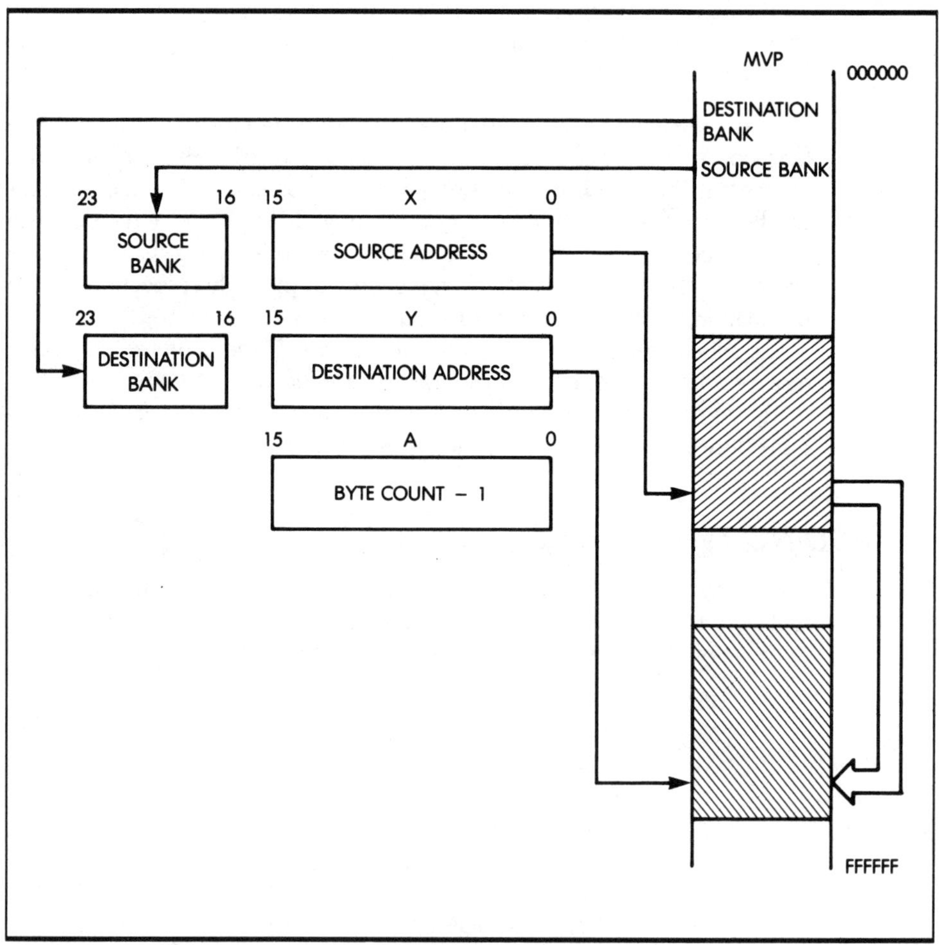

Figure 5.7: Registers and Memory for Block Move Positive

```
INY
CPY   #COUNT*2
BNE   NEXT
```

In this program, you do not need to know the absolute location of BLK1 and BLK2. The addresses could have been written by another part of the program before the block add was executed.

SUMMARY

I have now discussed addressing modes and analyzed those available on the 65816. You have seen that the 65816 offers many possible addressing mechanisms. To program the 65816 efficiently, you must understand these mechanisms. They will be used throughout the remainder of this book.

EXERCISES

5-1: *Use the block addition program to perform a 32-bit addition.*

5-2: *Use the block addition program to perform a 64-bit addition.*

5-3: *Modify the block addition program so that the result is stored in a separate block starting at address BLK3.*

5-4: *Modify the block addition program to perform a subtraction rather than an addition.*

5-5: *Write a program to add the first 10 bytes of a table stored at location BASE. The result will have 16 bits. (This is a checksum computation.)*

5-6: *Can you solve the same problem in Exercise 5-5 without using the indexing mode?*

5-7: *Reverse the order of the 10 bytes of this table. Store the result of the addition at address REVER.*

5-8: *Search the same table for its largest element. Store it at memory address LARGE.*

INPUT/OUTPUT TECHNIQUES

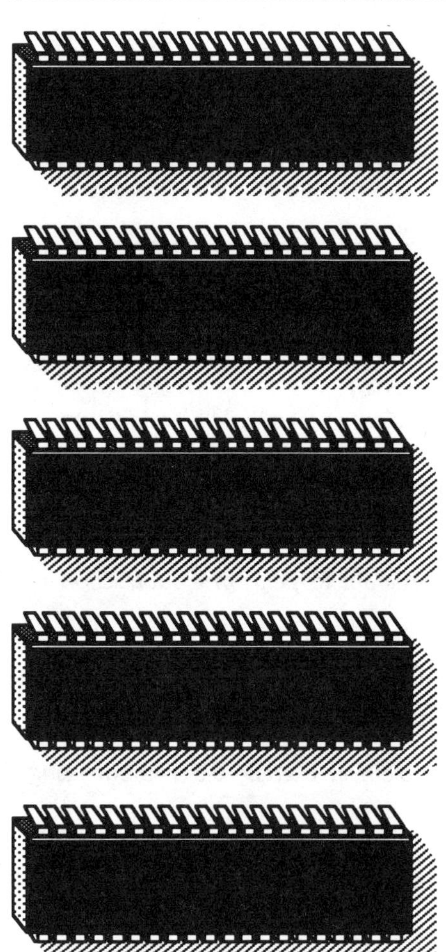

6

SO FAR IN THIS BOOK, you have seen how to exchange information between the memory and the various registers of the processor; you have learned how to manage registers; and you have learned how to use a variety of instructions to manipulate data. I will now examine input/output techniques and show you how to communicate with the external world.

The principal advantage of the 65816 architecture in this important area is its powerful interrupt structure, which provides, in addition to a regular interrupt mode, a nonmaskable interrupt mode. Also important in the use of these interrupt modes is the 65816's unique WAI instruction, which I will also explore in this chapter.

Input is the transfer of data from an outside peripheral (keyboard, disk, or physical sensor) to *internal* computer storage. *Output* is the transfer of data from within the microprocessor or the memory to an *external* device, such as a printer, CRT, disk, or actual sensors and relays. In this chapter, you will learn to perform the input/output operations required in most computer applications. You will also learn to manage several input/output devices simultaneously, and finally, I will discuss the subject of polling versus interrupts.

THE 65816 INPUT/OUTPUT INSTRUCTIONS

For input or output on the 65816, you can use any instruction that transfers data to or from memory. Input/output interfacing on the 65816 is called *memory-mapped interfacing* because input/output devices are interfaced to the 65816 in the same way that memory is interfaced. You can use *any* addressing mode for input or output; however, absolute addressing is commonly used, because the addresses of input/output devices rarely change once a system has been built.

GENERATING A SIGNAL

To generate a signal, the computer must turn an output device off or on. To do this, you must change an electrical voltage level in the device from a logical 0 to a logical 1, or from 1 to 0. For example, assume that an external relay is connected to bit 0 of a register called OUT1. To turn the relay on, you simply write *1* in the appropriate bit position of the register. I assume here that OUT1 represents the address of the device output register in the system. Here is a program that will turn the relay on:

```
TURNON LDA  #%00000001   LOAD PATTERN INTO A
       STA  OUT1         OUTPUT IT TO DEVICE
```

STA is the output instruction. The **%** symbol indicates a binary number.

In this example, I have assumed that the states of the other seven bits of the register OUT1 are irrelevant. However, this is often not the case, as these bits might be connected to other relays. You can improve this simple program by turning the relay on without changing the state of any other bit in the register. Assume that you can read and write the contents of this register. The improved program is:

```
TURNON LDA  OUT1         READ CONTENTS OF OUT1
       ORA  #%00000001   FORCE BIT 0 TO 1 IN A
       STA  OUT1
```

This program first reads the contents of OUT1, then performs an inclusive-OR on its contents. It changes bit position 0 to 1, and leaves the rest of the register intact (see Figure 6.1).

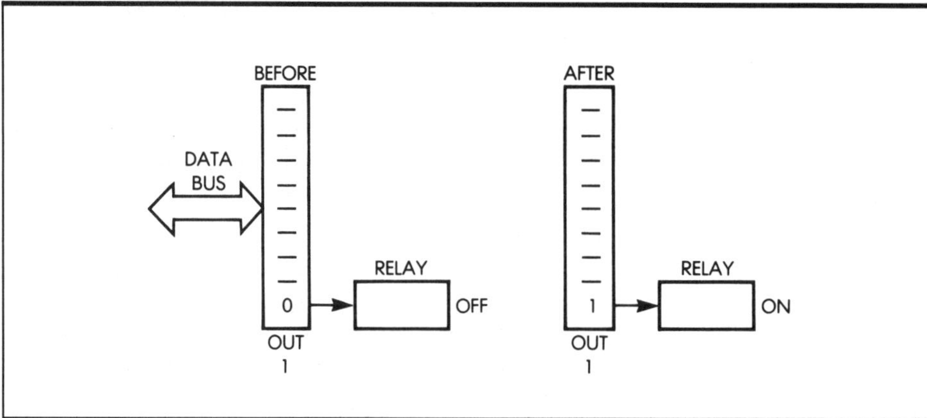

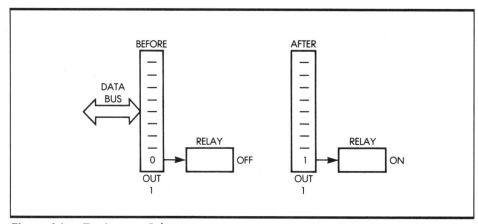

Figure 6.1: Turning on a Relay

PULSES

You can generate a *pulse* in the same way that you changed the voltage *level*. You first turn an output bit on, then turn it off. This results in a pulse, as illustrated in Figure 6.2. In this example, however, you must solve an additional problem: you need to generate the pulse for a specified length of time. Thus, you must generate a computed delay.

DELAY GENERATION AND MEASUREMENT

You can generate a delay by using both software and hardware methods. I will first generate one using software; then I will generate one using a hardware counter, called a *programmable interval timer* (PIT).

Programmed delays are achieved by *counting*. A counter register is first loaded with a value, then decremented. The program loops on itself and continues decrementing until the counter reaches the value 0. The total

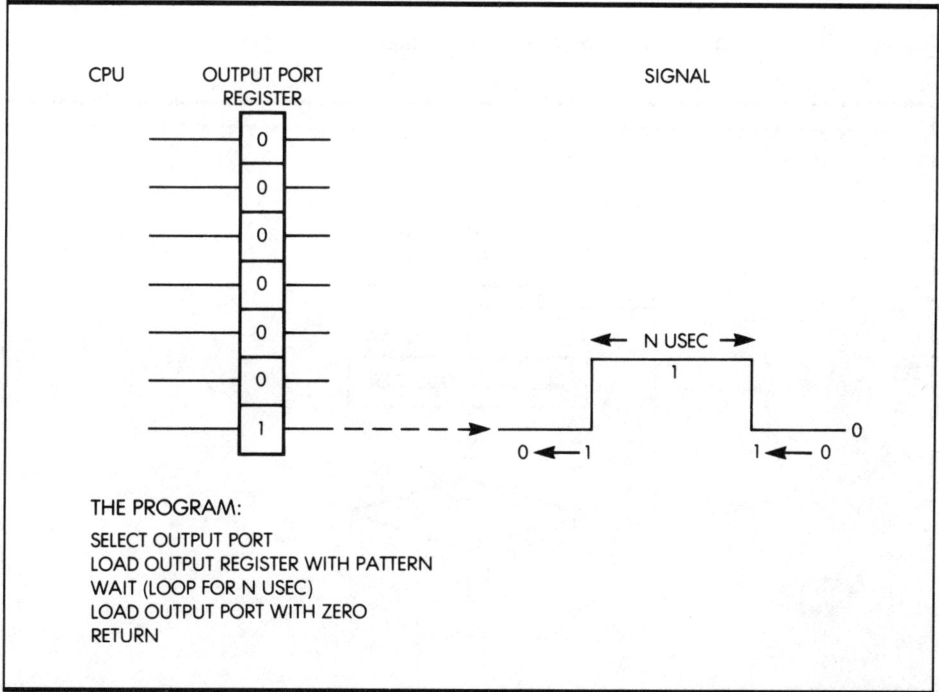

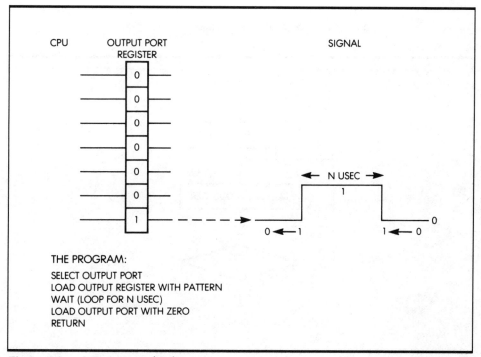

Figure 6.2: A Programmed Pulse

length of time used by this process implements the required delay. As an example, let's generate a delay of 27 clock cycles:

```
DELAY   LDA   #5      A IS COUNTER
NEXT    DEC   A       DECREMENT
        BNE   NEXT    LOOP TIL ZERO
```

The first instruction loads A with the value 5, and the next instruction decrements A. The last instruction causes a branch to NEXT, as long as A does not decrement to 0. When A finally decrements to 0, the program exits from this loop and executes whatever instruction follows. The logic of the program is simple and appears in the flowchart in Figure 6.3.

Let's now compute the effective delay that the program will implement. To do this, use Appendix E to look up the number of cycles required by each instruction. Appendix E shows that LDA in the immediate mode requires two clock cycles. If the processor is in the 16-bit accumulator mode, three cycles are required. DEC also requires two cycles, and finally, BNE uses three cycles. The timing is, therefore, two cycles for the first instruction, plus five for the next two, multiplied by the number of times the loop is executed.

$$\text{Delay} = 2 + (5 \times 5) = 27 \text{ cycles}$$

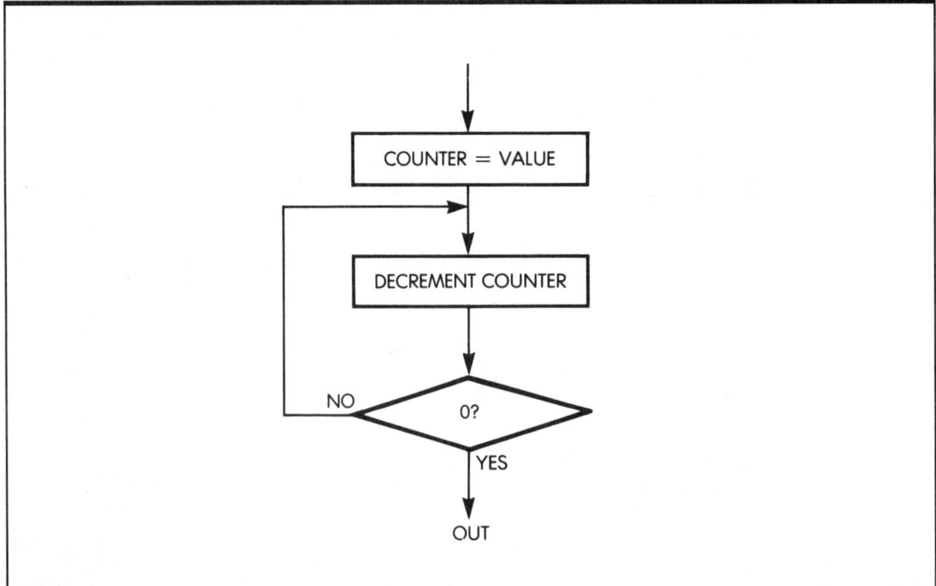

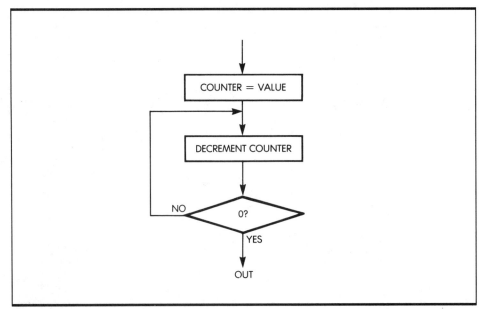

Figure 6.3: Basic Delay Flowchart

Assuming a 0.5 microsecond clock, the programmed delay will be 13.5 microseconds. (*Note:* The delay loop just described is used by most input/output programs. Be sure you understand it.)

To implement a longer delay, you simply add extra instructions in the program between the instructions DEC and BNE. The simplest way to do this is to add several NOP instructions. (The NOP instruction does nothing for two cycles.)

LONGER DELAYS

To generate longer delays using software, you can use a wider counter. For example, you can use the 16-bit mode to hold a 16-bit count. To simplify, assume that the lower count is 0. You load the lower byte with 0 (the maximum count), and it will go through a decrementation loop. When it is decremented to 0, the upper byte of the counter is decremented by 1. When the upper byte is decremented to 0, the program terminates. If the delay generation requires more precision, the lower count can have a non-null value. In that case, you would write the program as explained and add the three-line delay generation program described above.

Here is a 32-bit delay program:

```
DEL32   LDA   #COUNTH   COUNTER HIGH (16 BITS)
        STA   COUNTR
DEL16   LDA   #COUNTL   COUNTER LOW (16 BITS)
LOOP    DEC   A         DECREMENT IT
        BNE   LOOP      LOOP UNTIL ZERO
        DEC   COUNTR    DECREMENT HIGH COUNTER
        BNE   DEL16     REPEAT UNTIL ZERO
```

Naturally, you could generate still longer delays by using more than two words. Actually, this example is analogous to the way an odometer works on a car. When the rightmost wheel goes from 9 to 0, the next wheel to the left is incremented by 1. This is the general principle when you are counting with multiple discrete units.

The main disadvantage of this method, however, is that when the computer is counting delays, the microprocessor does nothing else for hundreds of milliseconds or even seconds. If the computer has nothing else to do, then this is acceptable. In general, though, the microcomputer should be available for other tasks. Therefore, long delays are normally not implemented by software. In fact, even short delays may be objectionable in a system, if the system is to provide guaranteed response time in certain situations. (In such situations, you must use hardware delays.) Another disadvantage of the software delay is that if the program is interrupted, timing accuracy may be lost.

HARDWARE DELAYS

Hardware delays are implemented by using a *programmable interval timer,* or *timer* for short. When you use a programmable interval timer, a register of the timer is loaded with a value. The timer automatically decrements the counter periodically. The programmer can usually adjust or select the amount of time between decrements. When the timer has decremented to 0, it normally sends an interrupt to the microprocessor. It may also set a status bit, which the computer can periodically sense. (I discuss interrupts later in this chapter.)

Other timer operating modes may include starting from 0 and counting the duration of the signal or the number of pulses received. When it is functioning as an interval timer, the timer is said to operate in a *one-shot* mode. When counting pulses, the timer is said to operate in a *pulse counting* mode. Some timer devices may even include multiple registers and several optional facilities that the programmer can select.

SENSING PULSES

The problem with sensing pulses is the reverse of the problem with generating pulses, and it includes one more difficulty: an output pulse is generated under program control, whereas an input pulse occurs *asynchronously* with the program. You can use two methods to detect a pulse: *polling* and *interrupts.*

Using the polling technique, the program continuously reads the value of a given input register and tests a bit position, perhaps bit 0. Assume that bit 0 was originally 0. (Thus, when a pulse is received, this bit takes the value 1.) The program continuously monitors bit 0 until it takes the value 1. When a one is found, the pulse has been detected. Here is a program that does this:

```
POLL    LDA     INPUT           READ INPUT REGISTER
        BIT     #%00000001      TEST FOR 0
        BEQ     POLL            KEEP POLLING IF ZERO
```

Conversely, assume that the input line is normally 1, and you want to detect a zero. This is the usual case for detecting a start bit, when monitoring a line connected to a Teletype. Here is the program:

```
POLL    LDA   INPUT       READ INPUT REGISTER
        BIT   #%0000001   SET Z BIT
        BNE   POLL        TEST IS REVERSED
START         . . .
```

MONITORING THE DURATION

You monitor the duration of a pulse in the same way that you compute the duration of an output pulse. You may use either a hardware or software technique. When you monitor a pulse by using software, a counter is regularly incremented by 1, then the presence of the pulse is verified. If the pulse is still present, the program loops upon itself. If the pulse disappears, the count contained in the counter register is used to compute the effective duration of the pulse. Here is a program that monitors pulse duration:

```
DURTN   LDX   #0           CLEAR COUNTER
AGAIN   LDA   INPUT        READ INPUT
        BIT   #%00000001   MONITOR BIT 0
        BEQ   AGAIN        WAIT FOR A 1
LONGER  INX                INCREMENT COUNTER
        LDA   INPUT
        BIT   #%00000001   CHECK BIT 0
        BNE   LONGER       WAIT FOR A 0
```

Naturally, you assume that the maximum duration of the pulse will not cause register X to overflow. However, if X does overflow, you will have to change the program to take that into account (or there will be a programming error!).

Since you now know how to sense and generate pulses, I will show you how to capture and transfer large amounts of data. You can then apply this knowledge to actual input/output devices.

PARALLEL BYTE TRANSFER

Assume here that eight bits of transfer data are available in parallel at address INPUT (see Figure 6.4). Also assume that the status information is contained in bit 7 of address STATUS. The microprocessor must read the data byte at this location whenever a status byte indicates that it is valid.

I will now write a program that reads and automatically saves each byte of data as it comes in. For simplicity, assume that the number of bytes to be read is known in advance and contained in location COUNT. But if this information is not available, you need to test for a *break character,* such as a *rubout,* or perhaps the * character. You have learned how to do this already.

The flowchart for this example appears in Figure 6.5. You test the status information until bit 7 becomes 1, indicating that a byte is ready. When the byte is ready, you read it and save it at an appropriate memory location. You then decrement the counter and test whether it has decremented to 0. If so, the task is completed; if not, you read the next byte. Here is a simple program that implements this algorithm:

```
PARAL   LDX     COUNT   READ COUNT INTO X
WATCH   LDA     STATUS  LOOK FOR DATAREADY TRUE
```

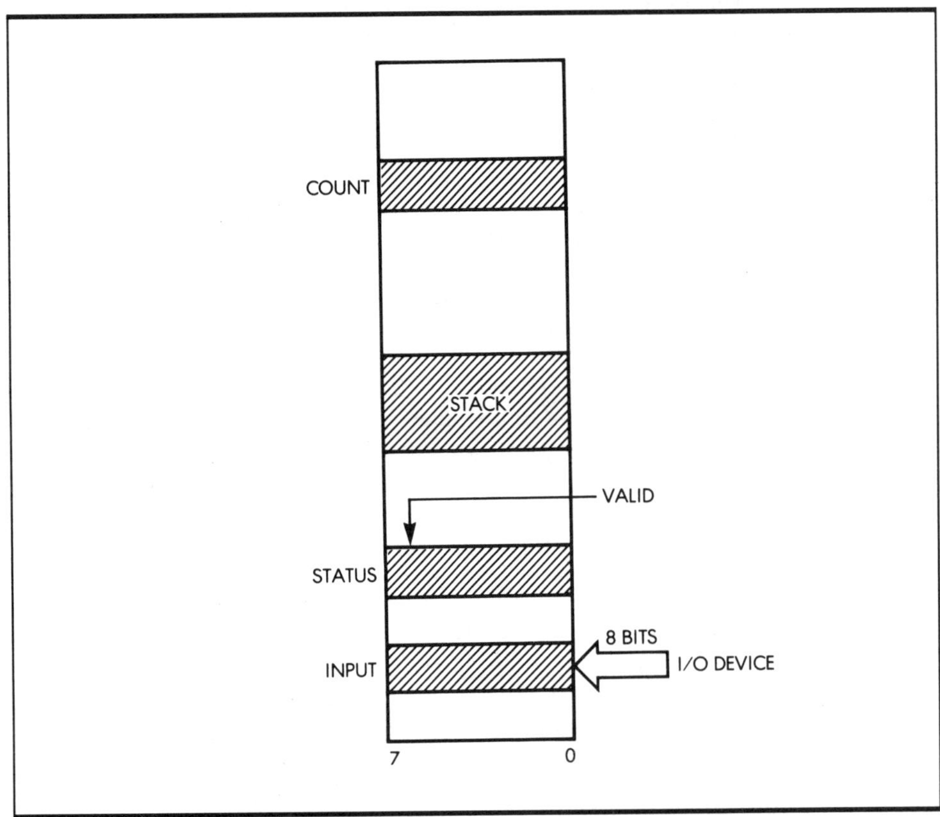

Figure 6.4: Memory for Parallel Byte Transfer

```
BPL     WATCH   LOOP TIL READY
LDA     INPUT   READ DATA
PHA             SAVE DATA ON STACK
DEX             DECREMENT COUNT
BNE     WATCH   REPEAT UNTIL ZERO
```

Assume here that the *data ready* flag is automatically cleared when STATUS is read. This is usually the case on a device controller.

The first instruction initializes the counter register X:

```
PARAL   LDX     COUNT
```

The next instructions read the status information and cause a loop to occur when bit 7 of the status register is 0. The LDA instruction sets the

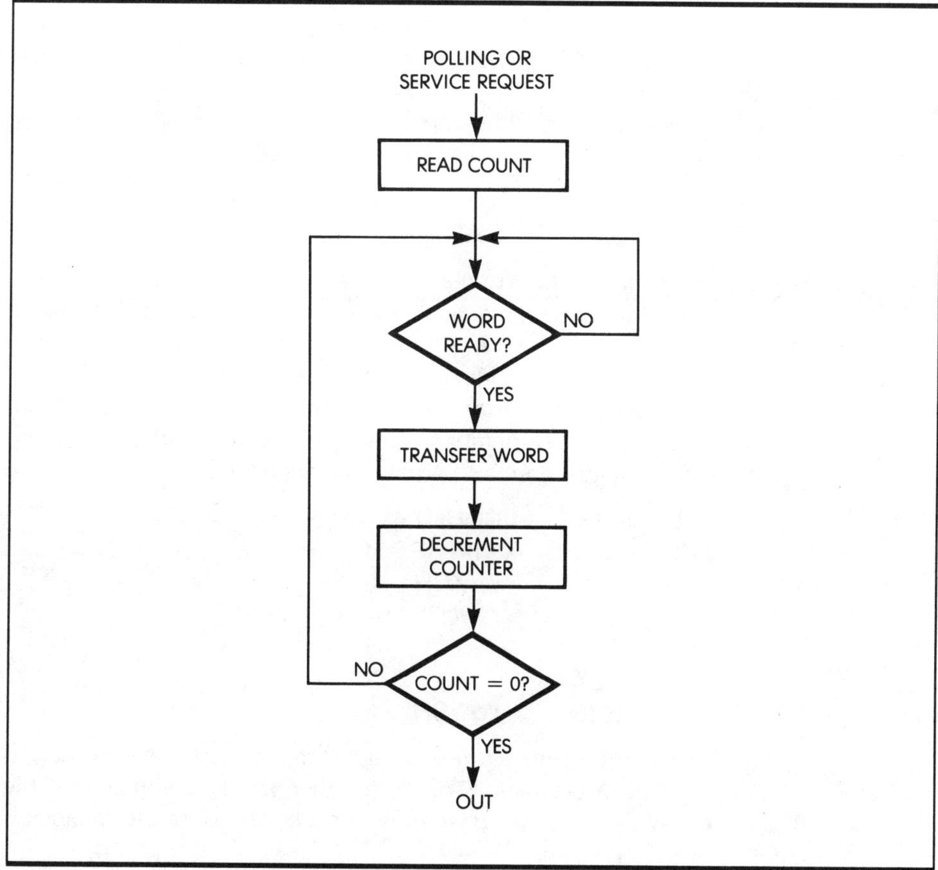

Figure 6.5: Flowchart for Parallel Byte Transfer

status bits. Bit 7 causes the N bit to be set. The M bit in the status register must be 0 so that the accumulator will be in the 8-bit mode.

```
        LDA     STATUS
        BPL     WATCH
```

When BPL fails, the data is valid and you can read it:

```
        LDA     INPUT
```

The byte has now been read from address INPUT and must be saved. Assuming that a sufficient stack area is available, you can use the instruction

```
        PHA
```

which saves A on the stack. If the stack is full, or if the number of bytes to be transferred is large, you cannot push them on the stack, and you will have to transfer them to a designated memory area, using, for example, an index register.

The byte of data has now been read and saved. You simply decrement the byte counter and test whether you are finished:

```
        DEX
        BNE     WATCH
```

You keep looping until the counter eventually decrements to 0.

This nine-instruction program, called a *benchmark program,* is designed to test a given processor for a specific operation. For example, you can compute the maximum transfer speed of the parallel transfer program—a program designed for maximum speed and efficiency. Assume that COUNT is contained in memory. Now examine the duration of each instruction (these figures are also given in Appendix E):

```
PARAL   LDX     COUNT   4 or 5
WATCH   LDA     STATUS  4
        BPL     WATCH   3
        LDA     INPUT   4
        PHA             3
        DEX             2
        BNE     WATCH   3
```

You can obtain the minimum execution time by assuming the data is ready every time you sample STATUS. In other words, if you assume the BPL will fail every time, the length of time necessary to transfer a block is then:

$$4 + [(4 + 3 + 4 + 3 + 2 + 3) \times \text{COUNT}]$$

If you neglect the first 4 cycles necessary to initialize the counter register, the time used to transfer one byte is 19 clock cycles, which is 9.5 microseconds with a 2 MHz clock. The maximum data transfer rate is:

$$\frac{1}{9.5(10^{-6})} = 105\text{K per second}$$

You have now learned to perform high-speed parallel transfers. Let's examine a more complex case.

BIT SERIAL TRANSFER

A serial input is one in which the bits of information (zeros or ones) come in successively on a line. These bits may come in at regular intervals, called *synchronous* transmission, or they may come at random intervals as bursts of data, called *asynchronous* transmission. I will now develop a program that works in both cases.

The principle of the capture of sequential data is simple. You watch an input line, which you assume to be line 0. When a bit of data is detected on this line, you read the bit in and shift it into a holding register. When you have assembled eight bits, you preserve the byte of data in the memory and assemble the next one.

To simplify this example, assume that you know the number of bytes to be received. Otherwise, you might have to watch for a special break character and stop the bit serial transfer at that point. Figure 6.6 shows the flowchart for this program. Here is the program:

```
SERIAL  STZ   WORD     CLEAR INPUT WORD
        LDX   #COUNT   PUT BYTE COUNT INTO X
LOOP    LDA   INPUT    READ PORT
        BPL   LOOP     WAIT FOR BIT 7 = 1
        LSR   A        SHIFT DATA BIT INTO CARRY
        ROL   WORD     SAVE CARRY IN WORD
        BCC   LOOP     CONTINUE UNTIL 8 BITS IN
        LDA   WORD     PUT WORD IN A
        PHA            SAVE WORD ON STACK
        LDA   #$01     RESET MARKER BIT
        STA   WORD     AND STORE IN WORD
        DEX            DECREMENT BYTE COUNTER
        BNE   LOOP     ASSEMBLE NEXT WORD
```

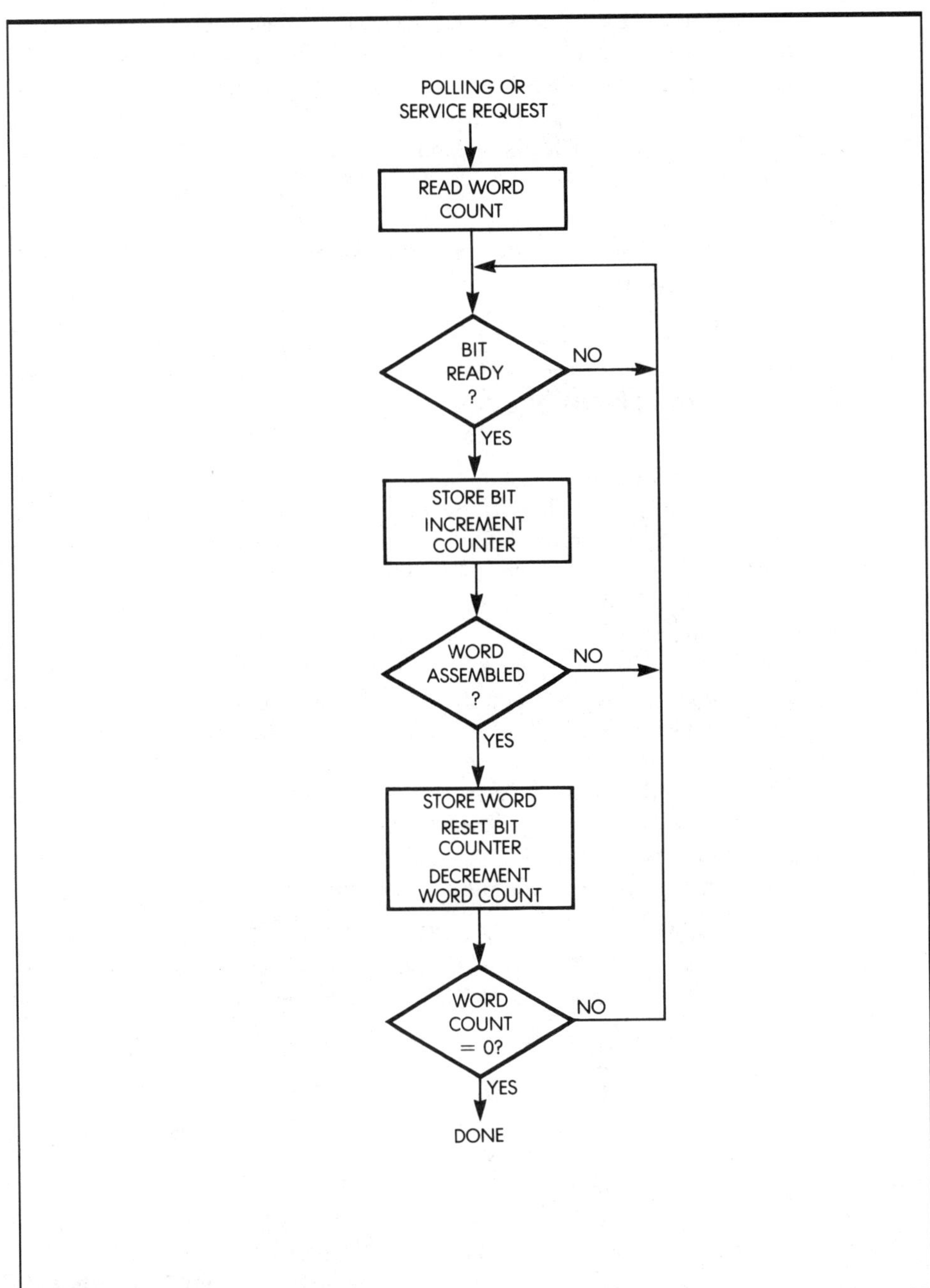

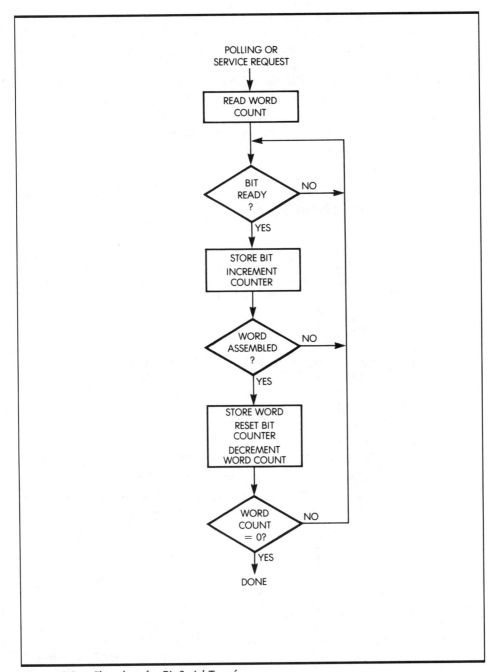

Figure 6.6: Flowchart for Bit Serial Transfer

I have designed this program for efficiency. It uses new techniques that I will explain later in this chapter (see Figure 6.7). The conventions are the following: The index register X is assumed to contain a count of the number of bytes to be transferred. The memory location WORD is used to assemble eight consecutive bits coming in. The address INPUT refers to an input register. Bit position 7 of this register is assumed to be a status flag or a clock bit. (When it is 0, the data is invalid; when it is 1, the data is valid.) Assume that the data itself appears in bit position 0 of this same address. (In many instances, the status information appears on a different register than the data register. Since this is in the same address, it should be a simple task, then, to modify this program accordingly.) In addition, assume that the first bit of data to be received by this program is guaranteed to be a one. This 1 indicates that the real data follows. However, if this is not the case, as you will later see, there is an obvious modification to correct this problem.

The program corresponds to the flowchart in Figure 6.6. The first few lines of the program implement a waiting loop, which tests whether a bit

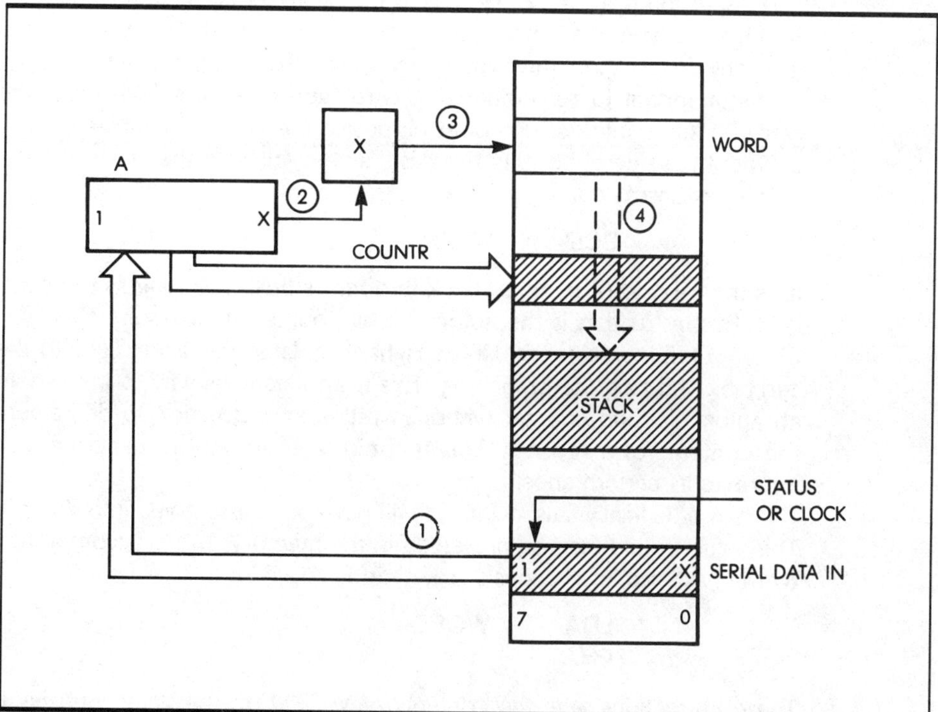

Figure 6.7: Registers for Serial-to-Parallel

is ready. To determine whether a bit is ready, you first read the input register, then test the negative bit (N). As long as this bit is 0, the instruction BPL succeeds, and the program branches back to the loop. Whenever the status (or clock) bit becomes true (1), then BPL fails and the next instruction is executed. This initial sequence of instructions corresponds to arrow 1 in Figure 6.7.

At this point, A contains a one in bit position 7, and the actual data bit is in bit position 0. The first data bit to arrive will be a one. However, the following bits may be either 0 or 1. To preserve the data bit that has been collected in position 0, the instruction

```
LSR     A
```

shifts the contents of A to the right by one position. This causes the rightmost bit of A, the data bit, to fall into the carry bit. You now preserve this data bit into WORD (this process is illustrated by arrows 2 and 3 in Figure 6.7) with the instruction:

```
ROL     WORD
```

This instruction reads the carry bit into the rightmost bit position of WORD. At the same time, the leftmost bit of WORD falls into the carry bit. (If you have any doubts about the rotation operation, refer to Chapter 4.)

It is important to remember that a rotation operation both saves the carry bit (here, into the rightmost bit position) and reconditions the carry bit with the value of bit 7. In this case, a zero falls into the carry.

The next instruction

```
BCC     LOOP
```

tests the carry and branches back to address LOOP, as long as the carry is 0. This instruction is the automatic bit counter. As a result of the first ROL, WORD contains 00000001. Eight shifts later, the 1 will fall into the carry bit and stop the branching. This is an ingenious way to implement an automatic loop counter without wasting an instruction to decrement the contents of a register. This technique shortens the program and improves its performance.

When BCC finally fails, eight bits will have been assembled into WORD. This value should then be preserved in the memory. This is accomplished by the next two instructions (arrow 4 in Figure 6.7):

```
LDA     WORD
PHA
```

These instructions save the contents of WORD on the stack. But this is possible only if there is enough room in the stack. Provided this condition is met, this is usually the fastest way to preserve a byte in the memory. The stack pointer is updated automatically. If you were not pushing a byte on the stack, you would have to use one more instruction to update a memory pointer.

After the first byte of data has been saved, there is no guarantee that the first data bit to come in will be a one. It could be a zero. You must, therefore, reset the contents of WORD to 00000001, so that you can continue to use the carry bit as a bit counter. You can do this with the next two instructions:

```
LDA     #$01
STA     WORD
```

Finally, you decrement the byte counter, since a byte has been assembled, and test whether you have reached the end of the transfer. This is accomplished by the next two instructions:

```
DEX
BNE     LOOP
```

The above program has been designed for speed, so that you can capture a fast input stream of data bits. Once the program terminates, it is naturally advisable to immediately read from the stack the bytes that have been saved there, and transfer them into another part of the memory where they may be processed. I performed such a block transfer in Chapter 5.

This program is more complex than the previous ones. Let's look at it again in more detail, and examine some possible trade-offs (see Figure 6.6).

Referring to the bit serial transfer program, you see that from time to time a bit of data comes into bit position 0 of INPUT. For example, there might be three ones in succession. You must, therefore, *differentiate between the successive bits* coming in. This is the function of the clock signal.

The *clock* (or status) signal tells you when the input bit is valid. Therefore, before you read a bit, you must test the status bit. If the status is 0, you must wait. If it is 1, the data bit is good. I assume here that the status signal is connected to bit 7 of register INPUT.

Once you have captured a data bit, you want to preserve it in a safe location. Then you want to shift it left, so that you can get the next bit.

Unfortunately, in this program the accumulator is used to read and test both data and status. If you were to accumulate data in the A accumulator, bit position 7 would be erased by the status bit.

In this example, the first bit to come in is assumed to be a special signal, guaranteed to be a one. However, in general, it could also be a zero. You could modify the program to handle data as the first bit. Note that you have saved the assembled byte in the stack; however, you could have saved it in some other memory area.

THE HARDWARE ALTERNATIVE

As usual for most standard input/output algorithms, you can implement the serial-to-parallel conversion through hardware. The hardware chip to do this, called a UART, automatically accumulates the bits. If you want to reduce the component count, you should use this program or a variation of it.

BASIC INPUT/OUTPUT SUMMARY

So far, you have learned how to perform elementary input/output operations and how to manage a stream of parallel data or serial bits. You are now ready to communicate with real input/output devices.

COMMUNICATING WITH INPUT/OUTPUT DEVICES

To exchange data with input/output devices, you must first ascertain whether data is available, and if so, if you want to read it; or you must ascertain whether the device is ready to accept data, and if so, if you want to send it. You can use two procedures to do this: handshaking and interrupts.

HANDSHAKING

Handshaking is generally used as a communication tool between two asynchronous devices—two devices that are not synchronized. For example, if you want to send a byte to a parallel printer, you must first make sure that the input buffer of the printer is available. You must, therefore, ask the printer, "Are you ready?" The printer will respond either yes or no. If it is not ready, you must wait. If it is ready, you can send the data (see Figure 6.8).

Conversely, before reading data from an input device, you must verify whether the data is valid. You ask, "Is data valid?" The device responds

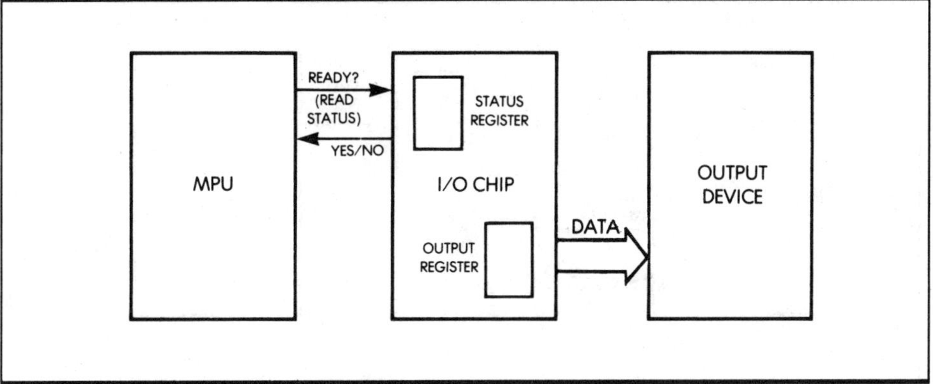

Figure 6.8: Handshaking (Output)

either yes or no, which is indicated either by status bits or by some other means (see Figure 6.9).

As an analogy, if you wish to exchange information with someone who is doing something else at the time, you need to ascertain that that person is ready to communicate with you. The usual rule of courtesy is to shake hands; data exchange may then follow. This is also the procedure normally used in communicating with input/output devices. Let's examine a simple example.

SENDING A CHARACTER TO THE PRINTER

In this example, the character you wish to print is assumed to be in memory location CHAR. Here is the program you can use to print it:

```
WAIT    LDA     STATUS
        BPL     WAIT     WAIT TIL READY
        LDA     CHAR     GET CHARACTER
        STA     PRINTD   PRINT IT
        BRA     WAIT     GO FOR NEXT
```

This program is straightforward and uses the handshaking procedure described previously. The data paths appear in Figure 6.10.

The character (called DATA) is located at memory location CHAR. First, the status of the printer is checked. Whenever bit 7 of the status register becomes 1, it indicates that the printer is ready for output—its output buffer is available. At this point, the character is loaded into the accumulator and then output to the printer via the accumulator. As long as the status bit remains 0, the program will remain in a loop, called WAIT.

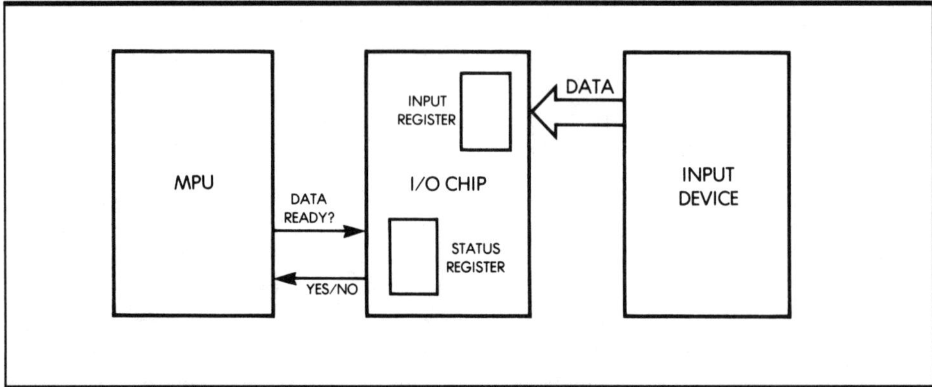

Figure 6.9: Handshaking (Input)

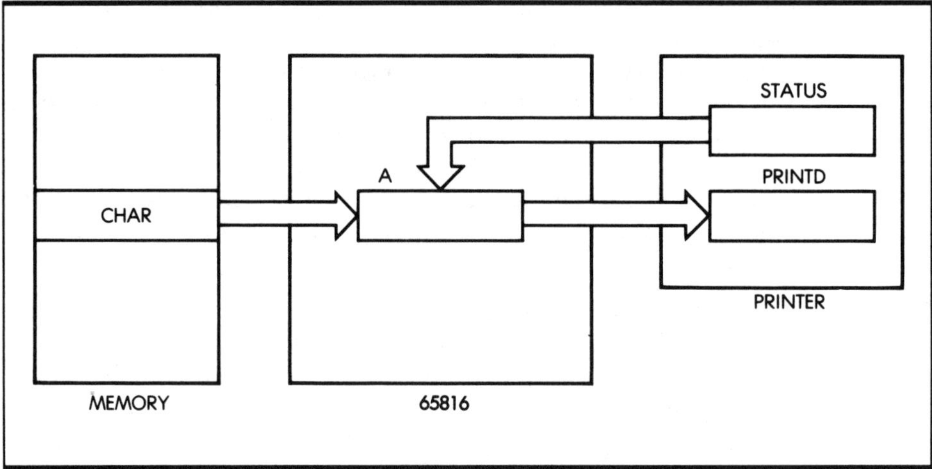

Figure 6.10: Data Paths for the Printer

Let's now complicate the output procedure by requiring a code conversion and by outputting to several devices at a time.

OUTPUT TO A 7-SEGMENT LED

You can use a traditional 7-segment light-emitting diode (LED) to display the digits 0 through 9, or even 0 through F hexadecimal by lighting combinations of its seven segments. Figure 6.11 shows a 7-segment LED. Figure 6.12 shows the characters generated with this LED. The segments of the LED are labeled A through G in both figures.

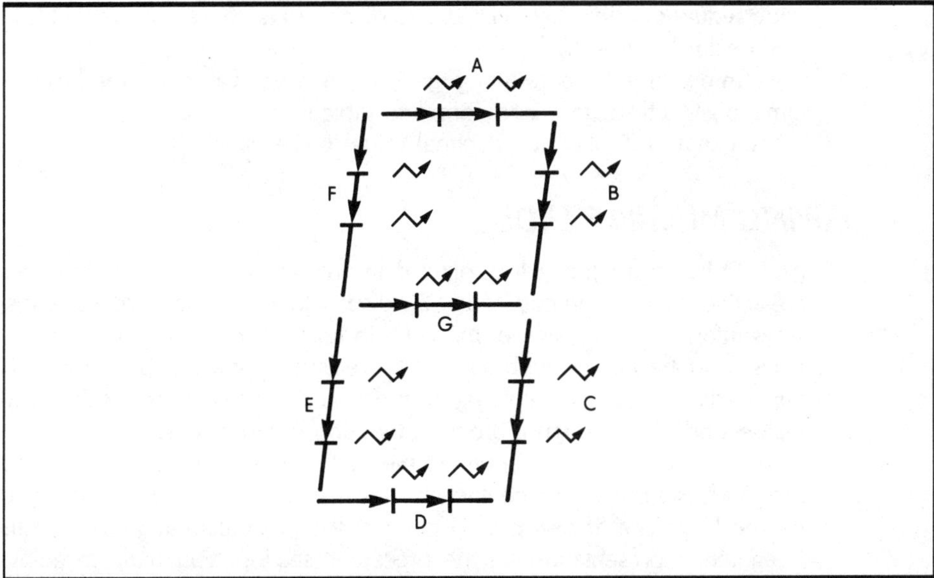

Figure 6.11: 7-Segment LED

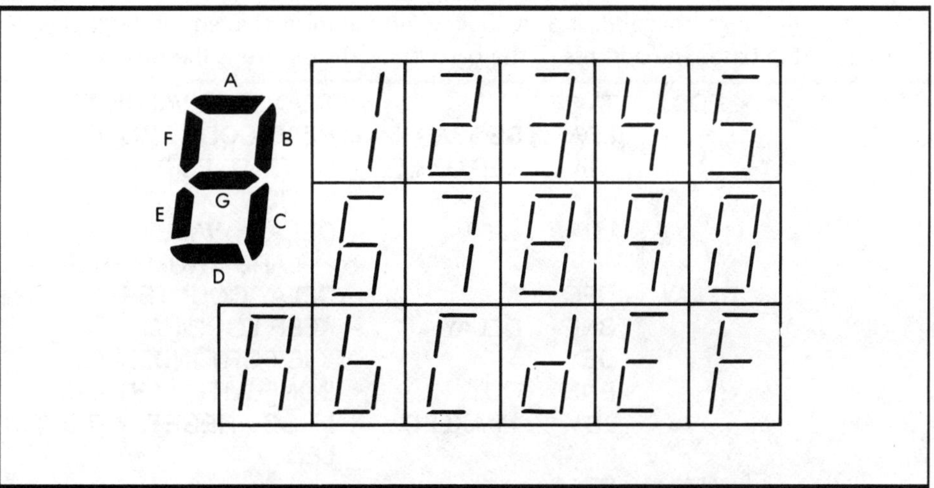

Figure 6.12: Hexadecimal Characters Generated with a 7-Segment LED

For example, you can display 0 by lighting the segments ABCDEF. Now assume that bit 0 of an output port is connected to segment A, that 1 is connected to segment B, and so on, and that bit 7 is not used. The binary code required to light up FEDCBA (to display 0) is, therefore, 0111111. In hexadecimal, this is 3F.

As an exercise, try computing the 7-segment equivalent for the hexadecimal digits 0 through F, and complete Table 6.1.

You can also display hexadecimal values on *several* LEDs.

DRIVING MULTIPLE LEDS

An LED has no memory. It displays data only as long as its segment lines are active. To keep the cost of an LED display low, the microprocessor displays information on *each of the LEDs* in turn. The rotation between the LEDs must be fast enough so that there is no apparent blinking. This implies that the time spent going from one LED to the next is less than 100 milliseconds. Let's design a program that accomplishes this.

You can use register Y to point to the LED on which you want to display a digit. A is assumed to contain the hexadecimal value to be displayed on the LED. The first step is to convert the hexadecimal value into its 7-segment representation. In the preceding section, you built an equivalence table. Since you are accessing the table, you can use the indexed addressing mode, where the displacement index is provided by the hexadecimal value. This means that you can obtain the 7-segment code for the hexadecimal digit 3 by looking up the third element of the table after the base. The address of the base is SEGBAS. Here is the program:

```
LEDS    TAX                  TRANSFER VALUE TO X
        LDA    SEGBAS,X      READ CODE FROM TABLE
        STA    SEGADR,Y      OUTPUT FOR SET DURA-
                               TION
        LDA    #$50          DELAY VALUE = ANY
                               LARGE NUMBER
DELAY   DEC    A             DELAY COUNTER
        BNE    DELAY         KEEP LOOPING
        DEY                  Y IS PORT INDEX
        BNE    OUT           DONE WITH LAST LED?
        LDY    #MAXLED       IF SO, RESET Y TO TOP
                             LED
OUT     RTS
```

The program assumes that the SEGADR points to the base address of the LEDs, and that Y is added to SEGADR to point to the next LED to be illuminated. The A accumulator contains the digits to be displayed.

This program first looks up the 7-segment code corresponding to the hexadecimal value contained in the accumulator. The X register is used as

Hex	LED code	Hex	LED code	Hex	LED code	Hex	LED code
0	3F	4		8		C	
1		5		9		D	
2		6		A		E	
3		7		B		F	

Table 6.1: LED Codes for Hexadecimal Digits

an index into SEGBAS. The code for the hexadecimal digit is added to the base address of the table:

```
LEDS    TAX
        LDA     SEGBAS,X
```

The next instruction outputs the 7-segment code to the address specified, by using Y as a displacement for the segment address:

```
        STA     SEGADR,Y
```

A delay loop is then implemented so that the code from the table is displayed for an appropriate duration. Here I have arbitrarily chosen a constant, 50 hexadecimal. The next three instructions implement the delay loop:

```
        LDA     #$50
DELAY   DEC     A
        BNE     DELAY
```

Once the delay has been implemented, you simply decrement the LED pointer displacement and make sure you loop around to the highest LED address, if the smallest LED address has been reached:

```
        DEY
        BNE     OUT
        LDY     #MAXLED
OUT     RTS
```

This program is assumed to be written as a subroutine; the last instruction is, therefore, RTS (return from subroutine).

You have now learned to solve common input/output problems. Now consider the case of a common peripheral: the Teletype.

TELETYPE INPUT/OUTPUT

The *Teletype* is a serial device that sends and receives bytes of information in a serial format. (The ASCII table appears in Appendix B.) In addition, every character is preceded by a *start* bit, and terminated by two *stop* bits. In the 20-milliamp current loop interface, which is most frequently used, the state of the line is normally a one. This is used to indicate to the processor that the line has not been cut. A start is a 1-to-0 transition. This indicates to the receiving device that data bits follow. The standard Teletype is a 10-cps (characters per second) device. I have just established that each character requires 11 bits. This means the Teletype will transmit 110 bits per second—or that it is a 110-baud device. I will now design a program to send bits to the Teletype serially at the correct speed.

One hundred ten bits per second implies that bits are separated by 9.09 ms (milliseconds). This will have to be the duration in a program of the delay loop to be implemented between transmission or reception of successive bits. Figure 6.13 shows the format of a Teletype Word. Figure 6.14 displays the flowchart for bit input. Here is the program:

```
TTYIN   STZ   CHAR     CLEAR INPUT CHAR
START   LDA   STATUS
        BPL   START    DATA READY?
        JSR   DELAY1   CENTER OF PULSE
        LDA   TTYBIT   START BIT
        STA   TTYBIT   ECHO IT
        JSR   DELAY9   NEXT PULSE 9MS
        LDX   #$08     BIT COUNT
NEXT    LDA   TTYBIT   READ DATA BIT
        STA   TTYBIT   ECHO IT
        LSR   A        SAVE IT IN CARRY
        ROR   CHAR     PRESERVE IT IN CHAR
        JSR   DELAY9   EXT PULSE 9MS
        DEX            DECREMENT BIT COUNT
        BNE   NEXT
        LDA   TTYBIT   READ STOP BIT
        STA   TTYBIT   ECHO IT
        JSR   DELAY9   SKIP SECOND STOP
        RTS
```

Let's examine this program in detail.

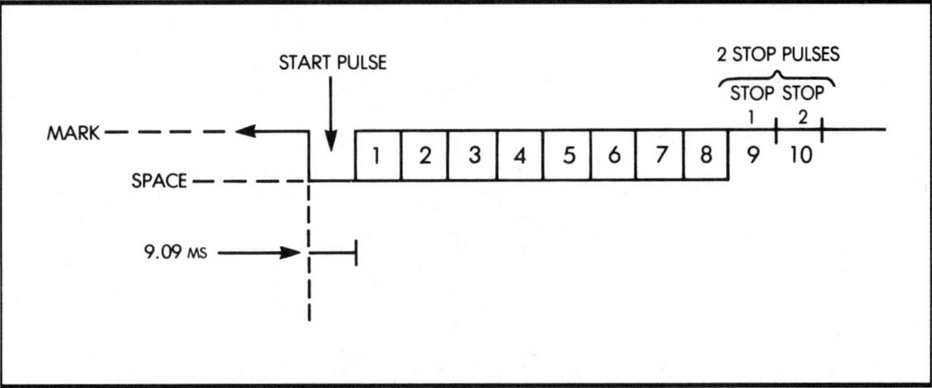

Figure 6.13: Format of a Teletype Word

First, you clear a memory location, then test the status of the Teletype to determine if a character is available:

```
TTYIN   STZ     CHAR
START   LDA     STATUS
        BPL     START
```

Then, you implement a 4.5 ms delay to sense the start bit in the middle of the pulse:

```
        JSR     DELAY1
```

DELAY1 is the delay subroutine that implements the required delay. The first bit to come is the start bit. It should be echoed to the Teletype, but ignored by the rest of the program. This is done by the next few instructions:

```
        LDA     TTYBIT
        STA     TTYBIT
```

You must now wait for the first data bit. The necessary delay is equal to 9.09 ms and is implemented by a subroutine:

```
        JSR     DELAY9
```

The X index register is used as a counter and loaded with the value 8, because eight data bits are captured:

```
        LDX     #$08
```

Next, each data bit is read into A, in turn, then echoed. The data bit is assumed to arrive in bit position 0 of A. The data bit is then preserved in

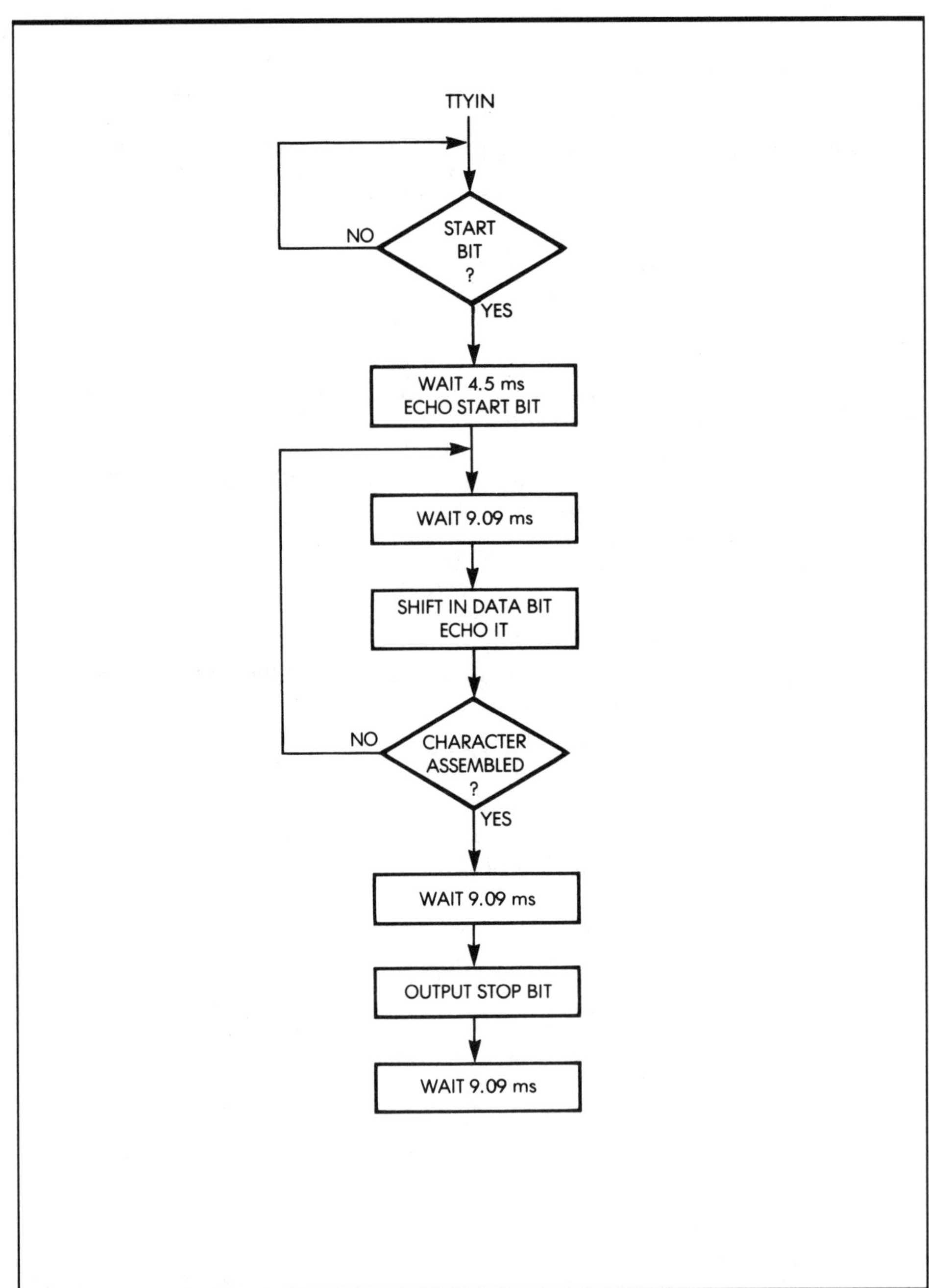

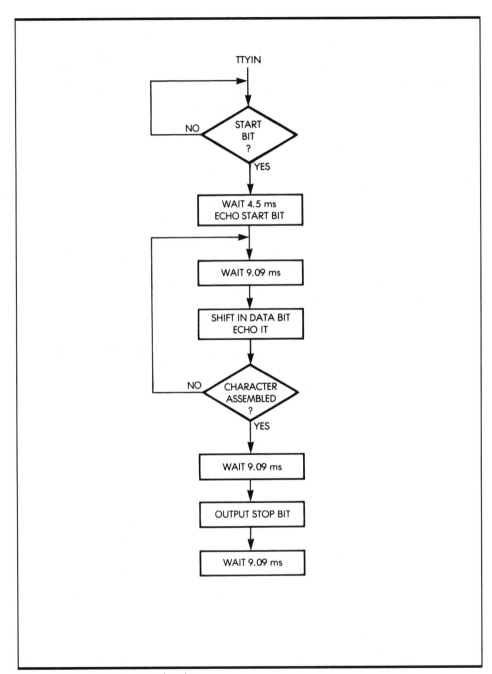

Figure 6.14: TTY Input with Echo

CHAR, where it is shifted in. The transfer from A to CHAR is performed through the carry bit:

```
NEXT    LDA     TTYBIT
        STA     TTYBIT
        LSR     A
        ROR     CHAR
```

Figure 6.15 illustrates this sequence.

Next, the usual 9 ms delay is implemented, the bit counter is decremented, and the loop is entered again—as long as the eight bits have not been captured:

```
        JSR     DELAY9
        DEX
        BNE     NEXT
```

Finally, the stop bit is captured and echoed. It is usually sufficient to send a single stop bit; however, two could be sent back by using two more instructions:

```
        LDA     TTYBIT
        STA     TTYBIT
        JSR     DELAY9
        RTS
```

Let's examine the program. The logic is quite simple: whenever a bit is read from the Teletype (at address TTYBIT), it is echoed back to the Teletype. This is a standard feature of the Teletype. Whenever you press a key,

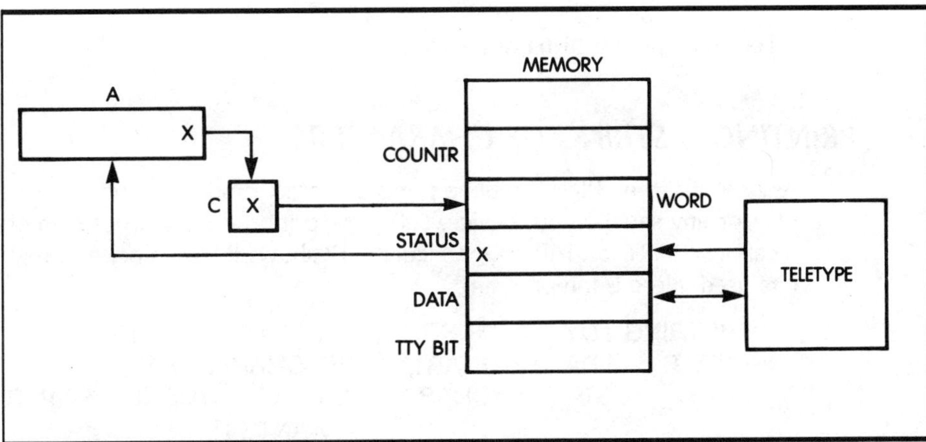

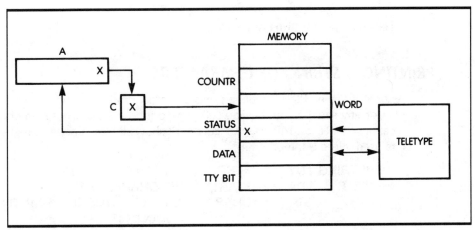

Figure 6.15: Teletype Input

the information is transmitted to the processor and then back to the printing mechanism of the Teletype. This verifies that the transmission lines are working and that the processor is operating when a character is, indeed, printed correctly on the paper.

Using the above program, let's now write a PRINTC program that prints the contents of memory location CHAR on the Teletype. Figure 6.16 shows the relevant flowcharts. Here is the program:

```
PRINTC  LDX   #11      COUNTER = 11 BITS
        CLC            CLEAR CARRY = START BIT
        LDA   CHAR     GET CHARACTER
        ROL   A        CARRY BIT INTO A
NEXT    STA   TTYBIT   OUTPUT BIT
        JSR   DELAY9
        ROR   A        NEXT BIT
        SEP   #$01     SET CARRY BIT
        DEX            BIT COUNT
        BNE   NEXT
        RTS
```

The X register is used as a bit counter for the transmission. The contents of bit 0 of register A are sent to the Teletype line (TTYBIT). Note how the carry is used to provide a ninth bit (the start bit). Also, note that the carry is cleared by:

```
        CLC
```

At the end of the program, the carry is set to 1 to generate a stop bit:

```
        SEP   #$01
```

Let's now print a string of characters.

PRINTING A STRING OF CHARACTERS

Assume that the PRINTC routine prints a character on the printer, the display, or any serial output device. Let's now print the contents of memory locations START to START + N. Figure 6.17 shows the memory and registers used. Here is the program:

```
PSTRING LDY   #NBR     LENGTH OF STRING
NEXT    LDA   START,Y  GET CHARACTER
        STA   CHAR     PUT IT WHERE PRINTC
                          WANTS IT
        JSR   PRINTC   PRINT IT
```

```
DEY
BNE     NEXT     DO IT AGAIN
RTS
```

PERIPHERAL SUMMARY

I have now described the basic programming techniques used to communicate with typical input/output devices. In addition to the data transfer, you need to condition one or more control registers within each I/O device, so as to condition correctly the transfer speeds, the interrupt mechanism, and various other options. Consult the user's manual to

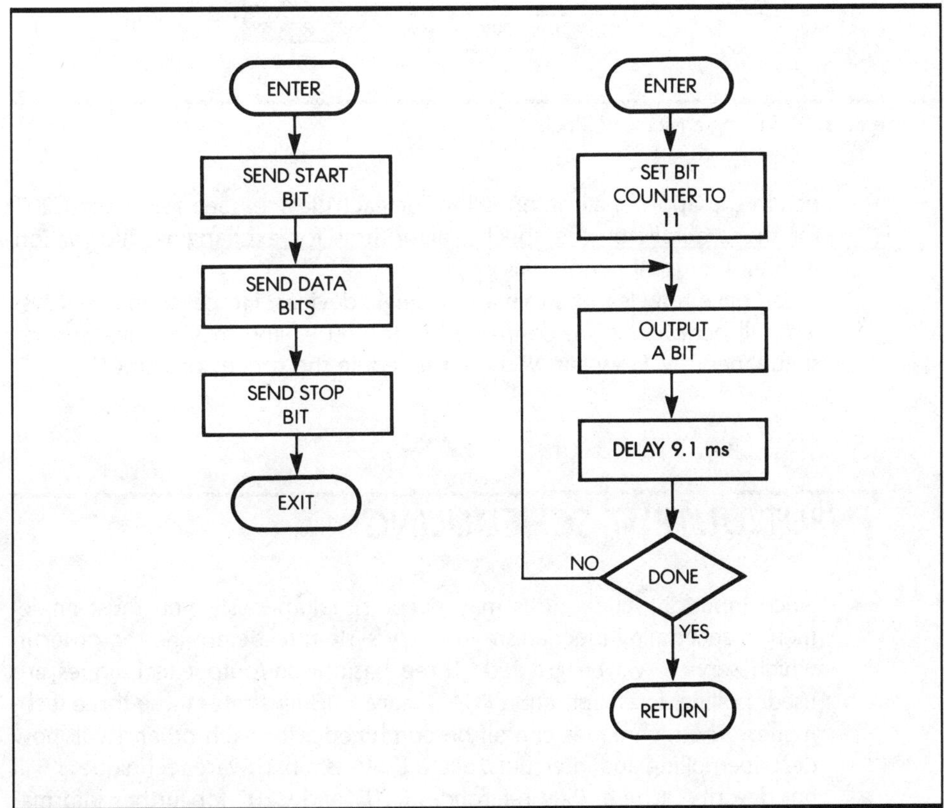

Figure 6.16: Teletype Output

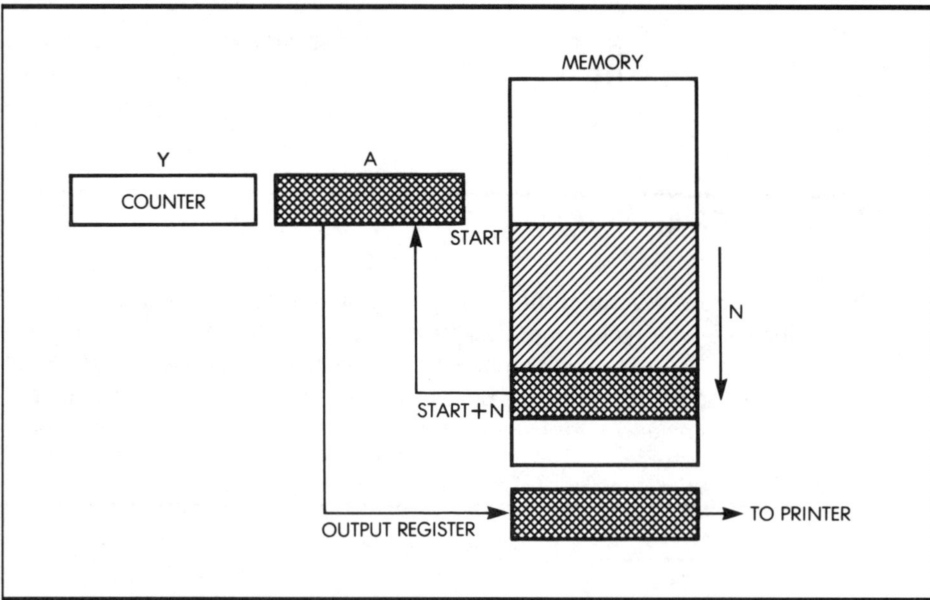

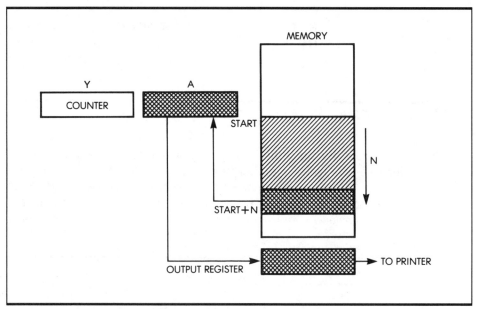

Figure 6.17: Printing a Memory Block

obtain the appropriate information for each device. (See reference C207 for more details on the specific algorithms for exchanging information with all the usual peripherals.)

You have now learned to manage single devices. However, in a real system, all peripherals are connected to the buses and may request service simultaneously. How can you then schedule the processor's time?

INPUT/OUTPUT SCHEDULING

Since input/output requests may occur simultaneously, you must implement a scheduling mechanism in every system to determine the order in which service will be granted. Three basic input/output techniques are used: polling, interrupt, and DMA. Figure 6.18 illustrates these three techniques. The techniques can all be combined with each other. I will now describe polling and interrupts. Since DMA is a hardware technique, I will not describe it here. (See references C201 and C207 for further information on DMA.)

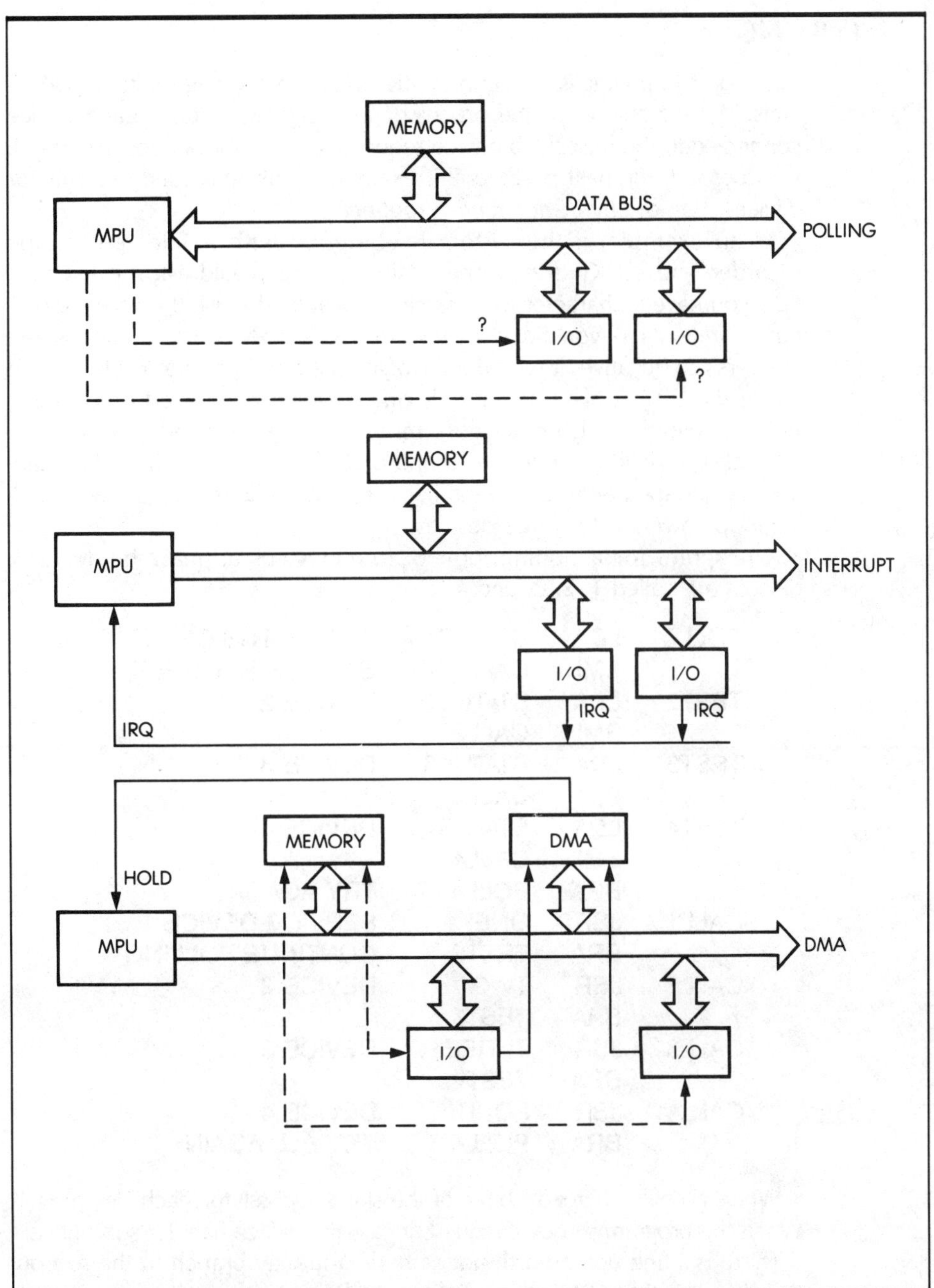

Figure 6.18: Three Methods of I/O Control

POLLING

Conceptually, polling is the simplest method for managing multiple peripherals. With this strategy, the processor interrogates, in turn, each device connected to the buses. If a device requests service, the service is granted. If it does not, the next peripheral is examined. Polling is used not only for devices, but for *any device service routine.*

As an example, if the system is equipped with a Teletype, a tape recorder, and a CRT display, the polling routine would ask the Teletype, "Do you have a character to transmit?" It would also ask the Teletype *output routine,* "Do you have a character to send?" Then, assuming the answers are negative, it would interrogate the tape-recorder routines, and finally, the CRT display. Even if only one device is connected to a system, polling would be used to determine whether it needs service. As examples of polling, Figures 6.19 and 6.20 show the flowcharts for reading a papertape reader and printing on a printer. Figure 6.21 shows a polling loop flowchart for three devices.

A program for a polling loop of four devices appears below. The devices are called 1, 2, 3, and 4.

```
POLL4   LDA   STATUS1   GET STATUS OF DEVICE 1
        BMI   CALL1     SERVICE REQUEST
TEST2   LDA   STATUS2   DEVICE 2
        BMI   CALL2
TEST3   LDA   STATUS3   DEVICE 3
        BMI   CALL3
TEST4   LDA   STATUS4   DEVICE 4
        BMI   CALL4
        BRA   POLL4     TRY AGAIN
CALL1   JSR   ONE       SERVICE DEVICE 1
        BRA   TEST2     CONTINUE POLLING
CALL2   JSR   TWO       DEVICE 2
        BRA   TEST3
CALL3   JSR   THREE     DEVICE 3
        BRA   TEST4
CALL4   JSR   FOUR      DEVICE 4
        BRA   POLL4     TRY ALL AGAIN
```

When a device is ready, bit 7 of the status register for each device is 1. When the program senses a request, it calls the device handler subroutine.

There is a fine point worth noting here. You may branch to the subroutine directly with a BMI, thus eliminating the second part of the program, which carries out the JSR instruction. Use of the branch requires the

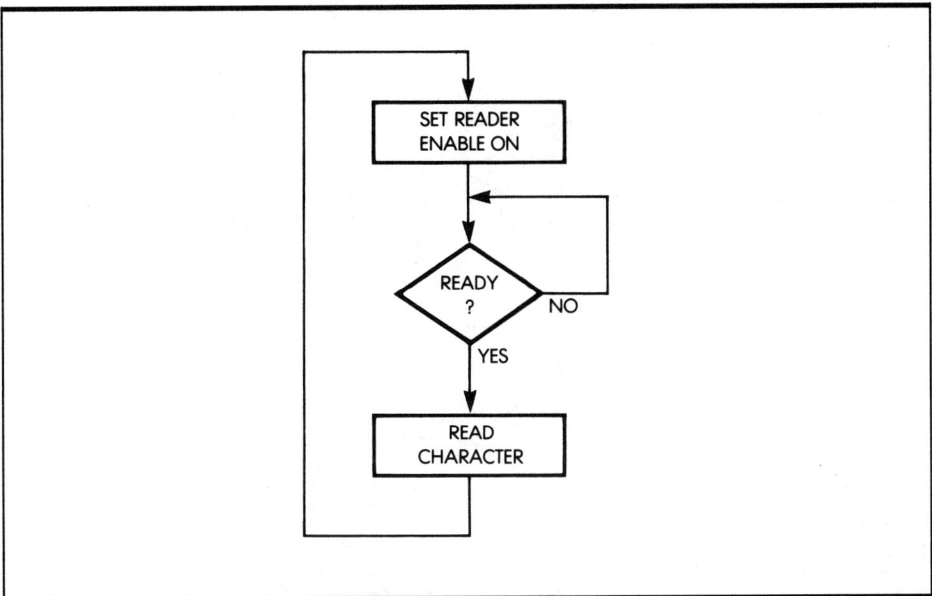

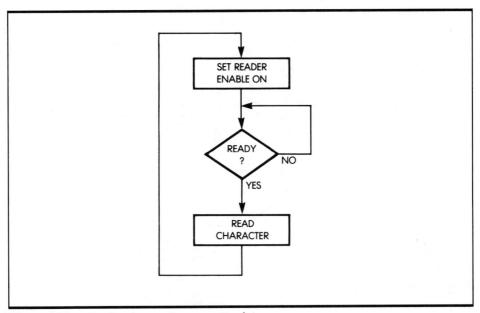

Figure 6.19: Reading from a Papertape Reader

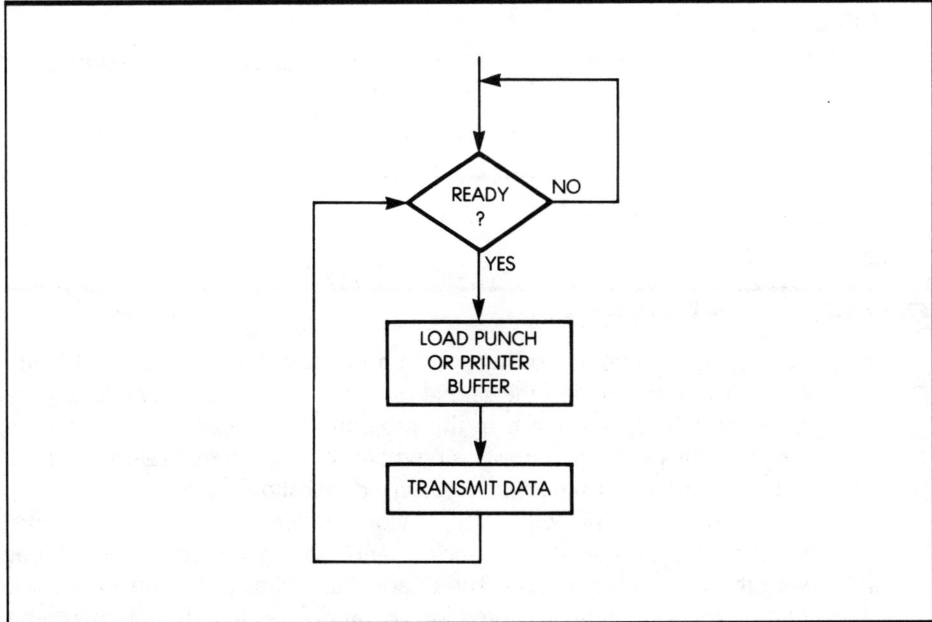

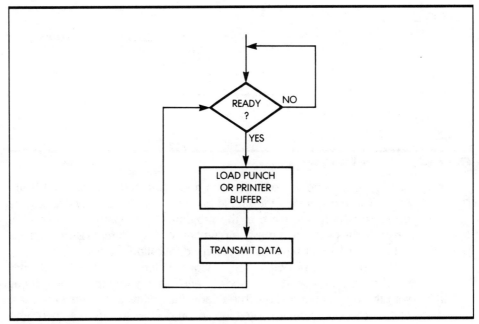

Figure 6.20: Printing on a Punch or Printer

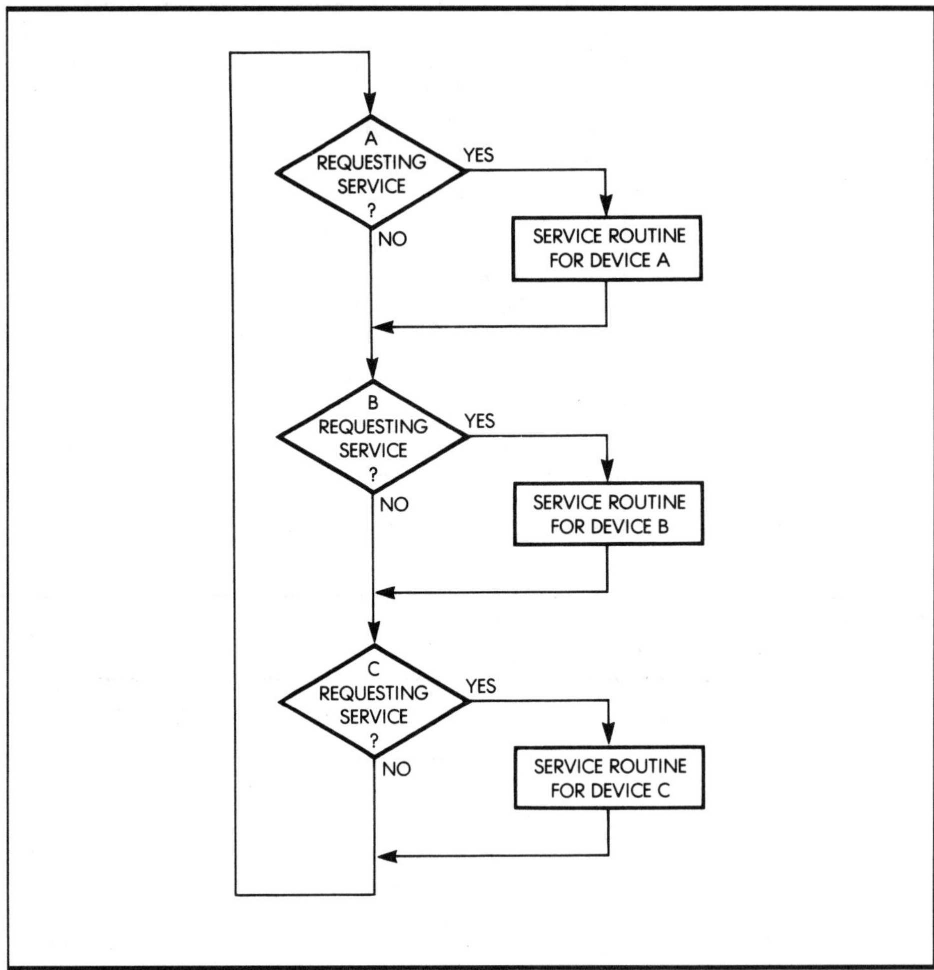

Figure 6.21: Polling Loop Flowchart

handler subroutine to "know" which address to return to when it is finished. This means that if the simple branch is used, the handler could be called from only one place in the program. If the handler is used elsewhere in the program, it must be rewritten with a different return address. Subroutines help eliminate unnecessary duplication of code.

The advantages of polling are obvious. Polling is simple. It does not require hardware assistance, and it keeps all input/output synchronous with the program operation. The disadvantages are just as obvious. Most of the processor's time is wasted looking at devices that do not need service. In addition, by wasting so much time, the processor might then be late in giving service to a device.

Another mechanism is, therefore, desirable to guarantee that the processor's time is used for performing useful computations, rather than needlessly polling devices all the time. However, polling *is* used extensively whenever a microprocessor has nothing better to do, as it keeps the overall organization simple. Let's examine an essential alternative to polling: interrupts.

INTERRUPTS

Figure 6.18 illustrates the concept of interrupts. A special hardware line, the interrupt line, is connected to a specialized pin of the microprocessor. You may connect multiple input/output devices to this interrupt line. Then, when any one of them needs service, it sends a level or pulse on this line. An interrupt signal is the service request from an input/output device to the processor. Let's examine the response of the processor to this interrupt.

In all cases, when an interrupt occurs, the processor completes the instruction it is currently executing (otherwise, such an interruption would create chaos inside the microprocessor). Next, the microprocessor branches to an interrupt-handling routine, which processes the interrupt. Branching to this subroutine implies that the contents of the program counter must be saved on the stack. *An interrupt must, therefore, cause the automatic preservation of the program counter on the stack.* In addition, the processor status register (P) should also be preserved automatically, as its contents will be altered by any subsequent instruction. Finally, if the interrupt-handling routine should modify any internal registers, these internal registers should also be preserved on the stack (see Figures 6.22 and 6.23).

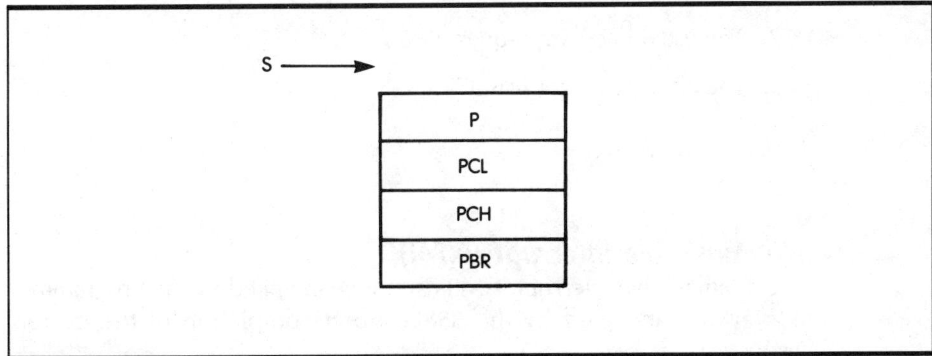

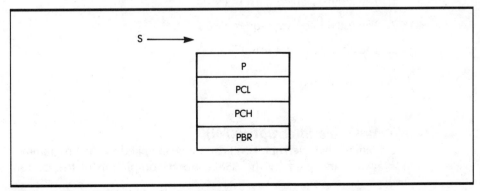

Figure 6.22: 65816 Stack after Interruption

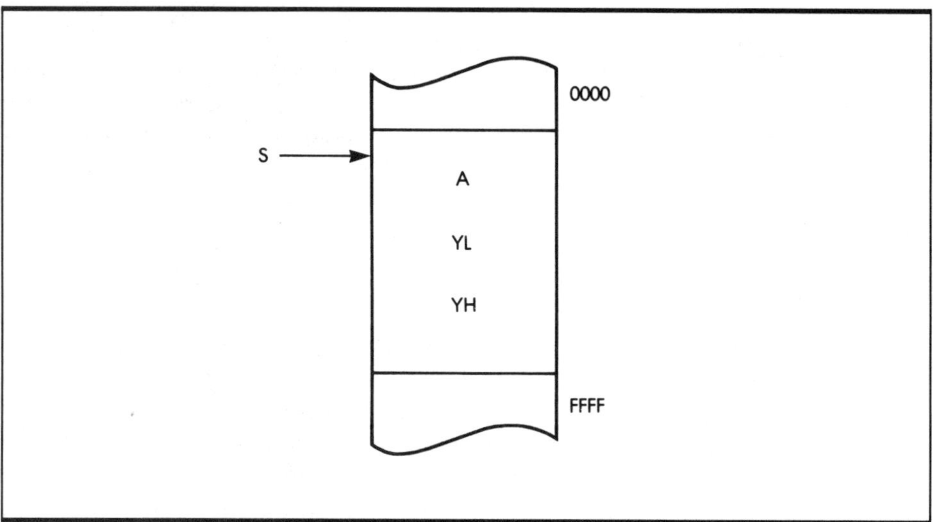

Figure 6.23: Saving Some Working Registers

65816 INTERRUPTS

An *interrupt* is a signal sent to the microprocessor that may request service at any time. This signal is asynchronous to the program. Whenever a program branches to a subroutine, such branching is *synchronous* to program execution—scheduled by the program. An interrupt, however, can occur at any time, and it generally suspends the execution of the current program (without the program knowing it). Because it may happen at any time relative to program execution, it is called *asynchronous.*

Three interruption mechanisms are provided on the 65816:

1. The nonmaskable interrupt (NMI)
2. The usual interrupt request (IRQ)
3. The abort interrupt (ABORT)

Let's examine them.

The Nonmaskable Interrupt (NMI)

The nonmaskable interrupt (NMI) cannot be inhibited by the programmer. It is always accepted by the 65816 upon completion of the current instruction.

The NMI causes the automatic push of the program counter, the program bank register, and the status register onto the stack (S). A new program counter is loaded from the data in memory locations 00FFEA and 00FFEB. The starting address of the NMI handler is stored with the high byte in 00FFEB and the low byte in 00FFEA, as shown in Figure 6.24.

The NMI is used in case of "emergencies," such as a power failure. It does not offer the flexibility of the maskable interrupts. The address of the NMI handler must be placed in location 00FFEB:00FFEA, before an interrupt occurs. The interrupt handler must finish before the next NMI occurs, otherwise the stack may fill the memory.

The Interrupt Request (IRQ)

The interrupt request, a *maskable* interrupt, is the most commonly used interrupt mechanism. The maskable interrupt is ignored or masked when the interrupt disable bit (I) in the status register is set to 1. When the I bit is 0, IRQ interrupts are accepted by the processor.

When an IRQ occurs and the I bit is 1, the PC, PBR, and P registers are pushed onto the stack. The PC of the IRQ handler is fetched from memory

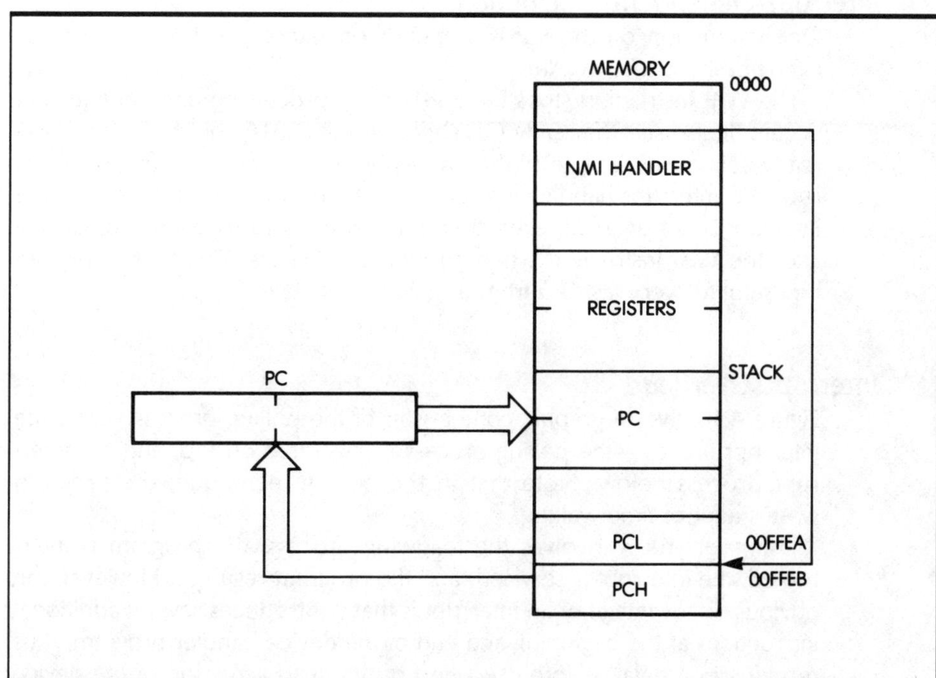

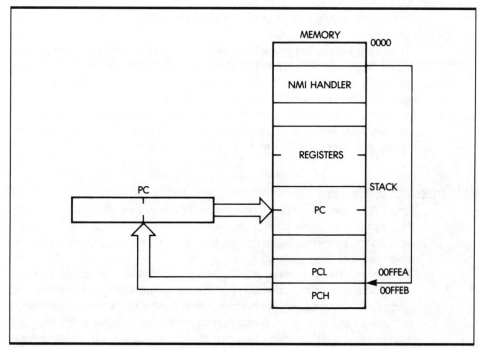

Figure 6.24: Nonmaskable Interrupt Sequence

locations 00FFEF:00FFEE. This process is the same for the NMI. Usually, the program need not handle more than one IRQ at a time. However, the program may clear the I bit and accept more IRQs, if necessary.

The IRQ and NMI handlers are terminated with an RTI instruction, which restores the P, PC, and PBR registers from the stack. The I bit in the status register must be set to 0 after the IRQ handler finishes (just before the RTI instruction), otherwise no more IRQ interrupts will be accepted.

The Abort Interrupt Request (ABORT)

The *abort interrupt request* is similar to the NMI, as it is not maskable. The abort occurs when the abort input pin goes to 0. The instruction being executed will be completed without modifying the internal registers. When the instruction is finished, the PBR, PC, and P registers are stored on the stack and the new PC is fetched from 00FFE8:00FFE9. An abort is used to stop an instruction from executing if the hardware detects a problem accessing memory.

Interrupt-Dependent Instruction

One instruction on the 65816 depends on interrupts. It is the *wait for interrupt* instruction (WAI).

The WAI instruction stops the 65816 from processing until an interrupt occurs. It also sets the ready (RDY) pin on the 65816 chip to 0. This is the ready acknowledge state of the processor. If the disable bit for interrupts is 0, the interrupt handler is executed when an interrupt occurs. If the interrupt is not enabled, execution of the program proceeds immediately after the WAI instruction when an interrupt occurs. This instruction can be useful for very fast I/O from a device.

Interrupt Overhead

Figure 6.18 gives a graphic comparison of the polling process versus the interrupt process—the polling process is illustrated on top, and the interrupt process below. Note that in the polling technique, the program wastes a lot of time waiting.

Using interrupts involves the following process: the program is interrupted, the interrupt is serviced, and the program resumes. However, the obvious disadvantage of an interrupt is that it introduces several additional instructions at the beginning and end of the device handler program, thus resulting in a delay before execution of the first instruction of the device handler. This delay is additional overhead.

Now that I have clarified the operation of the interrupt lines, consider two remaining problems, involving:

- Multiple devices triggering an interrupt at the same time
- An interrupt occurring while another is being serviced

MULTIPLE DEVICES CONNECTED TO A SINGLE INTERRUPT LINE

Whenever an interrupt occurs, the processor branches to a specified address. Before it can do any effective processing, the interrupt handler must determine which device triggered the interrupt. You can use a polling method to find the device that interrupted the processor. The microprocessor asks each device, in turn, "Did you trigger the interrupt?" If the answer is negative, it interrogates the next one. The following program illustrates this process:

```
POLINT  LDA   STATUS1    READ STATUS
        BMI   ONE        HANDLE DEVICE IF IT INTER-
                         RUPTED
        LDA   STATUS2
        BMI   TWO
        . . .
```

SIMULTANEOUS INTERRUPTS

Another problem is that a new interrupt may be triggered during the execution of an interrupt-handling routine. Let's examine what happens when this occurs, and see how the stack can solve this problem. I previously indicated that this was another essential role of the stack; now I will demonstrate its use. Figure 6.25 illustrates multiple interrupts.

The contents of the stack are shown at the bottom of the illustration. (Time elapses from left to right in the illustration.) Looking at time T0 on the left, program P is in execution. Moving to the right, at time T1 interrupt I1 occurs. Assume that the interrupt mask was enabled, authorizing I1. Program P is suspended, as shown at the bottom of the illustration. The stack contains, at the least, the program counter and the status register of program P, plus any optional registers that might be saved by the interrupt handler or I1 itself.

At time T1, interrupt I1 starts executing until time T2. At time T2, interrupt I2 occurs. Assume that interrupt I2 has a higher priority than

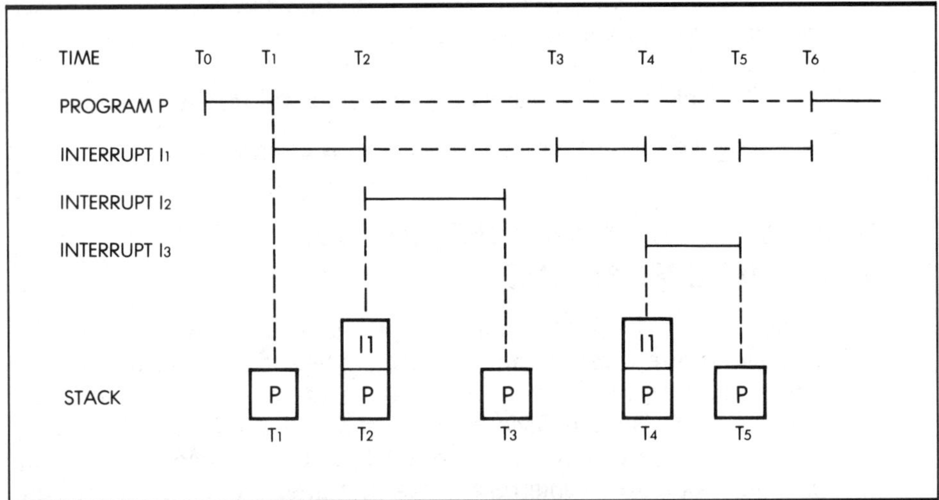

Figure 6.25: Stack Contents during Multiple Interrupts

interrupt I1. If it had a lower priority, it would be ignored until I1 had been completed. At time T2, the registers for I1 are stacked (as shown at the bottom of the illustration). Again, the contents of the program counter and the status register are pushed onto the stack. In addition, the routine for I2 might decide to save additional registers. At time T3, I2 executes to completion.

When I2 terminates, the contents of the stack are automatically pulled back into the 65816 (as illustrated at the bottom of Figure 6.25). Thus, I1 resumes execution automatically. Unfortunately, at time T4 an interrupt I3 of higher priority occurs again. You can see at the bottom of the illustration that the registers for I1 are again pushed onto the stack. Interrupt I3 executes from T4 to T5 and terminates at T5. At that time, the contents of the stack are pulled into the 65816, and interrupt I1 resumes execution. This time it runs to completion and terminates at T6. At T6, the remaining registers saved in the stack are pulled into the 65816, and program P can resume execution. You can verify that the stack is empty at this point. In fact, the number of dashed lines indicating program suspension *also* indicate the number of levels in the stack.

In practice, however, microprocessor systems are normally connected to a small number of devices using interrupts. It is, therefore, unlikely that a high number of simultaneous interrupts will occur in such a system.

I have now shown you how to solve all the problems usually associated with interrupts. Their use is simple, and even novice programmers can use them to advantage.

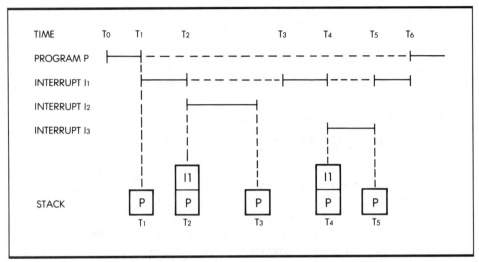

SUMMARY

In this chapter, I have presented the techniques used to communicate with the outside world, ranging from elementary input/output routines to more complex programs for communication with actual peripherals. You have learned how to develop all the usual programs and have even examined the efficiency of benchmark programs in the case of a parallel transfer and a parallel-to-serial conversion. Finally, you have learned to schedule the operation of multiple peripherals using polling and interrupts.

Naturally, you may connect many exotic input/output devices to a system. With the array of techniques presented so far, and with an understanding of the peripherals involved, you should now be able to solve most common problems.

In the next chapter, I will examine the actual characteristics of the input/output interface chips usually connected to a 65816. I will then discuss the basic data structures available for use.

EXERCISES

6-1: *What are the maximum and the minimum delays that can be implemented with the simple three-instruction delay loop program?*

6-2: *Modify the three-instruction delay loop program to obtain a delay of about 100 ms.*

6-3: *Write a program to implement a 100 ms delay (typical of a Teletype).*

6-4: *Assume that the number of bytes to be transferred to memory is greater than 256. Determine the impact on the maximum data transfer rate.*

6-5: *Compute the maximum speed at which the serial bit transfer program can read serial bits. Look up in Appendix E the number of cycles required by every instruction in the table, then compute the time that will elapse during execution of this program. To compute the length of time used by a loop, simply multiply the total duration of this loop, expressed in microseconds, by the number of times it will be executed. Also, when computing* *the maximum speed, assume that a data bit will be ready every time the input location is sensed.*

6-6: *Can you explain why bit 7 is used for status and bit 0 for data in the bit serial transfer program? Does it matter?*

6-7: *Modify the bit serial transfer program, assuming that the first bit to come in is valid data (not to be discarded), and that it can be 0 or 1. (Hint: The bit counter should still work correctly if you initialize it with the correct value.)*

6-8: *Modify the bit serial transfer program to save the assembled byte in the memory area starting at BASE.*

6-9: *Modify the bit serial transfer program so that the transfer stops when the S character is detected in the input stream.*

6-10: *Modify the bit serial transfer program, assuming that the data is available in bit position 0 of location INPUT and the status information is available in bit position 0 of address INPUT + 1.*

6-11: *You must usually send a start order to use a printer. Modify the printer program to generate such an order, assuming that you obtain the start command by writing a one in bit position 0 of the STATUS register, which is assumed to be bidirectional.*

6-12: *Modify the printer program to print a string of* n *characters, where* n *is assumed to be less than 255.*

6-13: *Modify the printer program to print a string of characters until it encounters a carriage-return code.*

6-14: *You must usually turn off the segment drivers for an LED before it can display new digits. Modify the LED program by adding the necessary instructions (output 00 as the character code, prior to outputting the character).*

6-15: *What would happen to the LED display if the DELAY label in the LED program were moved up by one line position? Would this change the timing? Would it change the appearance of the display?*

6-16: *Assuming that the LED program is a subroutine, notice that it uses the register X internally and modifies its contents. If the subroutine freely* *uses the memory area designated by SAVEX, can you add instructions at the beginning and end of this program to guarantee that, when the subroutine returns, the contents of the register X will be the same as when the subroutine was entered?*

6-17: *Same exercise as above, but assume that the memory area SAVEX, etc., is not available to the subroutine. (Hint: Remember that there is a built-in mechanism in every computer for preserving information in chronological order.)*

6-18: *Write the delay routine that results in the 9.09 ms delay (DELAY9 subroutine).*

6-19: *Assume that the area available to the stack is limited to 300 locations in a specific program. Also, assume that all the registers must always be saved and that the programmer allows interrupts to be nested—that is, to interrupt each other. What is the maximum number of simultaneous interrupts that can be handled? Will any other factor contribute to reducing further the maximum number of simultaneous interrupts?*

6-20: *A 7-segment LED display can also display digits other than the hex alphabet. Compute the codes for: H, I, J, L, O, P, S, U, Y, g, h, i, j, l, n, o, p, r, t, u, y.*

6-21: *Refer to the flowchart for interrupt management (Figure 6.26) and answer the following questions:*

a. *What is done by hardware? What is done by software?*
b. *What is the use of the mask?*
c. *How many registers should be preserved?*
d. *How is the interrupting device identified?*
e. *What does the RTI instruction do? How does it differ from a subroutine return?*
f. *Suggest a way to handle a stack overflow situation.*
g. *What is the overhead ("lost time") introduced by the interrupt mechanism?*

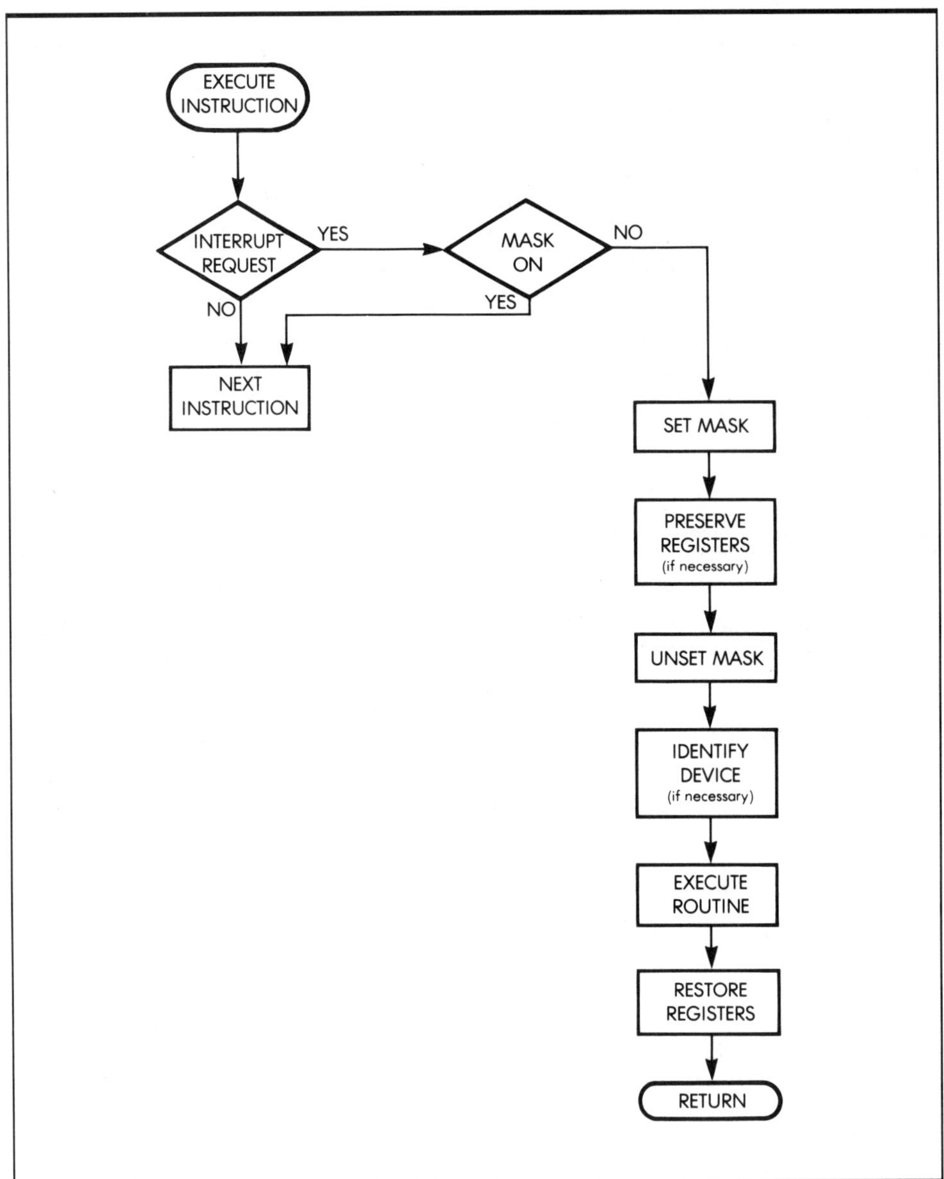

Figure 6.26: Flowchart for Interrupt Management

INPUT/OUTPUT DEVICES

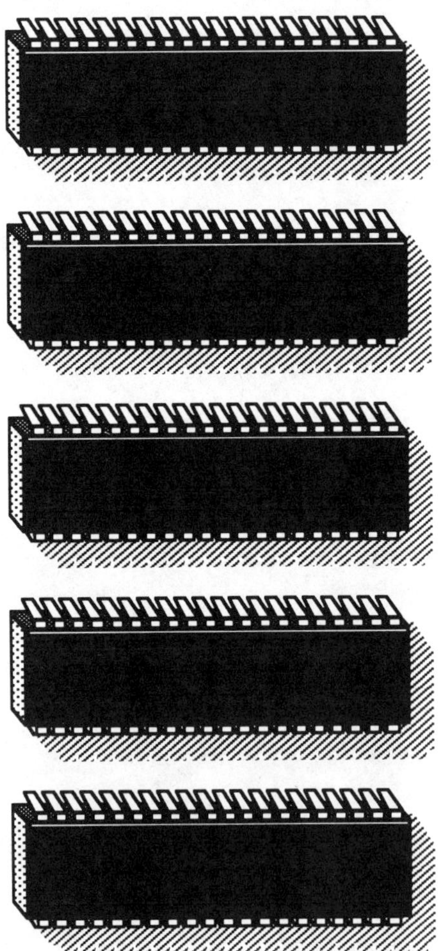

7

WITH THE PROGRESS OF VLSI, more elaborate input/output chips have been developed. As a result, the task of programming a system includes not only programming the microprocessor itself, but also programming the *input/output chips.* In fact, it is often more difficult to remember how to program the various control options of an input/output chip than it is to program the microprocessor itself. This is not because the programming is more difficult, but because each device has its own idiosyncrasies. In this chapter, I will examine the most general input/output device—the programmable input/output chip (the PIO)—and then look at some input/output devices from The Western Design Center.

The 65816 was designed as a 16-bit processor, but it can interface easily with any of the extensive 65xx family of I/O chips developed for 8-bit processors. The 65816 can also interface with most 6800 I/O devices.

THE "STANDARD" PIO

Although there is no "standard" PIO, most manufacturers produce PIOs that are similar in function. A *PIO* provides a multiport connection for input/output devices. (A *port* is a set of eight input/output lines.) At the very least, each input/output device needs a *data buffer* to stabilize the contents of the data bus on output. Most PIOs are equipped with a buffer for each port.

In Chapter 6, I established that a microcomputer can use a *handshaking* procedure or *interrupts* to communicate with an I/O device. The PIO uses a similar procedure to communicate with a peripheral. Therefore, to implement a handshaking function, each PIO must be equipped with at least *two control lines per port.*

A microprocessor also needs to read the status of each port. Thus, each port must be equipped with one or more *status bits.* Finally, the PIO has several options for configuring its resources. To specify these programming options, a programmer must be able to access a special register in the PIO called the *control register.* In some cases, the status information is part of the control register.

One essential faculty of the PIO is that each line may be configured as *either* an input line or an output line. Figure 7.1 shows a diagram of a PIO. It is up to the programmer to specify whether a line will be input or output. To program the direction of the lines, a *data-direction register* is provided for each port. A zero in a bit position of the data-direction register specifies an input. A one specifies an output.

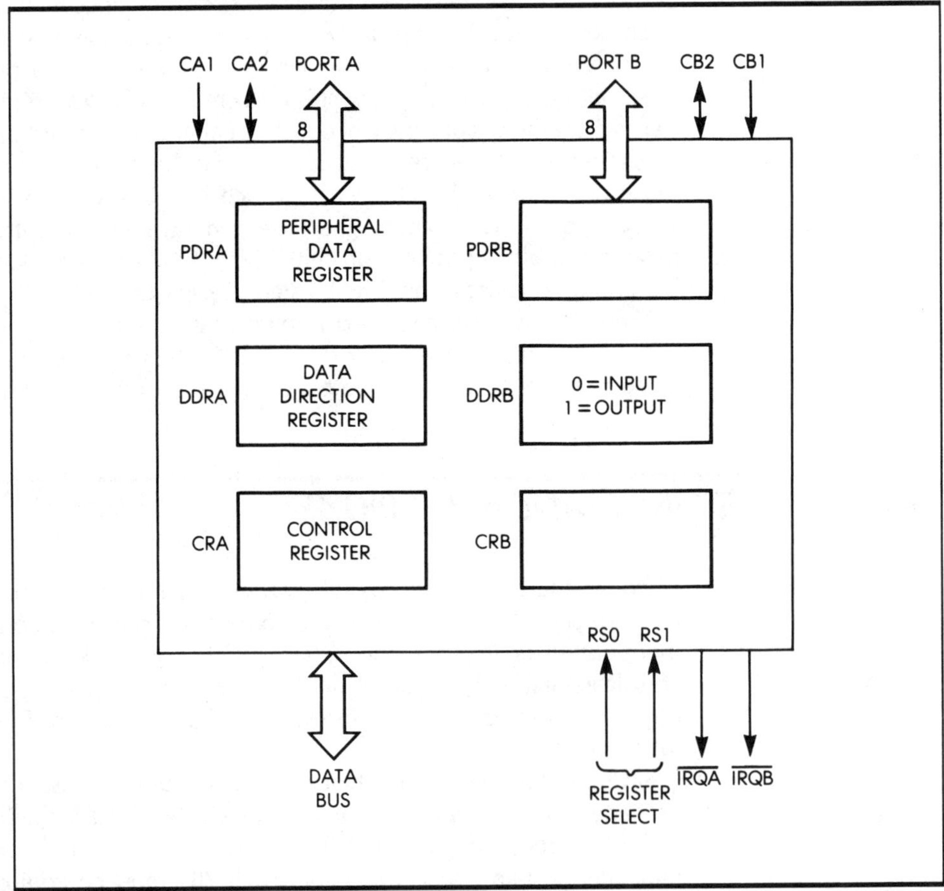

Figure 7.1: Typical PIO

It may be surprising that a zero is used for input and a one for output, when usually a zero corresponds to output and a one to input. This change is quite deliberate: whenever power is applied to the system, it is important that all the I/O lines are configured as *input.* Otherwise, if the microcomputer is connected to some dangerous peripheral, the peripheral may be activated by accident. When a reset is applied, all registers are normally cleared, which results in configuring all lines of the PIO as inputs. The connection to the microprocessor appears on the left of the illustration in Figure 7.1. The PIO connects to the 8-bit data bus, the microprocessor address bus, and the microprocessor control bus. The programmer simply specifies the address of any register to be accessed within the PIO.

THE INTERNAL CONTROL REGISTER

The control register of the PIO provides several options for generating or sensing interrupts, or for implementing automatic handshake functions. I will not provide a complete description of these facilities here. However, very simply, in a practical system that uses a PIO, you must usually refer to the data sheet that shows the effects of setting the various bits of the control register. When the system is initialized, the programmer must load the control register of the PIO with the correct contents for the expected application.

PROGRAMMING A PIO

Let's now look at a typical sequence, using a PIO channel (assuming an input):

1. *Load the control register* by using a programmed transfer between a 65816 register (usually the accumulator) and the PIO control register. The options and operating mode of the PIO are set when the register is loaded (see Figure 7.2). The loading is normally done only once, at the beginning of a program.
2. *Load the direction register* to specify the direction in which the I/O lines will be used (see Figure 7.3).
3. *Read the status register* to check if a valid byte is available on input (see Figure 7.4).

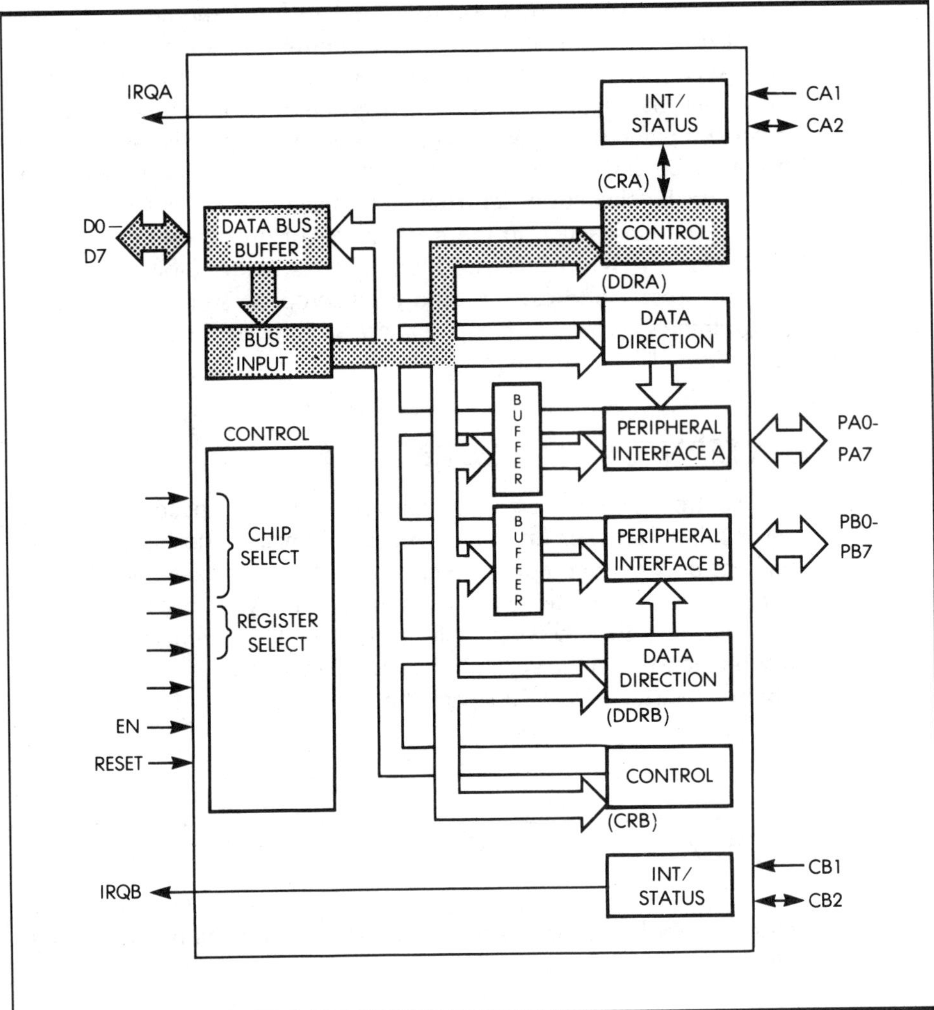

Figure 7.2: Using a PIO: Load Control Register

4. *Read the port;* the byte is read into the 65816 (see Figure 7.5).

THE WESTERN DESIGN CENTER 65SC21 PIA

The 65SC21 PIA (peripheral interface adapter) is a two-port PIO with an architecture that is essentially the same as the standard model I have just described. Figure 7.6 shows the actual pinout of a 65SC21.

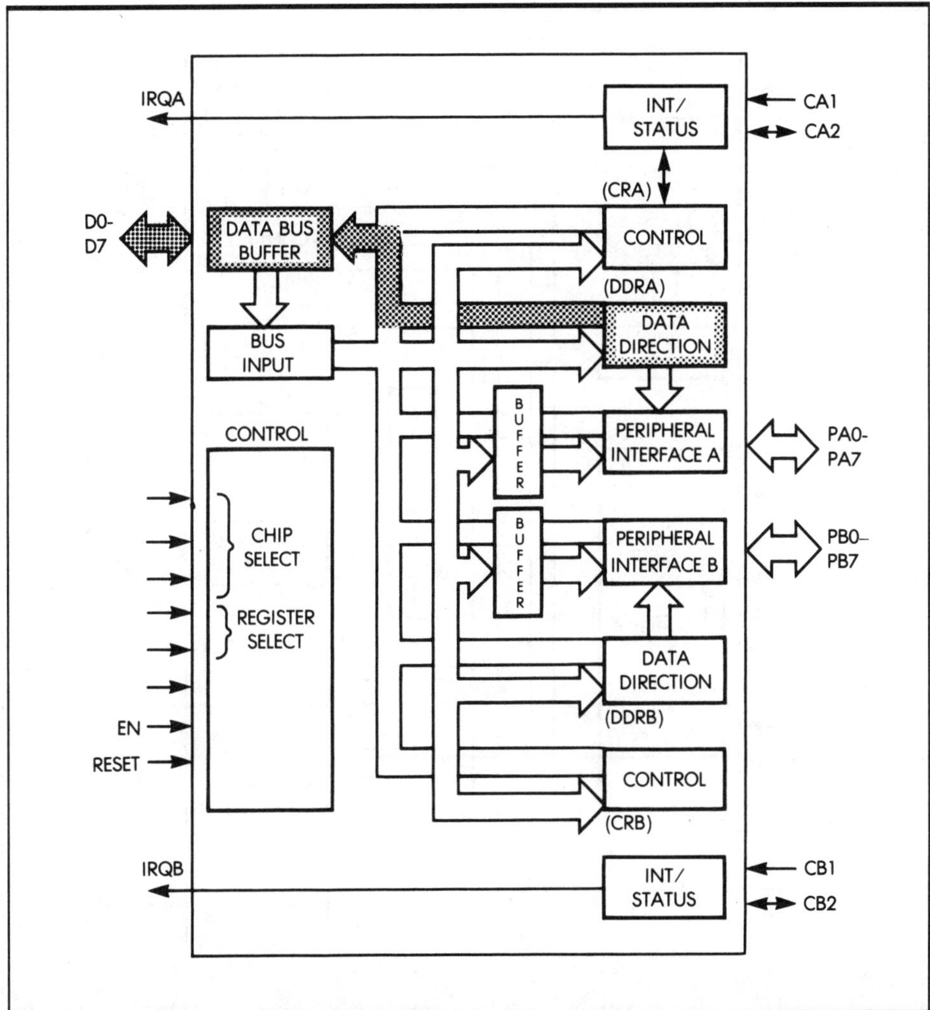

Figure 7.3: Using a PIO: Load Data Direction

The control register for each port has bits that control the conditions under which an interrupt can be generated and the conditions when the handshake bits change state.

PROGRAMMING THE WESTERN DESIGN CENTER PIO

Let's now examine a typical sequence for using a PIO:

1. *Load the control register* to set the handshake bits mode.

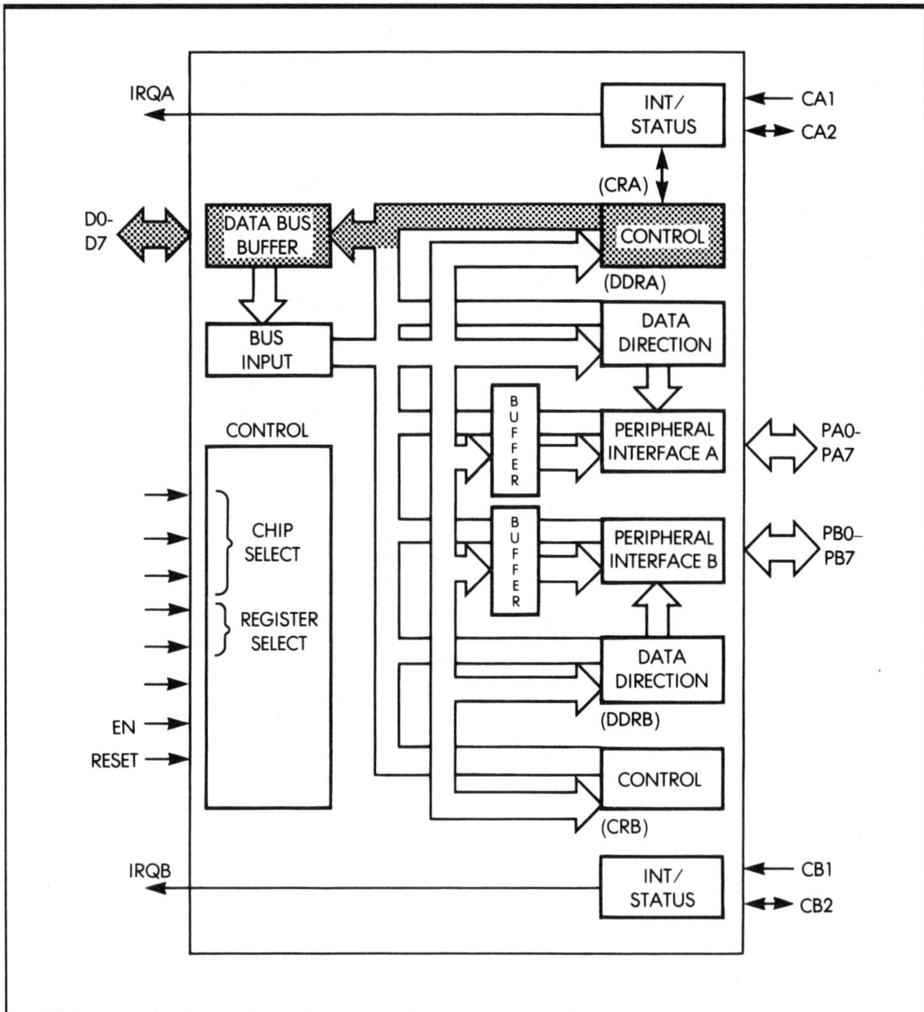

Figure 7.4: Using a PIO: Read Status

2. *Load the data direction register* of port A to specify that lines 0 to 5 are inputs and lines 6 and 7 are outputs.
3. *Read a word* by reading the contents of the input buffer.

THE 65816 ACIA

The W65SC51 ACIA (asynchronous communications interface adapter) is a peripheral chip designed to facilitate asynchronous communications in

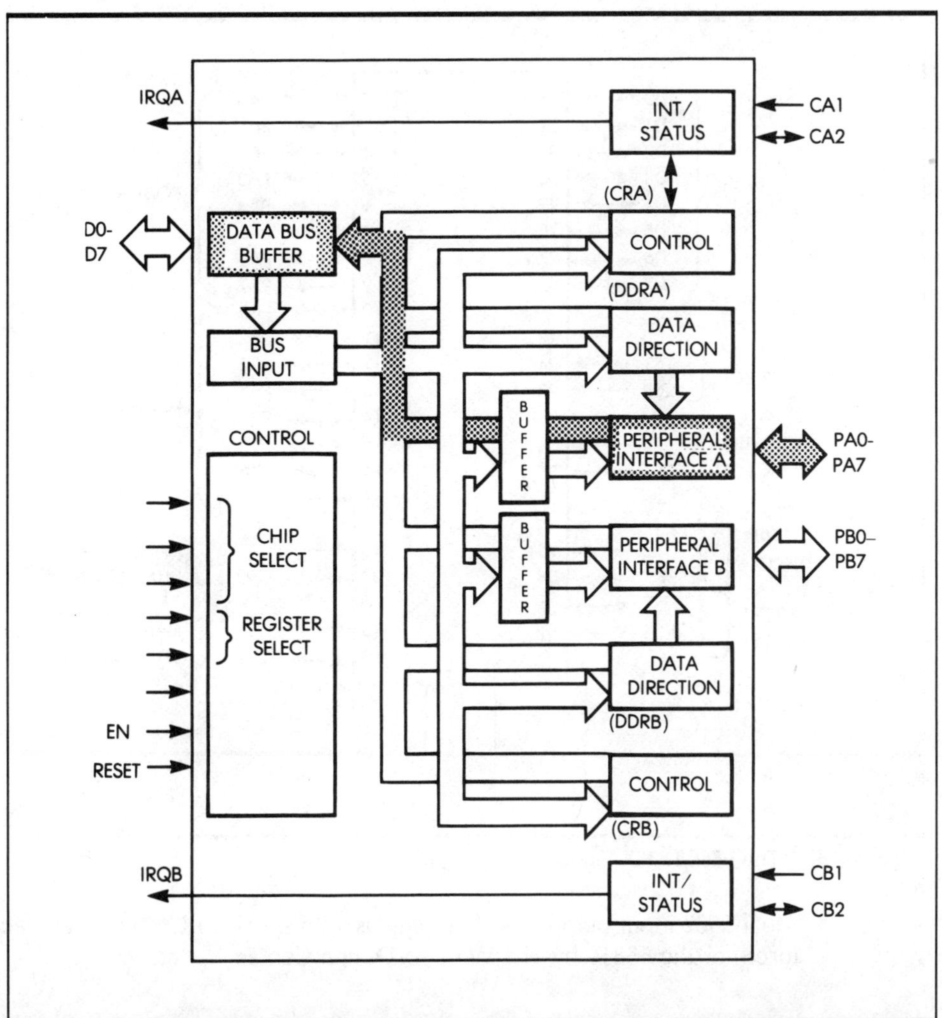

Figure 7.5: Using a PIO: Read Input

serial form. It includes a UART (universal asynchronous receiver-transmitter). The essential function of the ACIA is serial-to-parallel and parallel-to-serial conversion. The ACIA also offers a choice of data format and interrupt modes.

OTHER I/O CHIPS

Because the 65816 is commonly used as an upgraded replacement for the 6502, it has been designed so that it can be used with almost any of the

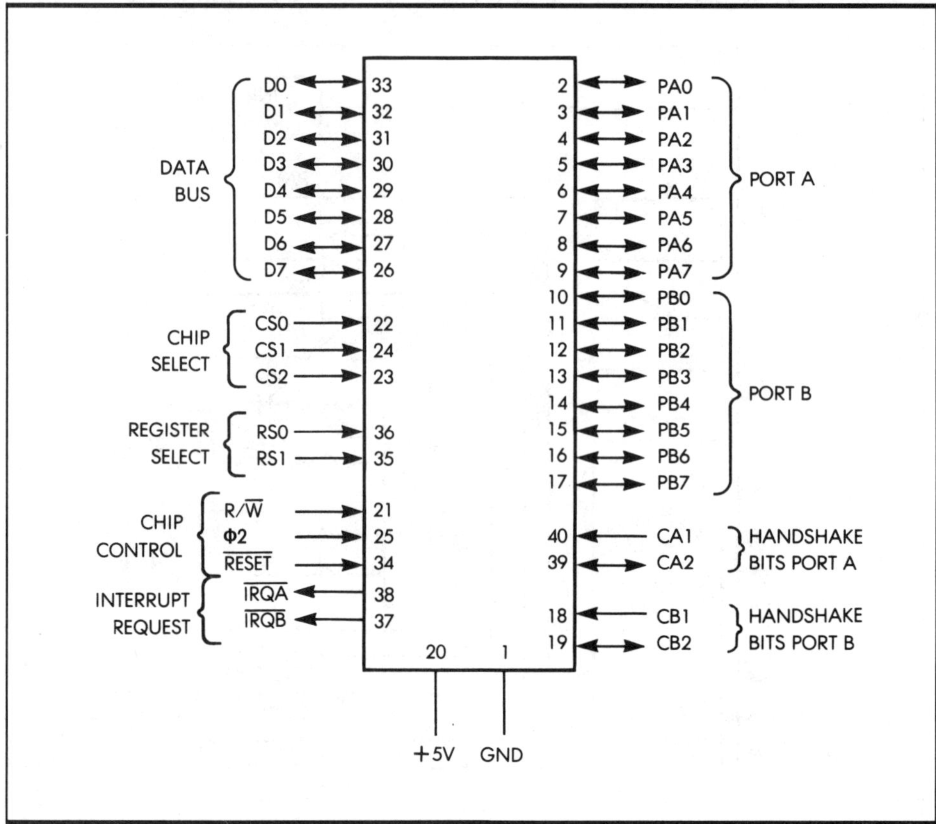

Figure 7.6: The 65SC21 PIA Pinout

usual 6502 input/output chips, as well as with specific I/O chips manufactured for the 65816 by The Western Design Center.

SUMMARY

To make effective use of input/output components, you need to understand the function of each bit or group of bits within the various control registers. These complex new chips automate several procedures previously carried out by software or special logic. In particular, many of the handshaking procedures are automated within components, such as the ACIA. Interrupt handling and detection may also be internal.

You should now be familiar with the functions of the basic signals and registers of I/O devices. Naturally, in the future, new components will be introduced that offer a hardware implementation of even more complex algorithms.

APPLICATION EXAMPLES

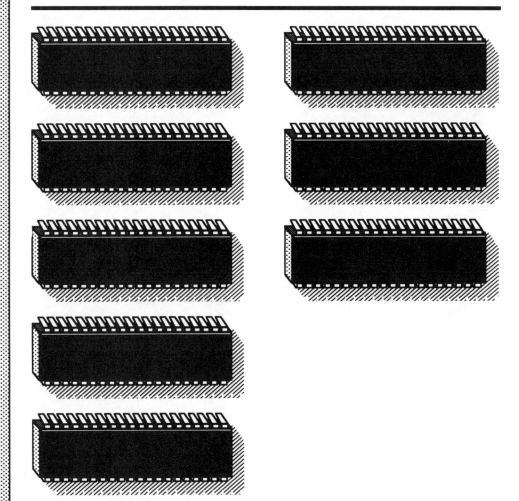

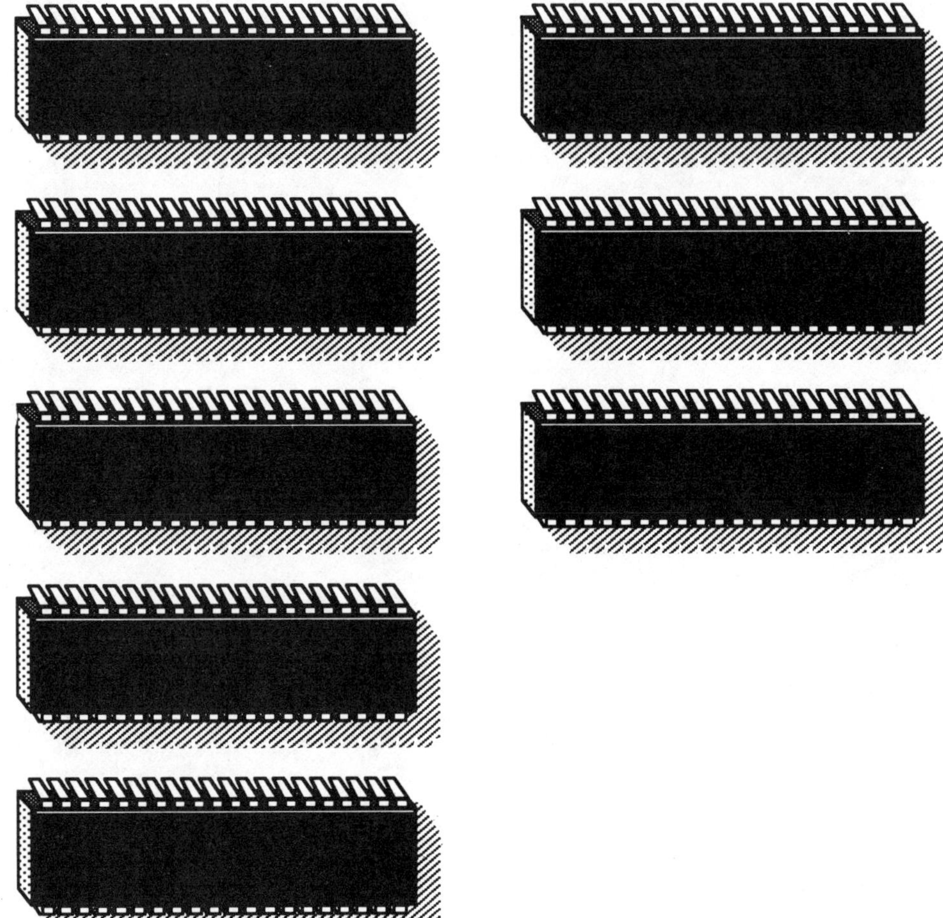

8

IN THIS CHAPTER, you can sharpen your new programming skills by developing a collection of utility programs that fetch characters from an I/O device and process them in various ways. These programs give you a chance to apply the knowledge and techniques you have learned so far to develop several routines that are useful in many applications. The development of these routines demonstrates how the architecture of the 65816 can make the programming of such common algorithms exceptionally straightforward.

Before beginning, let's clear an area of the memory in which to put the characters from the I/O device. Clearing memory is not always necessary; I do it here as a programming example.

CLEARING A SECTION OF MEMORY

I will start by clearing (zeroing) the contents of the memory from address BASE to address BASE + LENGTH, where LENGTH is less than 256 bytes. The program is:

```
ZEROM   LDX     #LENGTH    LOAD X WITH LENGTH
        LDA     #0         CLEAR ACCUMULATOR
CLEAR   STA     BASE,X     CLEAR LOCATION
        DEX                DECREMENT COUNTER
        BNE     CLEAR      END OF SECTION?
        RTS
```

In this program, I assume that the length of the section of memory is equal to LENGTH. I use the X index register as a pointer to the current byte to be cleared and as a counter. If LENGTH is greater than 256, the 16-bit indexing mode should be used.

You could use this utility in a memory test program to zero the contents of a block. The memory test program would then verify that the contents of the block remain zero.

GETTING CHARACTERS IN

I will now write a program that reads characters from an I/O device. Assuming that the computer you are using has a keyboard as an input device, each time you type a character, the character will be saved in an area of memory called the BUFFER, until a special character called *space* is encountered. (Appendix B gives the code number for *space*.) The subroutine GETCHAR fetches one character from the keyboard and puts it in the A accumulator. I assume that 256 characters (maximum) will be fetched before the program encounters a space character.

```
STRING  LDX   #0        SET INDEX TO ZERO
NEXT    JSR   GETCHAR   GET A CHARACTER
        CMP   #SPC      CHECK FOR SPACE
        BEQ   OUT       FOUND IT?
        STA   BUFFER,X  STORE CHAR IN BUFFER
        INX             INCREMENT POINTER
        BRA   NEXT      GET NEXT CHAR
OUT     RTS
```

At the end of this routine, you have a string of characters in the memory buffer. You can now process them in various ways.

TESTING A CHARACTER

This program determines if the character at memory location LOC is equal to 0, 1, or 2:

```
ZOT     LDA   LOC       GET CHARACTER
        CMP   #0        IS IT A ZERO?
        BEQ   ZERO      BRANCH ROUTINE
        CMP   #1        A ONE?
        BEQ   ONE
        CMP   #2        A TWO?
        BEQ   TWO
        BRA   NOTFND    FAILURE
```

You simply read the character, then use the CMP instruction to check its value.

Let's now run a different test.

BRACKET TESTING

This program determines if the ASCII character at memory location LOC is a digit between 0 and 9:

```
BRACK   LDA   LOC    GET CHARACTER
        AND   #$7F   MASK OUT PARITY BIT
        CMP   #$30   ASCII 0
        BCC   OUT    CHAR TOO LOW?
        CMP   #$39   ASCII 9
        BEQ   IN     CHAR IS 9
        BCS   OUT    CHAR TOO HIGH?
IN      LDA   #0     FORCE ZERO FLAG
OUT     RTS
```

ASCII 0 is represented in hexadecimal by 30 or by B0, depending upon whether the parity bit is used or not. Similarly, ASCII 9 is represented in hexadecimal by 39 or by B9.

The purpose of the second instruction of the program is to delete bit 7 (the parity bit) in case it was used, so the program is applicable to both cases. The value of the character is then compared to the ASCII values for 0 and 9. When using a comparison instruction, the Z bit is set if both the contents of the register and the operand are equal. The carry bit is set if there is a borrow. This means that the carry bit is set if the value of the operand is less than or equal to the contents of the register.

The instruction LDA #0 forces a zero into the Z bit. The Z bit is used to indicate to the calling routine that the character in LOC was indeed in the interval (0,9). You could also use other conventions, such as loading a digit into the accumulator, to indicate the results of the test.

When using an ASCII table, note that parity is used often. For example, the ASCII representation for 0 is 0110000, a 7-bit code. If, however, you use odd parity and guarantee that the total number of ones in a word is odd, then the code becomes 10110000 (or B0 in hexadecimal). An extra 1 is added to the left side of the code. Let's now develop a program to generate parity.

GENERATING PARITY

This program generates even parity in bit position 7:

```
PARITY  LDA   CHAR     GET CHARACTER
        STZ   ONECNT   CLEAR COUNT OF ONES
        LDX   #7       COUNT 7 BITS
BITCNT  LSR   A        SHIFT CHAR RIGHT
        BCC   NOINC    C = ZERO SKIP
        INC   ONECNT   COUNT CARRY BITS
NOINC   DEX            LOOP TILL
        BNE   BITCNT   7 BITS ARE TESTED
        LSR   ONECNT   CHECK IF A IS EVEN
        BCC   DONE     IF EVEN THEN DONE
        LDA   CHAR     GET CHARACTER
        ORA   #$80     SET BIT 7
        STA   CHAR
DONE    RTS
```

This program shifts a character and then counts the number of ones in it. If the number of ones is even, the parity bit is not set; if the number is odd, the parity bit is set.

The memory location ONECNT is used as working space for this program. Shifting destroys the character, but it is preserved in CHAR.

CODE CONVERSION: ASCII TO BCD

Converting ASCII to BCD is simple. In this example, you see that the hexadecimal representation of ASCII characters 0 to 9 is either 30 to 39 or B0 to B9, depending on parity. The BCD representation is obtained simply by dropping the 3 or the B—masking the left nibble (4 bits):

```
ASCBCD  JSR    BRACK    CHECK THAT CHAR IS 0 TO 9
        BNE    ILLEGAL  EXIT IF ILLEGAL CHAR
        LDA    CHAR     GET CHARACTER
        AND    #$0F     ZERO HIGH NIBBLE
        STA    BCDCHR   STORE RESULT
```

In full BCD notation, the first byte contains the count of BCD digits, the next contains the sign, and every successive nibble contains a BCD digit (I assume no decimal point). The last nibble of the block may not be used.

CONVERTING HEX TO ASCII

In the example, the A register contains one hexadecimal digit. You simply need to add a 3 (or a B) into the left nibble:

```
AND     #$F      ZERO LEFT NIBBLE
CLC              PREPARE TO ADD
ADC     #$30     ASCII
CMP     #$3A     CORRECTION NEEDED?
BCC     OUT
ADC     #7       CORRECTION FOR A TO F
```

FINDING THE LARGEST ELEMENT OF A TABLE

The beginning address of the table is contained at memory address BASE. The first entry of the table is the number of bytes it contains. The following program searches for the largest element of the table. Its value is then stored in A, and its position is stored in INDEX.

This program uses registers A and Y, and indexed addressing, to search a table anywhere in memory (see Figure 8.1):

```
MAX      LDY   #0        CLEAR INDEX
         LDA   BASE,Y    BYTES IN TABLE
         TAY             PUT BYTE COUNT IN Y
         LDA   #0        INITIALIZE MAX VALUE
LOOP     CMP   BASE,Y    COMPARE ENTRY
         BCS   NOSWIT    BRANCH IF LESS THAN MAX
         LDA   BASE,Y    SET NEW POSITION
         STY   INDEX     LOAD NEW MAX
NOSWIT   DEY             DECREMENT COUNTER
         BNE   LOOP      KEEP GOING UNTIL ZERO
         RTS
```

This program tests the *n*th entry. If it is greater than A, the entry goes into A, and its location is remembered in INDEX. The (n − 1) entry is then tested, and so on. This program works for positive integers only.

SUM OF N ELEMENTS

This program computes the 32-bit sum of N entries of a table. Each entry is 16 bits. The starting address of the table is contained at memory address BASE, in page zero. The first entry of the table contains the number of elements in N. The 32-bit sum is left in memory locations SUMLO and SUMHI. If the sum requires more than 32 bits, only the lower 32 bits are kept. (The high-order bits are said to be truncated.)

This program modifies registers A and Y. It assumes 256 elements maximum (see Figure 8.2):

```
SUMIG   REP   #$30     SET PROCESSOR TO 16-BIT
                       MODE
        LDY   #0       INITIALIZE Y TO ZERO
        LDA   BASE,Y   READ LENGTH INTO A
        TAY            TRANSFER COUNT TO Y
        STZ   SUMLO    CLEAR RESULT
        STZ   SUMHI
        CLC            CLEAR CARRY FOR ADC
ADLOOP  LDA   BASE,Y   GET TABLE ENTRY
        ADC   SUMLO    COMPUTE PARTIAL SUM
        STA   SUMLO    STORE IT
        BCC   NOCARY   CHECK FOR CARRY
        INC   SUMHI    ADD CARRY TO HIGH WORD
        CLC            FOR NEXT SUM
NOCARY  DEY            DECREMENT WORD COUNT
        BNE   ADLOOP   KEEP ADDING TIL END
        RTS
```

This program should be self-explanatory.

CHECKSUM COMPUTATION

A *checksum* is a digit or set of digits computed from a block of successive characters. The checksum is computed at the time the data is stored and then put at the end. To verify the integrity of the data, the data is read, and the checksum is recomputed and compared with the stored value. A discrepancy indicates an error or failure.

You can use several algorithms. In this example, exclusive-OR operates on all the bytes in a table of N elements, and leaves the results in the

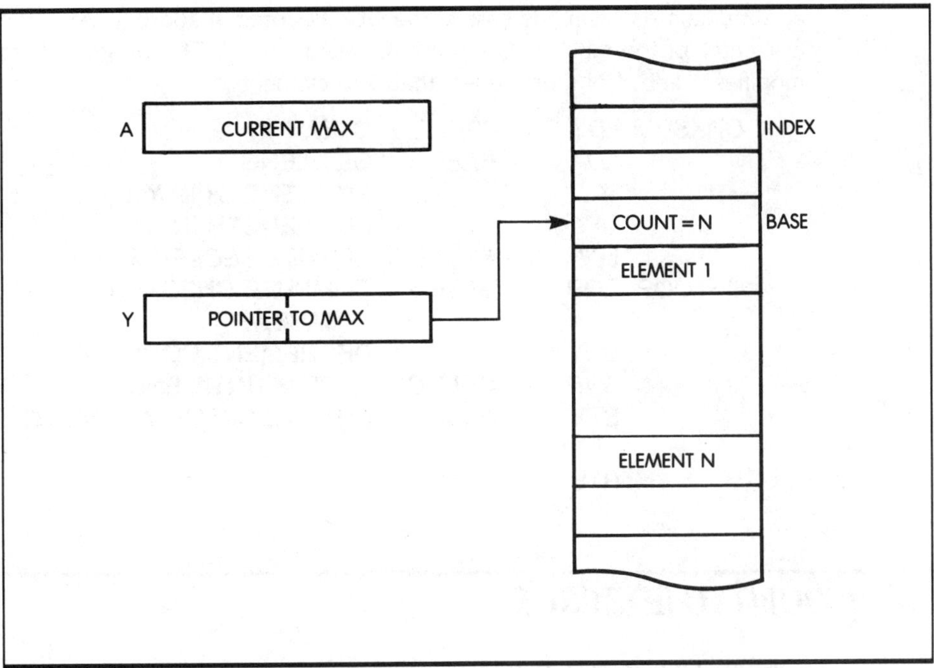

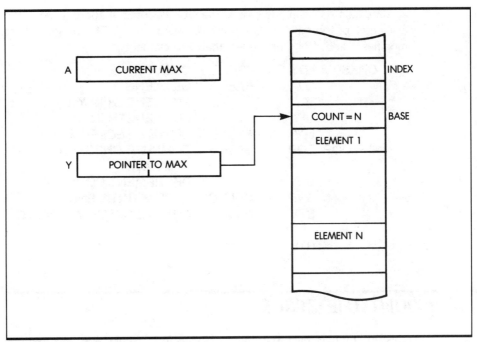

Figure 8.1: Largest Elements in a Table

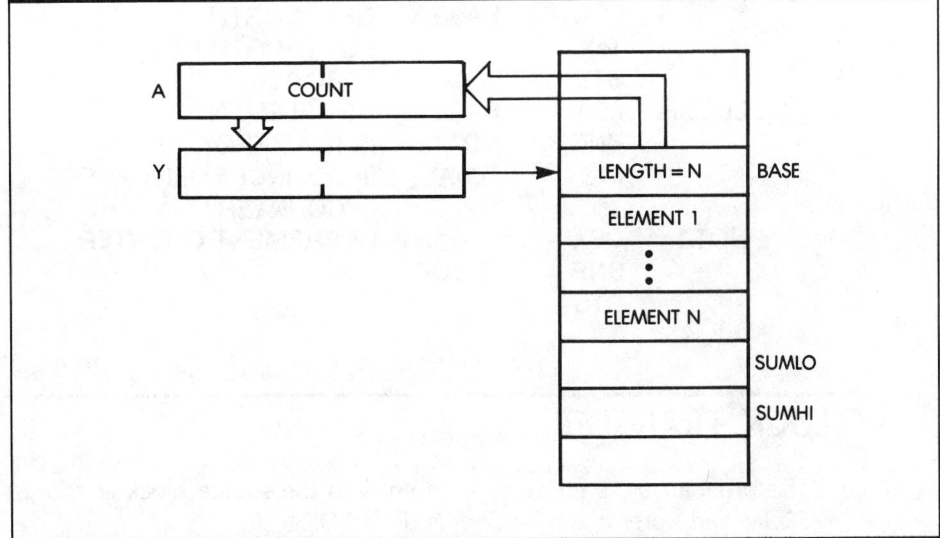

Figure 8.2: Sum of N Elements

accumulator. As usual, the base of the table is stored at address BASE. The first entry of the table is its number of elements, N. The program then modifies A and Y. N must be less than 256 elements.

```
CHKSUM LDY    #0       CLEAR Y
       LDA    BASE,Y   GET LENGTH
       TAY             PUT LENGTH IN Y
       TAX             PUT LENGTH IN X
       LDA    #0       CLEAR CHECKSUM
CHLOOP EOR    BASE,Y   COMPUTE CHECKSUM FOR
                         BASE,Y
       DEY             DECREMENT COUNTER
       BNE    CHLOOP   REPEAT UNTIL END
       STA    BASE,X   PUT CHECKSUM AT END OF
                         TABLE
       RTS
```

COUNT THE ZEROS

This program counts the number of zeros in the table, and puts the total in location TOTAL. It modifies A and X.

```
ZEROS  LDX    #0       CLEAR X
       LDA    BASE,X   GET LENGTH
       TAX             PUT LENGTH IN X
       STZ    TOTAL    ZERO TOTAL
ZLOOP  LDA    BASE,X   GET ELEMENT
       BNE    NOTZ     IS IT A ZERO?
       INC    TOTAL    IF SO, INCREMENT ZERO
                         COUNTER
NOTZ   DEX             DECREMENT COUNTER
       BNE    ZLOOP
       RTS
```

BLOCK TRANSFER

This program picks up every third entry in the source block at address FROM and stores it in a block at address TO:

```
FER3   LDA    #LENGTH  GET LENGTH
       STA    COUNT    STORE IN COUNT
```

```
        LDY    #0       SET UP POINTERS
        TYX
LOOP    LDA    FROM,X   GET AN ENTRY
        STA    TO,Y     STORE IT
        INX
        INX
        INX             POINT TO THIRD
        INY             POINT TO NEXT
        DEC    COUNT
        BNE    LOOP
```

BUBBLE-SORT

Bubble-sort is a sorting technique used to arrange the elements of a table in ascending or descending order. The bubble-sort technique derives its name from the fact that the smallest element "bubbles up" to the top of the table. Every time an element collides with a "heavier" element, it jumps over it.

Figures 8.3 and 8.4 show practical examples of a bubble-sort. The list to be sorted contains the numbers 10, 5, 0, 2, and 100, and must be sorted in descending order (0 on top). The algorithm is simple. The flowchart for the algorithm appears in Figure 8.5.

The two top (or else the two bottom) elements are compared. If the lower element is less (lighter) than the top element, they are exchanged. Otherwise, they are left alone. For practical purposes, the exchange, if it occurs, is indicated by a flag called EXCHANGED. The process is then repeated on the next pair of elements, until all elements have been compared two by two.

Figure 8.3 illustrates this first pass in steps 1, 2, 3, 4, 5, and 6, going from the bottom up. (Equivalently, you could go from the top down.) If no elements have been exchanged, the sort is complete. If an exchange has occurred, you must start over again. In Figure 8.4, you can see that four passes are necessary. This process is simple, and widely used.

One possible complication resides in the actual mechanism of the exchange. When exchanging A and B, you may not write

A = B

or

B = A

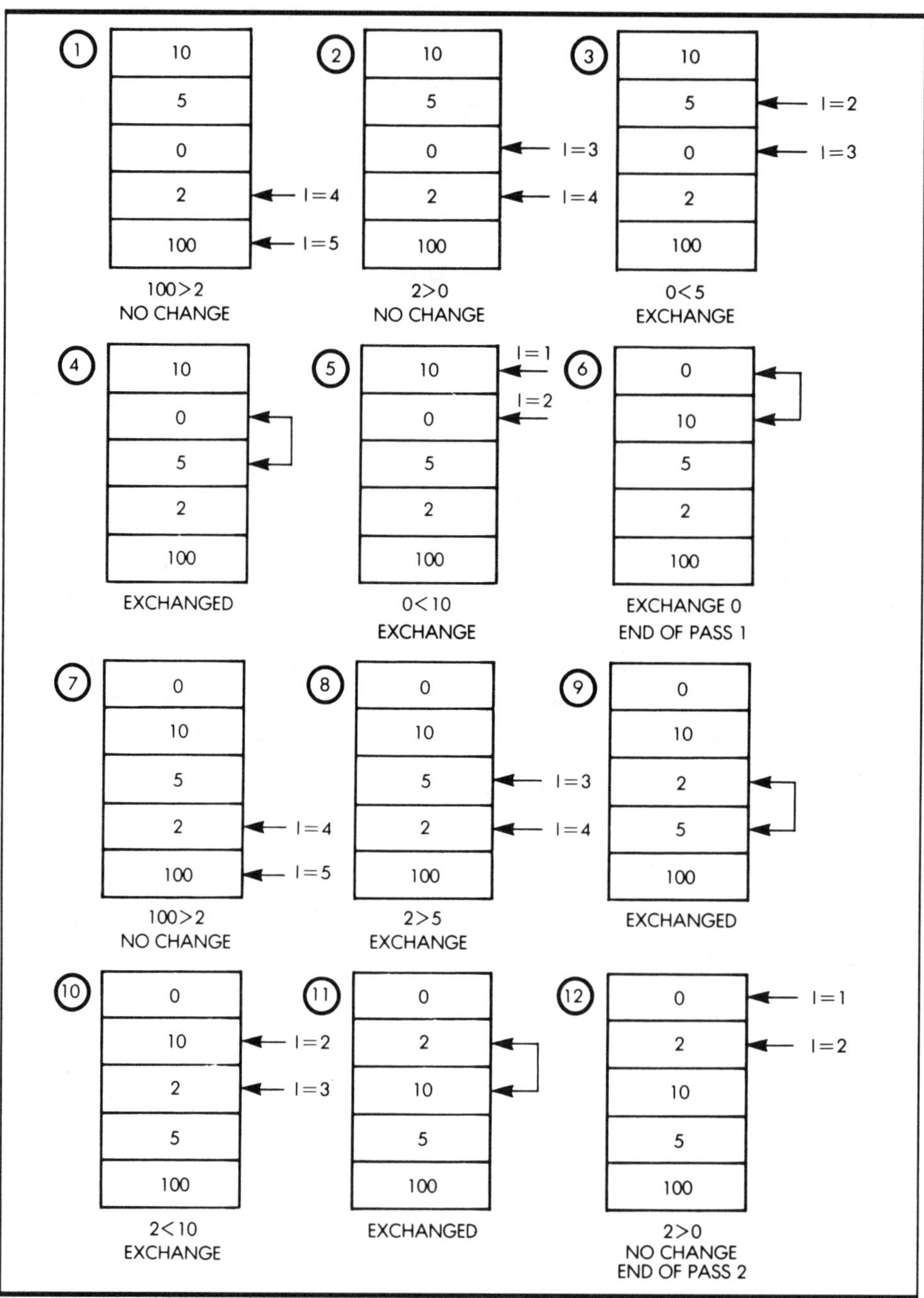

Figure 8.3: Bubble-Sort Example, Phases 1 to 12

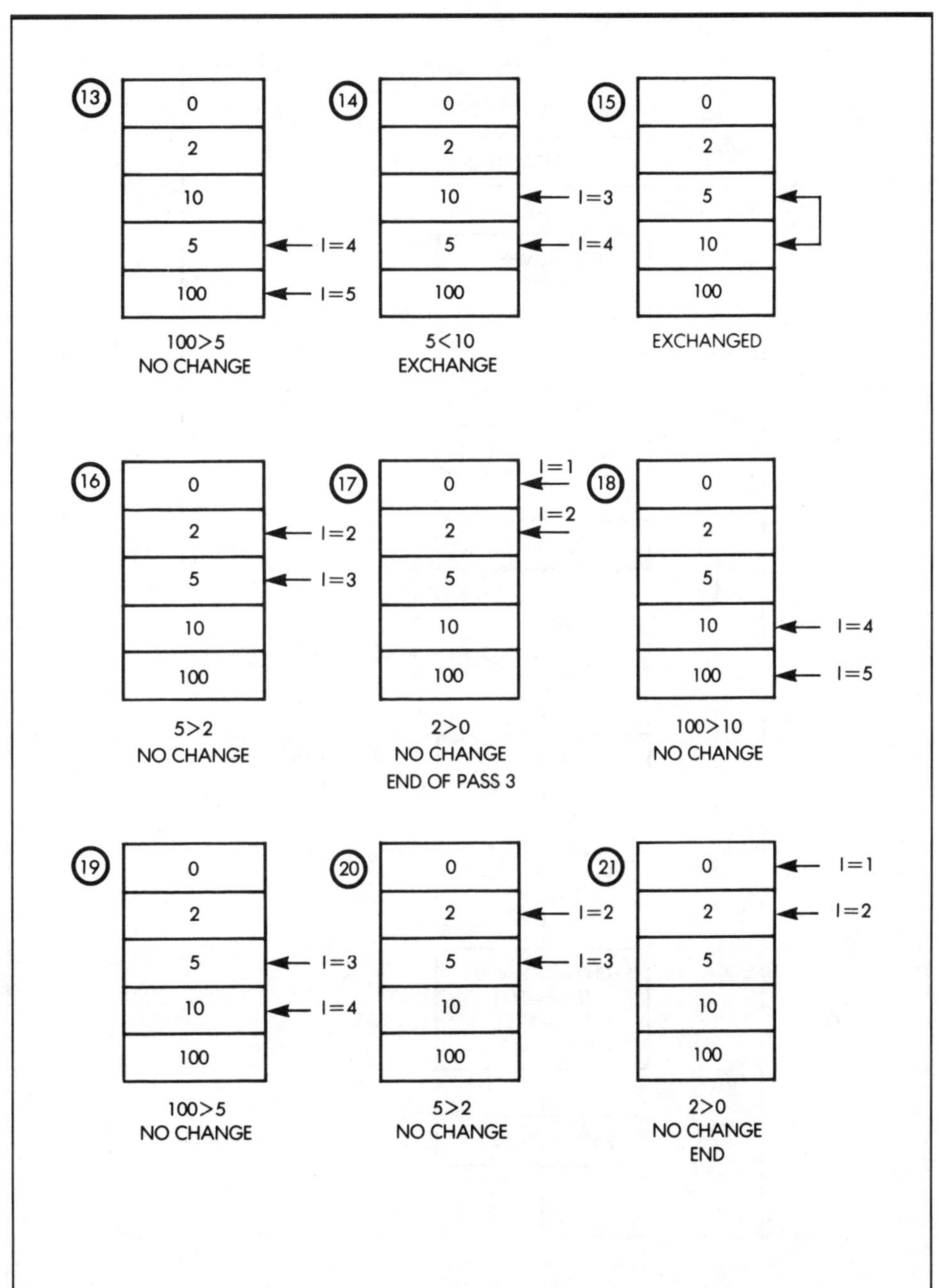

Figure 8.4: Bubble-Sort Example, Phases 13 to 21

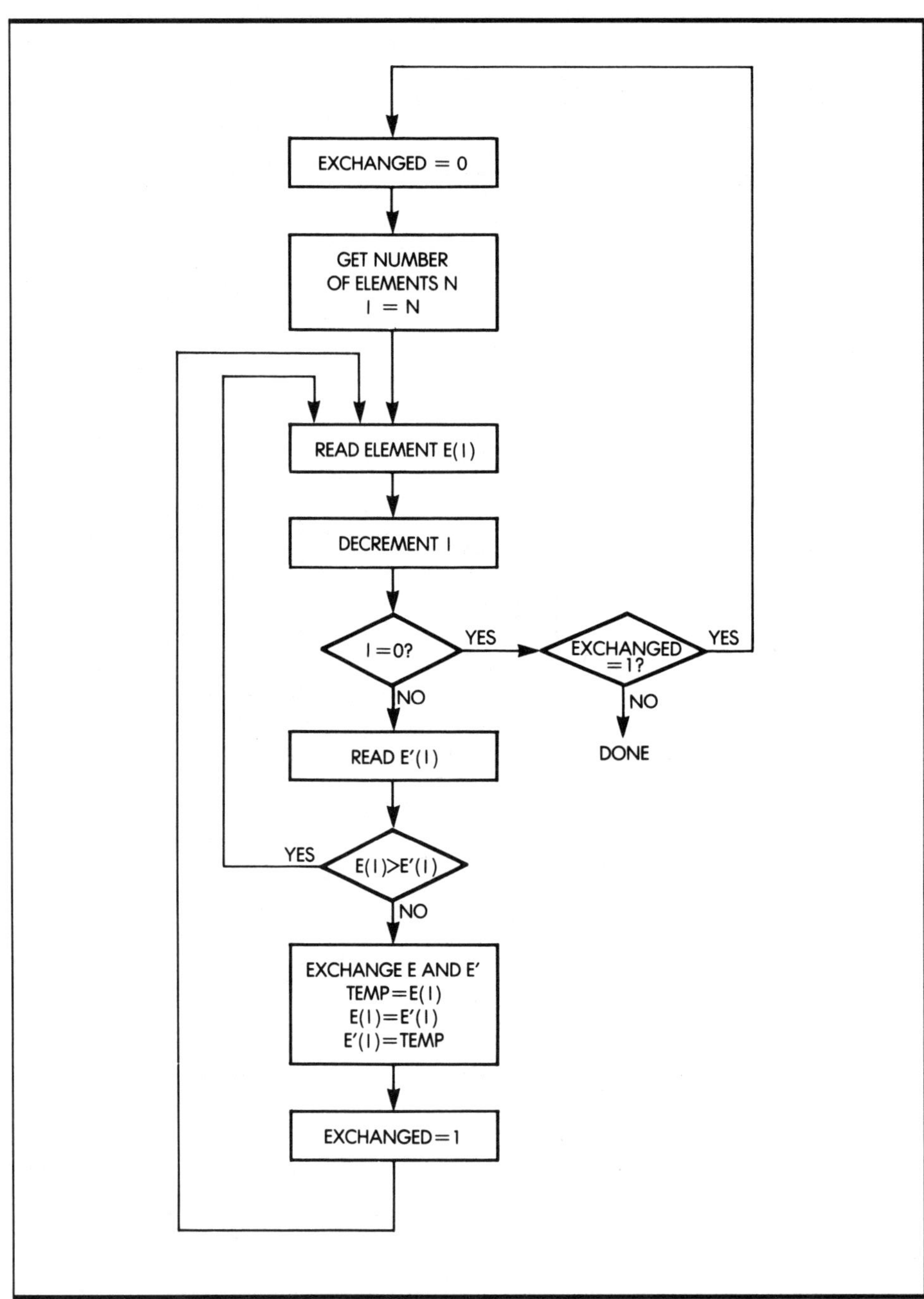

Figure 8.5: Bubble-Sort Flowchart

as this would result in the loss of the previous value of A. (Try it on an example.) The correct solution is to use a temporary variable or location to preserve the value of A. For example, you may use:

TEMP = A
A = B
B = TEMP

This process, called *circular permutation,* works. (Try it on an example.)

All programs implement the exchange in this way. Figure 8.5 illustrates the process. Figure 8.6 shows the register and memory assignments. The program is:

```
BUBBLE  LDX    #0       CLEAR X
        LDA    BASE,X   GET LENGTH
        TAX             PUT LENGTH IN X
        STZ    EXCHG    CLEAR EXCHANGE FLAG
NEXT    LDA    BASE,X   A = CURRENT ENTRY
        DEX             POINT TO NEXT ELEMENT
        BEQ    NOSWIT   DONE WITH ONE PASS
        CMP    BASE,X   COMPARE WITH NEXT
        BCS    NEXT     GO TO NOSWITCH IF
                          CURRENT >= NEXT
        TAY             SAVE A
        LDA    BASE,X   GET NEXT
        INX             POINT TO LAST
        STA    BASE,X   STORE IN LAST
        TYA
        DEX
        STA    BASE,X   STORE LAST IN NEXT
        INC    EXCHG    SET EXCHANGE FLAG
        BRA    NEXT     GET NEXT ELEMENT
NOSWIT  LDA    EXCHG    EXCHANGED = 0?
        BNE    BUBBLE   RESTART IF NOT = 0
        RTS
```

SUMMARY

You have just explored common utility routines that use combinations of the various techniques described in previous chapters. In several of these

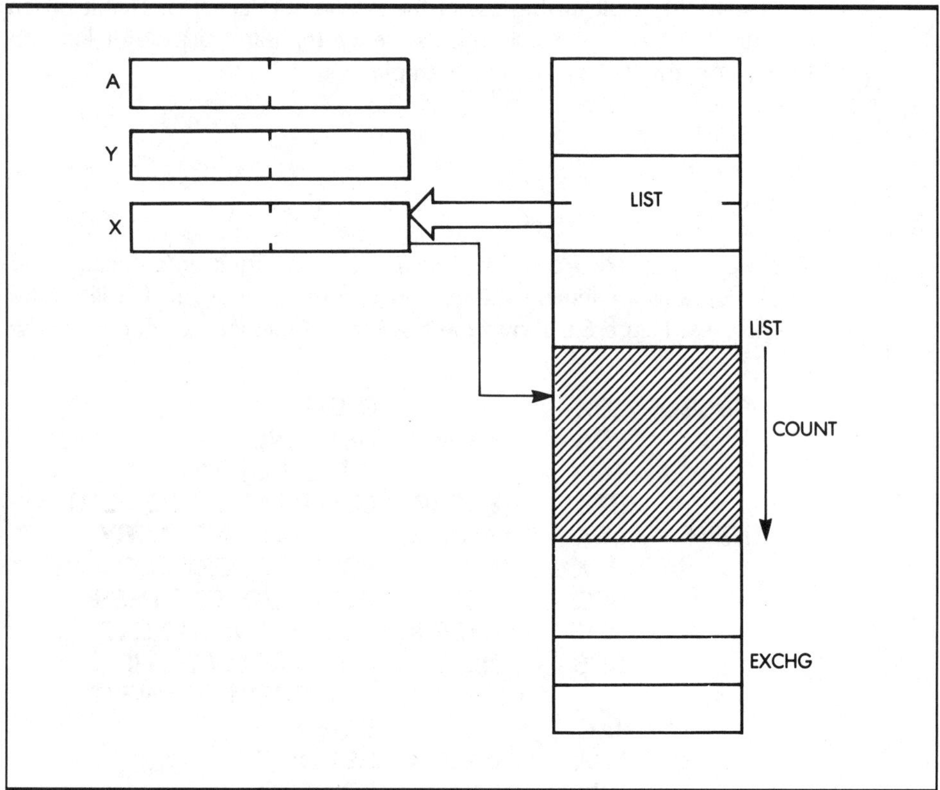

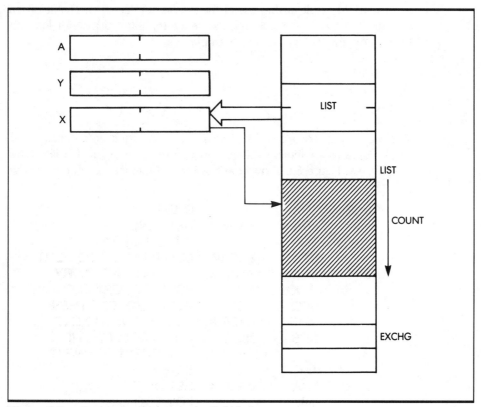

Figure 8.6: Registers and Memory for Bubble-Sort

routines, I used a special data structure, called a table, that is useful for designing programs. There are other techniques you can use to structure data; I discuss them in the next chapter.

EXERCISES

8-1: *Write a memory test program that:*

- *Zeros a 256-word block and verifies that each location is 0*
- *Writes all ones and verifies the contents of the block*
- *Writes 01010101 and verifies the contents*
- *Writes 10101010 and verifies the contents*

8-2: *Modify the program you wrote for Exercise 8-1 so that it fills the memory section with alternating bytes of zeros and ones.*

8-3: *Try to improve the STRING program by:*

- *Echoing the character back to the device (for a Teletype, for example)*
- *Checking that the input string is no longer than 256 characters*

8-4: *Is the following program equivalent to the Bracket Testing program?*

```
LDA    LOC
SEC
SBC    #$30
BMI    OUT
SEC
SBC    #10
BPL    OUT
CLC
ADC    #10
```

8-5: *Determine if an ASCII character contained in an accumulator is a letter of the alphabet.*

8-6: *Using the Parity Generation program as an example, verify the parity of a word. You must compute the correct parity, then compare it to the one that is expected.*

8-7: *Write a program to convert BCD to ASCII.*

8-8: *Write a program to convert BCD to binary (more difficult).* (Hint: *$N_3N_2N_1N_0$ in BCD is*

$$((((N_3 \times 10) + N_2) \times 10 + N_1) \times 10) + N_0$$

in binary.)

8-9: *Convert HEX to ASCII, assuming a packed format (two hex digits in A).*

8-10: *Modify the program that finds the largest element in a table so that it also works for negative numbers in two's complement.*

8-11: *Will the program in Exercise 8-10 also work for ASCII characters?*

8-12: *Write a program that sorts* n *numbers in ascending order.*

8-13: *Write a program that sorts* n *names (three characters each) in alphabetical order.*

8-14: *Modify the Sum of N Elements program to:*

- *Compute a 16-bit sum*
- *Compute a 24-bit sum*
- *Detect any overflow*

8-15: *Modify the Count the Zeros program to count:*

- *The number of stars (the * character)*
- *The number of letters of the alphabet*
- *The number of digits between 0 and 9*

DATA STRUCTURES

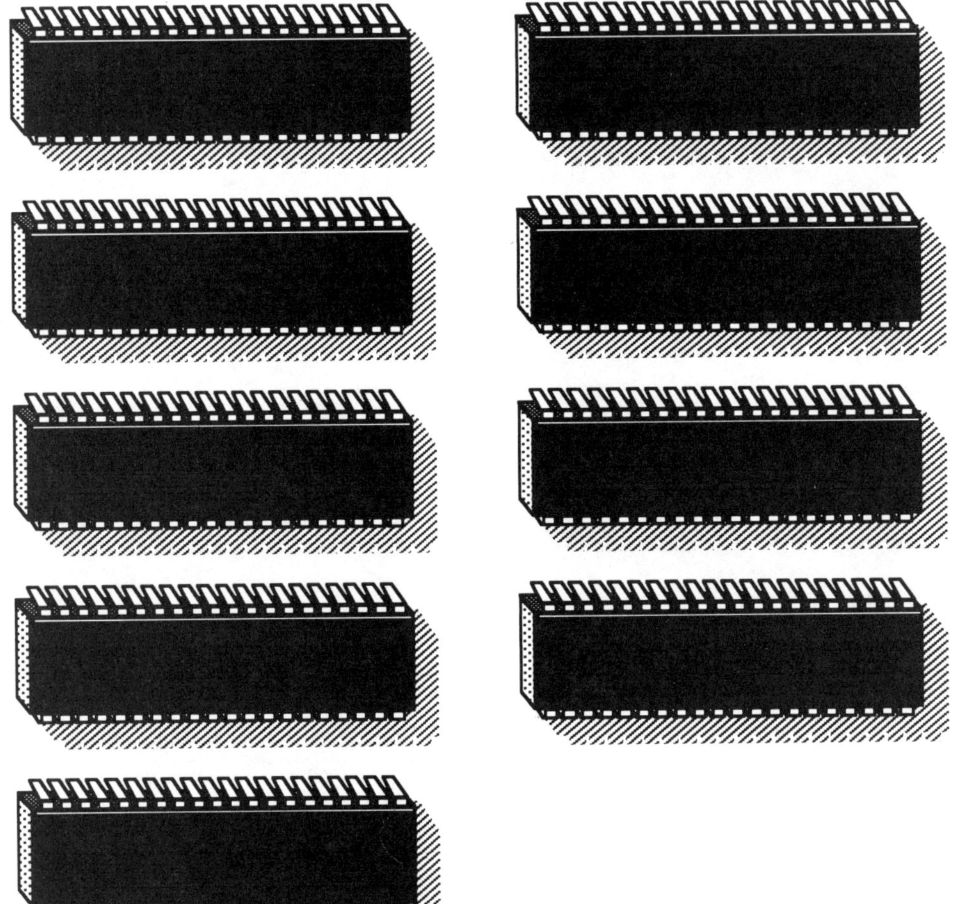

9

TO DESIGN A GOOD PROGRAM, you need both a good algorithm design and a good data structure design. Since most simple programs do not involve significant data structures, up to this point I have only concentrated on designing and coding good algorithms in a given machine language. I will now focus on the design of data structures, so that you can develop more complex programs. I have already used two data structures in this book: the table and the stack. I will now examine several other, more general, data structures.

PART I—THEORY

The material presented in Part I of this chapter is theoretical in concept; it involves the logical organization of data in any system. I have limited the material in this chapter to that which is essential for understanding common data structures. I will begin by reviewing the most common data structure: the pointer.

POINTERS

A *pointer* is a number that designates the location of actual data. Every pointer is an address. However, every address is not necessarily a pointer. An address is a pointer only if it points to some type of data or structured information. In this book, you have already encountered a typical pointer—the stack pointer, which points to the top of the stack (or just over the top of the stack). The stack is a common data structure. Another example is indirect addressing: the indirect address is always a pointer to the data that is to be retrieved.

LISTS

Almost all data structures are organized as lists. Let's examine several types of lists.

A SEQUENTIAL LIST

A *sequential list*—either a table or a block—is probably the simplest data structure (see Chapter 8). *Tables* are normally organized by a specific criterion, such as alphabetical or numerical ordering. Because of this, it is easy to retrieve an element in a table (for example, by using indexed addressing).

A *block* normally refers to a group of data that has definite limits, but whose contents are not ordered. A block may contain a string of characters, it may be a sector on a disk, or it may be some logical area (called a segment) of the memory. Generally, it is not easy to access a random element of a block; directories facilitate the retrieval of blocks of information.

A DIRECTORY

A *directory* is a list of tables or blocks. For example, a file system normally uses a directory structure. As a simple example, the master directory of a system may include a list of users' names (see Figure 9.1). The entry for user *John* points to John's file directory. In this case, the *file directory* is a table of pointers containing the names and locations of all of John's files. In this case, it is a two-level directory. This flexible directory system allows the inclusion of additional intermediate directories—a convenient feature for users.

A LINKED LIST

In a system, there are often blocks of information that represent data, events, or other structures that cannot be moved around easily. If they could be easily moved, you would probably assemble them into a table to sort or structure them. Assume, for example, that you want to leave several blocks where they are, but you also want to establish an ordering among them, such as first, second, third, or fourth. To do this, you can use a linked list (see Figure 9.2). In this illustration, a list pointer, called FIRSTBLOCK, points to the beginning of the first block. A dedicated location within Block 1, such as the

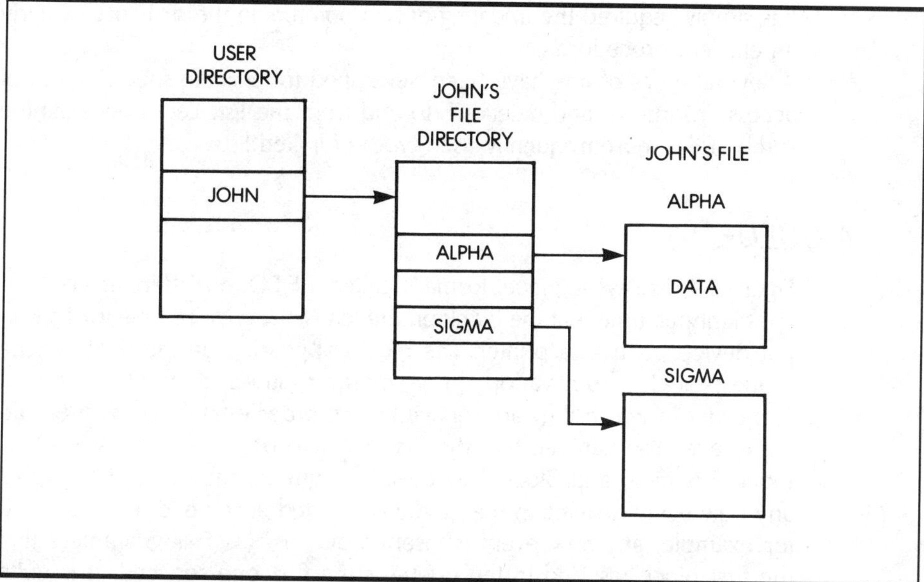

Figure 9.1: A Directory Structure

first or last word, contains a pointer to Block 2, called PTR1. The process is then repeated for Block 2 and Block 3. Since Block 3 is the last entry in the list, by convention PTR3 contains either a special *nil* value or points to itself. This is done so that the program can detect the end of the list. This structure is economical, as it requires only one pointer per block and frees you from having to physically move the blocks in the memory.

Let's now examine how a new block is inserted (see Figure 9.3). Assume that the new block is at address NEWBLOCK, and is to be inserted between Block 1 and Block 2. Pointer PTR1 is simply changed to the value NEWBLOCK, so that it now points to Block X. PTRX now contains the former value of PTR1 (it points to Block 2). The other pointers in the structure are left unchanged. You can see that the insertion of a new block

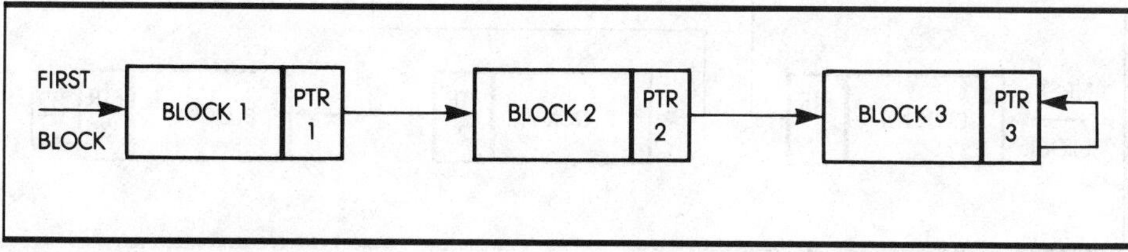

Figure 9.2: A Linked List

has simply required the updating of two pointers in the structure—clearly an efficient procedure.

Several types of lists have been developed to facilitate specific types of access, insertions, and deletions, to and from the list. Let's now examine some of the more frequently used types of linked lists.

A QUEUE

Figure 9.4 displays a *queue,* formally called a FIFO, or first-in, first-out list. For clarity, assume that the block on the left is a service routine for an output device, such as a printer. The blocks appearing on the right are the request blocks, from various programs or routines, to print characters. The order in which they are serviced is the order established by the waiting queue. You can see that the first event to obtain service is Block 1; Block 2 is next; and Block 3 follows. In a queue, the convention is that any new event arriving in the queue is inserted at the end. In Figure 9.4, for example, any new event is inserted after PTR3. This guarantees that the first block inserted in the queue is the first one serviced. It is quite common in a computer system to have queues for several events, whenever they must wait for a scarce resource such as the processor or some input/output device.

A STACK

I have already discussed the stack structure, a last-in, first-out (LIFO) structure. The last element deposited on top is the first one to be removed. A stack may be implemented as either a sorted block or a list. Because most stacks in microprocessors are used for high-speed events, such as

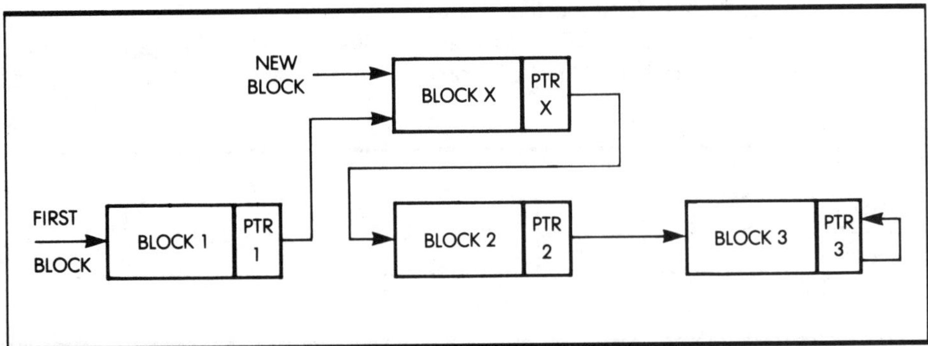

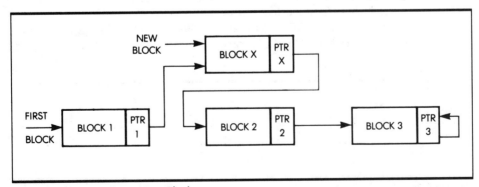

Figure 9.3: Inserting a New Block

subroutines and interrupts, a continuous block (rather than a linked list structure) is usually allocated to the stack.

LINKED LIST VERSUS BLOCK

Similarly, a queue could be implemented as a block of reserved locations. Advantages of using a continuous block include fast retrieval and the elimination of pointers. A disadvantage is that it is usually necessary to dedicate a fairly large block to accommodate the worst-case size of the structure. In addition, it is often difficult or impractical to insert or remove elements from within the block. Since memory is traditionally a scarce resource, blocks have usually been reserved for fixed-size structures or for structures, such as the stack, that require the maximum speed of retrieval.

A CIRCULAR LIST

Round robin is a common name for a *circular list*. A circular list is a linked list in which the last entry points back to the first (see Figure 9.5). In the case of a circular list, a *current-block* pointer is often kept. In the case of events or programs waiting for service, a *current-event* pointer is moved by one position to the left or right each time. In a round robin, all blocks

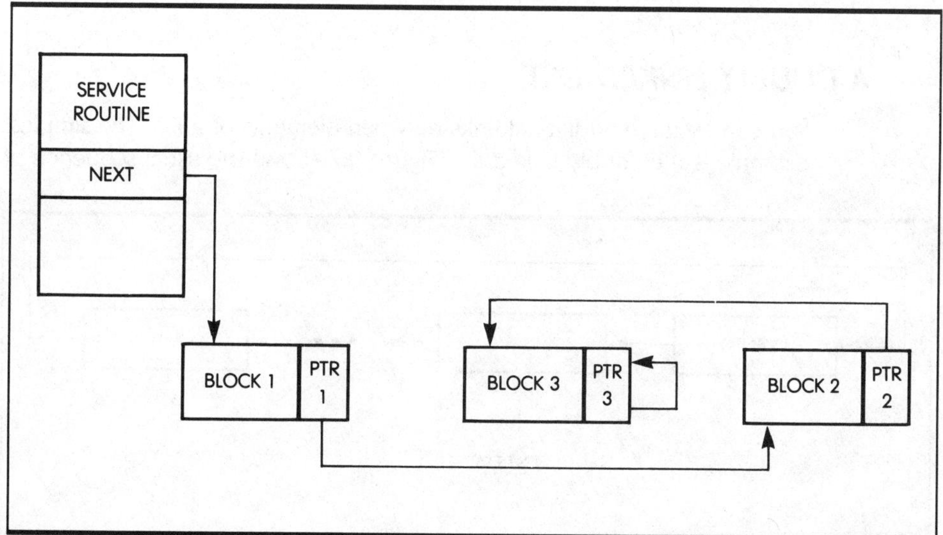

Figure 9.4: A Queue

have the same priority. However, a circular list may also be used as a subcase of other structures, to facilitate the retrieval of the first block after the last one when performing a search.

A polling program is a good example of a circular list. It usually proceeds in a round robin fashion, interrogating all peripherals and then coming back to the first one.

A TREE STRUCTURE

You can use a tree structure whenever a logical relationship (called a *syntax*) exists among all elements of a structure. A simple example of a tree structure is a descendant or genealogical tree (see Figure 9.6). The tree in Figure 9.6 shows that Smith has two children: a son, Robert, and a daughter, Jane. Jane, in turn, has three children: Liz, Tom, and Phil. Tom has two children: Max and Chris. Robert, on the left of the illustration, has no descendants.

This tree is a structured tree. The directory in Figure 9.1 is an example of a simple, two-level tree.

Trees are used to advantage whenever you can classify elements according to a fixed structure, thus facilitating insertion and retrieval. In addition, you can use trees to arrange groups of information in a structured way, so that you can easily use them for later processing, such as in a compiler or interpreter design.

A DOUBLY LINKED LIST

You can establish additional links between elements of a list. The simplest example is the doubly linked list. Figure 9.7 shows the usual sequence of

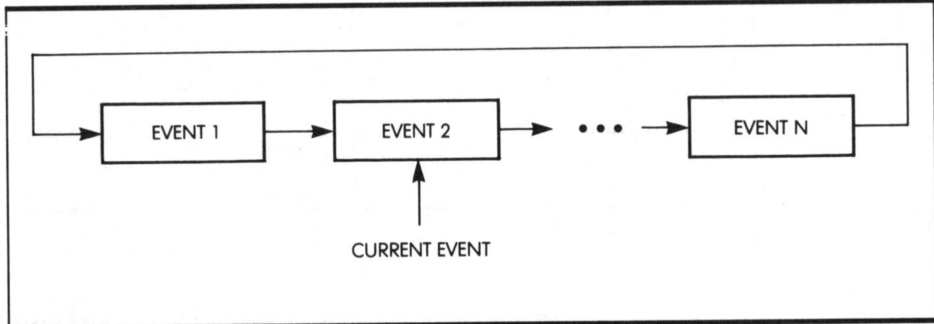

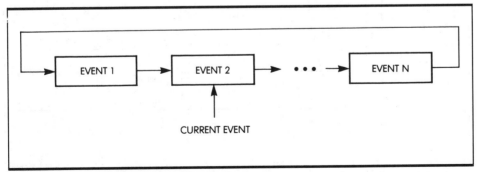

Figure 9.5: A Round Robin Is a Circular List

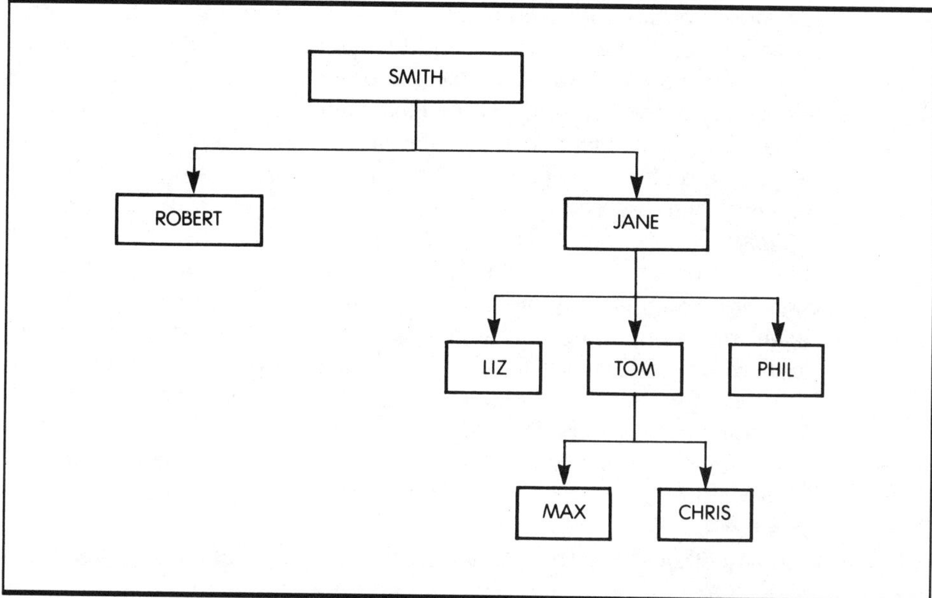

Figure 9.6: A Genealogical Tree

links from left to right, plus another sequence of links from right to left. The goal is to allow easy retrieval of the elements just before and after the element being processed. This method does, however, cost an extra pointer per block.

SEARCHING AND SORTING

The process of searching and sorting elements of a list depends directly on the type of structure used for the list. Programmers have developed many searching algorithms for the most frequently used data structures. As an

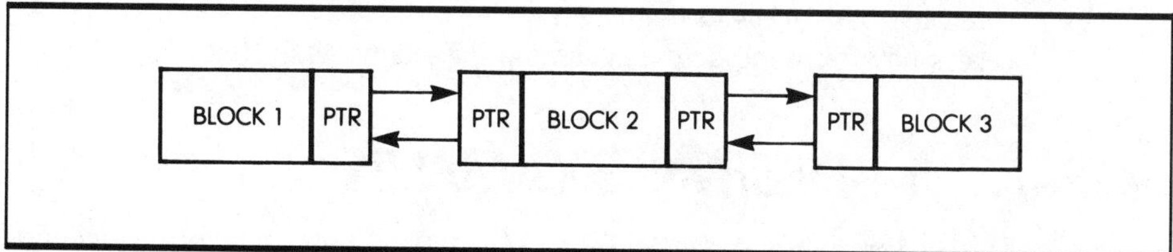

Figure 9.7: A Doubly Linked List

example, you used indexed addressing in Chapter 8 to search through a table for a particular element. Recall that you can use indexed addressing whenever the elements of a table are ordered by known criteria. Such elements can then be retrieved by their numbers.

Sequential searching refers to the linear scanning of an entire block. This technique is clearly inefficient, but you may need to use it when the elements are not ordered.

Binary or *logarithmic searching* attempts to find an element in a sorted list by dividing the *search interval* (the list being searched) in half at every step. For example, assume you are searching an alphabetical list. You might start in the middle of a table and determine if the name you are looking for is before or after that point. If it is after, you can eliminate the first half of the table and look at the middle element of the second half. You compare this entry again to the one you are looking for, restrict your search to one of the two halves, and so on. The maximum length of a search is then guaranteed to be log2n, where *n* is the number of elements in a table.

Many other search techniques exist; however, I cannot describe them all here.

SECTION SUMMARY

In this section, I have offered only a brief presentation of the usual data structures used by programmers. Although most common data structures have been organized into types and given a name, the overall organization of data in a complex system may use any combination of data structures, or even require programmers to invent more appropriate ones. The array of possibilities is limited only by your imagination. Similarly, several well-known sorting and searching techniques have been developed for coping with the usual data structures. A comprehensive description is beyond the scope of this book. In this section, I have stressed the importance of designing appropriate structures for manipulating data and provided the basic tools to that effect.

Let's now examine actual programming examples in detail.

PART II—DESIGN EXAMPLES

This section offers design examples for typical data structures, including the table, the sorted list, and the linked list. In particular, you will learn to program searching, insertion, and deletion algorithms for these structures.

To thoroughly understand the design examples, you must understand the concepts presented in the first part of this chapter. The programs I present here use many of the addressing modes of the 65816 and integrate many of the concepts and techniques presented in previous chapters.

I will now introduce three structures: a simple list, an alphabetic list, and a linked list, plus directory. For each structure, I will develop three programs: SEARCH, ENTER, and DELETE.

DATA REPRESENTATION FOR THE LIST

In the example shown in Figure 9.8, note that both the simple list and the alphabetic list use a common representation for each list element. Each element, or *entry*, includes a 3-byte label, and an *n*-byte block of data, where *n* is between 1 and 253. Thus, at most, each entry uses one page (256 bytes). Within each list, all elements are the same length (see Figure 9.9). Note that the programs operating on these two simple lists use some common variable conventions:

ENTLEN	length of an element: for example, if each element has 9 bytes of data, ENTLEN = 3 + 9 = 12
TABASE	base of the list or table in memory
POINTR	running pointer to the current element
OBJECT	current entry to be located, inserted, or deleted
TABLEN	number of entries

All labels are assumed to be distinct. Changing this convention would require a minor change in the programs.

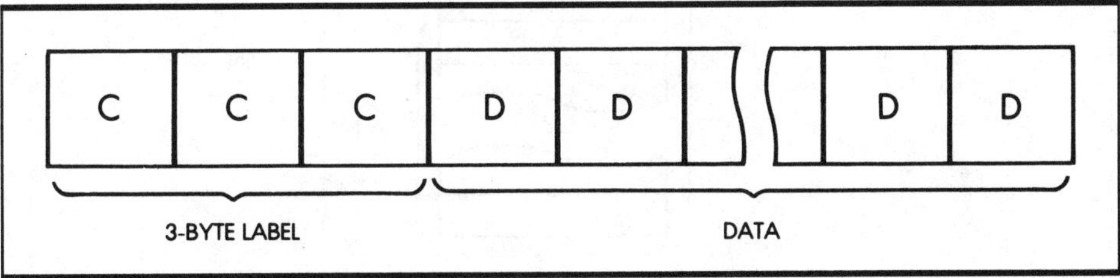

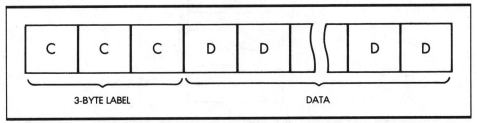

Figure 9.8: A Single List Entry

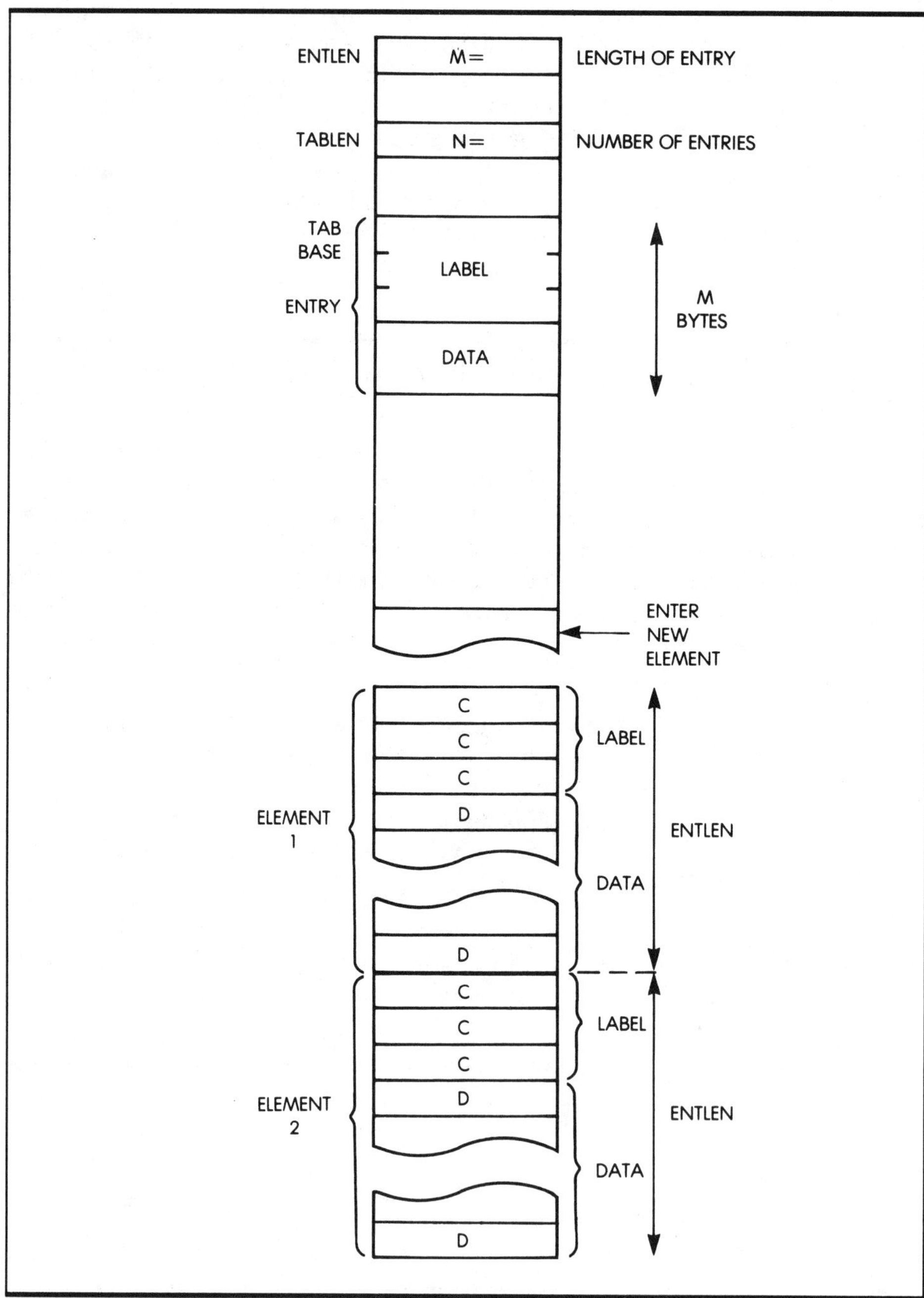

Figure 9.9: Typical List Entries in the Memory

SIMPLE LIST

In this example, I have organized a simple list as a table of *n* elements. The elements are not sorted (see Figure 9.10). The program searches by scanning the list until it either finds an entry or reaches the end of the table. The program inserts a new entry by appending it to the existing ones. When deleting, the entries in higher memory locations, if any, are shifted down to keep the table continuous. Let's examine these functions in more detail.

SEARCHING

Consider a serial search technique, where each entry's label field is compared in turn to the OBJECT's label, letter by letter. If the 16-bit mode is used, only two comparisons are needed to check the three bytes of the label, but the entry length must be an even number. This program uses the absolute indexed addressing mode and the direct indirect indexed mode.

The search proceeds in an obvious way. Figure 9.11 shows the corresponding flowchart for the program, called SEARCH (see Listing 9.1).

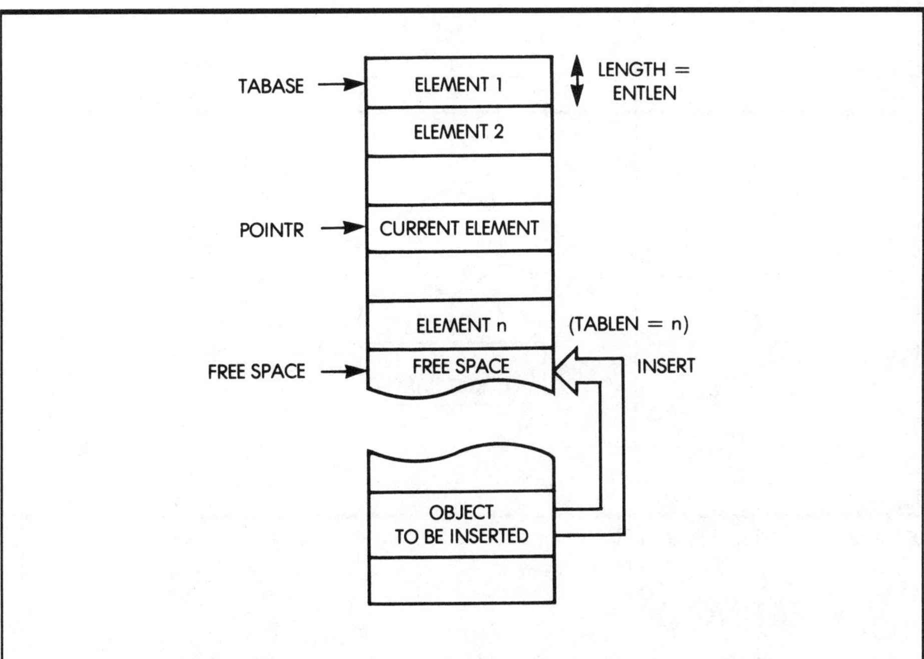

Figure 9.10: The Simple List

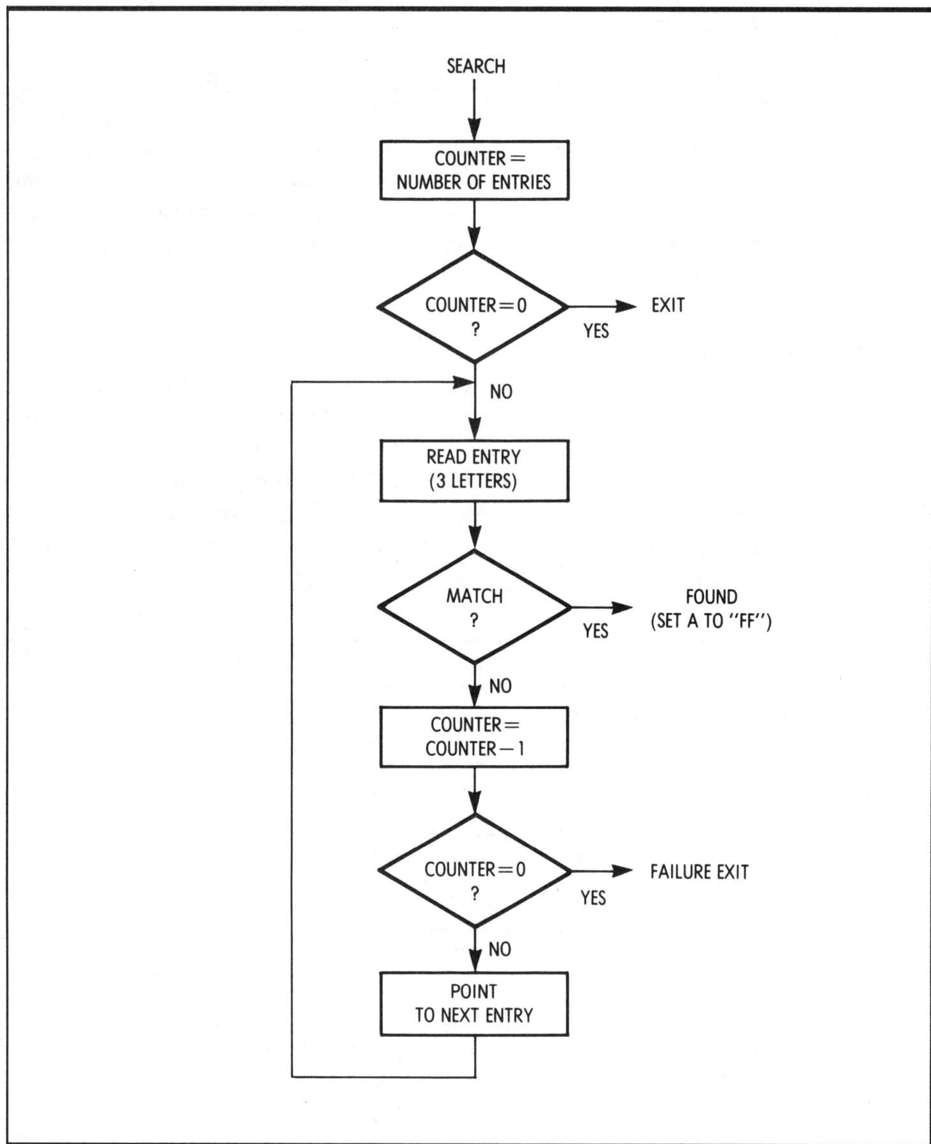

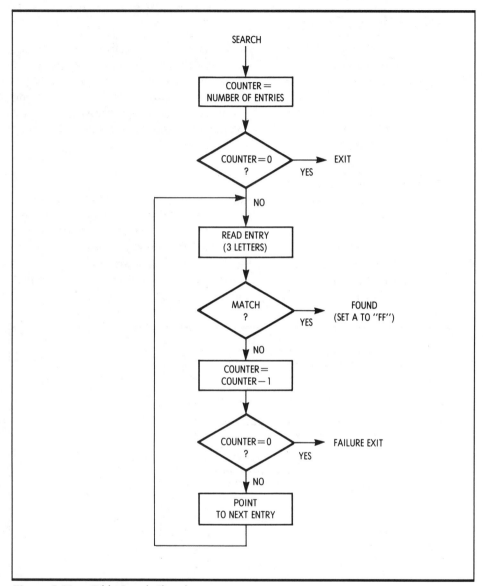

Figure 9.11: Table Search Flowchart

INSERTING

When you insert a new element, the first available memory block ENTLEN bytes long at the end of the list is used (see Figure 9.10). The pro-

```
SEARCH   LDA   #TABASE        SET POINTR TO
         STA   POINTR         START OF TABLE
         LDX   #TABLEN        GET TABLE LENGTH
         BEQ   OUT            QUIT IF EMPTY
ENTRY    LDY   #0
         LDA   OBJECT,Y
         CMP   (POINTR),Y     COMPARE FIRST TWO BYTES
         BNE   NOGOOD
         INY                  POINT TO 2ND AND 3RD BYTES
         LDA   OBJECT,Y
         CMP   (POINTR),Y     COMPARE NEXT TWO BYTES
         BEQ   FOUND
NOGOOD   DEX                  CHECK IF ALL ENTRIES
         BEQ   OUT            HAVE BEEN CHECKED
         LDA   #ENTLEN        POINT TO NEXT ENTRY
         CLC
         ADC   POINTR
         STA   POINTR
         BRA   ENTRY
FOUND    LDA   #$FFFF
OUT      RTS
```

Listing 9.1: SEARCH Program for a Simple List

gram first checks that the new entry is not already in the list. All labels are assumed to be distinct in this example. If the entry is not found, the program increments the list length TABLEN, and moves the OBJECT to the end of the list. Figure 9.12 shows the corresponding flowchart for the program, called NEW (see Listing 9.2). The 16-bit mode is being used, so only half as many transfers as there are bytes in the list need to be done.

DELETING

To delete an element from the list, the elements following that element in the list at higher addresses are merely moved up by one element position. The length of the list must also be decremented (see Figure 9.13). The corresponding program is called DELETE (see Listing 9.3).

ALPHABETIC LIST

Unlike a simple list, an alphabetic list or table keeps all of its elements sorted in alphabetical order. This allows the use of faster search techniques than can be used with a simple list.

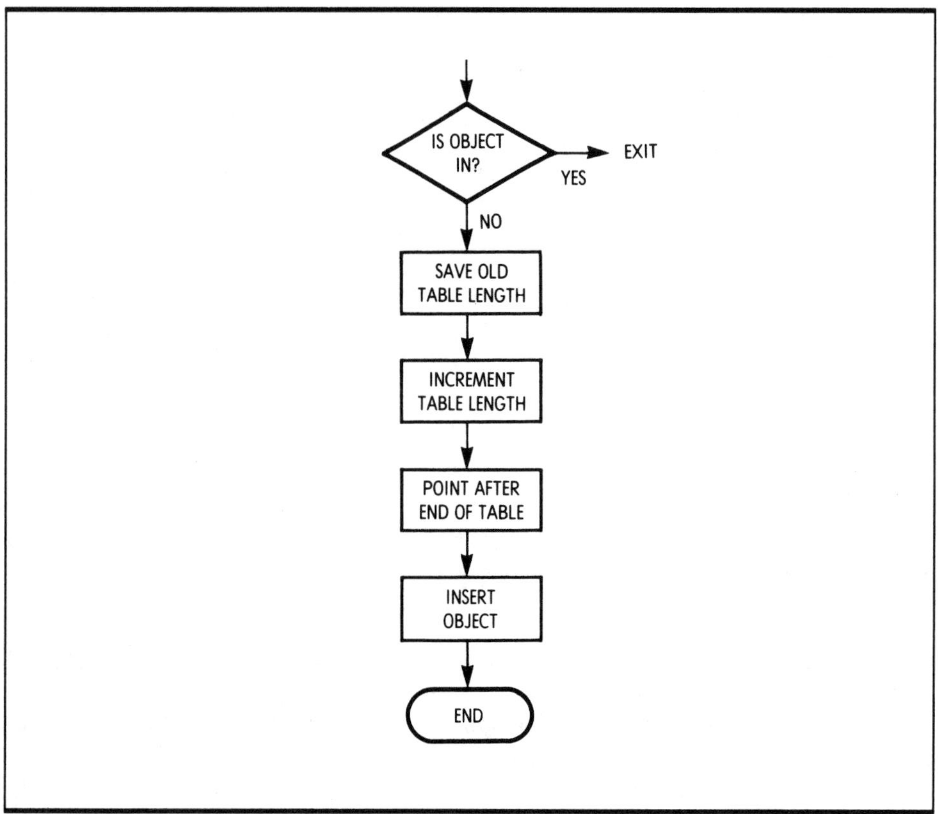

Figure 9.12: Table Insertion Flowchart

SEARCHING

The search algorithm is a classic binary search. Recall that this technique is essentially analogous to the one used to find a name in a telephone book, where you start somewhere in the middle of the book and then, depending on the entries found, go either forward or backward to find the desired entry. This method is fast and reasonably simple to implement.

The binary search flowchart appears in Figure 9.14. Listing 9.4 shows the program.

The alphabetic list keeps the entries in alphabetical order and retrieves them using a binary or logarithmic type search. Figure 9.15 shows an example of a binary search. The search is somewhat complicated because it is necessary to keep track of several conditions. The major problem is to avoid searching forever for an object that is not there. In such a case, the entries with higher and lower alphabetic values would be alternately

```
NEW       CLC                       SET TO NATIVE MODE
          XCE
          REP     #$30              SET TO 16-BIT MODE
          JSR     SEARCH
          BNE     OUTN              FOUND IF NOT 0
          LDA     TABLEN
          BEQ     INSERT            INSERT IF TABLEN 0
          LDA     POINTR
          CLC
          ADC     #ENTLEN           POINT BEYOND END OF TABLE
          STA     POINTR
INSERT    INC     TABLEN
          LDY     #0
          LDA     #ENTLEN           DIVIDE LENGTH BY 2
          LSR     A                 BECAUSE 16 BITS ARE MOVED
          TAX                       EACH TIME
LOOPN     LDA     OBJECT,Y          MOVE OBJECT TO END OF TABLE
          STA     (POINTR),Y
          INY
          INY
          DEX
          BNE     LOOPN             LOOP UNTIL ALL WORDS ARE MOVED
OUTN      SEC                       SET TO EMULATION MODE
          XCE
          RTS
```

Listing 9.2: NEW Program for a Simple List

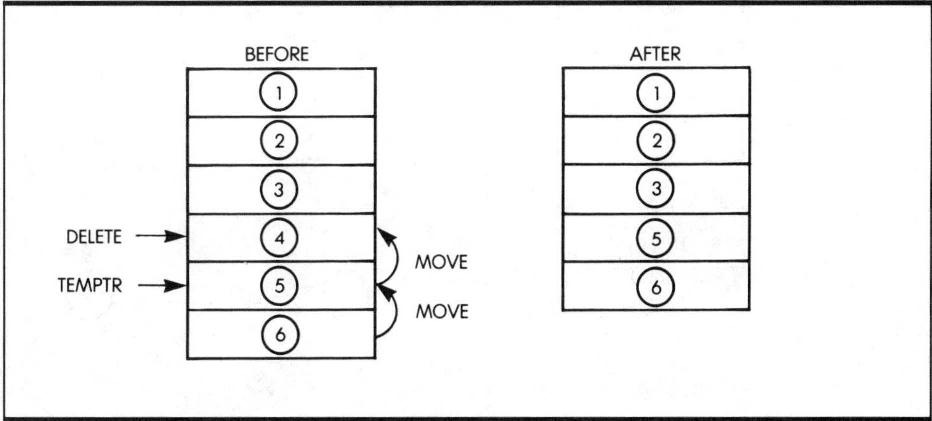

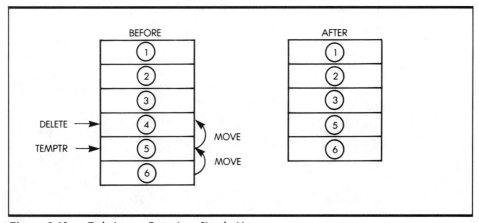

Figure 9.13: Deleting an Entry in a Simple List

tested forever. To avoid such an occurrence, a flag is maintained in the program to preserve the value of the carry flag after an unsuccessful comparison. When the INCMNT value, which shows the amount by which the pointer was incremented, reaches the value 1, the CLOSENOW flag is

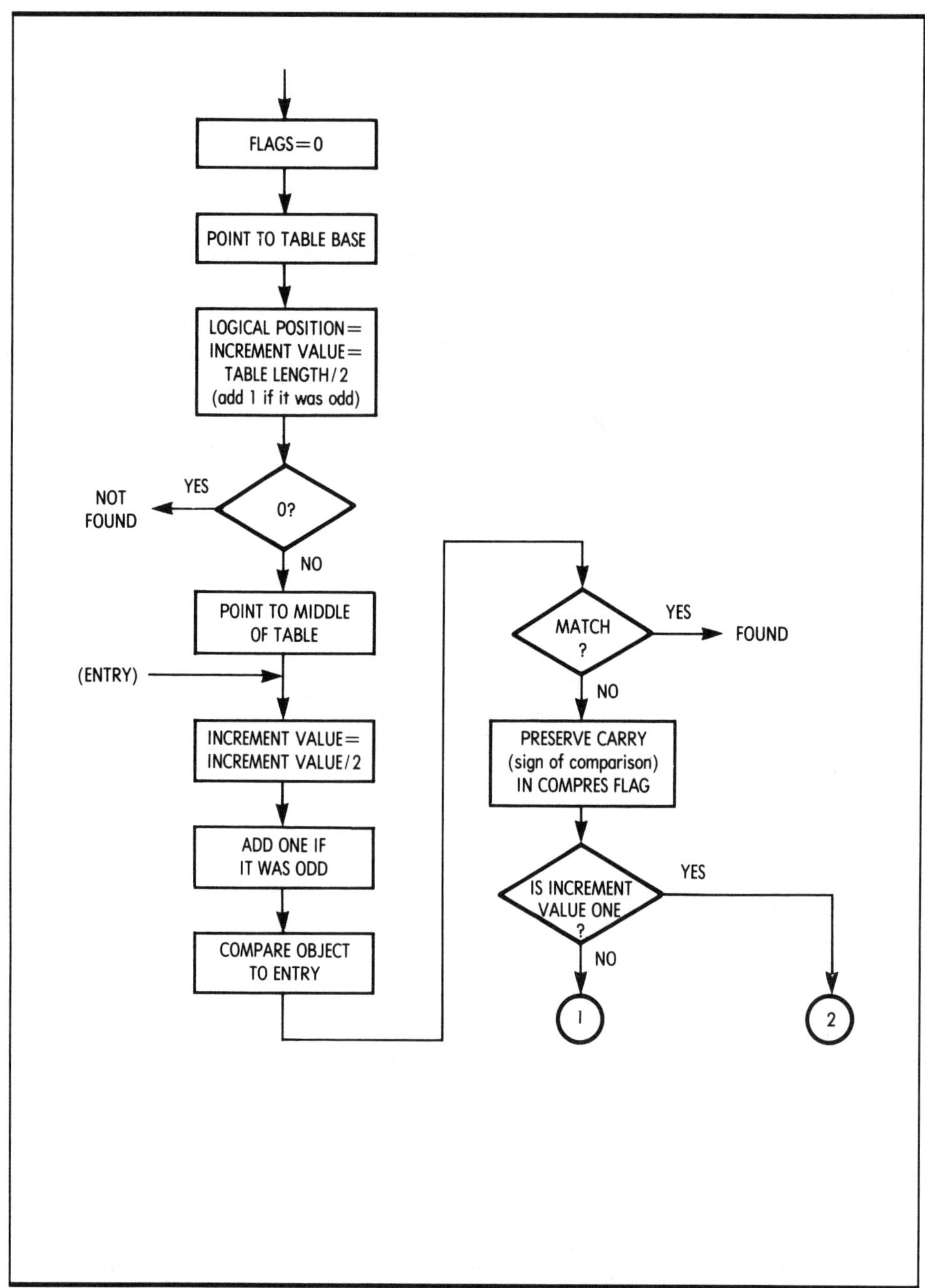

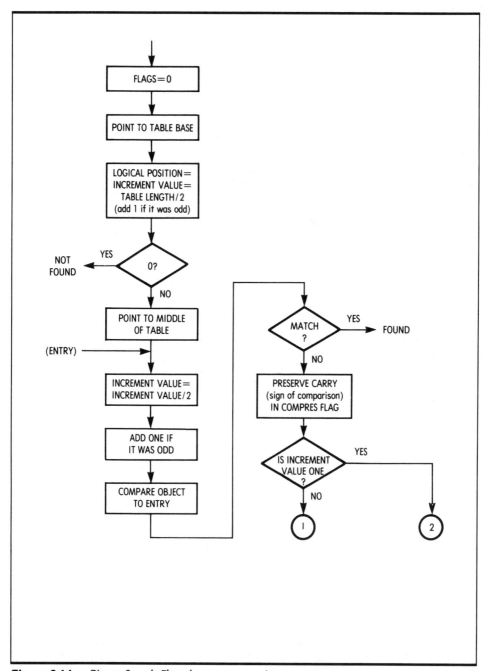

Figure 9.14: Binary Search Flowchart

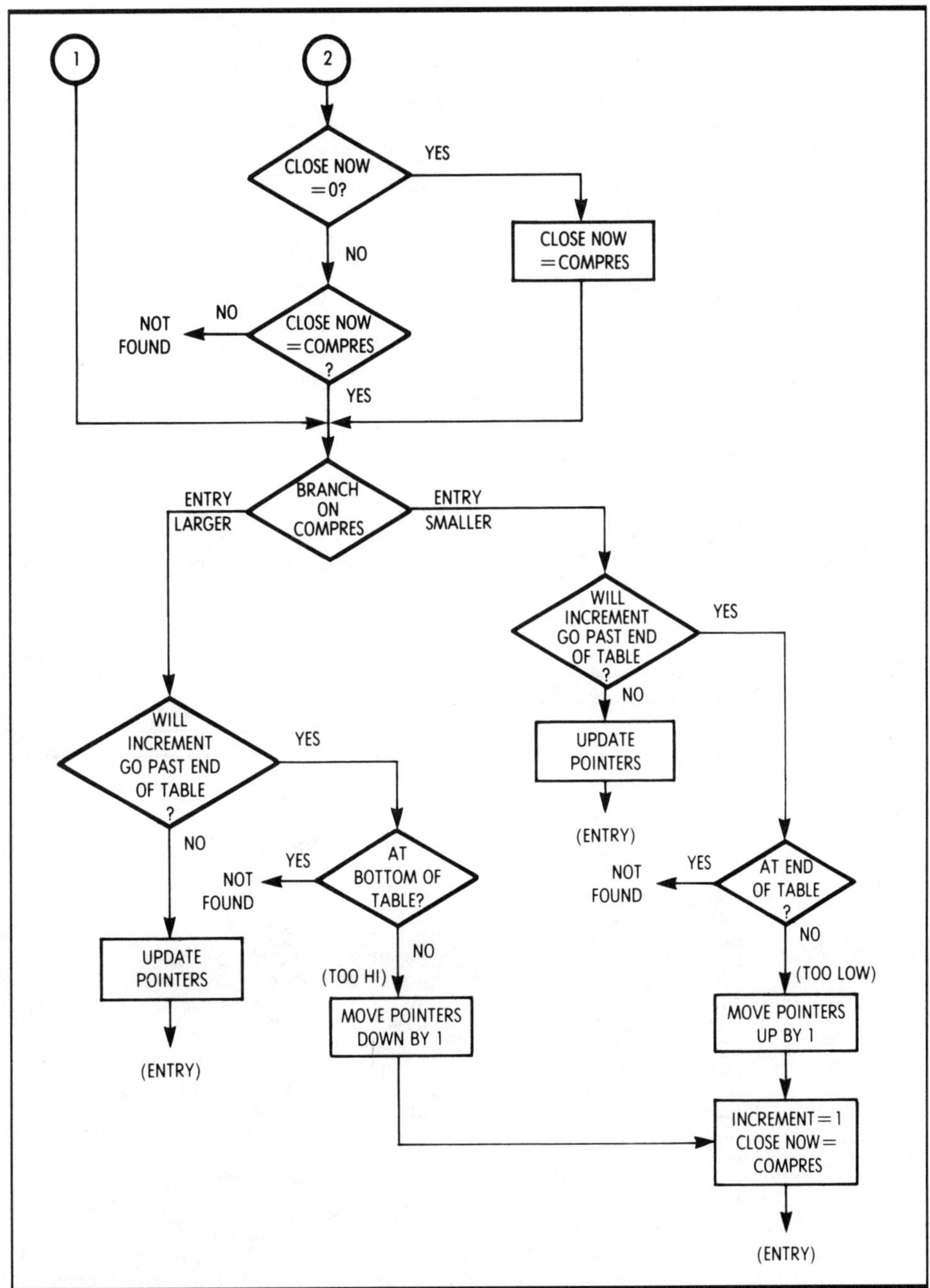

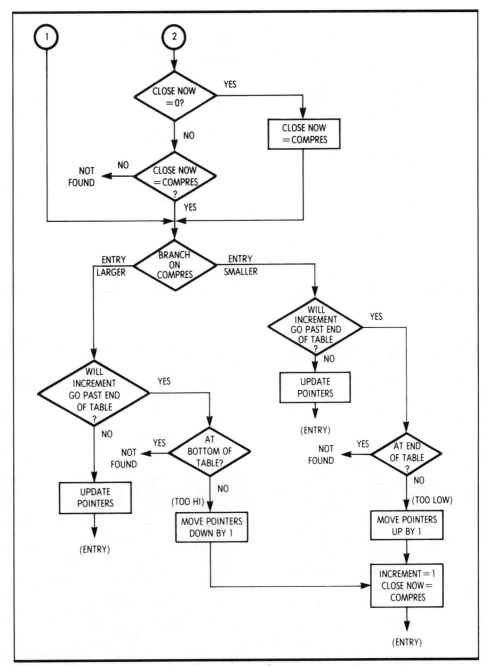

Figure 9.14: Binary Search Flowchart (continued)

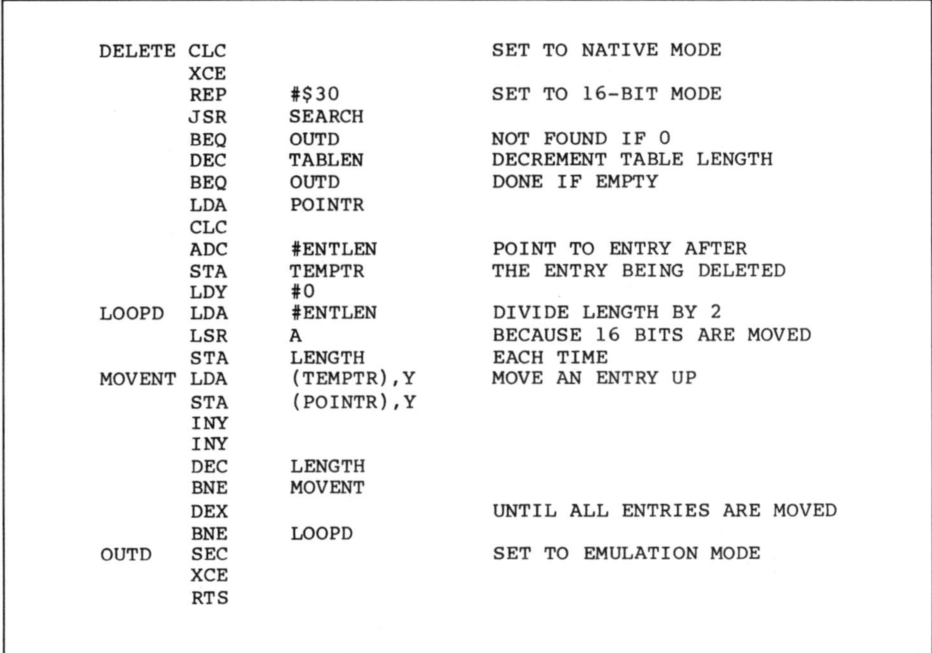

```
DELETE CLC                          SET TO NATIVE MODE
       XCE
       REP     #$30                 SET TO 16-BIT MODE
       JSR     SEARCH
       BEQ     OUTD                 NOT FOUND IF 0
       DEC     TABLEN               DECREMENT TABLE LENGTH
       BEQ     OUTD                 DONE IF EMPTY
       LDA     POINTR
       CLC
       ADC     #ENTLEN              POINT TO ENTRY AFTER
       STA     TEMPTR               THE ENTRY BEING DELETED
       LDY     #0
LOOPD  LDA     #ENTLEN              DIVIDE LENGTH BY 2
       LSR     A                    BECAUSE 16 BITS ARE MOVED
       STA     LENGTH               EACH TIME
MOVENT LDA     (TEMPTR),Y           MOVE AN ENTRY UP
       STA     (POINTR),Y
       INY
       INY
       DEC     LENGTH
       BNE     MOVENT
       DEX                          UNTIL ALL ENTRIES ARE MOVED
       BNE     LOOPD
OUTD   SEC                          SET TO EMULATION MODE
       XCE
       RTS
```

Listing 9.3: DELETE Program for a Simple List

```
SEARCH  STZ     CLOSE               CLEAR FLAGS
        STZ     CMPRES
        LDA     #TABASE             POINT TO BEGINNING
        STA     POINTR
        LDA     TABLEN
        BNE     DIV
        BRL     OUT                 QUIT IF TABLEN 0
DIV     LSR     A                   DIVIDE TABLEN BY 2
        ADC     #0                  ADD BACK ODD BIT
        STA     LOGPOS              SAVE LOGICAL POSITION
        STA     INCMNT              SAVE INCREMENT
        LDX     LOGPOS
        DEX
        BEQ     ENTRY               IF LOGPOS=0 POINTR IS READY
LOOP    LDA     #ENTLEN             MULTIPLY ENTLEN BY LOGPOS
        CLC                         BY ADDING ENTLEN LOGPOS TIMES
        ADC     POINTR              ADD RESULT TO POINTR
        STA     POINTR
        DEX
        BNE     LOOP
```

Listing 9.4: Binary SEARCH Program for an Alphabetic List

```
ENTRY    LDA      INCMNT             DIVIDE INCMNT BY 2
         LSR      A
         ADC      #0
         STA      INCMNT
         LDY      #0
         LDA      OBJECT,Y
         CMP      (POINTR),Y         COMPARE OBJECT TO TABLE ENTRY
         BNE      NOGOOD
         INY
         LDA      OBJECT,Y
         CMP      (POINTR),Y
         BNE      NOGOOD
         BRL      FOUND              OBJECT FOUND IN TABLE
NOGOOD   LDY      #$FFFF
         BCC      TESTS              C=0 IF OBJ<POINTR
         LDY      #1
TESTS    STY      CMPRES             STORE IN COMPARISON RESULT FLAG
         LDY      INCMNT
         DEY                         IS INCMNT 1?
         BNE      NEXT               CHECK CLOSE FLAG
         LDA      CLOSE              IF CLOSE FLAG NOT SET
         BEQ      MAKCLO             SET CLOSE FLAG
         SEC
         SBC      CMPRES             SEE IF GONE PAST WHERE
         BEQ      NEXT               OBJECT SHOULD BE
         BRL      OUT                IF PAST NOT FOUND
MAKCLO   LDA      CMPRES             MAKE CLOSE=COMPRES
         STA      CLOSE
NEXT     BIT      CMPRES
         BMI      SUBIT
         LDA      TABLEN             SEE IF ADDITION OF INCMNT WILL
         SEC                         RUN PAST END OF TABLE
         SBC      LOGPOS
         BEQ      OUT                CHECK IF AT END OF TABLE
         SBC      INCMNT
         BCC      TOOHI
         LDX      INCMNT             OK TO INCREMENT POINTR
ADDER    LDA      #ENTLEN            MULTIPLY ENTLEN BY INCMNT
         CLC
         ADC      POINTR             ADD RESULT TO POINTR
         STA      POINTR
         DEX
         BNE      ADDER
         LDA      LOGPOS
         CLC
         ADC      INCMNT
         STA      LOGPOS
         BRL      ENTRY
TOOHI    INC      LOGPOS             POINT TO NEXT ENTRY
         LDA      #ENTLEN
         CLC
         ADC      POINTR
         STA      POINTR
         BRA      SETCLO
```

Listing 9.4: Binary SEARCH Program for an Alphabetic List (continued)

```
SUBIT   LDA    LOGPOS       SEE IF INCREMENT WILL RUN PAST
        SEC                 THE OTHER END OF THE TABLE
        SBC    INCMNT
        BEQ    TOOLOW
        BCC    TOOLOW
        STA    LOGPOS       SAVE NEW LOGICAL POSITION
        LDX    INCMNT
SUBLOP  LDA    POINTR       MULTIPLY ENTLEN BY INCMNT
        SEC
        SBC    #ENTLEN
        STA    POINTR       SUBTRACT RESULT FROM POINTR
        DEX
        BNE    SUBLOP
        BRL    ENTRY
TOOLOW  LDX    LOGPOS
        DEX
        BEQ    OUT          IF LOGPOS 1 OBJECT NOT IN TABLE
        DEC    LOGPOS
        LDA    POINTR       POINT TO PREVIOUS ENTRY
        SEC
        SBC    #ENTLEN
        STA    POINTR
SETCLO  LDA    #1
        STA    INCMNT
        LDA    CMPRES
        STA    CLOSE
        BRL    ENTRY
OUT     LDA    #$FFFF
FOUND   RTS
```

Listing 9.4: Binary SEARCH Program for an Alphabetic List (continued)

set to 1. The COMPRES (comparison result) flag stores the carry bit from the last comparison. When CLOSENOW is set, the value of COMPRES is compared with the carry bit of the most recent comparison. If they are not equal, the search terminates because the object cannot be found.

The carry bit for the last comparison is returned in A for use by the NEW program. This allows the NEW program to determine whether a new element goes before or after the entry pointed to by the SEARCH program.

The other major problem that you must deal with is the possibility of running off one end of the table when adding or subtracting the increment. You can solve this by performing a test add or subtract of that increment to the logical position or element number. The program then compares this number to 1 and the table length. If it is greater than the table length or less than 1, the program adjusts it to fall within the table boundaries.

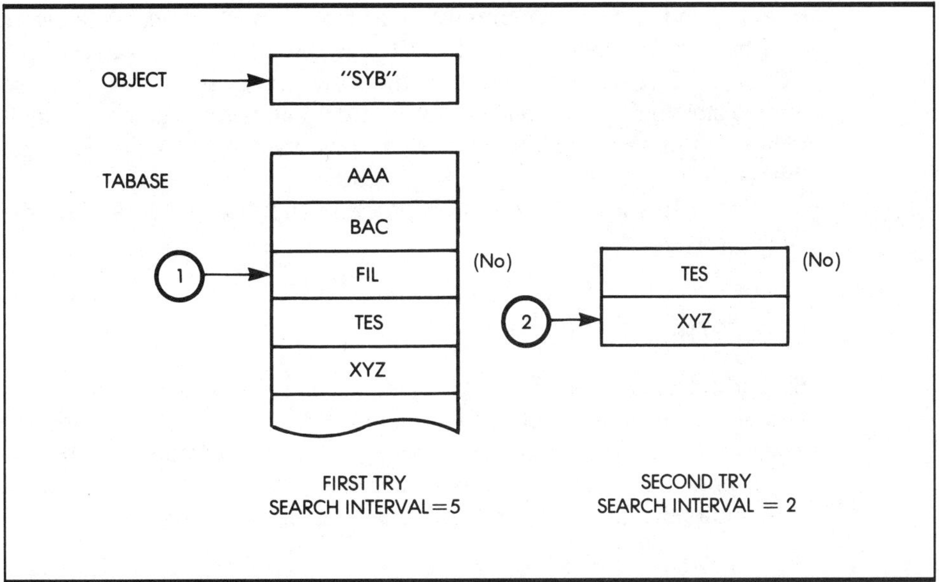

Figure 9.15: A Binary Search

The following variables are used in the program:

LOGPOS	logical position (element number)
INCMNT	value by which the pointer will be incremented or decremented if the next comparison fails
CLOSE	short for CLOSENOW
CMPRES	short for comparison result

An additional complication to this program occurs because the search interval at times can be either even or odd. Since the interval is divided by two to form the increment, you use an LSR instruction. If the bit falling off the right end is not added back into the accumulator, then only even or odd numbered elements would be checked, depending on the value of the table length. This would cause erroneous results.

Study the Binary SEARCH program in Listing 9.4 with care, as it is much more complex than the linear search.

ELEMENT INSERTION

To insert a new element, you must conduct a binary search. If the program finds the element in the table, it does not need to insert it. But if it does not find it, the program must insert that element immediately before or after the last element to which it was compared. The value of the COMPRES flag indicates whether the new object should be inserted immediately before or after the last element compared. All the elements following the new location are moved down by one block position, and the new object is inserted.

Figure 9.16 shows the insertion process, and Listing 9.5 displays the NEW program.

ELEMENT DELETION

Similarly, a binary search is conducted to find the object. If the search fails, the element does not need to be deleted. If the search succeeds, the element is deleted, and all the following elements are moved up by one block position. A corresponding example appears in Figure 9.17. Figure 9.18 shows the flowchart, and Listing 9.6 displays the program.

LINKED LIST

The linked list is assumed to contain, as usual, the three alphanumeric characters for the label, followed by 1 to 250 bytes of data, then a 2-byte

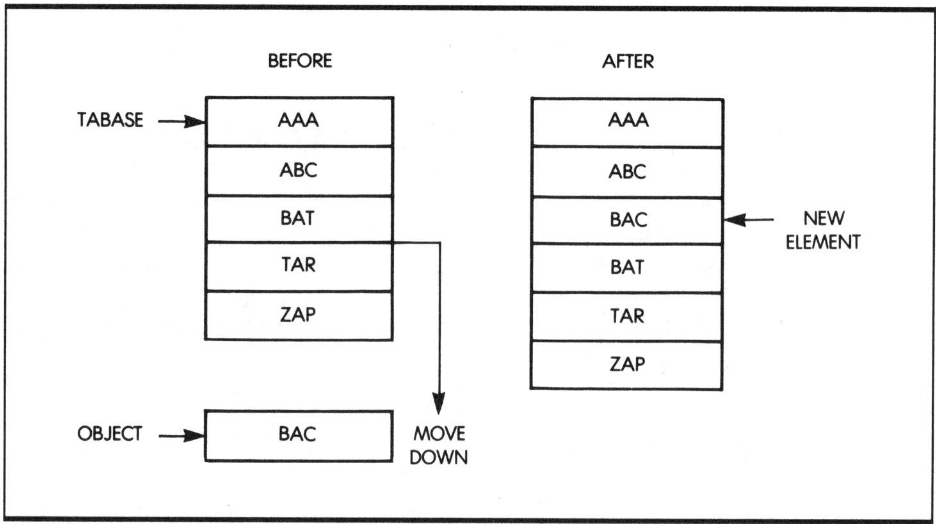

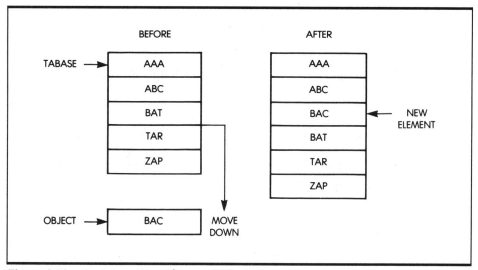

Figure 9.16: Inserting a New Element, BAC

```
NEW      CLC                          SET TO NATIVE MODE
         XCE
         REP      #$30                SET TO 16-BIT MODE
         JSR      SEARCH
         BEQ      OUTN                FOUND IF ZERO
         LDA      TABLEN              IF TABLE EMPTY
         BEQ      INSERT              INSERT
         BIT      CMPRES
         BPL      LOSIDE
         DEC      LOGPOS              SET LOGICAL POSITION
         BRA      SETUP               OBJECT GOES AFTER POINTR
LOSIDE   LDA      #ENTLEN             OBJECT GOES BEFORE POINTR
         CLC
         ADC      POINTR
         STA      POINTR
SETUP    LDA      TABLEN
         SEC                          SET HOW MANY ENTRIES TO
         SBC      LOGPOS              MOVE TO MAKE ROOM FOR OBJECT
         BEQ      INSERT              INSERT IF 0 TO MOVE
         TAX
         TAY
         DEY
         BEQ      SETEMP              SKIP IF POINTING TO LAST ENTRY
UPLOOP   LDA      #ENTLEN             ADD ENTLEN TO POINTR UNTIL
         CLC                          POINTING TO THE LAST ENTRY
         ADC      POINTR
         STA      POINTR
         DEY
         BNE      UPLOOP
SETEMP   LDA      POINTR              PREPARE TO MOVE ENTRIES
         CLC
         ADC      #ENTLEN
         STA      TEMPTR
         LDA      #ENTLEN
         LSR      A                   DIVIDE BY 2
         STA      LENGTH
         LDY      #0
ANOTHR   LDA      (POINTR),Y          MOVE AN ENTRY
         STA      (TEMPTR),Y
         INY
         INY
         DEC      LENGTH
         BNE      ANOTHR
         LDA      POINTR
         SEC
         SBC      #ENTLEN
         STA      POINTR
         DEX                          UNTIL ALL ENTRIES ARE MOVED
         BNE      SETEMP              TO MAKE SPACE FOR OBJECT
         LDA      #ENTLEN
         CLC
         ADC      POINTR              POINTR TO WHERE OBJECT GOES IN TABLE
         STA      POINTR
INSERT   LDY      #0
         LDA      #ENTLEN
```

Listing 9.5: NEW Program for an Alphabetic List

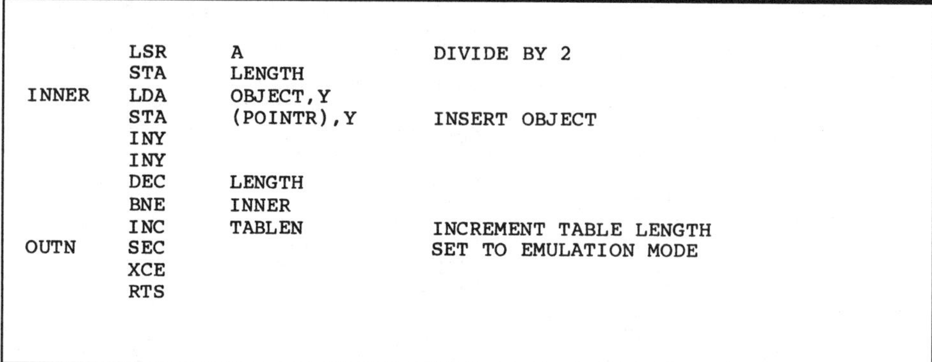

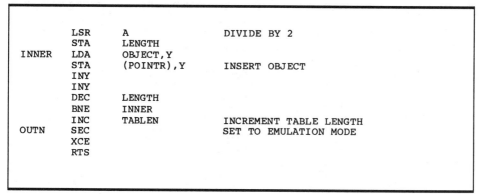

```
        LSR     A               DIVIDE BY 2
        STA     LENGTH
INNER   LDA     OBJECT,Y
        STA     (POINTR),Y      INSERT OBJECT
        INY
        INY
        DEC     LENGTH
        BNE     INNER
        INC     TABLEN          INCREMENT TABLE LENGTH
OUTN    SEC                     SET TO EMULATION MODE
        XCE
        RTS
```

Listing 9.5: NEW Program for an Alphabetic List (continued)

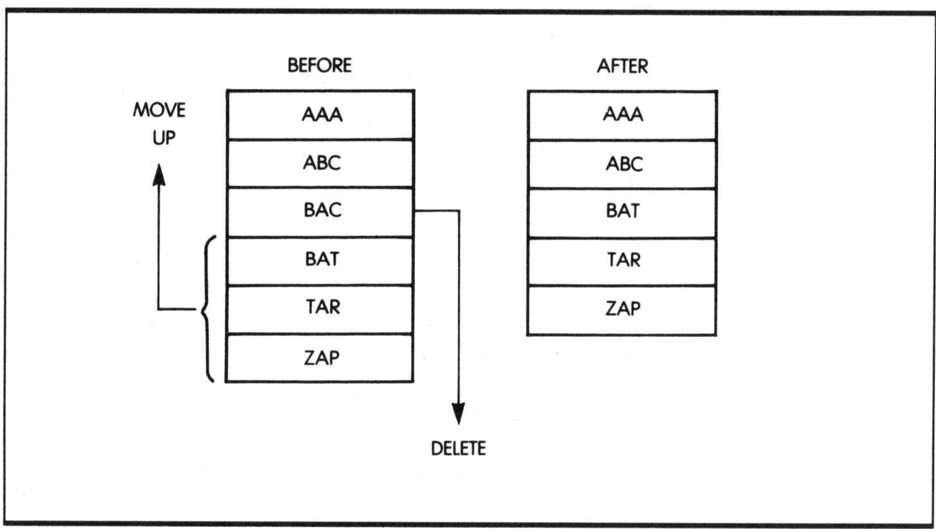

Figure 9.17: Deleting an Element, BAC

pointer that contains the starting address of the next entry, and finally, a 1-byte marker. Whenever this 1-byte marker is set to 1, it prevents the insert routine from substituting a new entry in place of the existing one. Figure 9.19 shows the structure of an entry.

Further, a directory contains a pointer to the first entry for each letter of the alphabet, facilitating retrieval. The program assumes that the labels are ASCII alphabetic characters. All pointers at the end of the list are set to a NIL value (which is here equal to the table base minus 1), as this value should never occur within the linked list.

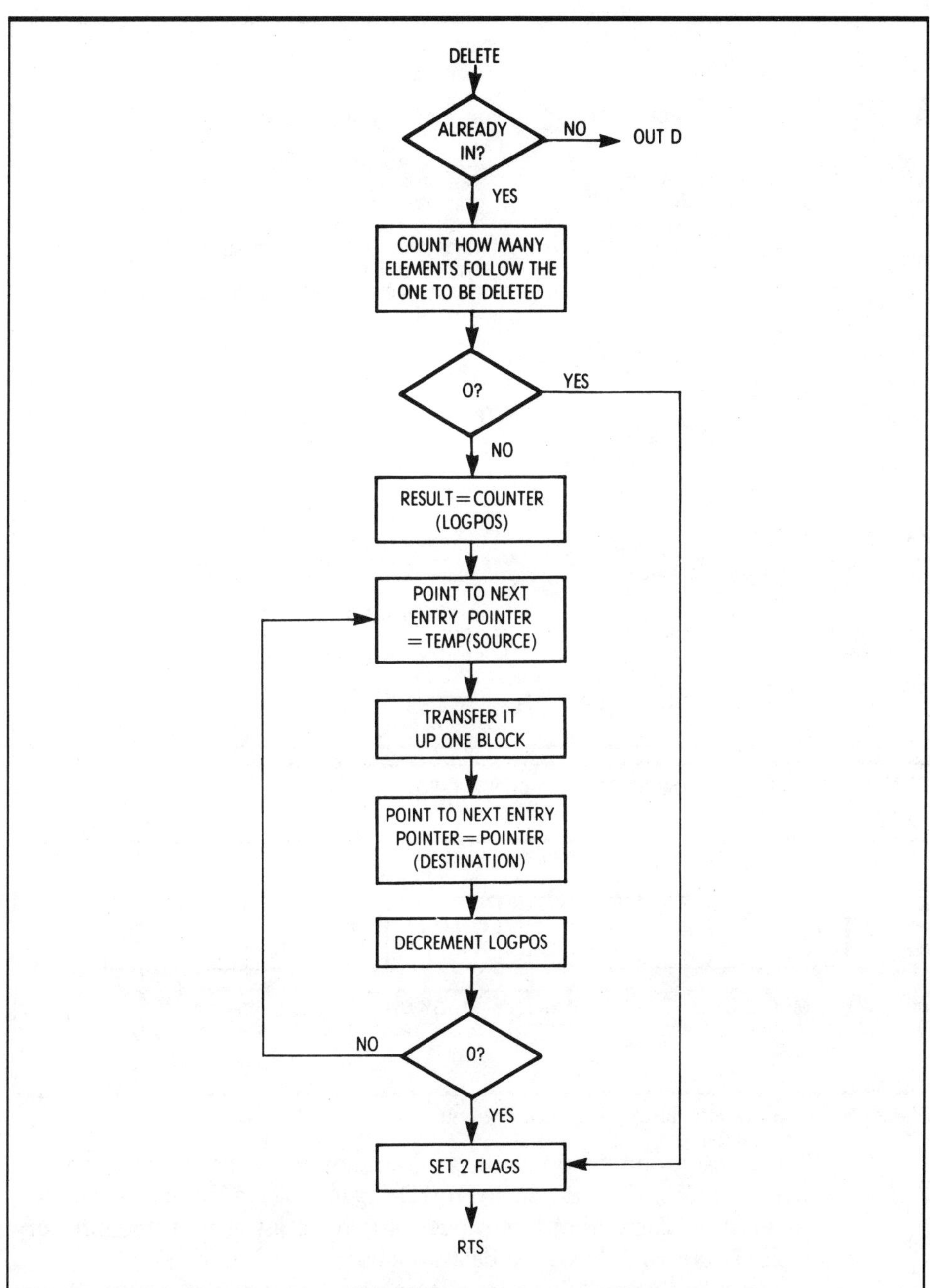

Figure 9.18: Deletion Flowchart for an Alphabetic List

```
DELETE  CLC                     SET TO NATIVE MODE
        XCE
        REP     #$30            SET TO 16-BIT MODE
        JSR     SEARCH
        BNE     OUTD            NOT ZERO NOT FOUND
        LDA     TABLEN          SEE HOW MANY ENTRIES ARE IN
        SEC                     THE TABLE AFTER OBJECT
        SBC     LOGPOS
        BEQ     DECER           IF NONE ALMOST FINISHED
        STA     LOGPOS          SAVE COUNT IN LOGPOS
        LDA     #ENTLEN         POINT TEMPTR AFTER OBJECT IN TABLE
        CLC
        ADC     POINTR
        STA     TEMPTR
        LDY     #0
BIGLOP  LDA     #ENTLEN
        LSR     A               DIVIDE BY 2
        STA     LENGTH
WORD    LDA     (TEMPTR),Y      MOVE ENTRIES
        STA     (POINTR),Y
        INY
        INY
        DEC     LENGTH
        BNE     WORD
        DEC     LOGPOS
        BNE     BIGLOP          UNTIL TABLE HAS NO GAP
DECER   DEC     TABLEN          DECREMENT TABLE LENGTH
OUTD    SEC                     SET TO EMULATION MODE
        XCE
        RTS
```

Listing 9.6: DELETE Program for an Alphabetic List

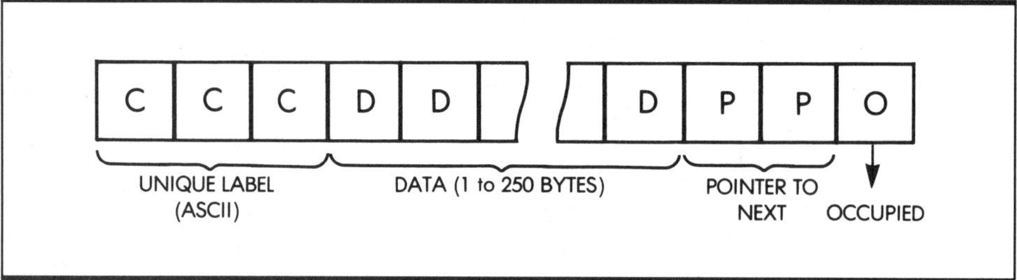

Figure 9.19: Data Structure of a Linked List Entry

The insertion and deletion programs perform the obvious pointer manipulations. They use the INDEXED flag to indicate if a pointer pointing to an object came from a previous entry in the list or from the directory table. Figure 9.20 shows the data structure.

An application for this data structure would be a computerized address book, where each person is represented by a unique three-letter code

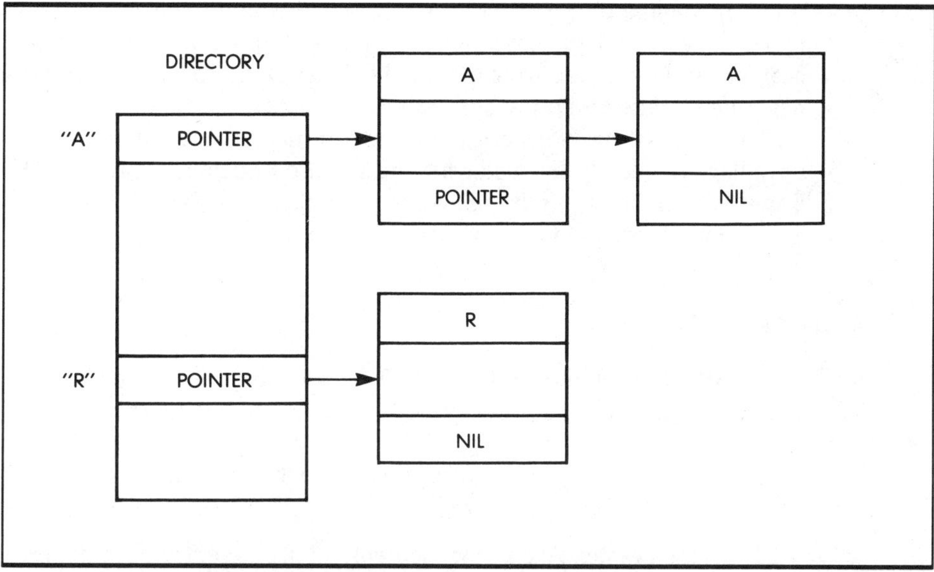

Figure 9.20: Linked List Structure

(perhaps the usual initials), and the data field contains a simplified address plus the telephone number (up to 250 characters). Let's examine the structure in more detail. The entry format also appears in Figure 9.19. As usual, the conventions are:

ENTLEN total element length (in bytes)
TABASE address of base list

Here, REFBASE points to the base address of the directory, or the *reference table.*

Each two-byte address within this directory points to the first occurrence of the letter to which it corresponds in the list. Thus, each group of entries with an identical first letter in its labels actually forms a separate list within the whole structure. This feature facilitates searching and is analogous to an address book. Note that no data are moved during a deletion; only pointers are changed, as in every well-behaved linked-list structure.

If no entry starting with a specific letter is found, or if there is no entry alphabetically following an existing one, the pointers will point to the beginning of the table minus 1 (NIL). The letters in the three-character code are assumed to be alphabetic letters in ASCII code. Changing this would require changing the constant in the PRETAB routine.

The end-of-table marker is set to the value of the beginning of the table minus 1 (NIL). By convention, the NIL pointers, found at the end of a string or within a directory location that does not point to a string, are set to the value of the table base minus 1, in order to provide a unique identification. Some other convention could be used, but the NIL pointer must never be confused with the address of an entry.

Insertions and deletions are performed in the usual way (see Part I of this chapter), merely by modifying the required pointers. The INDEXED flag is used to indicate if the pointer to the object is in the reference table or in another string element.

SEARCHING

The SEARCH program (see Listing 9.7) uses a subroutine called PRETAB. The search principle, as shown in Figure 9.21, is straightforward:

1. Get the directory entry corresponding to the letter of the alphabet in the first position of the OBJECT's label. PRETAB does this.
2. Get the pointer. Access the element. If NIL, the entry does not exist.
3. If not NIL, match the element against the OBJECT. If they are not the same, get the pointer to the next entry down the list.
4. Go back to 2.

```
SEARCH  LDA     #1              INITIALIZE INDEXD FLAG
        STA     INDEXD
        JSR     PRETAB          GET REF. POINTR FOR START
        LDA     (INDLOC),Y      PUT IN POINTR
        STA     POINTR
ENTRY   CMP     #TABASE-1       SEE IF END OF TABLE
        BEQ     NOTFND          DONE IF IT IS
        LDY     #0
        LDA     OBJECT,Y
        CMP     (POINTR),Y      COMPARE OBJECT
        BCC     NOTFND          NOT IN TABLE
        BNE     NOGOOD          TRY NEXT ENTRY
        INY
        LDA     OBJECT,Y
        CMP     (POINTR),Y
        BCC     NOTFND
        BEQ     FOUND
NOGOOD  LDA     POINTR
        STA     OLD             SAVE POINTR FOR LATER
        LDY     #ENTLEN-4
```

Listing 9.7: SEARCH Program for a Linked List

```
         LDA     (POINTR),Y       GET POINTR FROM ENTRY
         STA     POINTR           STORE IN POINTR
         STZ     INDEXD
         BRA     ENTRY
NOTFND   LDA     #$FFFF
FOUND    RTS

PRETAB   LDY     #0
         SEP     #$20             SET TO 8-BIT ACCUMULATOR MODE
         LDA     OBJECT,Y         GET FIRST BYTE OF OBJECT
         SEC
         SBC     #$41             REMOVE ASCII OFFSET
         ASL     A                MULTIPLY BY 2
         REP     #$30             BACK TO THE 16-BIT MODE
         CLC
         ADC     #REFBAS          INDEX TO REFERENCE TABLE
         STA     INDLOC
         RTS
```

Listing 9.7: SEARCH Program for a Linked List (continued)

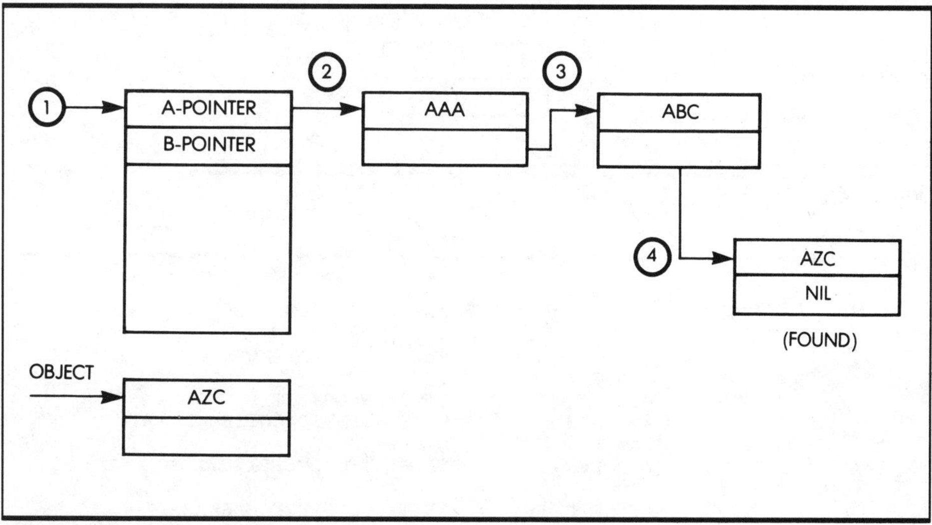

Figure 9.21: A Search in a Linked List

INSERTING

The insertion is essentially a search followed by an insertion once a NIL has been found (see Figure 9.22). The program allocates a block of storage for the new entry by looking for an occupancy marker set at *available*. The program, called NEW, appears in Listing 9.8.

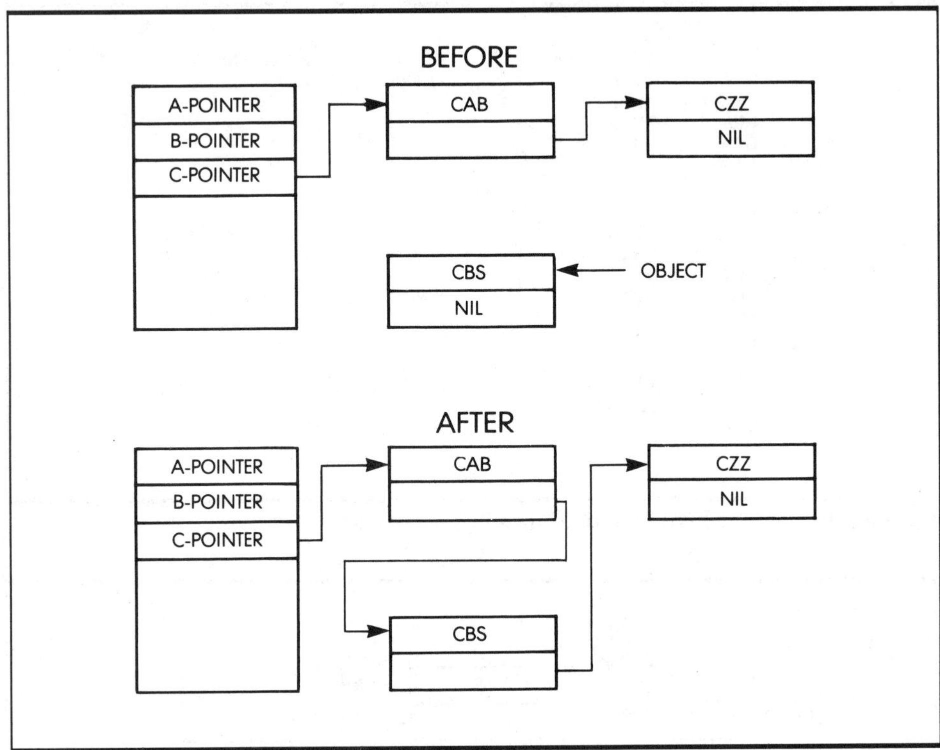

Figure 9.22: Example of Insertion in a Linked List

```
NEW     CLC                          SET TO NATIVE MODE
        XCE
        REP     #$30                 SET TO 16-BIT MODE
        JSR     SEARCH
        BEQ     OUTN                 STOP IF OBJECT FOUND
        LDA     #TABASE              LOOK FOR UNOCCUPIED ENTRY
        STA     TEMPTR
        LDY     #ENTLEN-2            OFFSET TO OCCUPIED FLAG
LOOP    LDA     #1
        CMP     (TEMPTR),Y           TEST OCCUPANCY MARKER
        BNE     INSERT
        LDA     TEMPTR               POINT TO NEXT BLOCK
        CLC
        ADC     #ENTLEN
        STA     TEMPTR
        BRA     LOOP
INSERT  LDA     #ENTLEN-4            LENGTH OF OBJECT
```

Listing 9.8: NEW Program for a Linked List

```
        LSR     A               DIVIDE BY 2
        STA     LENGTH
        LDY     #0
LOPE    LDA     OBJECT,Y        MOVE OBJECT
        STA     (TEMPTR),Y
        INY
        INY
        DEC     LENGTH
        BNE     LOPE
        LDA     POINTR          PUT POINTR INTO ENTRY
        STA     (TEMPTR),Y
        INY
        INY
        LDA     #1
        STA     (TEMPTR),Y      STORE OCCUPIED FLAG
        LDA     INDEXD          TEST IF IT WAS IN REF. TABLE
        BNE     SETINX          AND NEEDS ADJUSTING
        DEY
        DEY
        LDA     TEMPTR
        STA     (OLD),Y         CHANGE PREVIOUS ENTRY'S POINTR
        BRA     OUTN
SETINX  JSR     PRETAB          GET ADDRESS
        LDA     TEMPTR          LOAD NEW ADDRESS
        STA     (INDLOC),Y
OUTN    SEC                     SET TO EMULATION MODE
        XCE
        RTS
```

Listing 9.8: NEW Program for a Linked List (continued)

DELETING

The element is deleted by setting its occupancy marker to *available* and adjusting the pointer to it from the directory or the previous element. An example appears in Figure 9.23. The program, called DELETE, appears in Listing 9.9.

SUMMARY

If you are a beginning programmer, it is not essential for you to understand the details of data structure implementation and management. However, as you program more complex problems, you will need to learn about data structures. The examples presented in this chapter were designed to help you understand and solve the common problems encountered with these structures.

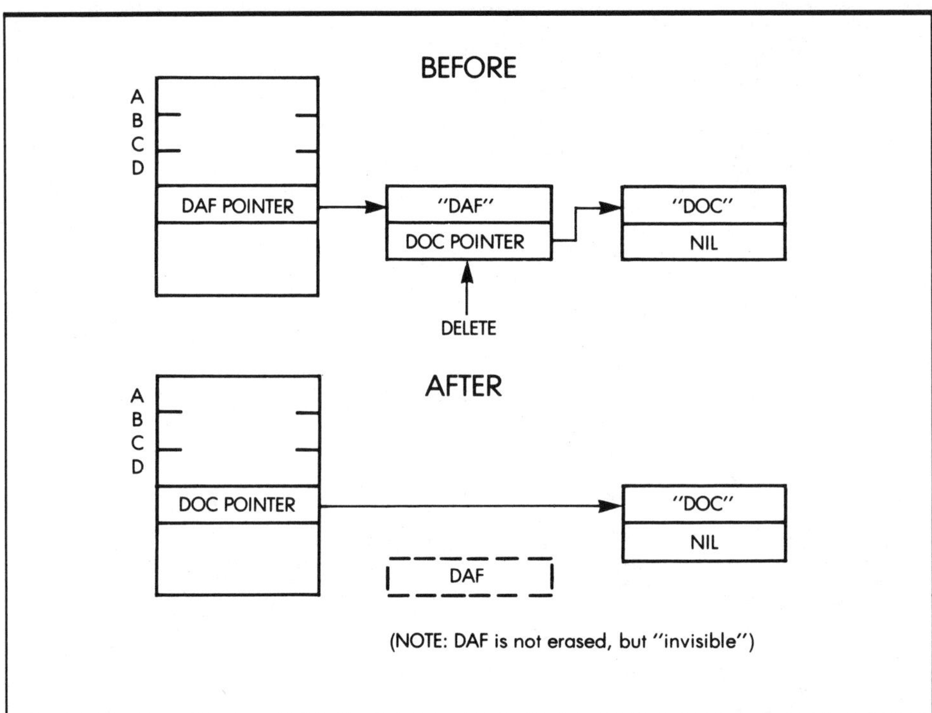

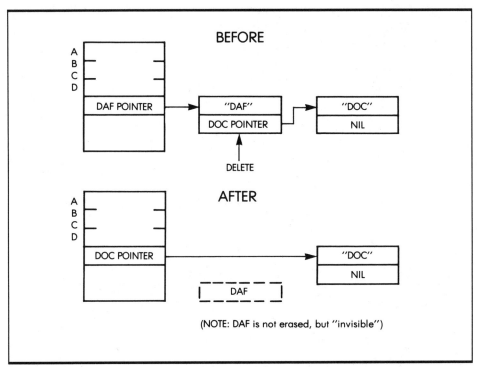

Figure 9.23: Example of Deletion in a Linked List

```
DELETE  CLC                     SET TO NATIVE MODE
        XCE
        REP     #$30            SET TO 16-BIT MODE
        JSR     SEARCH
        BNE     OUTD
        LDY     #ENTLEN-4
        LDA     (POINTR),Y      GET POINTR FROM ENTRY
        STA     TEMPTR
        INY
        INY
        LDA     #0
        STA     (POINTR),Y      CLEAR OCCUPIED MARK
        LDA     INDEXD          CHECK IF REF. TABLE NEEDS UPDATE
        BEQ     PREINX
        JSR     PRETAB          GET POINTR INTO REFERENCE TABLE
        JMP     MOVEIT
PREINX  LDA     OLD
        CLC
        ADC     #ENTLEN-4
```

Listing 9.9: DELETE Program for a Linked List

```
         STA     INDLOC          POINT TO PREVIOUS ENTRY'S POINTR
MOVEIT   LDA     TEMPTR
         LDY     #0
         STA     (INDLOC),Y      STORE POINTR
OUTD     SEC                     SET TO EMULATION MODE
         XCE
         RTS
```

Listing 9.9: DELETE Program for a Linked List (continued)

EXERCISES

9-1: *Examine Figure 9.24. At address 15 in the memory, there is a pointer to Table T. Table T starts at address 500. What are the actual contents of the pointer to T?*

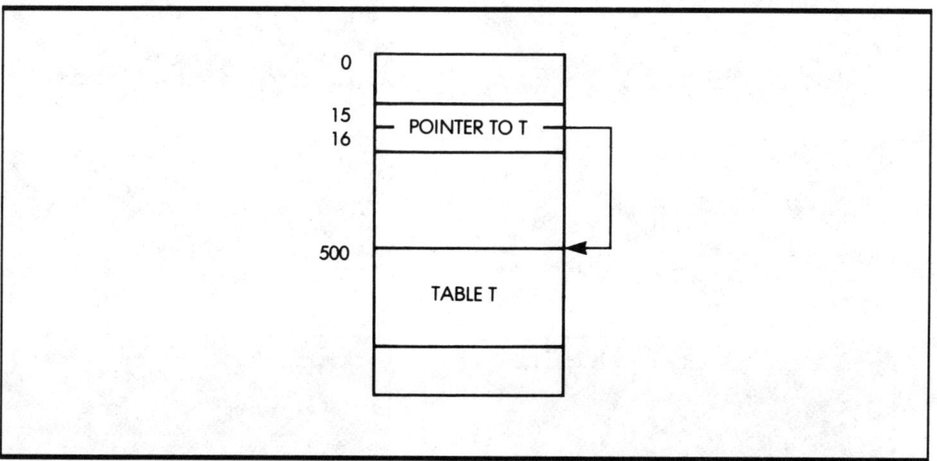

Figure 9.24: Pointer to T

9-2: *Draw a diagram showing how Block 2 would be removed from the structure in Figure 9.2.*

PROGRAM DEVELOPMENT

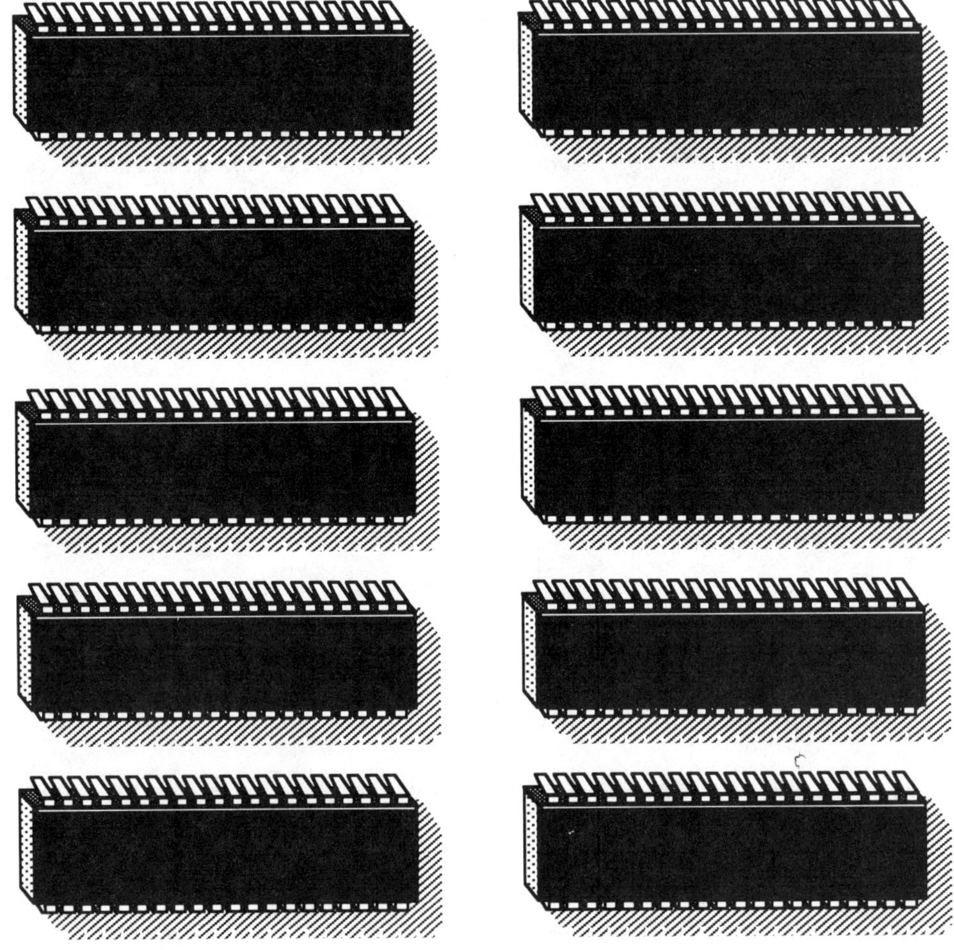

10

You have now reached the point where you should seriously consider developing actual programs. Before proceeding to this task—which is the goal of all your efforts—you should give careful consideration to the options and tools available for developing programs. There are several levels of hardware and software resources available. Which level is appropriate depends on the specific application. This chapter presents and evaluates all the available resources.

PROGRAMMING CHOICES

You may write a program either in binary or hexadecimal, in an assembly-level language, or in a high-level language. Let's discuss these alternatives. Figure 10.1 shows the different levels of programming.

HEXADECIMAL CODING

Most programs are conceived using assembly-language mnemonics. The actual translation of such mnemonics into the corresponding binary code requires an assembler. When there is no assembler, you must manually perform the translation from mnemonics into binary. Because translating into binary is tedious and error-prone, programmers often use hexadecimal. Also, many single-board microcomputers require the entry of programs in hexadecimal mode.

Note: In Chapter 1, I showed that one hexadecimal digit represents four binary bits. Therefore, two hexadecimal digits can represent the contents of a byte. Appendix D gives the hexadecimal equivalent of the 65816 instructions.

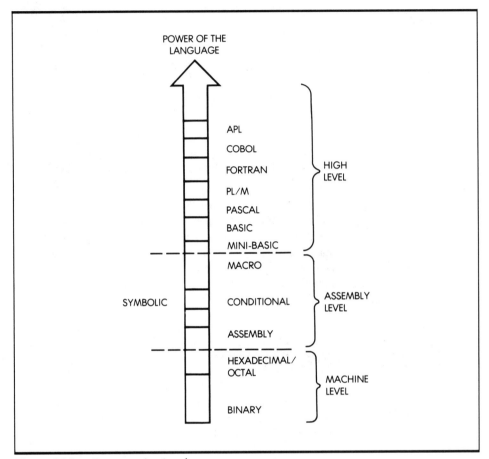

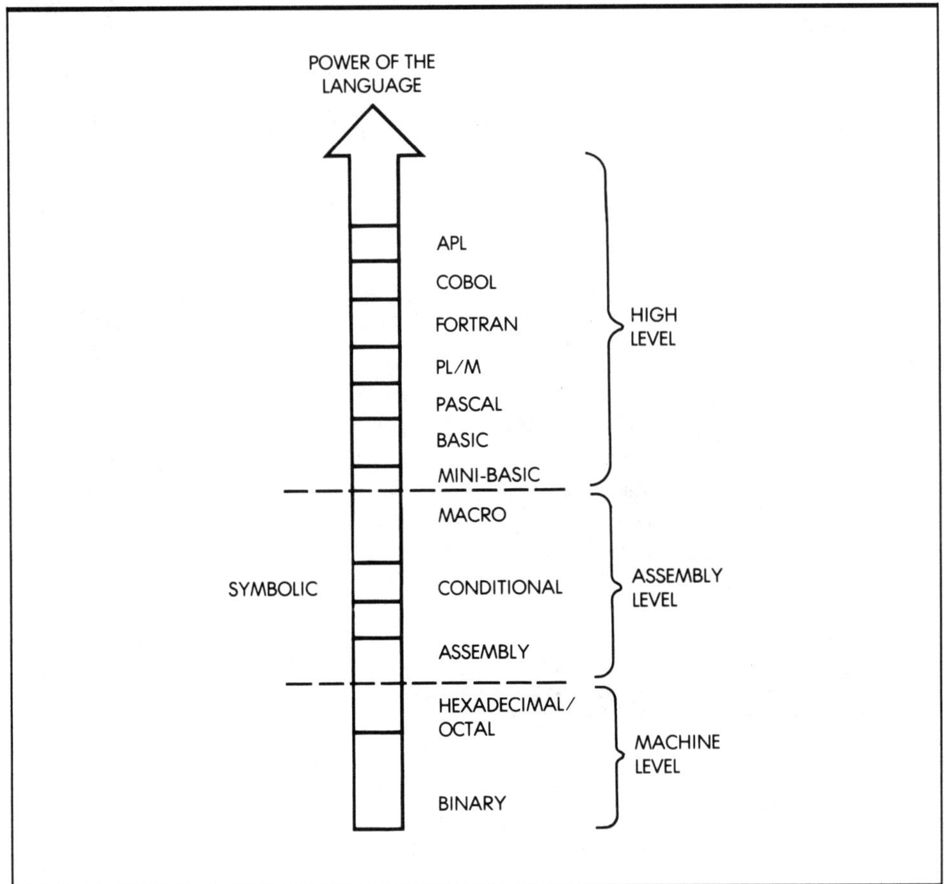

Figure 10.1: Programming Levels

Although it is reasonable to translate a program into hexadecimal by hand for a few instructions (for example, 10 to 100), when a program is larger this process becomes tedious and error-prone. Although most single-board microcomputers do not have an assembler and a full alphanumeric keyboard (to limit cost), they do provide a hexadecimal keyboard and 7-segment LED displays for program entry and debugging.

In summary, hexadecimal coding is not a desirable way to enter a program into a computer; it is simply an economical way. The cost of an assembler and the required alphanumeric keyboard is traded off against the increased time and effort required to enter the program into the memory. Therefore, if you have to use hexadecimal coding, it is wise to first write the program in assembly-language mnemonics, then convert it into hexadecimal code. This is because a program written in assembly language is easier to understand and debug.

ASSEMBLY LANGUAGE PROGRAMMING

Assembly-level programming includes both those programs written in symbolic form but entered into the system in hexadecimal form, and those entered in symbolic assembly-level form. Let's now examine the entry of a program directly in its assembly language representation.

When you are entering a program in assembly language, you must have an assembler program available that can read the mnemonic instructions of the program and translate them into the required bit patterns, using one to four bytes, as specified by the encoding of the instructions. A good assembler also offers several additional facilities for writing a program. In particular, it might offer *directives* or *pseudo-operations* that modify the value of symbols, and it might also facilitate symbolic addressing.

Note: If you use symbolic labels, you can insert an extra instruction between a branch and the point to which it branches without rewriting the entire program. The assembler automatically adjusts all the labels during the translation process. In addition, you can debug the program in symbolic form if an assembler is available.

Later in this chapter, I will review the various software resources normally available on a system. I will first, however, examine the third alternative: high-level language programming.

HIGH-LEVEL LANGUAGE

You can also write a program in a high-level language, such as BASIC, FORTRAN, or Pascal. A high-level language offers powerful instructions that make programming faster and easier than assembly language. These instructions are translated by a complex program into the final binary representation that a microcomputer can execute. Typically, each high-level instruction is translated into many individual binary instructions by a program called a compiler or an interpreter. A *compiler* translates all the instructions of a program into object code, and then executes the resulting code. By contrast, an *interpreter* interprets a single instruction and executes it, then translates the next one and executes it. An interpreter offers the advantage of interactive response, but results in low efficiency when compared to a compiler. I will not cover these topics further here. Instead, I will show you how to program an actual microprocessor in assembly-level language.

SOFTWARE SUPPORT

I will begin by reviewing the main software facilities available in a complete system for convenient software development. As I proceed, I will summarize the definitions introduced previously and define the remaining important programs available in a software development system.

The *assembler* translates the mnemonic representation of instructions into their binary equivalent. It normally translates one symbolic instruction into one binary instruction (which may occupy between one and four bytes). The resulting binary code, called the *object code,* is directly executable by the microcomputer. The assembler also produces a complete mnemonic listing of the program, and a symbol definition list (examples of listings appear later in this chapter). In addition, the assembler lists syntax errors (such as misspelled or illegal instructions), branching errors, and duplicate or missing labels. It does not, however, detect *logical* errors. (Such errors are *your* problem.)

A *compiler* translates high-level language instructions into their binary form. An *interpreter,* on the other hand, is similar to a compiler, but it often does not generate an intermediate code; it simply executes the high-level instructions directly.

The *monitor* is the basic program that is indispensable for using the hardware resources of the system. It continuously monitors the input devices for input; it also manages the rest of the devices. As an example, a minimal monitor for a single-board microcomputer, equipped with a keyboard and LEDs, continuously scans the keyboard for user input and displays the specified contents on the light-emitting diodes. In addition, it must recognize several limited commands from the keyboard, such as START, STOP, CONTINUE, LOAD MEMORY, or EXAMINE MEMORY. On a large system that provides complex file management or task scheduling, the monitor is often qualified as the *executive* program. The overall set of facilities is called the *operating system;* if the files are residing on a disk, the operating system is qualified as the *disk operating system,* or DOS.

An *editor* facilitates the entry and modification of text or programs. It allows users to conveniently enter, append, and insert characters; add and remove lines of text; and search for characters or strings. The editor is an important resource for convenient and effective text entry.

A *debugger* is a facility necessary for debugging programs. When a program does not work correctly, there may typically be no indication of the cause. In such a case, the programmer may want to insert breakpoints in the program to suspend the execution of the program at specified addresses and to examine the contents of registers or memory at these points. The debugger is useful for suspending a program; examining, displaying, and modifying the contents of its registers or memory; and then resuming execution. A good debugger also offers several additional facilities that allow the programmer to examine data in symbolic form (hexadecimal, binary, or other usual representations), as well as to enter data in this format.

A *loader* or *linking loader* places various blocks of object code at specified positions in the memory and adjusts their respective symbolic pointers, so that they can reference each other.

A *simulator* or an *emulator* program simulates the operation of a device (usually the microprocessor) so you can develop a program on a simulated processor prior to placing it on the actual board. Using this approach, you can suspend the program, modify it, and keep it in RAM memory. The disadvantages of a simulator are the following:

1. It usually simulates only the processor itself, not input/output devices.
2. The execution speed is slow, so the instruction cycle times are much longer. It is, therefore, not possible to test real-time devices; and synchronization problems may still occur, even though the logic of the program may be found to be correct.

An *emulator* is essentially a simulator in real time. An emulator uses one processor to simulate another one, and it simulates it in complete detail.

Utility routines are essentially the routines necessary in most applications. They are usually the routines that users wish the manufacturer had provided. They may include multiplication, division, and other arithmetic operations, as well as block move routines, character tests, input/output device handlers (or drivers), and others. Figure 10.2 shows a memory map for a typical program development system.

THE PROGRAM DEVELOPMENT SEQUENCE

I will now describe a typical sequence for developing an assembly-level program. I will assume that all the usual software facilities are available, so that I can demonstrate their value. If they are not available in a particular system, you can still develop programs, but the convenience will be decreased and, therefore, the amount of time necessary to debug the program is likely to be increased.

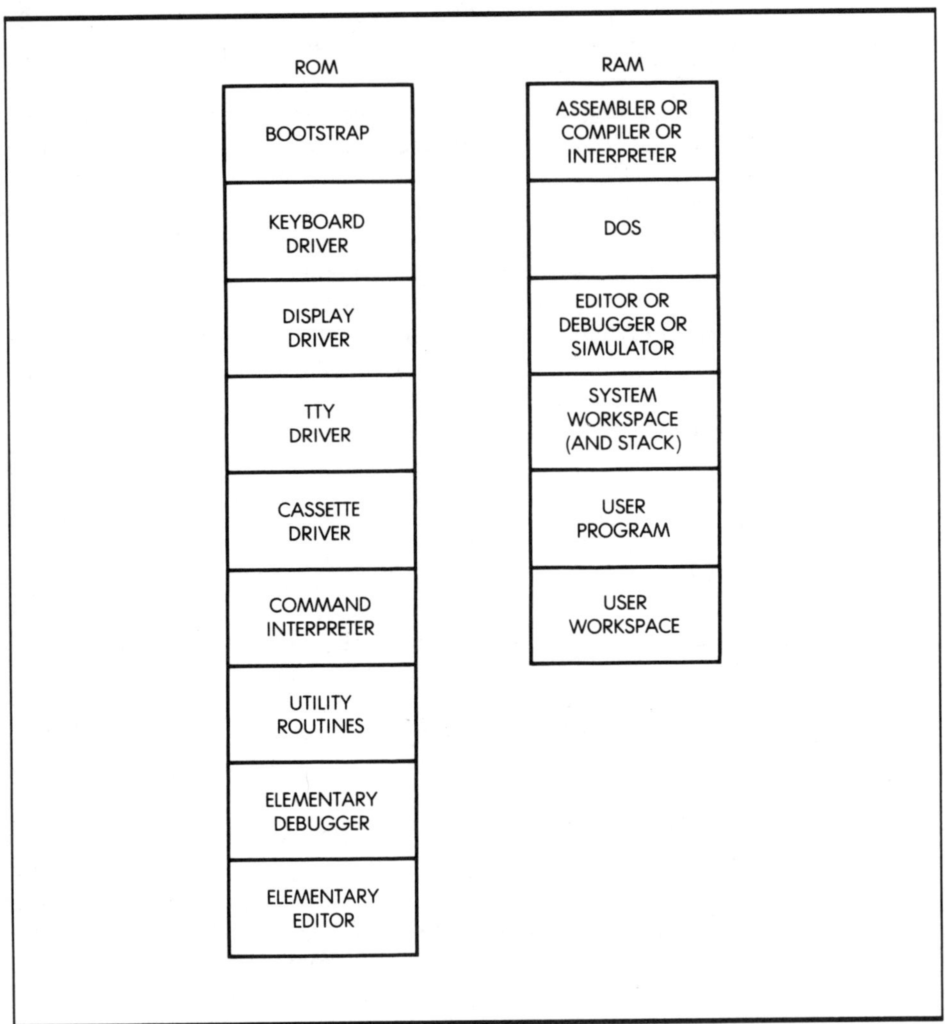

Figure 10.2: A Typical Memory Map

Recall that the normal approach for developing an assembly-level program is as follows:

1. To design an algorithm and the data structures for the problem to be solved.
2. To develop a comprehensive set of flowcharts, which represent the program flow.

3. To translate the flowcharts into the assembly-level language for the microprocessor (this is the *coding* phase) and enter the program on the computer. A program can be entered in the RAM memory of the system under the control of the editor.

4. Once you have entered the program, you can test a section of it, such as one or more subroutines.

You must first, however, use the assembler to translate the program into binary code. If the assembler does not already reside in the system, you must load it from external memory, such as a disk. Assembly will result in an object program that is ready to be executed.

A program is not normally expected to work correctly the first time. To verify its correct operation, you can use the debugger to set breakpoints at crucial locations to test whether the intermediate results are correct.

Whenever you find incorrect data, you have detected an error in the program. At this point, you should refer to the program listing and verify that the coding is correct. If you cannot find an error in the programming, you should refer to the flowchart—the error might be a logical one.

If you have checked the flowcharts by hand and believe them to be reasonably correct, the error probably stems from the coding. Therefore, you must now modify a section of the program. If the symbolic representation of the program is still in the memory, you can simply reenter the editor, modify the required lines, and then go through the preceding sequence again. In some systems, the memory available may not be large enough. In such a case, you will need to flush out the symbolic representation of the program onto a disk or cassette prior to executing the object code. Naturally, in this case, you would have to reload the symbolic representation of the program from its support medium, prior to entering the editor again.

You can then repeat this procedure until the results of the program are correct. I stress here that prevention is much more effective than a cure. A correct design typically results in a program that runs correctly very soon after the usual typing mistakes or obvious coding errors have been removed. However, a sloppy design may result in programs that take an extremely long time to debug. The debugging time is generally much longer than the actual design time. In short, it is always worth investing more time in the design in order to shorten the debugging phase.

Using the previous approach, you can test the overall organization of the program, but you cannot test it in real time with input/output devices. The direct solution for testing input/output devices is to transfer the program onto an EPROM, install it on the board, and then see if it works.

However, there is another solution. You can use an *in-circuit emulator.* An in-circuit emulator uses the 65816 microprocessor (or any other one) to emulate a 65816 in (almost) real time. (It emulates the 65816 physically.) The emulator is equipped with a cable terminated by a 40-pin connector, identical to the pinout of the 65816. If you insert this connector in the real application board you are developing, the signals generated by the emulator will be exactly like those of the 65816, but perhaps a little slower. The essential advantage of this approach is that the program under test can continue to reside in the RAM memory of the development system. Because an in-circuit emulator generates the real signals that communicate with the real input/output devices you wish to use, you can continue to develop the program using all the resources of the development system (editor, debugger, symbolic facilities, file system), while testing input/output in real time.

In addition, a good emulator provides special facilities, such as a *trace.* In short, a trace provides a film of the events that occurred prior to the breakpoint or malfunction. It is a recording of the last instructions and the status of the buses in the system prior to a breakpoint. Such a facility is of great value, since when an error is found it is usually too late—the instruction or data that caused the error has occurred prior to the detection. Using a trace, you can find the segment of the program that caused the error to occur. If the trace is not long enough, you can set an earlier breakpoint.

This completes the description of the usual sequence of events involved in developing a program. Let's now review the hardware alternatives available for developing programs.

HARDWARE ALTERNATIVES

Many different hardware systems are available for program development. The different systems vary in cost and capabilities. The more expensive and complex the system, the more tools it provides for developing programs.

SINGLE-BOARD MICROCOMPUTER

The single-board microcomputer offers the lowest-cost approach to program development. It is normally equipped with a hexadecimal keyboard, some function keys, and six LEDs, which can display addresses and data. Since a single-board microcomputer is equipped with a small amount of memory (typically 1K or 2K), an assembler is not usually available. At best, a single-board microcomputer has a small monitor and virtually no editing or debugging facilities, except for a few commands. You must, therefore, enter all programs in hexadecimal form; they are then displayed in hexadecimal form on the LEDs.

A single-board microcomputer has, in theory, the same hardware power as any other computer. However, because of its restricted memory size and keyboard, it does not support all the usual facilities of a larger system and, therefore, program development is much slower. Because developing programs in hexadecimal format is a tedious task, a single-board microcomputer is best suited for educational and training purposes, where programs of limited length are developed. Single-boards are probably the least expensive way to learn programming through actual practice. They cannot, however, be used for complex program development unless additional memory boards are attached and the usual software aids are made available.

THE DEVELOPMENT SYSTEM

A development system is a microcomputer system equipped with a significant amount of RAM memory (32K, 48K), the required input/output devices (a CRT display, a printer, disks, and usually, a PROM programmer), and perhaps an in-circuit emulator. A development system is specifically designed to facilitate program development in an industrial environment. It normally offers all, or most, of the software facilities mentioned in the preceding section. In principle, it is the ideal software development tool. Many types of personal computers (PCs) can be used as development systems, because the hardware and software to develop programs can be added to the PC.

A limitation of a microcomputer development system is that it may not have enough memory to support a compiler or interpreter. However, it does offer all the required facilities for developing programs in assembly-level language.

LOW-COST HOME COMPUTER

Home computer hardware is naturally analogous to that of a development system. The main difference is that it is normally not equipped with the sophisticated software development aids available on a development system. As an example, many home computers, or hobby-type microcomputers, offer only elementary assemblers and minimal editors and file systems. They normally do not have the facilities to attach a PROM programmer, an in-circuit emulator, or a powerful debugger. They represent, therefore, an intermediate step between the single-board microcomputer and the full microprocessor development system. For users who wish to develop programs of modest complexity, they are probably the best compromise. Still, they can offer the advantage of low cost and a reasonable array of software development tools.

TIME-SHARING SYSTEM

You can rent terminals that connect to time-sharing networks. These terminals share the time of a larger computer (a minicomputer or mainframe) and benefit from the advantages of the large installations. *Cross assemblers* are available for all microcomputers on virtually all commercial time-sharing systems. Some personal computers also have cross assemblers. Formally, a cross assembler is an assembler for microprocessor X, which resides on processor Y. The nature of the computer being used is irrelevant. For example, you can write a program in 65816 assembly-level language, and the cross assembler will translate it into the appropriate binary pattern. The difference, however, is that the program *cannot* be executed at that point. It can only be executed by a simulated processor, if one is available, provided it does not use any input/output resources. Therefore, this solution is used only in industrial environments.

IN-HOUSE COMPUTER

Whenever a large in-house computer is available, cross assemblers may also be available to facilitate program development. If such a computer offers time-shared service, this option is analogous to the one above. If it offers only batch service, this is probably one of the most inconvenient methods of program development, since submitting programs in batch mode at the assembly level for a microprocessor results in a very long development time.

SUMMARY OF HARDWARE RESOURCES

There are three broad categories of hardware systems. A single-board microcomputer is available for those who have only a minimal budget and want to learn how to program. Using a single-board microcomputer, you can develop all the simple programs in this book and many more.

Eventually, however, you will feel the limitations of this approach; for example, when you want to develop programs having more than a few hundred instructions.

A full development system is available for users of the more sophisticated personal computers. Any solution short of the full development system will cause a significantly longer development time. The trade-off is clear: hardware resources versus programming time. Naturally, if the programs being developed are simple, there are less expensive approaches. But if the programs are complex, it is difficult to justify any hardware savings when buying a development system, since programming costs are by far the dominant cost of any project.

For a beginning programmer, an inexpensive home computer typically offers sufficient, although minimal, facilities. Good development software is now becoming available for many of the hobby computers.

Let's now analyze in more detail the one indispensable resource: the assembler.

THE ASSEMBLER

I will now present the formal syntax or definition of assembly-level language. An assembler allows the convenient symbolic representation of a user's program, and makes it simple for the assembler program to convert these mnemonics into their binary representation. The ORCA/M macro-assembler from the Byte Works, Inc. is an example of a typical assembler. I tested the programs in this book with the ORCA/M assembler.

ASSEMBLER FIELDS

When you type in a program for the assembler, several fields are used. They are:

- *The label field* (optional), which may contain a symbolic address for the instruction that follows.
- *The instruction field,* which includes the opcode and any operands. (You may distinguish a separate operand field.)
- *The comment field* (optional), which is intended to clarify the program.

These fields appear on the programming form in Table 10.1.

	HEX INSTRUCTION				SYMBOLIC			COMMENTS
ADDRESS	1	2	3	4	LABEL	OPCODE	OPERAND	

Table 10.1: Microprocessor Programming Form

Once you have fed a program into the assembler, the assembler produces a *listing* of it. When it generates a listing, the assembler provides three additional fields, usually on the left of the page. An example of assembler output appears in Figure 10.3.

On the far left of the output is the line number. Each line you type is assigned a symbolic line number. The next field to the right is the actual address field, which shows (in hexadecimal) the value of the program counter that points to that instruction. Even further to the right is the hexadecimal representation of the instruction.

I have now shown one possible use of an assembler. Even if you are designing programs for a single-board microcomputer that accepts only

```
0001  0000                         KEEP TEST
0002  0000               MAIN      START
0003  0000
0004  0000  A20D                   LDX  #MSG2-MSG1     MESSAGE LENGTH
0005  0002  A000                   LDY  #0
0006  0004  B91200       LB1       LDA  MSG1,Y         LOAD A CHAR
0007  0007  200F00                 JSR  COUT           TYPE THE CHAR
0008  000A  C8                     INY                 POINT TO NEXT CHAR
0009  000B  CA                     DEX                 DECREMENT COUNTER
0010  000C  D0F6                   BNE  LB1            LOOP UNTIL 0
0011  000E  60           RTS
0012  000F
0013  000F  6C3600       COUT      JMP  ($36)
0014  0012
0015  0012  48454C4C     MSG1      DC   C'HELLO WORLD.'
0016  001E  0D                     DC   H'0D'
0017  001F               MSG2      ANOP
0018  001F                         END

Local Symbols

COUT   00000F LB1    000004 MSG1    000012 MSG2    00001F
```

Courtesy of the Byte Works Inc.

Figure 10.3: Example of Assembler Output

hexadecimal, you should still write the program in assembly-level language, provided you have access to a system equipped with an assembler. You can then run the programs on the system, using the assembler. The assembler automatically generates the correct hexadecimal codes on the system. This simple example shows the value of additional software resources.

TABLES

When the assembler translates the symbolic program into its binary representation, it performs two essential tasks:

1. It translates the mnemonic instructions into their binary encoding.

2. It translates the symbols used for constants and addresses into their binary representations.

To facilitate program debugging, the assembler shows, at the end of the listing, the hexadecimal value of each symbol used. This is called the *symbol table.*

Some symbol tables list not only the symbol and its value, but also the line numbers where the symbol occurs—thereby providing an additional reference.

ERROR MESSAGES

During the assembly process, the assembler detects syntax errors and includes them as part of the final listing. Typical diagnostics include: undefined symbols, label already defined, illegal opcode, illegal address, and illegal addressing mode. Many additional diagnostics are desirable, and are usually provided. Such features vary with each assembler.

THE ASSEMBLY LANGUAGE

I have already discussed *opcodes.* I will define here the symbols, constants, and operators you can use as part of the assembler syntax.

SYMBOLS

Symbols are used to represent numerical values, either data or addresses. Symbols may include up to ten characters, and they must start with an alphabetic character. The number of characters allowed in a symbol depends on the assembler being used. The characters are restricted to letters of the alphabet, numbers, and the underline character (_). Also, you may not choose names identical to the opcodes utilized by the 65816, the names of the registers (A, B, C, D, X, Y, S, PC, DBR, and PBR), or the various names used as pseudo-operators by the assembler. The names of these assembler directives are listed in the corresponding section of this chapter.

Assigning a Value to a Symbol

Labels are special symbols with values that do not need to be defined by the programmer. The value is automatically defined by the assembler program when it finds that label. Thus, the label value automatically corresponds to the number of the line where it appears. There are special pseudo-instructions available for forcing a new starting value for labels or for assigning them a specific value. However, you must define any other symbols used for constants or memory addresses prior to use.

You can use a special assembler *directive* to assign a value to a symbol. This directive is essentially an instruction to the assembler that will not be translated into an executable statement. For example, the constant LOG is defined as:

```
LOG         EQU         $302
```

This assigns the value 302 hexadecimal to the symbol LOG.

CONSTANTS OR LITERALS

Constants may be expressed in decimal, hexadecimal, octal, or binary, or as alphanumeric strings. To differentiate between the bases used to represent numbers, you must use a symbol. To load a zero into accumulator A, you simply write:

```
LDA         #0
```

The absence of a symbol always means decimal.

A hexadecimal number is preceded by the symbol **$**. To load the value FF into A, you write:

```
LDA         #$FF
```

An octal symbol is preceded by an **@**. A binary symbol is preceded by a **%**. For example, to load the value 11111111 into A, you write:

```
LDA         #%11111111
```

You can also use literal ASCII characters in the literal field. The ASCII symbol must be preceded and followed by a single or double quote. For example, to load the symbol S into A, you write:

```
LDA         #'S'
```

OPERATORS

To further facilitate the writing of symbolic programs, assemblers allow the use of operators. At a minimum, they usually allow plus and minus, so that you can specify, for example:

```
LDA         ADDRESS
LDX         ADDRESS + 1
```

It is important to understand that the expression ADDRESS + 1 is computed by the assembler, to determine the actual memory address that must be inserted as the binary equivalent. It is computed at *assembly time,* not at program-execution time.

In addition, other operators may be available, such as multiply and divide—a convenience when accessing tables in memory. There may also be available more specialized operators, such as greater than and less than, which truncate a two-byte value into its high and low byte, respectively.

Naturally, an expression may *evaluate* to a positive or negative value. Logical expressions evaluate to a zero or a one.

Finally, a special symbol traditionally represents the current value of the address of the line. This symbol (*) means "current location" (value of PC).

EXPRESSIONS

The 65816 assembler specifications allow a wide range of expressions with arithmetic and logical operations. Table 10.2 displays these operations. Let's examine the order of precedence of the various operations:

- Operations within parentheses and .NOT. are evaluated first.
- Multiplication, division, and all of the logical operators take precedence over addition and subtraction.
- Operators with the same precedence are evaluated left to right.
- Comparisons of expressions have the lowest priority.

ADDRESSING MODES

It is necessary to distinguish the different addressing modes used in the 65816 with special symbols. If a symbol is not used, the assembler normally chooses an 8-bit or 16-bit address unless the assembler can determine the type of addressing required by context. (*Note:* The assembler chooses direct-page addressing [8-bit] whenever possible.) To force direct-page addressing, you must put the symbol < before the operand. Similarly, you can force absolute addressing by putting the symbol ¦ or ! before the operand, and use > to force absolute long addressing.

The symbols <, ¦, and > are needed because the assembler can use an expression for an address. If the expression evaluates to a value less than 256, direct addressing is assumed, but you may want to use absolute or absolute long addresssing. The symbols force a certain type of addressing regardless of an expression's value. Refer to Chapter 5 for more information on addressing mode notation.

OPERATOR	FUNCTION
+	ADDITION
–	SUBTRACTION
*	MULTIPLICATION
/	DIVISION
!	BIT SHIFT
.NOT.	BOOLEAN NEGATION
.AND.	LOGICAL AND
.OR.	LOGICAL OR
.EOR.	LOGICAL EXCLUSIVE OR
=	EQUAL
<>	NOT EQUAL
<=	LESS THAN OR EQUAL
>=	GREATER THAN OR EQUAL
<	LESS THAN
>	GREATER THAN

Table 10.2: Assembler Operators

ASSEMBLER DIRECTIVES

Directives are special orders, given by the programmer to the assembler, that result in storing values into symbols or in memory or in controlling the execution of the assembler. To provide a specific example, I will now review a few of the assembler directives available on the 65816 assembler. I begin with:

```
ORG        NN
```

This directive sets the assembler address counter to the value NN. In other words, the first executable instruction encountered after this directive will reside at the value NN. You can use this directive to locate different segments of a program at different memory locations.

The directive

```
LABEL •    EQU          NN
```

assigns a value to a label.

The declare constant directive

```
DC         H'N'
```

assigns the 8-bit hexadecimal (H) value N to a byte residing at the current program counter. You may use a label with DC.

The same directive is used to form a two-byte constant:

```
DC        H'NN'
```

This directive assigns the value NN to the two-byte memory word residing at the current program counter. You may assign binary, integer, and floating-point constants by using the letters B, I, and F, respectively.

You may also use the define constant directive to form a character string:

```
DC        C'string'
```

This directive places the 7-bit ASCII characters in STRING in successive bytes in memory. The single-quote character ' is a delimiter for the string.

The declare storage bytes directive

```
DS        NN
```

allocates NN bytes of space at the present location in the program. You may use a label with DS.

The 65816 directive

```
65816     ON
65816     OFF
```

tells the assembler whether to assemble 65816 instructions or only 6502 instructions. If the 65816 directive is off, then 65816 instructions, such as BRL, will be flagged as errors.

The long accumulator directive

```
LONGA     ON
LONGA     OFF
```

tells the assembler to use 16-bit numbers for the immediate addressing modes that use the accumulator. You should use LONGA ON when you set the M bit in the status register to 0. You should use LONGA OFF when the M bit is 1. It is your responsibility to tell the assembler what mode the processor is in, because the assembler cannot figure this out for itself.

The long index register directive

```
LONGI     ON
LONGI     OFF
```

tells the assembler to use 16-bit numbers for immediate addressing modes that use the index registers. You should use LONGI ON when you set the X bit in the status register to 0. You should use LONGI OFF when the X bit is 1. It is again your responsibility to tell the assembler what mode the processor is in.

The start program segment directive

```
START        LABEL
```

tells the assembler to begin a program segment with the name in LABEL. Each program segment must be followed by an end directive. There must be at least one START directive in every program.

The end directive

```
END
```

marks the end of a program segment. It directs the assembler to print the local symbol table and prepare for the next segment. END is the last statement of a program.

SUMMARY

This chapter has presented the techniques and the hardware and software tools required to develop a program; it has also examined various trade-offs and alternatives. These techniques range from a single-board microcomputer to a full development system at the hardware level, and from binary coding to high-level programming at the software level.

CONCLUSION

In this book, I have covered all the important aspects of programming the 65816, ranging from the basic definitions and concepts to the internal manipulation of the 65816 registers, the management of input/output devices, and the implementation of software development aids. These concepts apply to other microprocessors as well as to the 65816.

What is the next step? There is no substitute for experience. Once you have studied the examples in this book and completed the exercises, you should be ready to move ahead and create *your own programs.*

APPENDIXES

APPENDIX A

HEX	0	1	2	3	4	5	6	7	8	9	A	B	C	D	E	F	00	000
0	0	1	2	3	4	5	6	7	8	9	10	11	12	13	14	15	0	0
1	16	17	18	19	20	21	22	23	24	25	26	27	28	29	30	31	256	4096
2	32	33	34	35	36	37	38	39	40	41	42	43	44	45	46	47	512	8192
3	48	49	50	51	52	53	54	55	56	57	58	59	60	61	62	63	768	12288
4	64	65	66	67	68	69	70	71	72	73	74	75	76	77	78	79	1024	16384
5	80	81	82	83	84	85	86	87	88	89	90	91	92	93	94	95	1280	20480
6	96	97	98	99	100	101	102	103	104	105	106	107	108	109	110	111	1536	24576
7	112	113	114	115	116	117	118	119	120	121	122	123	124	125	126	127	1792	28672
8	128	129	130	131	132	133	134	135	136	137	138	139	140	141	142	143	2048	32768
9	144	145	146	147	148	149	150	151	152	153	154	155	156	157	158	159	2304	36864
A	160	161	162	163	164	165	166	167	168	169	170	171	172	173	174	175	2560	40960
B	176	177	178	179	180	181	182	183	184	185	186	187	188	189	190	191	2816	45056
C	192	193	194	195	196	197	198	199	200	201	202	203	204	205	206	207	3072	49152
D	208	209	210	211	212	213	214	215	216	217	218	219	220	221	222	223	3328	53248
E	224	225	226	227	228	229	230	231	232	233	234	235	236	237	238	239	3584	57344
F	240	241	242	243	244	245	246	247	248	249	250	251	252	253	254	255	3840	61440

5		4		3		2		1		0	
HEX	DEC	HEX	DEC	HEX	DEC	HEX	DEC	HEX	DEC	HEX	DEC
0	0	0	0	0	0	0	0	0	0	0	0
1	1,048,576	1	65,536	1	4,096	1	256	1	16	1	1
2	2,097,152	2	131,072	2	8,192	2	512	2	32	2	2
3	3,145,728	3	196,608	3	12,288	3	768	3	48	3	3
4	4,194,304	4	262,144	4	16,384	4	1,024	4	64	4	4
5	5,242,880	5	327,680	5	20,480	5	1,280	5	80	5	5
6	6,291,456	6	393,216	6	24,576	6	1,536	6	96	6	6
7	7,340,032	7	458,752	7	28,672	7	1,792	7	112	7	7
8	8,388,608	8	524,288	8	32,768	8	2,048	8	128	8	8
9	9,437,184	9	589,824	9	36,864	9	2,304	9	144	9	9
A	10,485,760	A	655,360	A	40,960	A	2,560	A	160	A	10
B	11,534,336	B	720,896	B	45,056	B	2,816	B	176	B	11
C	12,582,912	C	786,432	C	49,152	C	3,072	C	192	C	12
D	13,631,488	D	851,968	D	53,248	D	3,328	D	208	D	13
E	14,680,064	E	917,504	E	57,344	E	3,584	E	224	E	14
F	15,728,640	F	983,040	F	61,440	F	3,840	F	240	F	15

Appendix A: Hexadecimal Conversion Table

APPENDIX B

HEX LSD	MSD BITS	0 000	1 001	2 010	3 011	4 100	5 101	6 110	7 111
0	0000	NUL	DLE	SPACE	0	@	P	—	p
1	0001	SOH	DC1	!	1	A	Q	a	q
2	0010	STX	DC2	"	2	B	R	b	r
3	0011	ETX	DC3	#	3	C	S	c	s
4	0100	EOT	DC4	$	4	D	T	d	t
5	0101	ENQ	NAK	%	5	E	U	e	u
6	0110	ACK	SYN	&	6	F	V	f	v
7	0111	BEL	ETB	'	7	G	W	g	w
8	1000	BS	CAN	(	8	H	X	h	x
9	1001	HT	EM	)	9	I	Y	i	y
A	1010	LF	SUB	*	:	J	Z	j	z
B	1011	VT	ESC	+	;	K	[	k	{
C	1100	FF	FS	,	<	L	\	l	--
D	1101	CR	GS	—	=	M	]	m	}
E	1110	SO	RS	.	>	N	^	n	~
F	1111	SI	US	/	?	O	←	o	DEL

Appendix B: ASCII Conversion Table

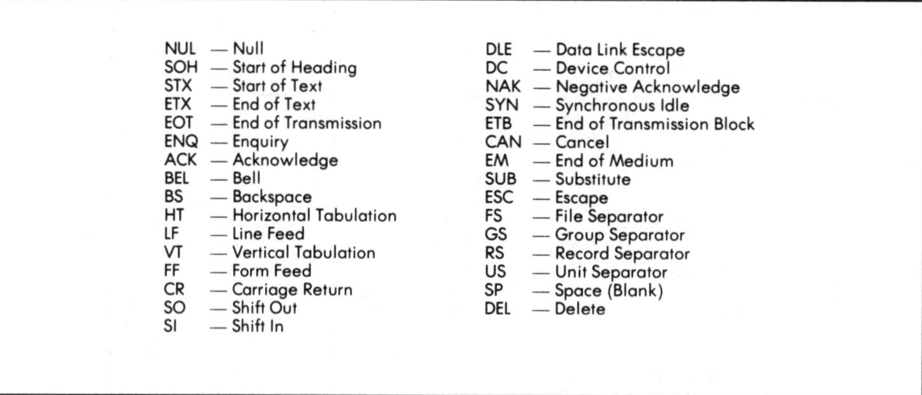

NUL — Null
SOH — Start of Heading
STX — Start of Text
ETX — End of Text
EOT — End of Transmission
ENQ — Enquiry
ACK — Acknowledge
BEL — Bell
BS — Backspace
HT — Horizontal Tabulation
LF — Line Feed
VT — Vertical Tabulation
FF — Form Feed
CR — Carriage Return
SO — Shift Out
SI — Shift In
DLE — Data Link Escape
DC — Device Control
NAK — Negative Acknowledge
SYN — Synchronous Idle
ETB — End of Transmission Block
CAN — Cancel
EM — End of Medium
SUB — Substitute
ESC — Escape
FS — File Separator
GS — Group Separator
RS — Record Separator
US — Unit Separator
SP — Space (Blank)
DEL — Delete

Appendix B: The ASCII Symbols

APPENDIX C

DECIMAL	BCD	DEC	BCD	DEC	BCD
0	0000	10	00010000	91	10010000
1	0001	11	00010001	91	10010001
2	0010	12	00010010	92	10010010
3	0011	13	00010011	93	10010011
4	0100	14	00010100	94	10010100
5	0101	15	00010101	95	10010101
6	0110	16	00010110	96	10010110
7	0111	17	00010111	97	10010111
8	1000	18	00011000	98	10011000
9	1001	19	00011001	99	10011001

Appendix C: Decimal to BCD Conversion Table

APPENDIX D

Operation, Operation Codes, and Status Register

MNE-MONIC	OPERATION	#	a	al	d	A	i	(d),y	[d],y	(d,x)	d,x	d,y	a,x	al,x	a,y	r	rl	(a)	(d)	[d]	(a,x)	s	d,s	(d,s),y	xyc	PROCESSOR STATUS CODE 7	6	5	4	3	2	1	0		MNE-MONIC
																										N	V	M	X	D	I	Z	C	E = 0	
		1	2	3	4	5	6	7	8	9	10	11	12	13	14	15	16	17	18	19	20	21	22	23	24	N	V	1	B	D	I	Z	C	E = 1	
ADC	A + M + C → A	69	6D	6F	65			71	77	61	75		7D	7F	79				72	67			63	73		N	V	.	.	.	.	Z	C		ADC
AND	A∧M → A	29	2D	2F	25			31	37	21	35		3D	3F	39				32	27			23	33		N	.	.	.	.	.	Z	.		AND
ASL	C ← [15/7 0] ← 0		0E		06	0A					16		1E													N	.	.	.	.	.	Z	C		ASL
BCC	BRANCH IF C = 0															90										.	.	.	.	.	.	.	.		BCC
BCS	BRANCH IF C = 1															B0										.	.	.	.	.	.	.	.		BCS
BEQ	BRANCH IF Z = 1															F0										.	.	.	.	.	.	.	.		BEQ
BIT	A∧M (NOTE 1)	89	2C		24						34		3C													M_7	M_6	.	.	.	.	Z	.		BIT
BMI	BRANCH IF N = 1															30										.	.	.	.	.	.	.	.		BMI
BNE	BRANCH IF Z = 0															D0										.	.	.	.	.	.	.	.		BNE
BPL	BRANCH IF N = 0															10										.	.	.	.	.	.	.	.		BPL
BRA	BRANCH ALWAYS															80										.	.	.	.	.	.	.	.	●	BRA
BRK	BREAK (NOTE 2)																					00				.	.	.	●	0	I	.	.		BRK
BRL	BRANCH LONG ALWAYS																82									.	.	.	.	.	.	.	.	★	BRL
BVC	BRANCH IF V = 0															50										.	.	.	.	.	.	.	.		BVC
BVS	BRANCH IF V = 1															70										.	.	.	.	.	.	.	.		BVS
CLC	0 → C						18																			.	.	.	.	.	.	.	0		CLC
CLD	0 → D						D8																			.	.	.	.	0	.	.	.		CLD
CLI	0 → 1						58																			.	.	.	.	.	0	.	.		CLI
CLV	0 → V						B8																			.	0	.	.	.	.	.	.		CLV
CMP	A-M	C9	CD	CF	C5			D1	D7	C1	D5		DD	DF	D9				D2	C7			C3	D3		N	.	.	.	.	.	Z	C		CMP
COP	CO-PROCESSOR																					02				.	.	.	.	0	I	.	.	★	COP
CPX	X-M	E0	EC		E4																					N	.	.	.	.	.	Z	C		CPX
CPY	Y-M	C0	CC		C4																					N	.	.	.	.	.	Z	C		CPY
DEC	DECREMENT		CE		C6	3A					D6		DE													N	.	.	.	.	.	Z	.		DEC
DEX	X - 1 → X						CA																			N	.	.	.	.	.	Z	.		DEX
DEY	Y - 1 → Y						88																			N	.	.	.	.	.	Z	.		DEY
EOR	A∀M → A	49	4D	4F	45			51	57	41	55		5D	5F	59				52	47			43	53		N	.	.	.	.	.	Z	.		EOR
INC	INCREMENTS		EE		E6	1A					F6		FE													N	.	.	.	.	.	Z	.		INC
INX	X + 1 → X						E8																			N	.	.	.	.	.	Z	.		INX
INY	Y + 1 → Y						C8																			N	.	.	.	.	.	Z	.		INY
JML	JUMP LONG TO NEW LOC.																	DC								.	.	.	.	.	.	.	.	★	JML
JMP	JUMP TO NEW LOC.		4C	5C														6C			7C					.	.	.	.	.	.	.	.		JMP
JSL	JUMP LONG TO SUB.			22																						.	.	.	.	.	.	.	.		JSL
JSR	JUMP TO SUB.		20																		FC					.	.	.	.	.	.	.	.		JSR
LDA	M → A	A9	AD	AF	A5			B1	B7	A1	B5		BD	BF	B9				B2	A7		A3	B3			N	.	.	.	.	.	Z	.		LDA
LDX	M → X	A2	AE		A6							B6			BE											N	.	.	.	.	.	Z	.		LDX
LDY	M → Y	A0	AC		A4						B4		BC													N	.	.	.	.	.	Z	.		LDY
LSR	0 → [15/7 0] → C		4E		46	4A					56		5E													0	.	.	.	.	.	Z	C		LSR
MVN	M → M BACKWARD																								54	.	.	.	.	.	.	.	.	★	MVN
MVP	M → M FORWARD																								44	.	.	.	.	.	.	.	.	★	MVP
NOP	NO OPERATION						EA																			.	.	.	.	.	.	.	.		NOP
ORA	A∨M → A	09	0D	0F	05			11	17	01	15		1D	1F	19				12	07			03	13		N	.	.	.	.	.	Z	.		ORA
PEA	Mpc + 1, Mpc + 2 → Ms - 1, Ms S - 2 → S																					F4				.	.	.	.	.	.	.	.	★	PEA
PEI	M(d), M(d + 1) → Ms - 1, Ms S - 2 → S																					D4				.	.	.	.	.	.	.	.	★	PEI
PER	Mpc + rl, Mpc + rl + 1 → Ms - 1, Ms S - 2 → S																					62				.	.	.	.	.	.	.	.	★	PER

Courtesy of Western Design Center, Inc.

Appendix D: The 65816 Instruction set: Operation, Operation Codes, and Status Register

APPENDIX D

Operation, Operation Codes, and Status Register (continued)

Mnemonic	Operation																									N	V	M	X	D	I	Z	C	New	Mnemonic
PHA	A → Ms, S - 1 → S																				48					.	.	.	.	.	.	.	.		PHA
PHB	DBR → Ms, S - 1 → S																				8B					.	.	.	.	.	.	.	.		PHB
PHD	D → Ms, Ms - 1, S - 2 → S																				0B					.	.	.	.	.	.	.	.	*	PHD
PHK	PBR → Ms, S - 1 → S																				4B					.	.	.	.	.	.	.	.	*	PHK
PHP	P → Ms, S - 1 → S																				08					.	.	.	.	.	.	.	.		PHP
PHX	X → Ms, S - 1 → S																				DA					.	.	.	.	.	.	.	.	●	PHX
PHY	Y → Ms, S - 1 → S																				5A					.	.	.	.	.	.	.	.	●	PHY
PLA	S + 1 → S, Ms → A																				68					N	.	.	.	.	.	Z	.		PLA
PLB	S + 1 → S, Ms → DBR																				AB					N	.	.	.	.	.	Z	.	*	PLB
PLD	S + 2 → S, Ms - 1, Ms → D																				2B					N	.	.	.	.	.	Z	.	*	PLD
PLP	S + 1 → S, Ms → P																				28					N	V	M	X	D	I	Z	C		PLP
PLX	S + 1 → S, Ms → X																				FA					N	.	.	.	.	.	.	.		PLX
PLY	S + 1 → S, Ms → Y																				7A					N	.	.	.	.	.	Z	.		PLY
REP	M∧P → P	C2																								N	V	M	X	D	I	Z	C	*	REP
ROL	[15/7 0] ← C		2E		26	2A					36		3E													N	.	.	.	.	.	Z	C		ROL
ROR	C → [15/7 0]		6E		66	6A					76		7E													N	.	.	.	.	.	Z	C		ROR
RTI	RTRN FROM INT.																				40					N	V	M	X	D	I	Z	C		RTI
RTL	RTRN FROM SUB. LONG																				6B					.	.	.	.	.	.	.	.	*	RTL
RTS	RTRN SUBROUTINE																				60					.	.	.	.	.	.	.	.		RTS
SBC	A - M - C̄ → A	E9	ED	EF	E5			F1	F7	E1	F5		FD	FF	F9				F2	E7		E3	F3			N	V	.	.	.	.	Z	C		SBC
SEC	1 → C						38																			.	.	.	.	.	.	.	1		SEC
SED	1 → D						F8																			.	.	.	.	1	.	.	.		SED
SEI	1 → I						78																			.	.	.	.	.	1	.	.		SEI
SEP	M∨P → P	E2																								N	V	M	X	D	I	Z	C	*	SEP
STA	A → M		8D	8F	85			91	97	81	95		9D	9F	99				92	87		83	93			.	.	.	.	.	.	.	.		STA
STP	STOP (1 → ϕ2)						DB																			.	.	.	.	.	.	.	.	●	STP
STX	X → M		8E		86							96														.	.	.	.	.	.	.	.		STX
STY	Y → M		8C		84						94															.	.	.	.	.	.	.	.		STY
STZ	00 → M		9C		64						74		9E													.	.	.	.	.	.	.	.	●	STZ
TAX	A → X						AA																			N	.	.	.	.	.	Z	.		TAX
TAY	A → Y						A8																			N	.	.	.	.	.	Z	.		TAY
TCD	C → D						5B																			N	.	.	.	.	.	Z	.	*	TCD
TCS	C → S						1B																			.	.	.	.	.	.	.	.	*	TCS
TDC	D → C						7B																			N	.	.	.	.	.	Z	.	*	TDC
TRB	Ā∧M → M		1C		14																					.	.	.	.	.	.	Z	.	●	TRB
TSB	A∨M → M		0C		04																					.	.	.	.	.	.	Z	.	●	TSB
TSC	S → C					3B																				N	.	.	.	.	.	Z	.	*	TSC
TSX	S → X					BA																				N	.	.	.	.	.	Z	.		TSX
TXA	X → A					8A																				N	.	.	.	.	.	Z	.		TXA
TXS	X → S					9A																				.	.	.	.	.	.	.	.		TXS
TXY	X → Y					9B																				N	.	.	.	.	.	Z	.	*	TXY
TYA	Y → A					98																				N	.	.	.	.	.	Z	.		TYA
TYX	Y → X					BB																				N	.	.	.	.	.	Z	.	*	TYX
WAI	0 → RDY					CB																				.	.	.	.	.	.	.	.	●	WAI
WDM	NO OPERATION (RESERVED)					42																				.	.	.	.	.	.	.	.	*	WDM
XBA	B ⟷ A					EB																				N	.	.	.	.	.	Z	.	*	XBA
XCE	C ⟷ E					FB																				.	.	.	.	.	.	.	E	*	XCE

Notes:
1. Bit immediate N and V flags not affected. When M = 0, M_{15} → N and M_{14} → V.
2. Break Bit (B) in Status register indicates hardware or software break.
3. * = New W65C816/802 Instructions
   ● = New W65C02 Instructions
   Blank = NMOS 6502

\+ Add
\- Subtract
∧ AND
∨ OR
⊻ Exclusive OR

Courtesy of Western Design Center, Inc.

Appendix D: (continued)

APPENDIX E

Detailed Instruction Operation

ADDRESS MODE		CYCLE	$\overline{VP}$,	$\overline{ML}$,	VDA,	VPA	ADDRESS BUS	DATA BUS	R/$\overline{W}$
1. Immediate #		1.	1	1	1	1	PBR,PC	Op Code	1
(LDY,CPY,CPX,LDX,ORA,		2.	1	1	0	1	PBR,PC+1	IDL	1
AND,EOR,ADC,BIT,LDA,	(1)(8)	2a.	1	1	0	1	PBR,PC+2	IDH	1
CMP,SBC REP,SEP)									
(14 Op Codes)									
(2 and 3 bytes)									
(2 and 3 cycles)									
2a. Absolute **a**		1.	1	1	1	1	PBR,PC	Op Code	1
(BIT,STY,STZ,LDY,		2.	1	1	0	1	PBR,PC+1	AAL	1
CPY,CPX,STX,LDX,		3.	1	1	0	1	PBR,PC+2	AAH	1
ORA,AND,EOR,ADC,		4.	1	1	1	0	DBR,AA	Data Low	1/0
STA,LDA,CMP,SBC)	(1)	4a.	1	1	1	0	DBR,AA+1	Data High	1/0
(18 Op Codes)									
(3 bytes)									
(4 and 5 cycles)									
2b. Absolute (R-M-W) **a**		1.	1	1	1	1	PBR,PC	Op Code	1
		2.	1	1	0	1	PBR,PC+1	AAL	1
(ASL,ROL,LSR,ROR		3.	1	1	0	1	PBR,PC+2	AAH	1
DEC,INC,TSB,TRB)		4.	1	0	1	0	DBR,AA	Data Low	1
(6 Op Codes)	(1)	4a.	1	0	1	0	DBR,AA+1	Data High	1
(3 bytes)	(3)	5.	1	0	0	0	DBR,AA+1	IO	1
(6 and 8 cycles)	(1)	6a.	1	0	1	0	DBR,AA+1	Data High	0
		6.	1	0	1	0	DBR,AA	Data Low	0
2c. Absolute (JUMP) **a**		1.	1	1	1	1	PBR,PC	Op Code	1
(JMP)(4C)		2.	1	1	0	1	PBR,PC+1	NEW PCL	1
(1 Op Code)		3.	1	1	0	1	PBR,PC+2	NEW PCH	1
(3 bytes)		1.	1	1	1	1	PBR, NEW PC	Op Code	1
(3 cycles)									
2d. Absolute (Jump to		1.	1	1	1	1	PBR,PC	Op Code	1
subroutine) **a**		2.	1	1	0	1	PBR,PC+1	NEW PCL	1
(JSR)		3.	1	1	0	1	PBR,PC+2	NEW PCH	1
(1 Op Code)		4.	1	1	0	0	PBR,PC+2	IO	1
(3 bytes)		5.	1	1	1	0	0,S	PCH	0
(6 cycles)		6.	1	1	1	0	0,S-1	PCL	0
(different order from N6502)		1.	1	1	1	1	PBR,NEW PC	Next Op Code	1
★3a. Absolute Long **al**		1.	1	1	1	1	PBR,PC	Op Code	1
(ORA,AND,EOR,ADC		2.	1	1	0	1	PBR,PC+1	AAL	1
STA,LDA,CMP,SBC)		3.	1	1	0	1	PBR,PC+2	AAH	1
(8 Op Codes)		4.	1	1	0	1	PBR,PC+3	AAB	1
(4 bytes)		5.	1	1	1	0	AAB,AA	Data Low	1/0
(5 and 6 cycles)	(1)	5a.	1	1	1	0	AAB,AA+1	Data High	1/0
★3b. Absolute Long (JUMP) **al**		1.	1	1	1	1	PBR,PC	Op Code	1
(JMP)		2.	1	1	0	1	PBR,PC+1	NEW PCL	1
(1 Op Code)		3.	1	1	0	1	PBR,PC+2	NEW PCH	1
(4 bytes)		4.	1	1	0	1	PBR,PC+3	NEW BR	1
(4 cycles)		1.	1	1	1	1	NEW PBR,PC	Op Code	1
★3c. Absolute Long (Jump to		1.	1	1	1	1	PBR,PC	Op Code	1
Subroutine Long) **al**		2.	1	1	0	1	PBR,PC+1	NEW PCL	1
(JSL)		3.	1	1	0	1	PBR,PC+2	NEW PCH	1
(1 Op Code)		4.	1	1	1	0	0,S	PBR	0
(4 bytes)		5.	1	1	0	0	0,S	IO	1
(7 cycles)		6.	1	1	0	1	PBR,PC+3	NEW PBR	1
		7.	1	1	1	0	0,S-1	PCH	0
		8.	1	1	1	0	0,S-2	PCL	0
		1.	1	1	1	1	NEW PBR,PC	Next Op Code	1

ADDRESS MODE		CYCLE	$\overline{VP}$,	$\overline{ML}$,	VDA,	VPA	RDY	ADDRESS BUS	DATA BUS	R/$\overline{W}$
4a. Direct **d**		1.	1	1	1	1		PBR,PC	Op Code	1
(BIT,STZ,STY,LDY,		2.	1	1	0	1		PBR,PC+1	DO	1
CPY,CPX,STX,LDX,	(2)	2a.	1	1	0	0		PBR,PC+1	IO	1
ORA,AND,EOR,ADC,		3.	1	1	1	0		0,D+DO	Data Low	1/0
STA,LDA,CMP,SBC)	(1)	3a.	1	1	1	0		0,D+DO+1	Data High	1/0
(18 Op Codes)										
(2 bytes)										
(3,4 and 5 cycles)										
4b. Direct (R-M-W) **d**		1.	1	1	1	1		PBR,PC	Op Code	1
(ASL,ROL,LSR,ROR		2.	1	1	0	1		PBR,PC+1	DO	1
DEC,INC,TSB,TRB)	(2)	2a.	1	1	0	0		PBR,PC+1	IO	1
(6 Op Codes)		3.	1	0	1	0		0,D+DO	Data Low	1
(2 bytes)	(1)	3a.	1	0	1	0		0,D+DO+1	Data High	1
(5,6,7 and 8 cycles)	(3)	4.	1	0	0	0		0,D+DO+1	IO	1
	(1)	5a.	1	0	1	0		0,D+DO+1	Data High	0
		5.	1	0	1	0		0,D+DO	Data Low	0
5. Accumulator **A**		1.	1	1	1	1		PBR,PC	Op Code	1
(ASL,INC,ROL,DEC,LSR,ROR)		2.	1	1	0	0		PBR,PC+1	IO	1
(6 Op Codes)										
(1 byte)										
(2 cycles)										
6a. Implied **i**		1.	1	1	1	1		PBR,PC	Op Code	1
(DEY, INY, INX, DEX, NOP,		2.	1	1	0	0		PBR,PC+1	IO	1
XCE, TYA, TAY,TXA, TXS,										
TAX,TSX,TCS,TSC,TCD,										
TDC,TXY,TYX,CLC,SEC,										
CLI,SEI,CLV,CLD,SED)										
(25 Op Codes)										
(1 byte)										
(2 cycles)										
★6b. Implied **i**		1.	1	1	1	1		PBR,PC	Op Code	1
(XBA)		2.	1	1	0	0		PBR,PC+1	IO	1
(1 Op Code)		3.	1	1	0	0		PBR,PC+1	IO	1
(1 byte)										
(3 cycles)										
● 6c. Wait For Interrupt										
(WAI)		1.	1	1	1	1	1	PBR,PC	Op Code	1
(1 Op Code)	(9)	2.	1	1	0	0	1	PBR,PC+1	IO	1
(1 byte)		3.	1	1	0	0	0	PBR,PC+1	IO	1
(3 cycles)	$\overline{IRQ,NMI}$	1.	1	1	1	1	1	PBR,PC+1	IRQ(BRK)	1
● 6d. Stop-The-Clock										
(STP)		1.	1	1	1	1	1	PBR,PC	Op Code	1
(1 Op Code)		2.	1	1	0	0	1	PBR,PC+1	IO	1
(1 byte)	$\overline{RES}$=1	3.	1	1	0	0	1	PBR,PC+1	IO	1
(3 cycles)	$\overline{RES}$=0	1c.	1	1	0	0	1	PBR,PC+1	RES(BRK)	1
	$\overline{RES}$=0	1b.	1	1	0	0	1	PBR,PC+1	RES(BRK)	1
	$\overline{RES}$=1	1a.	1	1	0	0	1	PBR,PC+1	RES(BRK)	1
See 21a Stack (Hardware interrupt)		1.	1	1	1	1	1	PBR,PC+1	BEGIN	1
7. Direct Indirect Indexed **(d),y**		1.	1	1	1	1		PBR,PC	Op Code	1
(ORA,AND,EOR,ADC,		2.	1	1	0	1		PBR,PC+1	DO	1
STA,LDA,CMP,SBC)	(2)	2a.	1	1	0	0		PBR,PC+1	IO	1
(8 Op Codes)		3.	1	1	1	0		0,D+DO	AAL	1
(2 bytes)		4.	1	1	1	0		0,D+DO+1	AAH	1
(5,6,7 and 8 cycles)	(4)	4a.	1	1	0	0		DBR,AAH,AAL+YL	IO	1
		5.	1	1	1	0		DBR,AA+Y	Data Low	1/0
	(1)	5a.	1	1	1	0		DBR,AA+Y+1	Data High	1/0

Courtesy of Western Design Center, Inc.

Appendix E: Detailed 65816 Instruction Operation

APPENDIX E

Detailed Instruction Operation (continued)

ADDRESS MODE		CYCLE	$\overline{VP}$	$\overline{ML}$	VDA	VPA	ADDRESS BUS	DATA BUS	R/$\overline{W}$
8. Direct Indirect		1.	1	1	1	1	PBR,PC	Op Code	1
Indexed Long **[d],y**		2.	1	1	0	1	PBR,PC+1	DO	1
(ORA,AND,EOR,ADC,	(2)	2a.	1	1	0	0	PBR,PC+1	IO	1
STA,LDA,CMP,SBC)		3.	1	1	1	0	0,D+DO	AAL	1
(8 Op Codes)		4.	1	1	1	0	0,D+DO+1	AAH	1
(2 bytes)		5.	1	1	1	0	0,D+DO+2	AAB	1
(6,7 and 8 cycles)		6.	1	1	1	0	AAB,AA+Y	Data Low	1/0
	(1)	6a.	1	1	1	0	AAB,AA+Y+1	Data High	1/0
9. Direct Indexed Indirect **(d,x)**		1.	1	1	1	1	PBR,PC	Op Code	1
(ORA,AND,EOR,ADC,		2.	1	1	0	1	PBR,PC+1	DO	1
STA,LDA,CMP,SBC)	(2)	2a.	1	1	0	0	PBR,PC+1	IO	1
(8 Op Codes)		3.	1	1	0	0	PBR,PC+1	IO	1
(2 bytes)		4.	1	1	1	0	0,D+DO+X	AAL	1
(6,7 and 8 cycles)		5.	1	1	1	0	0,D+DO+X+1	AAH	1
		6.	1	1	1	0	DBR,AA	Data Low	1/0
	(1)	6a.	1	1	1	0	DBR,AA+1	Data High	1/0
10a. Direct,X **d,x**		1.	1	1	1	1	PBR,PC	Op Code	1
(BIT,STZ,STY,LDY,		2.	1	1	0	1	PBR,PC+1	DO	1
ORA,AND,EOR,ADC,	(2)	2a.	1	1	0	0	PBR,PC+1	IO	1
STA,LDA,CMP,SBC)		3.	1	1	0	0	PBR,PC+1	IO	1
(11 Op Codes)		4.	1	1	1	0	0,D+DO+X	Data Low	1/0
(2 bytes)	(1)	4a.	1	1	1	0	0,D+DO+X+1	Data High	1/0
(4,5 and 6 cycles)									
10b. Direct,X(R-M-W) **d,x**		1.	1	1	1	1	PBR,PC	Op Code	1
(ASL,ROL,LSR,ROR,		2.	1	1	0	1	PBR,PC+1	DO	1
DEC,INC)	(2)	2a.	1	1	0	0	PBR,PC+1	IO	1
(6 Op Codes)		3.	1	1	0	0	PBR,PC+1	IO	1
(2 bytes)		4.	1	0	1	0	0,D+DO+X	Data Low	1
(6,7,8 and 9 cycles)	(1)	4a.	1	0	1	0	0,D+DO+X+1	Data High	1
	(3)	5.	1	0	0	0	0,D+DO+X+1	IO	1
	(1)	6a.	1	0	1	0	0,D+DO+X+1	Data High	0
		6.	1	0	1	0	0,D+DO+X	Data Low	0
11. Direct,Y **d,y**		1.	1	1	1	1	PBR,PC	Op Code	1
(STX,LDX)		2.	1	1	0	1	PBR,PC+1	DO	1
(2 Op Codes)	(2)	2a.	1	1	0	0	PBR,PC+1	IO	1
(2 bytes)		3.	1	1	0	0	PBR,PC+1	IO	1
(4,5 and 6 cycles)		4.	1	1	1	0	0,D+DO+Y	Data Low	1/0
	(1)	4a.	1	1	1	0	0,D+DO+Y+1	Data High	1/0
12a. Absolute,X **a,x**		1.	1	1	1	1	PBR,PC	Op Code	1
(BIT,LDY,STZ,		2.	1	1	0	1	PBR,PC+1	AAL	1
ORA,AND,EOR,ADC,		3.	1	1	0	1	PBR,PC+2	AAH	1
STA,LDA,CMP,SBC)	(4)	3a.	1	1	0	0	DBR,AAH,AAL+XL	IO	1
(11 Op Codes)		4.	1	1	1	0	DBR,AA+X	Data Low	1/0
(3 bytes)	(1)	4a.	1	1	1	0	DBR,AA+X+1	Data High	1/0
(4,5 and 6 cycles)									
12b. Absolute,X(R-M-W) **a,x**		1.	1	1	1	1	PBR,PC	Op Code	1
(ASL,ROL,LSR,ROR,		2.	1	1	0	1	PBR,PC+1	AAL	1
DEC,INC)		3.	1	1	0	1	PBR,PC+2	AAH	1
(6 Op Codes)		4.	1	1	0	0	DBR,AAH,AAL+XL	IO	1
(3 bytes)		5.	1	0	1	0	DBR,AA+X	Data Low	1
(7 and 9 cycles)	(1)	5a.	1	0	1	0	DBR,AA+X+1	Data High	1
	(3)	6.	1	0	0	0	DBR,AA+X+1	IO	1
	(1)	7a.	1	0	1	0	DBR,AA+X+1	Data High	0
		7.	1	0	1	0	DBR,AA+X	Data Low	0
★13. Absolute Long,X **al,x**		1.	1	1	1	1	PBR,PC	Op Code	1
(ORA,AND,EOR,ADC,		2.	1	1	0	1	PBR,PC+1	AAL	1
STA,LDA,CMP,SBC)		3.	1	1	0	1	PBR,PC+2	AAH	1
(8 Op Codes)		4.	1	1	0	1	PBR,PC+3	AAB	1
(4 bytes)		5.	1	1	1	0	AAB,AA+X	Data Low	1/0
(5 and 6 cycles)	(1)	5a.	1	1	1	0	AAB,AA+X+1	Data High	1/0
14. Absolute,Y **a,y**		1.	1	1	1	1	PBR,PC	Op Code	1
(LDX,ORA,AND,EOR,ADC,		2.	1	1	0	1	PBR,PC+1	AAL	1
STA,LDA,CMP,SBC)		3.	1	1	0	1	PBR,PC+2	AAH	1
(9 Op Codes)	(4)	3a.	1	1	0	0	DBR,AAH,AAL+YL	IO	1
(3 bytes)		4.	1	1	1	0	DBR,AA+Y	Data Low	1/0
(4,5 and 6 cycles)	(1)	4a.	1	1	1	0	DBR,AA+Y+1	Data High	1/0
15. Relative **r**		1.	1	1	1	1	PBR,PC	Op Code	1
(BPL,BMI,BVC,BVS,BCC,		2.	1	1	0	1	PBR,PC+1	Offset	1
BCS,BNE,BEQ,BRA)	(5)	2a.	1	1	0	0	PBR,PC+1	IO	1
(9 Op Codes)	(6)	2b.	1	1	0	0	PBR,PC+1	IO	1
(2 bytes)		1.	1	1	1	1	PBR,PC+Offset	Op Code	1
(2,3 and 4 cycles)									
★16. Relative Long **rl**		1.	1	1	1	1	PBR,PC	Op Code	1
(BRL)		2.	1	1	0	1	PBR,PC+1	Offset Low	1
(1 Op Code)		3.	1	1	0	1	PBR,PC+2	Offset High	1
(3 bytes)		4.	1	1	0	0	PBR,PC+2	IO	1
(4 cycles)		1.	1	1	1	1	PBR,PC+Offset	Op Code	1
17a. Absolute Indirect **(a)**		1.	1	1	1	1	PBR,PC	Op Code	1
(JMP)		2.	1	1	0	1	PBR,PC+1	AAL	1
(1 Op Code)		3.	1	1	0	1	PBR,PC+2	AAH	1
(3 bytes)		4.	1	1	1	0	0,AA	NEW PCL	1
(5 cycles)		5.	1	1	1	0	0,AA+1	NEW PCH	1
		1.	1	1	1	1	PBR,NEW PC	Op Code	1
★17b. Absolute Indirect **(a)**		1.	1	1	1	1	PBR,PC	Op Code	1
		2.	1	1	0	1	PBR,PC+1	AAL	1
(JML)		3.	1	1	0	1	PBR,PC+2	AAH	1
(1 Op Code)		4.	1	1	1	0	0,AA	NEW PCL	1
(3 bytes)		5.	1	1	1	0	0,AA+1	NEW PCH	1
(6 cycles)		6	1	1	1	0	0,AA+2	NEW PBR	1
		1.	1	1	1	1	NEW PBR,PC	Op Code	1
• 18. Direct Indirect **(d)**		1.	1	1	1	1	PBR,PC	Op Code	1
(ORA,AND,EOR,ADC,		2.	1	1	0	1	PBR,PC+1	DO	1
STA,LDA,CMP,SBC)	(2)	2a.	1	1	0	0	PBR,PC+1	IO	1
(8 Op Codes)		3.	1	1	1	0	0,D+DO	AAL	1
(2 bytes)		4.	1	1	1	0	0,D+DO+1	AAH	1
(5,6 and 7 cycles)		5.	1	1	1	0	DBR,AA	Data Low	1/0
	(1)	5a.	1	1	1	0	DBR,AA+1	Data Low	1/0
★19. Direct Indirect Long **[d]**		1.	1	1	1	1	PBR,PC	Op Code	1
(ORA,AND,EOR,ADC		2.	1	1	0	1	PBR,PC+1	DO	1
STA,LDA,CMP,SBC)	(2)	2a.	1	1	0	0	PBR,PC+1	IO	1
(8 Op Codes)		3.	1	1	1	0	0,D+DO	AAL	1
(2 bytes)		4.	1	1	1	0	0,D+DO+1	AAH	1
(6,7 and 8 cycles)		5.	1	1	1	0	0,D+DO+2	AAB	1
		6.	1	1	1	0	AAB,AA	Data Low	1/0
	(1)	6a.	1	1	1	0	AAB,AA+1	Data High	1/0
20a. Absolute Indexed Indirect **(a,x)**		1.	1	1	1	1	PBR,PC	Op Code	1
(JMP)		2.	1	1	0	1	PBR,PC+1	AAL	1
(1 Op Code)		3.	1	1	0	1	PBR,PC+2	AAH	1
(3 bytes)		4.	1	1	0	0	PBR,PC+2	IO	1
(6 cycles)		5.	1	1	0	1	PBR,AA+X	NEW PCL	1
		6.	1	1	0	1	PBR,AA+X+1	NEW PCH	1
		1.	1	1	1	1	PBR, NEW PC	Op Code	1

Courtesy of Western Design Center, Inc.

Appendix E: (continued)

APPENDIX E

Detailed Instruction Operation (continued)

	ADDRESS MODE		CYCLE	$\overline{VP}$	$\overline{ML}$	VDA	VPA	ADDRESS BUS	DATA BUS	R/$\overline{W}$
★20b.	Absolute Indexed Indirect		1.	1	1	1	1	PBR,PC	Op Code	1
	(Jump to Subroutine Indexed		2.	1	1	0	1	PBR,PC+1	AAL	1
	Indirect) **(a,x)**		3.	1	1	1	0	0,S	PCH	0
	(JSR)		4.	1	1	1	0	0,S-1	PCL	0
	(1 Op Code)		5.	1	1	0	1	PBR,PC+2	AAH	1
	(3 bytes)		6.	1	1	0	0	PBR,PC+2	IO	1
	(8 cycles)		7.	1	1	0	1	PBR,AA+X	NEW PCL	1
			8.	1	1	0	1	PBR,AA+X+1	NEW PCH	1
			1.	1	1	1	1	PBR,NEW PC	Next Op Code	1
21a.	Stack (Hardware		1.	1	1	1	1	PBR,PC	IO	1
	Interrupts) **s**	(3)	2.	1	1	0	0	PBR,PC	IO	1
	(IRQ,NMI,ABORT,RES)	(7)	3.	1	1	1	0	0,S	PBR	0
	(4 hardware interrupts)		4.	1	1	1	0	0,S-1	PCH	0
	(0 bytes)		5.	1	1	1	0	0,S-2	PCL	0
	(7 and 8 cycles)		6.	1	1	1	0	0,S-3	P	0
			7.	0	1	1	0	0,VA	AAVL	1
			8.	0	1	1	0	0,VA+1	AAVH	1
			1.	1	1	1	1	0,AAV	Next Op Code	1
21b.	Stack (Software		1.	1	1	1	1	PBR,PC	Op Code	1
	Interrupts) **s**	(3)	2.	1	1	0	1	PBR,PC+1	Signature	1
	(BRK,COP)	(7)	3.	1	1	1	0	0,S	PBR	0
	(2 Op Codes)		4.	1	1	1	0	0,S-1	PCH	0
	(2 bytes)		5.	1	1	1	0	0,S-2	PCL	0
	(7 and 8 cycles)		6.	1	1	1	0	0,S-3 (COP Latches)	P	0
			7.	0	1	1	0	0,VA	AAVL	1
			8.	0	1	1	0	0,VA+1	AAVH	1
			1.	1	1	1	1	0,AAV	Next Op Code	1
21c.	Stack (Return from		1.	1	1	1	1	PBR,PC	Op Code	1
	Interrupt) **s**		2.	1	1	0	0	PBR,PC+1	IO	1
	(RTI)	(3)	3.	1	1	0	0	PBR,PC+1	IO	1
	(1 Op Code)		4.	1	1	1	0	0,S+1	P	1
	(1 byte)		5.	1	1	1	0	0,S+2	PCL	1
	(6 and 7 cycles)		6.	1	1	1	0	0,S+3	PCH	1
	(different order from N6502)	(7)	7.	1	1	1	0	0,S+4	PBR	1
			1.	1	1	1	1	PBR,PC	New Op Code	1
21d.	Stack (Return from		1.	1	1	1	1	PBR,PC	Op Code	1
	Subroutine) **s**		2.	1	1	0	0	PBR,PC+1	IO	1
	(RTS)		3.	1	1	0	0	PBR,PC+1	IO	1
	(1 Op Code)		4.	1	1	1	0	0,S+1	PCL	1
	(1 byte)		5.	1	1	1	0	0,S+2	PCH	1
	(6 cycles)		6.	1	1	0	0	0,S+2	IO	1
			1.	1	1	1	1	PBR,PC	Op Code	1
★21e.	Stack (Return from		1.	1	1	1	1	PBR,PC	Op Code	1
	Subroutine Long) **s**		2.	1	1	0	0	PBR,PC+1	IO	1
	(RTL)		3.	1	1	0	0	PBR,PC+1	IO	1
	(1 Op Code)		4.	1	1	1	0	0,S+1	NEW PCL	1
	(1 byte)		5.	1	1	1	0	0,S+2	NEW PCH	1
	(6 cycles)		6.	1	1	1	0	0,S+3	NEW PBR	1
			1.	1	1	1	1	NEW PBR,PC	Next Op Code	1
21f.	Stack (Push) **s**		1.	1	1	1	1	PBR,PC	Op Code	1
	(PHP,PHA,PHY,PHX,		2.	1	1	0	0	PBR,PC+1	IO	1
	PHD,PHK,PHB)	(1)	3a.	1	1	1	0	0,S	Register High	1
	(7 Op Codes)		3.	1	1	1	0	0,S-1	Register Low	1
	(1 byte)									
	(3 and 4 cycles)									
21g.	Stack (Pull) **s**		1.	1	1	1	1	PBR,PC	Op Code	1
	(PLP,PLA,PLY,PLX,PLD,PLB)		2.	1	1	0	0	PBR,PC+1	IO	1
	(Different than N6502)		3.	1	1	0	0	PBR,PC+1	IO	1
	(6 Op Codes)		4.	1	1	1	0	0,S+1	Register Low	1
	(1 byte)	(1)	4a.	1	1	1	0	0,S+2	Register High	1
	(4 and 5 cycles)									
★21h.	Stack (Push Effective		1.	1	1	1	1	PBR,PC	Op Code	1
	Indirect Address) **s**		2.	1	1	0	1	PBR,PC+1	DO	1
	(PEI)	(2)	2a.	1	1	0	0	PBR,PC+1	IO	1
	(1 Op Code)		3.	1	1	1	0	0,D+DO	AAL	1
	(2 bytes)		4.	1	1	1	0	0,D+DO+1	AAH	1
	(6 and 7 cycles)		5.	1	1	1	0	0,S	AAH	0
			6.	1	1	1	0	0,S-1	AAL	0
★21i.	Stack (Push Effective		1.	1	1	1	1	PBR,PC	Op Code	1
	Absolute Address) **s**		2.	1	1	0	1	PBR,PC+1	AAL	1
	(PEA)		3.	1	1	0	1	PBR,PC+2	AAH	1
	(1 Op Code)		4.	1	1	1	0	0,S	AAH	0
	(3 bytes)		5.	1	1	1	0	0,S-1	AAL	0
	(5 cycles)									
★21j.	Stack (Push Effective		1.	1	1	1	1	PBR,PC	Op Code	1
	Program Counter Relative		2.	1	1	0	1	PBR,PC+1	Offset Low	1
	Address) **s**		3.	1	1	0	1	PBR,PC+2	Offset High	1
	(PER)		4.	1	1	0	0	PBR,PC+2	IO	1
	(1 Op Code)		5.	1	1	1	0	0,S	PCH+OFF+ CARRY	0
	(3 bytes)									
	(6 cycles)		6.	1	1	1	0	0,S-1	PCL+OFFSET	0
★22.	Stack Relative **d,s**		1.	1	1	1	1	PBR,PC	Op Code	1
	(ORA,AND,EOR,ADL,		2.	1	1	0	1	PBR,PC+1	SO	1
	STA,LDA,CMP,SDC)		3.	1	1	0	0	PBR,PC+1	IO	1
	(8 Op Codes)		4.	1	1	1	0	0,S+SO	Data Low	1/0
	(2 bytes)	(1)	4a.	1	1	1	0	0,S+SO+1	Data High	1/0
	(4 and 5 cycles)									
★23.	Stack Relative Indirect		1.	1	1	1	1	PBR,PC	Op Code	1
	Indexed **(d,s),y**		2.	1	1	0	1	PBR,PC+1	SO	1
	(ORA,AND,EOR,ADC,		3.	1	1	0	0	PBR+PC+1	IO	1
	STA,LDA,CMP,SDC)		4.	1	1	1	0	0,S+SO	AAL	1
	(8 Op Codes)		5.	1	1	1	0	0,S+SO+1	AAH	1
	(2 bytes)		6.	1	1	0	0	0,S+SO+1	IO	1
	(7 and 8 Cycles)		7.	1	1	1	0	DBR,AA+Y	Data Low	1/0
		(1)	7a.	1	1	1	0	DBR,AA+Y+1	Data High	1/0

Courtesy of Western Design Center, Inc.

Appendix E: (continued)

APPENDIX E

Detailed Instruction Operation (continued)

	ADDRESS MODE		CYCLE	$\overline{VP}$	$\overline{ML}$	VDA	VPA	ADDRESS BUS	DATA BUS	R/$\overline{W}$
★24a.	Block Move Positive		1.	1	1	1	1	PBR,PC	Op Code	1
	(forward) **xyc**		2.	1	1	0	1	PBR,PC+1	DBA	1
	(MVP)		3.	1	1	0	1	PBR,PC+2	SBA	1
	(1 Op Code)	N-2	4.	1	1	1	0	SBA,X	Source Data	1
	(3 bytes)	Byte	5.	1	1	1	0	DBA,Y	Dest. Data	0
	(7 cycles)	C=2	6.	1	1	0	0	DBA,Y	IO	1
	x = Source Address		7.	1	1	0	0	DBA,Y	IO	1
	y = Destination		1.	1	1	1	1	PBR,PC	Op Code	1
	c =Number of Bytes to Move -1		2.	1	1	0	1	PBR,PC+1	DBA	1
	x,y Decrement		3.	1	1	0	1	PBR,PC+2	SBA	1
	MVP is used when the	N-1	4.	1	1	1	0	SBA,X-1	Source Data	1
	destination start address	Byte	5.	1	1	1	0	DBA,Y-1	Dest. Data	0
	is higher (more positive)	C=1	6.	1	1	0	0	DBA,Y-1	IO	1
	than the source start address.		7.	1	1	0	0	DBA,Y-1	IO	1
			1.	1	1	1	1	PBR,PC	Op Code	1
	FFFFFF		2	1	1	0	1	PBR,PC+1	DBA	1
	Dest. Start	N Byte	3.	1	1	0	1	PBR,PC+2	SBA	1
		Last	4.	1	1	1	0	SBA,X-2	Source Data	1
	Source Start	C=0	5.	1	1	1	0	DBA,Y-2	Dest. Data	0
	Dest. End		6.	1	1	0	0	DBA,Y-2	IO	1
	Source End		7.	1	1	0	0	DBA,Y-2	IO	1
	000000		1.	1	1	1	1	PBR,PC+3	Next Op Code	1
★24b.	Block Move Negative		1.	1	1	1	1	PBR,PC	Op Code	1
	(backward) **xyc**		2.	1	1	0	1	PBR,PC+1	DBA	1
	(MVN)	N-2	3	1	1	0	1	PBR,PC+2	SBA	1
	(1 Op Code)	Byte	4.	1	1	1	0	SBA,X	Source Data	1
	(3 bytes)	C=2	5.	1	1	1	0	DBA,Y	Dest. Data	0
	(7 cycles)		6.	1	1	0	0	DBA,Y	IO	1
	x = Source Address		7.	1	1	0	0	DBA,Y	IO	1
	y = Destination		1.	1	1	1	1	PBR,PC	Op Code	1
	c = Number of Bytes to Move -1		2.	1	1	0	1	PBR,PC+1	DBA	1
	x,y Increment	N-1	3	1	1	0	1	PBR,PC+2	SBA	1
	FFFFFF	Byte	4.	1	1	1	0	SBA,X+1	Source Data	1
	Source End	C=1	5.	1	1	1	0	DBA,Y+1	Dest. Data	0
			6.	1	1	0	0	DBA,Y+1	IO	1
	Dest. End		7.	1	1	0	0	DBA,Y+1	IO	1
	Source Start		1.	1	1	1	1	PBR,PC	Op Code	1
	Dest. Start		2.	1	1	0	1	PBR,PC+1	DBA	1
		N Byte	3.	1	1	0	1	PBR,PC+2	SBA	1
	000000	C=0	4.	1	1	1	0	SBA,X+2	Source Data	1
	MVN is used when the		5.	1	1	1	0	DBA,Y+2	Dest. Data	0
	destination start address		6.	1	1	0	0	DBA,Y+2	IO	1
	is lower (more negative)		7.	1	1	0	0	DBA,Y+2	IO	1
	than the source start address.		1.	1	1	1	1	PBR,PC+3	Next Op Code	1

Notes:

(1) Add 1 byte (for immediate only) for M=0 or X=0 (i.e. 16 bit data), add 1 cycle for M=0 or X=0.

(2) Add 1 cycle for direct register low (DL) not equal 0.

(3) Special case for aborting instruction. This is the last cycle which may be aborted or the Status, PBR or DBR registers will be updated.

(4) Add 1 cycle for indexing across page boundaries, or write, or X=0. When X=1 or in the emulation mode, this cycle contains invalid addresses.

(5) Add 1 cycle if branch is taken.

(6) Add 1 cycle if branch is taken across page boundaries in 6502 emulation mode (E=1).

(7) Subtract 1 cycle for 6502 emulation mode (E=1).

(8) Add 1 cycle for REP,SEP.

(9) Wait at cycle 2 for 2 cycles after $\overline{NMI}$ or $\overline{IRQ}$ active input.

Abbreviations:

AAB Absolute Address Bank
AAH Absolute Address High
AAL Absolute Address Low
AAVH Absolute Address Vector High
AAVL Absolute Address Vector Low
C Accumulator
D Direct Register
DBA Destination Bank Address
DBR Data Bank Register
DO Direct Offset
IDH Immediate Data High
IDL Immediate Data Low
IO Internal Operation
P Status Register
PBR Program Bank Register
PC Program Counter
R-M-W Read-Modify-Write
S Stack Address
SBA Source Bank Address
SO Stack Offset
VA Vector Address
x,y Index Registers
★ = New W65C816/802 Addressing Modes
● = New W65C02 Addressing Modes
Blank = NMOS 6502 Addressing Modes

Courtesy of Western Design Center, Inc.

Appendix E: (continued)

BIBLIOGRAPHY

Mensch, William, Jr. ***CMOS W65C816 and W65C802 16-Bit Microprocessor Family.*** Data Sheet. Western Design Center, November 1985.

Zaks, Rodnay. ***From Chips to Systems: An Introduction to Microprocessors,*** Ref. 0-063. Berkeley, Calif.: SYBEX, 1981.

Zaks, Rodnay, and Lesea, Austin. ***Microprocessor Interfacing Techniques,*** 3rd ed., Ref. 0-029. Berkeley, Calif.: SYBEX, 1979.

INDEX

#, 46, 67
$, 67
<, 216
[ ], 219
*, 223, 236, 349
%, 230
!, 349
¦, 349

A register, 286–287
ABORT signal, 49
Absolute addressing, 209–210, 215–216, 229
Absolute indexed addressing, 218, 223
Absolute indexed indirect addressing, 221
Absolute long indexed addressing, 218
Accumulators, 33, 41–42, 56, 63
  exchanging, 204
  loading, 149
  pulling contents from stack, 167
  pushing contents onto stack, 160
  transferring to index registers, 189–190
ACIA (asynchronous communications interface adapter), 278–279
ADC instruction, 46, 57, 59, 66, 70, 115
Addition, 7–8, 70, 103
  8-bit, 55, 57, 65
  16-bit, 61–62, 68
  32-bit, 65
Address bus, 31–32, 35–36
Address register, 35, 213, 286–287
Addressing, 111, 207
Addressing modes, 102, 207–208
  absolute, 209–210, 215–216, 229
  absolute indexed, 218, 223
  absolute indexed indirect, 221
  absolute long indexed, 218
  combining, 213, 220
  direct, 210, 216
  direct indexed, 218, 223
  direct indirect indexed, 220, 226
  direct indirect long indexed, 220
  extended, 215
  immediate, 209, 215
  implied, 209, 215
  indexed, 210–211, 286, 307
  indirect, 212–213, 219, 300
  notation, 221–222
  relative, 210, 216–217, 221
Algorithms, 1–2, 63, 300
Alphanumeric data representation, 21
ALU (arithmetic-logical unit), 31, 33, 41
AND instruction, 87, 104, 116, 121, 194
Architecture of microcomputer, 31, 34
Arithmetic programs, 55
ASCII code, 21–22, 284–285, 355
ASL instruction, 17
Assembler, 338
Assembler program, 56, 337, 344, 348–349
Assembly-language representation, 45
Asynchronous branching, 262
Asynchronous transmission, 239, 244
Automatic sequencing, 40
Auxiliary circuits, 33

Bank address, 43
BASIC language, 9, 336
BCC instruction, 75, 118, 242
BCD arithmetic, 18–19, 60, 65–68, 285, 356–357
BCD representation, 18–19, 66–67
BCS instruction, 119
BE (bus enable) input, 51
Benchmark program, 238
BEQ instruction, 120
Binary
  addition, 67
  digits, 4
  division, 82, 84
  logic circuits, 4
  mode, 60
  numbers, 66
  representation, 22, 25
  search, 315–318
BIT instruction, 107, 121
Bit serial transfer, 239–241
Bit 7 (the sign bit), 14, 284
Bit 2, 107
Bits, 4, 61
  abbreviations for, 110
  grouping, 4
  manipulation, 100, 106
Blocks
  accessing elements in, 210
  adding, 225, 287–288
  indexing, 222
  moving, 153–154, 226
  printing, 256
  storing, 226
  transferring, 223–225
  zeroing, 283
BMI instruction, 122, 258
BNE instruction, 76, 123
Bootstrap, 32

BPL instruction, 124
BRA instruction, 125
Branch instructions, 71, 75–76, 100, 107, 110–111, 118–120, 122–125, 127–129, 210, 262
Branch relative byte, 216
Break character, 236
Breaks, 101, 111, 126
BRK instruction, 111, 126
BRL instruction, 111, 127
Bubble-sort, 290–294
Buffer, 33, 284
Bus enable input (BE), 51
Buses, 31–33, 35–36, 43
BVC instruction, 128
BVS instruction, 129

C (carry) bit, 8, 12, 15, 61, 82, 103, 108, 130, 180, 205
CALL instruction, 91, 100
CALL SUB instruction, 89–90
Carry flag, 68
CHAR, 245, 284
Characters, 284
  printing a string, 254
  search, 224
Checksum, 287
Chips, 33, 48
Circular permutation, 294
CLC instruction, 59, 67, 75, 103, 130
CLD instruction, 60, 131
CLI instruction, 132
Clock, 32, 49, 112
  cycles, 40, 47
  stopping, 185
  signals, 51
CLOSENOW flag, 314, 319
CLV instruction, 133
CMP instruction, 84, 134
Combination chips, 33
Comments, 57
Compiler, 337–338
Complementing bits, 10
COMPRES flag, 319
Conditional branch, 110
Conditional instruction, 34
Control bus, 31–32
Control instructions, 101, 111–112
Control register, 174–175
Controller sequencer, 43
Conversions, 279, 285, 356
COP instruction, 135
COUNT, 70
Counting, 70, 231, 233
CPU (central-processing unit), 31, 111
CPX instruction, 136
CPY instruction, 137
CRT, 229, 258
CU (control unit), 31

DATA, 245
D bit, 60, 107
D register, 42, 44, 158
Data bank register (DBR), 43, 56, 161, 168, 225
Data counters, 35
Data paths, 245–246
Data processing operations, 100, 104
  bit manipulation, 106
  categories of, 103
Data ready flag, 236
Data storage, 37
Data structures, 2, 63, 300–301
Data transfers, 70, 99, 102, 229, 235, 238–239
Debugger, 338
Debugging, 3, 95, 337–338
DEC instruction, 46, 103, 138
Decimal-binary table, 7
Decimal bit, 131, 181
Decimal mode, 60
Decoder, 43
Decoding, 33, 40, 45
Decrementing, 138–140
Delays, 155, 231–234, 251
Device controller, 237
Device handler, 258
DEX instruction, 76, 139
DEY instruction, 140
Diamonds, 2
Direct addressing, 210, 216
Direct binary representation, 5
Direct indexed addressing, 218, 223
Direct indirect indexed addressing, 220, 226
Direct indirect long indexed addressing, 220
Direct page addressing mode, 111
Direct page register (D), 42
Direct register, 193
  pulling contents from stack, 169
  pushing contents onto stack, 162
Directives, 350–351
Directories, 301
Disable bit, 132, 182
Displacement byte, 210
Division, 82, 84, 86
DMA technique, 256
DOS (disk operating system), 338

E bit, 48–49, 51, 107, 205
EBCDIC code, 21
Editor, 338
Emulation mode, 49, 107
Emulator, 338
EOR instruction, 14, 87, 105, 141
Errors, 337, 347
Exponent, 19–20
Extended addressing. *See* Absolute addressing

Fetching, 39, 41, 47
FIFO (first in/first out) list, 303
Fixed format representation, 16–17
Floating-point representation, 19–20
Flowcharting, 2–3
FORTRAN, 336
FROM, 223

GETCHAR subroutine, 284

Handshaking, 244–245
Hardware, 2, 341–342
Hardware stack (S), 37, 93
Hexadecimal, 23–25, 67, 247, 249, 286, 354

Immediate addressing, 209, 215
Immediate operation, 46
Implied addressing, 209, 215
INC instruction, 45, 47, 103, 142
Inclusive-OR operation, 104
INCMNT value, 314
Incrementing, 45, 142–144, 225
Index registers, 37, 43, 70, 211, 213, 225
Indexed addressing, 210–211, 286, 307
INDEXED flag, 325
Indexed indirect addressing, 213
Indexing, 37, 70, 222
Indexing modes, 211–212
Indirect addressing, 211–213, 219–220, 300
Inherent addressing. *See* Implied addressing
Input/output devices, 49, 101–111, 229, 244–245, 250, 261, 284
Input/output instructions, 101, 111, 229
Input/output interfacing, 229
Instructions, program, 2, 56, 70
  categories, 99
  execution, 38, 47–48, 232
  formats, 44–45
  individual descriptions, 114
  representation, 45
Interface chips, 33
Internal processor status signals, 51

Interpreter, 337–338
Interrupt line, 261, 265
Interrupts, 37, 49, 132, 203, 229, 235, 244, 256, 261–262, 264–267
  disabling, 182
  reversing action, 176
  simulated, 101
INX instruction, 143
INY instruction, 144
IR (instruction register), 39–40, 43
IRQ interrupt, 49, 263

JML instruction, 145
JMP instruction, 111, 146, 210
JSL instruction, 93, 147
JSR instruction, 93, 148, 258
Jump instructions, 70–71, 93, 100, 110–111, 145–148, 210, 217, 219

Keyboard, 229

LDA instruction, 46, 48, 56, 70, 102, 149, 237
LDX instruction, 150
LDY instruction, 151
LEDs (light-emitting diodes), 22, 246–249
LENGTH, 283
LIFO (last-in/first-out) structure, 37
Lists, 301–306
LOC memory location, 87
Logical operations, 100, 104
Logical OR, 105
Long addressing, 213, 216
LOOP address, 242
Loop interface, 250
Loops, 73, 210, 237, 242, 258, 260
LSR instruction, 75, 78, 152, 242

M bit, 51, 64, 107, 238
Mantissa, 19–20
Megabyte, 44
Memory
  accessing location, 102
  adding, 115
  addressing, 37
  banks, 44
  clearing, 283
  moving blocks of, 153–154
  operand, 134, 136–137, 149
  zeroing, 283
Memory/index signal, 51
Memory-mapped I/O, 101, 339
ML (memory lock), 49
Mnemonic representation, 45
Monitor, 338

Monitor program, 32, 337
MPU (microprocessor unit), 31–32, 49
Multibyte operands, 62
Multiplication, 71, 73–74, 80, 94
MVN instruction, 153, 225
MVP instruction, 154, 225
M/X (memory/index) signal, 51

N (negative) bit, 109, 238
Native mode, 49
Negative numbers, 9–11
Nested calls, 91
NEW program, 328–330
Nibbles, 4
NIL pointers, 326
NMI interrupt, 49, 262–263
No-borrow condition, 64
NOP instruction, 112, 155

Octal representation, 23–24
One-byte instructions, 45–47
One-shot mode, 234
One's complement representation, 10
Opcode, 44, 347
Operands, 62–63
Operation codes, 357
OR instruction, 87, 156, 183, 195
ORA instruction, 104–105, 156
Overflow (V) bit, 12, 14–15, 51, 108, 133, 235
Overflow indicator, 14

P register, 41
Packed BCD, 18, 66
Packed BCD addition, 68–69
Page, 42
Parallel byte transfers, 135–137
Parity bit, 21, 284–285
Pascal, 336
Passing parameters, 94
PBR (program bank register), 43
PC (program counter), 35, 41–42, 90, 110
PEA instruction, 103, 157
PEI instruction, 103, 158
PER instruction, 103, 159
Peripherals, 229, 255, 257–258, 275
PHA instruction, 160
PHB instruction, 103, 161
PHD instruction, 162
PHK instruction, 163
PHP instruction, 164
PHX instruction, 165
PHY instruction, 166
Physical sensor, 229
PIA (peripheral interface adapter), 276
PIO (parallel input/output), 33
PLA instruction, 167
PLB instruction, 168
PLD instruction, 169
PLP instruction, 170
PLX instruction, 171
PLY instruction, 172
Pointers, 35, 213
Polling, 229, 234, 256, 258, 260–261, 264–265
POP instruction, 37
Ports, 274
Positive numbers, 9–11
PRINTC routine, 254
Printers, 229, 245–246
Printing
  character string, 254
  memory block, 256
Processor status register (P), 41
Program bank register (PBR), 43, 163, 176–177
Program counter (PC), 35, 41–42, 90, 110
Program loops. *See* Loops
Program representation, 4
Programming, 1–3, 95
Programs
  executing, 36, 90
  filling patches in, 155
  recursive, 94
  storing, 32
  suspending, 265
  test, 283
Pseudo-instructions, 60
Pull instruction, 37, 103
Pulses, 231, 234–235, 261
Push instruction, 103

Queue, 303

RAM (random-access memory), 32–33
RDY (ready) signal, 51
Read operation, 56
Rectangles, 2
Recursion, 94
Register addressing. *See* Address register
Registers, 33, 55–56, 59
Relative addressing, 210, 216–217, 221
Relays, 229–230
REP instruction, 106, 173
RES (reset) signal, 49
RETURN instruction, 89–91
ROL instruction, 81, 174
ROM (read-only memory), 32
ROR operations, 175

Rotate operations, 81, 83, 100, 105, 108, 174–175
RTI instruction, 111, 176
RTL instruction, 93, 177
RTS instruction, 76, 93, 178
Rubout, 236
R/W (read/write), 49

SBC instruction, 70, 179
Scheduling, 256–257
SEARCH program, 327
Searching, 307, 327
SEC instruction, 64, 68, 103, 180
SED instruction, 67, 68, 181
SEI instruction, 182
Sensors, 229
SEP instruction, 106, 183
Serial input, 239
Serial-to-parallel conversion, 244
Shift operations, 33, 35, 75, 78, 83, 100, 105, 108, 152
Short addressing, 210
Signals, 51, 101
Signed binary representation, 9
Simulator, 338
65816
  architecture, 229
  chips, 48
  data processing operations, 103
  improvements, 101
  instruction set, 101
  interfacing, 273
  internal organization, 41–42
  modes, 60
  peculiarities, 59–60
Skew operations, 100, 105
Skip operations, 100
SO (set overflow) input, 51
Software stack, 37
Sorting, 290
Speed of program execution, 4, 9, 70
STA instruction, 57, 70, 76, 184, 230
Stack instructions, 37, 103
Stack operations, 103
Stack pointer (S), 36, 43
Stack relative addressing mode, 217
Stacks, 36–38, 91, 94, 300
Start bit, 250
STATUS, 237–238
Status bits, 109, 245
  resetting, 173
  storing, 183
Status flag, 14–15, 34
Status register, 84, 107, 109, 176, 261
  pulling contents from stack, 170
Status Register (continued)
  pushing contents onto stack, 164
  testing bits in, 100
Stop bits, 250
STP instruction, 112, 185
STX instruction, 102, 186
STY instruction, 187
STZ instruction, 188
Subroutine library, 95
Subroutine return instruction, 88
Subtraction, 8, 70, 103
  16-bit, 64
  BCD, 68
Symbol table, 348
Symbolic representation, 25, 344, 349, 355
SYNC (synchronize) output, 51
Synchronization signals, 101
Synchronous branching, 262
Synchronous transmission, 239

Tables, 224, 286
  accessing elements in, 210
  computing sums of entries, 287
  indexing, 222
TAX instruction, 102, 189
TAY instruction, 190
TCD instruction, 191
TCS instruction, 192
TDC instruction, 193
Teletype, 250–251, 253, 255, 258
TEMP memory location, 80–81
Ten's complement, 68
Test instructions, 100
Testing operations, 107
Three-byte instructions, 46, 48
Timer, 234
Timesharing networks, 343
Timing, 232–234
TO, 223
TRB instruction, 107, 194
Truncating the result, 17
Truth table, 104
TSB instruction, 195
TSC instruction, 196
Two-byte instructions, 46, 48
Two's complement, 10–13
TXA instruction, 198
TXS instruction, 197, 199
TXY instruction, 200
TYA instruction, 201
TYX instruction, 202

UART, 244, 279
Unconditional jump, 110

Underflow, 16
Utility programs, 283, 338

V (overflow) bit, 12, 14–15, 51, 108, 133, 235
Vector, 49
Voltage level, 230–231
VP (vector pull), 49
VPA (valid program) address, 50

WAI instruction, 112, 203, 229, 264
WAIT, 245
Western Design Center, 273
WORD, 242
Write operation, 59
W65C802 signals, 49, 51

X bit, 51, 107
X index register, 43, 139, 224–225, 248, 251, 254
  loading, 150
  pulling contents from stack, 171
  pushing contents onto stack, 165
  storing, 186
  transferring, 198–200
XBA instruction, 102, 204, 215
XCE instruction, 107, 205

Y index register, 43, 140, 225, 248
  loading, 151
  pulling contents from stack, 172
  pushing contents onto stack, 166
  storing, 187
  transferring, 201–202

Z (zero) bit, 76, 84, 87, 108, 284
Zero-page addressing, 210